The Cover-Up at Omaha Beach

The Cover-Up at Omaha Beach

D-Day, the US Rangers, and the Untold Story of Maisy Battery

Gary Sterne

Foreword by Don Mann, SEAL Team Six (Ret.)

Skyhorse Publishing

FIRST NORTH AMERICAN EDITION 2014

First published in Great Britain in 2013 by Pen & Sword Military, an imprint of Pen & Sword Books Ltd

Skyhorse Publishing books may be purchased in bulk at special discounts for sales promotion, corporate gifts, fund-raising, or educational purposes. Special editions can also be created to specifications. For details, contact the Special Sales Department, Skyhorse Publishing, 307 West 36th Street, 11th Floor, New York, NY 10018 or info@skyhorsepublishing.com.

Skyhorse® and Skyhorse Publishing® are registered trademarks of Skyhorse Publishing, Inc.®, a Delaware corporation.

Visit our website at www.skyhorsepublishing.com.

Typeset in Ehrhardt by Mac Style, Bridlington, East Yorkshire, England

10 9 8 7 6 5 4 3 2

Library of Congress Cataloging-in-Publication Data

Sterne, Gary.
  The cover-up at Omaha Beach : D-Day, the US Rangers, and the untold story of Maisy Battery / Gary Sterne ; foreword by Don Mann, SEAL Team Six (Ret.). -- First North American edition.
      pages cm
  Includes index.
  ISBN 978-1-62914-327-9 (hardcover : alk. paper) 1. World War, 1939-1945--Campaigns--France--Normandy. 2. United States. Army. Ranger Battalion, 2nd. 3. United States. Army. Ranger Battalion, 5th. I. Title.
  D756.5.N6S75 2014
  940.54'21422--dc23

                              2014011474

            Jacket design by Jon Wilkinson

ISBN: 978-1-5107-0000-0
E-book ISBN: 978-1-62914-328-6

Printed in the United States of America

Contents

Contents

Foreword

*T*he *Cover-Up at Omaha Beach* is a very interesting, well-written, and accurate acount of the Rangers' untold experiences on D-Day.

In the decades since World War II, countless texts have been published on the amazing sagas that took place on the beaches of Normandy during the D-Day invasion. But many stories were never told. As explained by the author, most, if not all, books on D-Day do not even mention the Rangers at Maisy.

Every day we lose over seven hundred World War II veterans along with their untold stories. Gary Sterne's book is a prime example of a story that that did not emerge from those perilous times until now.

Sterne's book is not just another testament to the courage of America's Greatest Generation or that of the Army Rangers, but also is an attempt to correct history as we know it and to correct one of the largest mistakes made surrounding the history of D-Day – the omission of the Maisy Battery.

I felt as though I was in Normandy as I was reading about the Rangers' advance on Maisy. Sterne's methodical research on what he refers to as the 'D-Day myth' includes historical references from numerous after action reports and accounts from French locals from Maisy, the Rangers, the Allied forces, the German 352 infantry division, and German Grenadier Regiment 916, as well many other military accounts. The story is factual and fascinating!

I highly recommend this book to anyone interested in World War II history or the military in general or anybody just looking for a fantastic read.

—Don Mann, SEAL Team Six (Ret.)

Don Mann, a bestselling author and accomplished endurance athlete and mountaineer, played a crucial role in some of America's most daring military missions for more than two decades. A former member of Navy SEAL Team Six who was twice captured by enemy forces, he now focuses his attention on inspiring others to achieve goals they never thought they could. As a sought-after motivational speaker and trainer, Mann addresses a wide range of audiences around the United States – from major corporations to universities to professional sports teams – with a message that is equal parts inspiration and strategy. Mann's books include *Inside Seal Team Six*, *The Modern Day Gunslinger*, *The U.S. Navy SEAL Survival Handbook*, and the Thomas Crocker SEAL Team Six series of thrillers.

Preface

The purpose of this book is primarily to correct one of the largest 'mistakes' made surrounding the history of D-Day – that is the omission of the Maisy Battery in the history of the defence of France – 6 June 1944. At this point it would appear a grand and pretty laughable statement that so many people could apparently get the history of D-Day wrong. I agree it is a bold declaration, but this book – with its recollections of the Rangers, the re-construction of the Maisy Battery and the information it brings to light – hopefully will justify it.

I am often asked why I did it – uncover a place that only I believed had historical value. The answer is quite simple. I felt that 99.9 per cent of the thousands of books written about D-Day were inaccurate. Not because the facts that they repeat are in themselves inaccurate, but that the interpretation of those facts causes the reader to be misled. This stems not only from the accounts of individual units, but also because soldiers only have their own perspective on a battle and report just that, which inevitably creates misinterpretations afterwards by historians. If those 'facts' are repeated enough then they often become accepted reality, which few will question.

The book requires the reader to have some knowledge of D-Day, and in particular the story of two of the more dramatic battles that took place – one at Omaha Beach and the other at the gun battery of Pointe du Hoc. Both actions were undertaken by the US Army Rangers and were portrayed in the film *The Longest Day*, where the Rangers are seen dramatically landing on the beach at Vierville-sur-Mer, moving inland and also climbing the cliffs at Pointe du Hoc, only to find that the guns had been removed.

Over a long period of time I have conducted interviews with Second World War US Rangers and recorded the accounts of French people who lived and worked in the village of Maisy during the war. I have also gathered information and objects relating to D-Day from around the world and this has given me a unique collection of evidence. Equally, I will try to explain why certain things happened as a result of other things – mistakes that lead to accidents, people being in the wrong place at the wrong time, such as the friendly fire incident at Pointe du Hoc on 8 June and the Rangers landing at a different part of the beach on the 6th, which is widely recognised as having saved many of their lives, thus allowing the battalion to act as a more effective fighting unit. It was a positive situation created out of a necessary deviation to stay alive – an on-the-spot decision that worked.

I am hoping to tell more of the Rangers' story on D-Day and where appropriate I have included pieces from other members of the armed forces fighting alongside or near to the Rangers. In particular, the achievements of the 5th Battalion of the Rangers have often been overshadowed by the 2nd Battalion's efforts, as reported at Pointe du Hoc. Yet a number of men from the 5th Battalion were at Pointe du Hoc on D-Day. Equally, a number of men from the 2nd Battalion were at Maisy and did the same. This book is all about telling more of the Rangers' story in Normandy in greater detail and where possible, through the men themselves. These are their words and history.

I hope this book puts a different slant on D-Day in the American sector. I want people to see what happened and better understand the facts of the day with all the evidence in place now. To coin a well-used phrase, I think this book helps to 're-write D-Day history' more effectively.

In 100 per cent of history books I have read, the batteries at Maisy are not mentioned – they simply do not exist – therefore the logical assumption is that the gun battery at Pointe du Hoc 'must' have been the coastal gun battery covering the Omaha Sector on D-Day, or so the books will tell you. Indeed, it fits the layout for the defence in that sector when looked at strategically. The larger batteries on either side of Pointe du Hoc are Longues-sur-Mer and to the other side the battery of Crisbecq (St Marcouf). Pointe du Hoc sits naturally in between the two of them. One would reasonably deduce that interlocking fields of fire from these three large batteries would thus cover the approaches to the whole of the American landing beaches, as that was what they were designed to do.

The whole story started for me with the function of Pointe du Hoc on D-Day. The argument put forward in other books on the subject seems very plausible. The Rangers assaulted the cliffs at Pointe du Hoc and they did indeed find and destroy five guns in fields approximately 1 mile inland behind. Therefore, everybody repeats the story that the guns found behind Pointe du Hoc were the same guns that had previously been installed there and that they had simply been 'moved to protect them'.

By 'everybody', I mean the Rangers who were there, the American Government's 'After Action' Reports detailing events on the day and, as I have said, virtually every book ever written about D-Day. Trying to change such thinking is no easy task and the facts have to be substantiated. It fits as a story that the guns at the Pointe du Hoc Battery were moved because they were not there when the Rangers assaulted the site. As nobody has ever challenged this idea, it has become truth and history has recorded it as being so over the years.

The book *Historical Division US Army WAR DEPARTMENT Omaha Beachhead (6 June–13 June 1944)* (US Army, 1945) states the following:

> *About 0900hr, two Rangers went down a lane 200yd off the main road and found the missing battery of 5 guns. Cleverly camouflaged, they were sited for fire on either Omaha or Utah Beach and large ammunition stocks were ready at hand, but there were no enemy in or near the position. The patrol put two guns out of commission with incendiary grenades and went back for more grenades. While they were gone, a second patrol finished the job of disabling the guns and set fire to the powder. Word was sent back to the Pointe that the main objective had thus been accomplished.*

Remember it is not that these events did not happen, it is that in my opinion the interpretation of these events as they are recorded is incorrect.

When I found Maisy Battery, I knew of its existence from my own research, but few others did. I decided that the only way I could prove that Maisy had an operational role

in the D-Day defences was to find out what
happened at Pointe du Hoc and then make
an informed evaluation of the defences
in the sector. This is just as the Germans
would have done when they built them,
and in the various sectors they would have
dovetailed them to fit in with the rest of the
coastal defence system.

One must remember that I was
researching this at a time when the sixty-
year secrecy laws were still in force and
1944 records had not been released. In
contemporary accounts of the events errors

The memorial stone at Pointe du Hoc, with no mention
of the 5th Battalion.

have crept in, for example, in one of Stephen Ambrose's books on D-Day he states that
the cliffs at Pointe du Hoc are 300ft high. To the casual reader this simple mistake could
make the whole cliff assault a much harder proposition – in reality the cliffs are near to
100ft high. There is no mention of the 5th Battalion of the Rangers in the film *Saving
Private Ryan*, for example. It was the 2nd Battalion shown getting off the beach, yet the
5th Battalion were instrumental in the break-out from Omaha Beach, as you will read
later. Antony Beevor's best-selling book, *D-Day, the Battle for Normandy*, makes no
mention of Maisy at all, but quotes in graphic detail virtually every action in Normandy.
So why are so many books missing the Maisy Battery?

This book requires the reader to have an open mind, to put aside 'received wisdom'
and adopt a fresh approach, to stop thinking in terms of what has been written previously
and consider new ideas. If the events of the day are reported 'accurately' and yet miss off
one of the largest gun batteries in the sector, then is it not possible that the conclusions
drawn in those very same books are also incorrect?

Consider also that there is little or no mention of the 5th Battalion having been at
Pointe du Hoc before 8 June on a monument there. There is nothing there to acknowledge
their fight, yet elements of the 5th Battalion arrived on the 6th, 7th and 8th and fought
alongside the 2nd Battalion until relieved.

When visitors see the site at Maisy, or I tell them about the information I have –
which is difficult in a 5-minute conversation – some people understand it and others
do not. Visitors to Normandy come in many different categories – the people who have
seen the films, the collector, the holidaymaker, the historian, etc. Some have vast and
detailed knowledge and others have just read a book before their trip. This book sets out
the evidence and challenges the reader to look again at the D-Day story.

Chapter 1

Uncovering Maisy

The story you are about to read is one that certainly contains mystery, but it also features examples of mis-direction and bravery of the highest order. The information included in this book was known only to a few Second World War American veterans and a handful of people from the villages of Grandcamp and Maisy, who are now in old age. Even people who lived nearby and many of the US soldiers that fought in the vicinity were unaware of what existed there.

The reason for this is simple. It was buried. The site was buried physically under 1m to 3m of soil. A whole area of battlefield which in total covers approximately 144 acres was wiped off the face of the earth and buried before the end of the war, ensuring that the site drifted into obscurity – until 2004. For sixty years it simply vanished.

Fast forward to January 2004. It was a cold winter's day and the end of a fruitless search for me. I was driving around in drizzle looking for somewhere to build a Second World War museum. My brother and I had been looking at old maps for days – the general idea was to find a building that would provide both historical Second World War interest in itself and be an interesting backdrop for the proposed museum. I was looking for somewhere to house my collection of US and German militaria and artifacts related to D-Day and it was proving to be a far more difficult proposition than I had originally thought.

That was until I recalled that I had bought a US Army veteran's uniform some years earlier and that it had come in a box with a map and other personal items. I found the map, which was in itself not of particular interest, except for an area marked on the coast near Grandcamp-Maisy. This was about a mile from the sea and marked in red pencil with the words 'area of high resistance'. Knowing the area quite well, my brother and I went down the lane called Route des Perruques the following day. On arrival, I could see nothing other than three old and frankly fairly uninteresting looking gun casements facing Utah Beach. Certainly not the place to consider putting up a museum, I thought.

We turned the car around and headed back up the lane. But some 500yd later I slowed down to look at the map again. The area marked on the map was to my right in fields, not behind and to my left where we had just come from. I double-checked the field edges and decided that I was indeed looking at the correct place, but I could see absolutely nothing.

We stopped the car and debated the merits of getting out on such a miserable day. The wind was blowing sideways and the rain was starting to pick up. But something inside my head told me to get out of the car, so I did. There was a row of small 2ft-high posts every 10yd and a single-strand rusty barbed wire fence running along the roadside. I stepped over the wire and I walked into a series of overgrown fields, literally untouched and unploughed – just empty, unkempt fields. The vegetation had become

The bunker roof as it was first discovered. The chimney is in the foreground and the surrounding weeds were covering it from view. Over the years the soil had been washed away to reveal the roof top.

so dense over the years that the area had become a wilderness, forming almost a forest of weeds and scrub. In some areas there were brambles with inch-thick stems, while bushes and trees were impenetrable, but there was nothing visible to indicate that anything had been there during the Second World War.

It was a pretty awful day and there were no signs that the weather would improve, so I was intent on not going far. I walked probably only 100yd and found myself in a clearing and standing on concrete. It dawned on me that this was obviously the floor of a building which had been destroyed in combat and this was all that was left on the ground. Logically this must be what was marked on the map. Interesting, I thought, but that is nothing out of the ordinary in France. So I turned to leave, but as I did, I stepped back and nearly tripped up over a small chimney pot. It was then I realised that I was on the roof of a building – not standing on its floor. Whatever the building actually was, the top had been uncovered by years of rain and I was standing on it, and it was sunk in the ground beneath me.

We searched and searched for an entrance to the building and eventually found the top of a tunnel some 20yd away. Only about 12in of it was visible, but it was most definitely the top of a tunnel. At first it looked just like a wide rabbit hole that had given way over time due to the rain, but it had a ramp of soil going inside into the gloom and it was shouting out to be entered.

We went back home and returned more suitably dressed and armed with torches. If the building was still there underground, then logically it would have an entrance somewhere. We found the small mound on the surface where water had flowed in. Using the torches, we entered what turned out to be a concrete and brick entrance and slid down into the darkness. It opened out as the soil decreased and led us into a German ammunition store. The whole building that had been virtually invisible from the surface consisted of two big

This photograph gives you an idea how well covered and overgrown the site was. This particular building was a radio room on D-Day, but at the time of its discovery it was invisible beneath the weeds.

Many tunnels were only just visible where the soil had settled down over the years. The filling of this building was not done randomly. Soil could simply not get into tunnels and around corners by being bulldozed over the top. People had been engaged in literally filling them all the way up with soil to block them. It was not just a case of putting soil over entrances. The tunnel seen here, for example, turns a corner, is approx 6ft high and it is filled throughout. This is not something you could do easily unless you shovelled soil inside manually, but who would go to the trouble of doing that after the war? No farmer would bother to go to these lengths to bury dozens of bunkers when a simple piece of wood would have helped fill the entrance before it was buried. Maisy was well and truly buried – but not by any farmer.

This tunnel still had pieces of wartime debris on the floor and at one end it was buried with tons of soil which had poured inside.

storage areas on our left for large-calibre ammunition and another smaller room to the right, which would have been used for fuses. There was a 2m-thick concrete, bomb-proof roof and the floor was littered with ammunition and debris – just as it had been left when it was filled in. It was clearly part of a textbook German artillery position designed to be hidden from the Allies as they attacked the coast.

That sparked off my interest. After this initial discovery, we spent hours in the fields looking for emplacements and other things that would give us a clue as to the purpose of the bunkers. Over time, we stumbled across the central spine for mounting a large-calibre weapon, presumably a 155mm howitzer or 150mm cannon – the rest of the gun pit around it was buried, but it was not difficult to imagine what the area looked like. Water had washed away the soil around the central spine and created a pit with raised sides. It became obvious that the pits were for large guns and the bunkers and shelters around each pit were still there, just buried.

One area of the fields … long grass and heavily weeded areas. Nothing was visible and in this particular picture I am standing on what was a trench in 1944, now completely buried.

I was sure that this could be a piece of D-Day history that helped solve the long-

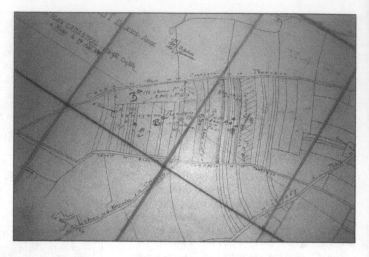

One of the old Maisy land plans from the 1900s. You can see that this area was owned by so many people.

standing Pointe du Hoc gun mystery. As a result, I approached one landowner after another and four years later, I had bought all the pieces of land that formed the site. I was the proud owner of a buried German Second World War position. But what position, that was the question.

The search began to find out what the site could have been. The Internet revealed only two websites with mentions of there being a gun battery at Maisy La Martiniere, and in one large-volume work on the Atlantic Wall it was referred too as having 'played no part in D-Day'. These books did not suggest there was a significant site on this land, so perhaps I had bought a dummy site – I honestly did not know. I could find no other recorded information about the site and there was nothing written about it in any of the major academic works on the subject, so I started to investigate myself.

I wrote to some members of the 2nd Rangers who were still alive via their association and to most who had fought at Pointe du Hoc. I logically assumed they would have come on towards the Maisy area after the Pointe du Hoc battle. Surely they would have information and know if anything existed on the site. I received replies from a number of Ranger veterans, with most of these telling me that the site that was attacked in the area was called Pointe du Hoc and that the battle was well researched. Many sent me details of their D-Day experiences, but nothing related to what I had found.

I then began to wonder what academics thought about Maisy. While I was in the process of buying the last couple of pieces of land I began corresponding via email with a professor at Texas University, whom I met some months later at Pointe du Hoc. It transpired that every year a group of students from Texas University visited Pointe du Hoc and that they were working on a seven-year study investigating what had happened to the guns at Pointe du Hoc. I was lucky as this was one of their annual student visits to Normandy to examine the site. I remember clearly walking over to discuss the Maisy site with their main man, but the problem was that I didn't own all of the Maisy site yet and therefore I couldn't really go into detail about its existence. However, I did want to pick his brains on what was known about the area, but I had to be careful what I said.

Following the original trenches was not difficult. The colour of the soil changed from brown to black where they had been filled in. Each trench had wooden duckboards in the bottom, similar to those found in First World War trenches and there were never ending amounts of spent American and German bullet cases.

One of the gun pits – you can see the central spine clearly now. This was the centre for the mounts that fixed a 155mm howitzer into place. This particular pit was buried under over a metre of soil.

I approached the Texas group and stood outside a stripey plastic cordon that they had erected around a slight mound on the ground. It was a little like the tape that is put round a crime scene on the TV and ironically I had stood on that very ground (without the tape) some weeks earlier. I thought it was a bit odd that they would put up tape so that they could sit and eat their sandwiches behind it, but what do I know?

I introduced myself to the professor and asked him if he remembered my emails to him. He did, which was good, and I asked him if he thought it would change their research if it was found that there was another gun battery covering this sector locally? I was trying to draw him out. I wanted him to tell me he knew about Maisy and if he thought it was insignificant – or that it was a dummy. It was important to me as I wanted some acknowledgement from his group that Maisy was at least known to exist.

I was fairly vague with my opening question, but at the same time trying to eke out any information they had. The professor was polite, but I remember his words well. He addressed me, and his attentive group of students:

It appears that Mr Sterne has not quite got the exact D-Day situation of gun batteries correct. We have Longues–sur–Mer to our right and the battery of Crisbecq to our left giving interlocking fields of fire ... there were no other significant coastal defence gun batteries in the area. Perhaps Mr Sterne needs to go and study his maps a little closer.

Another gun pit with its original gun mounting plate still fixed to the central spine. The gun wheels would be fixed to the baseplate and then the gun could be rotated around 360 degrees. Nothing was visible on this pit before we started to dig here and uncovering the original centre mounting plate intact was a real surprise.

At the time the guns were heavily camouflaged with netting and posts.

This photograph is taken from inside one of the 622 personnel shelters as the digger clears the outside trenches. Each stairway had to be dug out by hand and this was a long, physical process. Miles of trenches, bunkers and tunnels cover the fields at Maisy – its burial was not a small task.

502 headquarters complex – this was completely buried beneath the ground with only the roof visible after years of rainfall.

A small command shelter.

There are 2½ miles of trenches so far uncovered connecting all the gun pits and bunkers around the site.

Another ammunition store – three rooms and two different entrances both lead out to gun positions.

An ammunition tunnel leads out to a gun position.

A tunnel leading out to a gun pit past the commander's office at the centre of the site.

Emplacement after emplacement was dug out by hand and as the site was cleared the scale of the defences was revealed.

This elicited a laugh from his students, but stung me.

There was little I could actually say at that point, so I simply replied, 'OK, but can I remind you of this conversation in the future.' I left soon after, spitting feathers at having been embarrassed in front of so many students.

It made me more determined to look into the history of the Maisy site, so I increased my efforts to buy the remaining fields. I succeeded in doing this shortly after the meeting with the party from Texas. The next step was to dig up the site. Suffice to say, I spent eleven weeks with a 22-ton digger and began the process by starting to follow the German trenches. The colour of the trenches differed from the surrounding fields, so once I located one it was easy to follow the rest. I just followed one after another and uncovered dozens of structures. Eventually I had a large part of the Les Perruques Battery uncovered and had dug up building after building, not to mention about 2 miles of trenches, gun platforms, fortified positions and there was still more stretching out in all directions.

As I continued day after day the digging was causing a stir locally. Town officials would come past to look and I was asked by a local reporter for the *Ouest-France* newspaper if

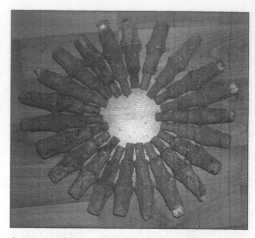

A pair of live, unfired 155mm howitzer shells being uncovered. These were later dug up and featured in an episode of the BBC series *Timewatch*, called *Bloody Omaha*.

Just some of the many 155mm shell-head fuses found scattered around the gun positions at Maisy.

I would discuss the site for a piece he was doing on Second World War, and I happily agreed to this.

That is when the fun started. I had let Pandora out of the box. Every newspaper in the world wanted to feature the 'new attraction' in Normandy and it was major headline news. Everyone was talking about the 'new' discovery that was going to change history. And that was also when the criticism began, as academics told me that no such place existed and I had created something that was a nothing, staged only for publicity purposes. I had

The day I found a German officer lying in a trench. I was a little stunned as his bones started to emerge from the trench. His body was lying with his water bottle, belt and buckle, torch and he was wearing his dog tags. He was later buried by the German Ambassador to France at the La Cambe German cemetery.

The pair of 155mm howitzer wheels from the first gun pit found at Mr Montagne's farm in 2009.

a lot of problems with the (old) mayor and the town was divided on what I had done, after all it could not have been a significant place or they would know about it, surely?

I knew it was for real. I had found ammunition by the bucket full, as well as fuses, equipment and objects that could only have been lost in combat conditions, such as gas masks, etc. I also discovered a German officer's skeleton, 155mm live ammunition and lots of evidence of German occupation and combat.

Once the papers got hold of the story they started to invent things to sensationalise it. I quickly found myself having to justify the newspapers' outlandish claims, which were often not ones that I had made, but newspapers do that. The sensible scholars knew differently and more information started to come to me via local people who remembered the Germans in their houses and remembered the site being attacked.

In the eyes of the public the site was seen for the first time in sixty years and it appeared across the world on the front pages of newspapers, in magazines and wildly on the Internet. In one weekend it appeared on nearly every television news report across the world and I was inundated with requests for interviews from magazines, newspapers and radio stations. I even had a friend call me from Australia saying I was on his 6pm TV news report! It was indeed big news.

But why was 'another German gun position' so interesting, after all as one historical analyst put it to the BBC, 'there are plenty of bunkers like this in Normandy', and strictly speaking he was right. But Maisy is far bigger than any simple bunker alone – and its position directly between Utah and Omaha Beaches is really what makes it special.

The answer to my quest for information came to me quite unexpectedly as I had never met a Second World War US Army Ranger veteran. It began with a discussion I had with one of the 2nd Rangers called Tom Herring, who gave me a clue. He suggested that perhaps it was the 5th Rangers who were involved in the Maisy battle not the 2nd, something I had not considered. Logically the 2nd had not been in that area so he assumed, that if it was Rangers, perhaps the 5th Battalion had been there. It sounded plausible so I wrote to the Ranger veterans association again and asked them if any 5th Battalion men remembered a place called Maisy. It was a long shot as naively I thought that anyone involved in Maisy would be long dead. As the 2nd Battalion of the Rangers knew nothing about it, then that was that. A huge percentage of the 5th Battalion of the Rangers were killed later on in the war at a place called Irsch-Zerf, so not many survived the war – I thought my chances of information were zero, but I asked anyway.

A number certainly did survive and I was contacted by a couple of men who remembered Maisy well. From then on the information really started to flow and I began to record their stories and remembrances of their time in Normandy. It is only right that I let them tell their story in their own words and I have tried where possible not to include information that has been used before. This is obviously difficult in places because the veterans tend to tell their experiences in the same way each time they are asked. I realised also that in some sources, such as the 'After Action' Reports, there is a degree of repetition with other publications. That is necessary because the objectives and purpose of particular missions will be the same as described in other books.

I hope this book is different in that it will tell a version of their story that you will have not read before. Hopefully, also I have gained information from these men that is not available elsewhere – if for no other reason than that I asked them different questions. I asked them about their feelings and how they reacted to certain things. I have sometimes put difficult questions to them about their colleagues and I am respectful of the fact that these were not always easy for them to respond to. This book is about what these brave men did in reality. If I was to sensationalise it in anyway, that would demean their efforts, so this is a real account of what they experienced and where possible written exactly in their own words.

From a historical documentary perspective, the book is also a collection of intelligence information. The reason for this is two-fold. First, it gives you a glimpse of what was actually known in Allied Headquarters about Maisy Battery before D-Day and, secondly, it tells you that information reported in many other books is not a full and accurate picture of the opposition the Germans had prepared for the American troops when they landed. If anything, the difficulties faced by the Rangers when they landed were actually worse than many books have thus far reported.

Why other books have not covered this subject I do not entirely know. It is perhaps that the authors did not have access to the pre-sixty-year TOP SECRET information, so they used the same information that others had, which was all that was available to them at the time. Perhaps is it also that in most other books attention has been focused on the activities of the Rangers on Omaha Beach and Pointe du Hoc – after all why would authors consider a gun battery elsewhere down the coast to be of interest. The big-selling, widely acclaimed books don't mention Maisy, so why should other authors?

Perhaps it is a mixture of the two, who knows for sure. I do however commend Cornelius Ryan for his research undertaken in the 1950s, which I have seen and it is superb. He did know Maisy existed, but the remit for his work, *The Longest Day*, only extended to 6 June 1944 – D-Day. Had he been able to cover other Ranger activities over a longer period, I am 100 per cent sure he would have written about Maisy.

What you are about to read is a true story ...

Chapter 2

The US Rangers on D-Day

It is important to understand the make-up of the Rangers and what set them apart from other American infantry units. **James Gabaree, A Company, 5th Battalion US Army Rangers**, sheds light on this:

As Rangers we were carefully selected individuals who were patriotic, courageous, intelligent, strong and must have more endurance than the average soldier. We were trained to act as a team member, but be capable of acting alone in order to complete the mission. Covert missions behind enemy lines and situations where regular army troops were stalled and unable to advance in combat were part of the Ranger training, 'Time to call in the Rangers', they would call. We were an elite group that very seldom took a defensive position, the mind set was to advance.

Before D-Day the Rangers were attached to the 116th Infantry and commanded by Lieutenant Colonel James Rudder. They were in a nutshell given two objectives. The first was the task of capturing the Pointe du Hoc Battery. This was a large German gun position sitting between the Utah and Omaha invasion sectors, a site said to contain six large field guns capable of firing at all the ships and landing vessels on D-Day. With an estimated range of 25,000yd, Pointe du Hoc was designated by Supreme Allied Commander Dwight Eisenhower as Target Number 1 in the whole of the invasion area. The second objective was blocking the Vierville–Grandcamp highway, thus preventing German re-inforcements arriving from the direction of Grandcamp intent on attacking the landing troops before they had a chance to make it off the beaches.

The 5th and 2nd Battalions were divided up. The 2nd Rangers were under the direct command of Colonel Rudder and the 5th Rangers were commanded by Lieutenant

2nd Battalion Rangers on the seafront at Weymouth.

Rangers standing in line waiting for food and drink on the seafront at Weymouth.

Colonel Max Schneider. Three companies, D, E and F, of the 2nd Battalion were to land from the sea and assault the cliffs at Pointe du Hoc, while the remaining 5th Battalion Ranger force, including companies A and B of the 2nd, were to wait off shore for a signal of success and then land at the Pointe. The plan was that they would then move inland and block the coastal highway, await the main invasion force and then push further inland. C Company of the 2nd was to attack and destroy the enemy positions at Pointe et Raz de la Percée. If the Rangers still at sea did not receive any communication from Pointe du Hoc at H-hour + 30 minutes, they would land on the western end of Omaha Beach at Vierville-sur-Mer and proceed overland at speed to Pointe du Hoc.

Each Ranger company consisted of about seventy-two men and was then divided into two platoons. There were six companies in each of the two battalions, listed A, B, C, D, E and F. Each company normally consisted of approximately sixty-five men, but as high casualties were expected these companies were increased in size by approx 15 per cent as they waited in Britain for their orders.

Their story inevitably starts in early June 1944 with the embarkation of the Rangers from Weymouth and Portland harbours. The harbours were perfect for the organisation of large quantities of vessels and the many different D-Day ships and boats were easily distributed around the extended sea walls. The size of the harbours allowed a huge number of vessels to shelter from the elements side by side, while all the different units were gathered together.

US meets Great Britain ... both countries posted sentries to guard their establishments. Here they are posted together on the Weymouth seafront at the clocktower.

George Miller, 1st Lieutenant, D Company, 5th Rangers:

We went aboard the HMS Prince Baudouin *about the 1 June, the next few days were spent keeping in top physical condition and making last-minute checks on equipment and reviewing plans of attack. We did celebrate rather heavily on the night of the 4th when we learned the operation was postponed for 24 hours.*

John Reville, Lieutenant, F Company, 5th Rangers:

Two weeks before D-Day we were finally told where we were going to land. We were behind barbed wire so we couldn't let the cat out of the bag. It was all about Pointe du Hoc. I remember Snyder – he had been in combat before. I do remember him making a speech … 'don't kill prisoners – for the simple fact that you can't keep that a secret – it will come out and what will happen – it is morally wrong and is going to make your job harder. When that German in there thinks that if he comes out he is going to get shot he won't – don't kill prisoners.'

Jack Burke, A Company, 5th Rangers:

On the trucks going to Weymouth the guys were in a good mood, all joking, singing and talking to the civilians as we rode through the towns. I had the feeling that we were finally going to do what we had been trained for over these many months in England and Scotland. I personally felt anxious while wondering how it would feel and how I would react in combat.

Rangers boarding their LCAs (Landing Craft Assault vessels) in Weymouth harbour.

Frank Kennard, 2nd Battalion Rangers:

Once we left the martialling area I never saw Rangers again until we were on Omaha Beach June 6. I also understand 2nd Bn 'paraded' on the quayside at Weymouth, but I wasn't part of it. I thought about many things … six months of uninterrupted (peaceful) living in private homes in England. We did vigorous physical training including a practice landing at Slapton Sands using the landing craft we would actually use in the invasion.

On leaving the hard standing we motored (in an endless column) to the port and parked in long columns. At a very large flat area there were hundreds of vehicles

After arriving in trucks from their camp the 2BTN walked down to the seafront at Weymouth through Greenhill gardens in full combat equipment.

Standing having a brew. Note the two men wearing camouflage painted helmets. They all have assault gas masks tied across their chests and two are wearing the famous 'assault vests'.

This man carries his Bangalore torpedo under his arm, as well as a mug of tea

2nd Battalion on the march with the Weymouth seafront in the background. They turned at the end of the esplanade where the Pavilion is today and waited along the harbour side to get into their LCAs.

Weighed down by the heavy equipment. This 5th Ranger is helped into his LCA.

Walking down the gangways alongside the larger landing ships.

Men of the 5th Battalion climbing into their LCA. Note the man carrying his M1 rifle with a grenade and launcher attached to the end.

Men of the 5th Battalion in their LCA.

Rangers with their full kit climb into an LCA. Note the waterproof gas masks carried by every man and the long tubular life vest being carried over each man's equipment.

Setting off from the quayside. Everyone is joking and sitting high on the boat ... this did not last long once the small wooden craft came within range of the German guns.

immediately adjacent to a quay on which there were permanent loading ramps. Over a long time each vehicle was directed to the quay where it turned around and backed down the ramp and onto its LC. The weather was Okay (no rain) and at no time was the procedure interrupted by enemy action (there was zero).

Leaving Weymouth harbour past the Nothe Fort.

I had two half-tracks with 75mm guns (referred to as a cannon platoon) and our invasion vessel was a small Landing Craft which also carried a couple of half-tracks with quad 50-calibre machine guns and one or two jeeps from the 741st AA/AWbn. Lt Conway Epperson with another two-gun platoon was aboard a different landing craft. Our vehicles were parked on the roadside in 'loading order' in 'notches' that had been carved on the shoulder of the road. They were all numbered with numerals corresponding to the number of the landing craft. At the appropriate time on June 3 (?) all of the units pulled out onto the road, thus forming an endless column. Travelling to the Port and, all along the way we had civilians cheering us on! We proceeded to a large flat area – a hard standing at Portland and in a highly controlled order went down a ramp onto our LC. We then sailed into the outer harbour and waited to form up with other LCs, in our landing wave (eight or ten LCs). Weather conditions were not bad. But the landing date was pushed forward from June 5 to 6 so we slept on board (I slept on a bunch of 10-in-1 ration boxes).

There was terrific planning and almost perfect execution of marshalling, loading and traveling in an absolutely AWESOME armada to the off-shore rendezvous area. Massive aerial and naval bombardment of the entire beachhead, along with no opposition produced a feeling THE LANDING FORCES COULD NOT AND WOULD NOT BE STOPPED.

D-Day was delayed, but we did not dis-embark. We cruised around in circles. It was raining and there was no shelter. Sometime on June 5 the landing was set for June 6 and all landing craft (except troop transports, but not LSTs) formed up into three enormously long columns maintaining a 'headway' of 300yd between each craft. Overhead there was an endless number of fighter planes all with special marking on the wings and fuselage (three white stripes) which we had never seen before. I thought it was an entirely new air force (not the 8th or RAF).

Frank Needham, a Wireless Operator in the British Army but embedded with the US Army, recalls the preparations for landing on Omaha Beach:

2nd Ranger Frank Kennard with his two halftracks mounted with 75mm asssult guns.

> *We were to land at H hour + 360 minutes and we were to land on Fox Red Beach. (on paper) I didn't like the look of Fox Red because to the east there was a 10-mile stretch of cliffs. Presumably there would be German defenders on this 10-mile stretch, yet there was to be no direct Allied attacking force – which suggested to me that Fox Beach might be very exposed from that side. I said nothing because I knew no details and assumed there would be an overwhelming force directed against Fox Red and we would just drive straight off! How naïve can you be?*
>
> *About 1 June, we moved off in a slow-moving convoy down to Weymouth harbour flanked the whole way by dozens of 'snowdrops' [military police]. Presumably to stop any deserters and to prevent contact by any civilians. Our little convoy of two 15cwt trucks broke off from the main convoy of tanks and trucks and went onto a narrow beach east of the harbour where great LSTs [Landing Ship Tanks] were lined up with their two bow doors open and the ramp down; all looking like big, ugly, beached whales with their mouths open to reveal a dark cavernous belly.*
>
> *We waited and waited whilst tanks and trucks were loaded, the time only relieved by a kind American lady in uniform, who gave us coffee, do-nuts and American paperbacks.*
>
> *I walked somewhat apprehensively up the ribbed steel ramp, finding a stairway to the top deck which was pretty well covered by American assault troops, infantry, tank crews and combat engineers.*
>
> *Geoff [a friend] had to finish off the waterproofing of the engine, it was already partially done, but now came extending and sealing the exhaust pipe above the top of the vehicle, temporarily covering and sealing the battery, ignition coil, generator, carburettor and spark plugs – all in readiness for the landing in the shallows on the French coast. At last the ramp was pulled up by two massive chains and the bow doors closed, then we moved to the outer harbour.*
>
> *We stayed in the outer harbour for a few days, living on K rations, but supplied with coffee by the sailors; wisely they did not want anyone brewing up on a ship loaded with all sorts of explosives. I slept on the open deck using a camouflage net as a bed. The Yanks were all saying that this was another exercise, but I didn't think so because we had all been so thoroughly briefed – it would not have been a secret any longer.*

The LST's were sent out to sea only to return the following morning, fuelling opinion that this was indeed just another exercise. However, they set sail again the next day and quickly formed up into a pattern with Frank's LST second in line. He continues:

> *The column stretched back to the distant horizon which was covered in a stupendous mass of shipping – too far back to be able to make out any individual ship. We set sail for the beach – two 15cwt radio trucks, six men and a useless vehicle (a truck damaged on the LCT). [The brief was] … to get off the beach as quickly as possible and onto the top of the cliffs; there to set up our radio link back to England.*

More Rangers veterans give their accounts of the run-up to D-Day.

Robert Gary, Private First Class, A Company, 2nd Rangers:

I trained in Bude. D and E Coys went to the Isle of Wight. We were spread out all over England. I was a mortar man and then I was given a sniper rifle. I had a choice when I got ready to land and I decided that the sniper rifle wasn't worth anything. Later on they gave me the rifle back!

Paul Louis Medeiros, E Company, 2nd Rangers:

We always knew that our outfit would play a key role, but we were entrusted with specific information about a month before D-Day, while cliff scaling in Swanage, England. I remember George Mackey, we called him Bill, winning all the money in an extended card game from all the guys in D and F companies, in the D-5 marshalling area just before boarding the boat. He came into our Squad tent and handed thousands of French francs (invasion currency just paid to us) to Private First Class Bill Bell and myself. He looked very sad and strange. We laughed and tried to give his money back to him. He said, 'No, I won't be needing it. You fellows have a drink for me when you get to Paris.' It was eerie. The tent was very still. Somehow you knew that he meant it. About three days later, I saw Bill stop a Jerry sniper's bullet and die. He never knew what hit him. His quiet, earnest words had been prophetic. He was a wonderful kid.

We were very well trained and informed soldiers. Colonel Rudder insisted that since his men were to do the dying they should always be entrusted with the reason WHY. We knew everything the Germans had at Pointe du Hoc and vicinity. Even the mine field around their position and the network of emplacements, how many enemy, etc. We did anticipate some possible underwater obstacles near the beach, which may have gone undetected by intelligence. The Germans didn't believe that anyone would land there and successfully assault those high, sheer cliffs.

There was a lot of speculation about what the French girls were like. The guys did a lot of dreaming. One can only guess as to how many of the dreams were fulfilled.

Loring Wadsworth, Sergeant, E Company, 2nd Rangers:

We went aboard five days in advance and would keep in shape by climbing all over the Ben Machree.

Maynard J. Priesman, C Company, 2nd Rangers:

It was the most beautiful sight I'd ever seen with the ships going in all directions. We gambled and played cards most of the time.

Regis McCloskey, F Company, 2nd Rangers:

Most of the boys spoke about their wives, kids or girlfriends, still others spoke about girls they wished they had with them at that time. I personally remember telling the boys all I wanted right then was a big tossed salad and the biggest cold bottle of beer in the world. We kidded a lot about saying our prayers. When we finally left the port on the afternoon of the 5th we all saw how rough the Channel was.

Lee Brown, T/4, 5th Rangers HQ Company:

I was 19 years, 4 months and 7 days old on D–Day. We were kept in a compound – that I think was in Weymouth and in the last few days towards D–Day we were told the plans for the invasion and were not allowed to leave. We were shown large maps and we understood our objective was Pointe du Hoc, if Rudder directed us to attack and Omaha was the back-up.

A German soldier looks through his binoculars prior to D-day ... they knew the Allies were coming – just not when!

I remember Lt Dee C. Anderson (I don't recall which company, but that he was a 5th Ranger) coming up to me in the last few days and asking if I was 'ready to meet my maker' – I responded, 'Yes, sir, I'm a Christian and I'm ready to die for my country.' Lt Anderson died the first day near the beach.

Robert Edlin, 1st Lieutenant, A Company, 2nd Rangers:

I know that our thoughts and words were that we were expendable troops – our job was clear cut. To knock out the battery at Pointe du Hoc at all costs. Cut the Vierville–Grandcamp highway and hold on until regular infantry could get to us. We felt reconciled to a lot of casualties.

Jack Snyder, 1st Lieutenant, 5th Rangers:

There were no rumours aboard ship. Every one of our men knew exactly what was expected of him and had been over every bit of enemy information that was available. Everyone was briefed on the latest intelligence.

James Gabaree:

Our assignment was to reach Pointe du Hoc and destroy the big guns. These 155 mm cannon could cover both Omaha and Utah Beaches and the incoming landing force, and were capable of destroying ships 10 or 12 miles out to sea.

Glen Erickson, 2nd Lieutenant, 6th Engineer Special Brigade, 149th Combat Engineer Battalion, 3rd Platoon:

In the evenings before D–Day we used to drive on the narrow roads to Exeter to army headquarters. I had a jeep driver whom I picked up at the motor company. They were dark and difficult roads to drive around with only limited lighting on the jeeps. Being subject to the BIGOT secrecy we couldn't use certain words and phrases. We were all very secretive before D–Day. Our companies were small ... there were many specialist units which would be attached to us. The brigade was only about 80–100 men. We didn't have the mission that the Rangers had, but we trained with them and worked alongside them.

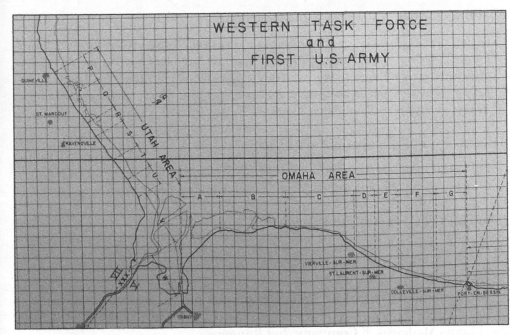

The official US invasion sector plan showing the two sectors, Omaha and Utah.

The original D-Day planning organisation map is seen above. The Utah Beach sector and the Omaha Beach sector can be seen stretching up to it. Omaha Beach, as it has now become known, is in actual fact only a part of the Omaha sector. The area marked A and B for example – if it had been used as a landing beach – would have been directly in front of the Maisy Battery. The Rangers were to attack the beaches between C, D and E. Their fellow Rangers were to attack the point of land that sticks out on the dotted line between B and C – a place called Pointe du Hoc.

Max Coleman, C Company, 5th Battalion:

On the evening of 5 June our chaplain, Captain Joseph R. Lacy, conducted separate services for Protestant, Catholic, Jewish. Captain Lacy was Catholic, but he recognised the great spiritual need of everyone. One thing he said stayed in my mind. He said, 'Tonight, I want you all to pray – but tomorrow I will do all the praying for you. What you will be doing will be a prayer in itself, and you won't have time to spend on you're knees.'

After the religious service, we were treated to a movie. The movie was Holiday Inn *starring Bing Crosby, and I am sure that a little excess moisture could be found in every eye as songs like 'White Christmas', 'Easter Parade', etc. were heard. The Channel was rough – and 0430hr we boarded LCAs to start the 10-mile dash to the coast of France, in a sea choppy enough to turn the stomach of Sinbad the Sailor.*

Joseph Lacy, Priest, 2nd and 5th Battalions:

I managed to visit and say mass and hold a general religious service aboard each of the five Ranger ships. I was with the outfit long enough to know many by name.

Carl Bombardier, F Company, 2nd Rangers:

We just slept or played cards, readied our equipment until we were about 10 miles from France. Then we boarded our LCAs which were sticking/over hanging the deck like lifeboats. I spent my time setting up a rocket launcher on our little LCA's deck. The British Navy were singing and joking, we were all in good spirits. I remember we sang 'Happy Birthday' to Ryan from Chicago.

Thomas Ryan, F Company, 2nd Rangers:

The morale was high. Being my birthday the Rangers in the LCA No. 888 sang 'Happy Birthday' to me. We were issued with small bags in case we had to vomit.

John Perry, A Company, 5th Rangers:

The morale of the troops was high, and the boys joked about who would come back and who wouldn't. Some of the men played cards, cleaned their weapons and made up charges to blow up barbed wire and pillboxes. The only thing we heard was that there were two divisions of Germans on the beach instead of 1 battalion which was predicted.

Paul Louis Medeiros, E Company, 2nd Rangers:

Our three companies were on a British ship, HMS Ben Machree. Our stay aboard was pleasant, the guys cracked jokes and kidded the British crew. We strung ¾in ropes from the masts to the deck and climbed them every day to keep our arms in shape for the job ahead. Also did a lot of PT. But underneath the jokes and laughter there was a keen edge. Everyone knew this was it and looked forward to it.

Francis Dawson, 5th Rangers:

I remember the crossing was very calm, that is no one was seasick until we departed the troop ship. The 5th Battalion was on a fast British ship, due to the size of the Battalion. We all had ample space to move about. We boarded ship about noon 4 June, we passed the time by numerous briefings and giving each platoon time for exercise above deck. The food served was excellent and plenty for both officers and enlisted men. The night of the 5th was a busy one, all weapons were checked, crew served weapons and demolition equipment were lashed to the assault boat and the men reconnoitred their way to their assault boat. The nights of 4 and 5 June I was quartered in a small stateroom with Lt Summers who was the weapons platoon leader. The two of us studied our maps and pieced them together and entered the targets by number on them so we could call for fire in needed. The room was under a gun turret so what little sleep was between the movement around the gun.

William Runge, Captain, F Company, 5th Rangers:

I was on the deck of a small Channel liner HMS Prince Baudouin with 200 Rangers watching a sight which looked like the sun on the horizon at night. It was the air force dropping 1,200 tons of bombs on Pointe du Hoc.

Alex Barber, T/3 Private First Class, F Company, 5th Rangers:

I was aboard the HMS Prince Baudouin. *The trip across was rough, for the water was choppy and the weather was bad. Most of the unit was kept busy cleaning and checking equipment and the members of the unit were constantly being briefed on the operations, for each man had to know his duties without a slip up. Some talked of what they intended to do at war's end, like settling down with English girls, and others said they were anxious to return to their homes in America.*

Burton Ranney, Staff Sergeant, F Company, 2nd Rangers:

I was very fortunate that I was never seasick at any time. We never slept that night. We didn't have too much room and I believe we were holed up in the eating area. Some fellows played cards, some sang, and played guitars; others just sat and talked. We cleaned weapons more that night than ever before. One man from E Company was cleaning a BAR rifle and it went off wounding three men playing cards at another table.

Rangers enjoying a meal courtesy of the Royal Navy.

We were kept pretty well informed on information available about D-Day and the enemy. We were told it was no picnic and that no one would be able to go back for at least three days. Everything would be going in and would keep going in to make room for more to come. We were briefed very completely up to the last, from air photos, on obstacles, pillboxes and enemy troops. Our morale was very high!

Avery Thornhill, B Company, 5th Rangers:

I took an overdose of seasick pills and slept until about 0300hr on 6 June, on awakening the firing had begun and no one was allowed on deck of the ship due to fragments from the anti-aircraft fire falling on deck.

The water was very rough and we had a hard time launching our little LCA. We were placed in the LCAs prior to the boats being launched and when we were halfway to the water a wave would pick up the LCA and almost put it back on the mother ship. Then the wave would recede leaving us hanging in the air. When the LCA returned to the length of the cables we got quite a jar. My company didn't lose a man in the launching or in the trip to the beach.

Emil Nelson Jr, F Company, 5th Rangers:

In our case we were preparing explosives on the fantail of an English manned ship. It seemed we were in a terrific state of suspense and we all signed each others French occupation notes [invasion money]. We heard that the Germans had over 200 subs in the Channel and many E-boats. We were also told to sleep dressed and ready to check out fast!

Gail Hamilton Belmont, Staff Sergeant, A Company, 2nd Rangers:

Most of the time on board ship was spent cleaning our weapons, studying photos of the beach we were going to land on, rehearsing in our minds how we were going to accomplish our assigned mission. There was conversation such as which company of the battalion would get across the beach first, whose platoon would reach their objective first, how far inland would we be at the end of the D-Day, etc. We were highly trained and probably didn't realise what combat would be like. Our outfit didn't go in much for rumours. It was the policy of the Battalion to keep everybody informed and abreast of the situation at all times. We did feel there was the possibility of the Germans employing gas or other chemical agents. The fact that we were issued a new type of assault gas mask, plus we had to wear impregnated clothing, which, when we hit the beach, only added to our grief.

Richard P. Sullivan, Major, Executive Officer, 5th Rangers:

Our troops had been trained and retrained to understand that the German enemy would possibly do anything to keep us from landing.

Robert Fitzsimmons, 1st Lieutenant, B Company, 2nd Rangers:

It was a quick trip – spent going over the routes we were to take after crossing the beach if we had to hit the beach. Our ultimate objective was to capture and destroy coastal guns on Pointe du Hoc that could fire on ships bringing men and supplies to Omaha and Utah Beaches.

Ralph Goranson, 2nd Rangers:

The crossing was quite normal and much like our previous training cruises, however the fact that this was the real thing did not seem to affect the men. They had attended church services and talked quietly among themselves. Because of their training they were ready and a good bit of their time was spent checking equipment, thinking of home and what it might be like on the beach next morning. Most of the men had a short, but good night's rest before we went over the side at 0330hr. With my company it was a last-minute review of two plans of action, an original and an alternate. Each man knew everything because if all officers and non-coms were casualties, a private had to be ready to lead the company and fulfil its missions.

Edgar LeRoy Arnold, Captain, B Company, 2nd Rangers:

My first platoon leader kept saying that he would never make it, that he would never get across the beach, that a bullet had his name on it. My job was to try and make him calm. This I tried to do. He was really not afraid to the point that he would back down, he apparently just had a feeling that his days were numbered. The men as well as the officers did not talk much. We did mention the beach defences and wondered if they were actually there as we were told and as indicated from photos. We talked about how soon we would get across the beach once we left the assault craft and reached the water's edge. We wondered if the cliffs would look the same as they did in the maps and photos.

Carl Weast, B Company, 5th Rangers:

On board the transport prior to boarding the landing craft, things were quiet, the last visit by the chaplain, pre-occupied soldiers, little talk – lots of thinking. We had fried eggs for breakfast at 0330hr – few ate. It was like a ferry boat ride until 0430hr when we loaded into the assault craft.

Lee Brown:

We entered the LCAs up high on the boat and were lowered down – we did not climb down the side of the Leopold into the LCA like others had too.

Glen Erickson:

Our Colonel had some serious arguments with the Navy on D-Day – I think he was later put under house arrest because he ordered our officers to pull side arms on the Navy landing craft men to get our men in closer. The Navy were anxious to get the landing craft in and out and were leaving us in too deep water – so most of our men ditched their helmets and gas gear. They were not necessary and it was very difficult … they lost a lot of gear.

I was sitting on my LST while this was happening and we were so thankful that the Navy destroyers which were firing virtually point blank at the targets could give some cover to the men on the beach. Our mission was to take the beach and stay there and at the time one other officer and I were to get to a certain point were the units would come in and we would tell them where they were supposed to be in line. That was my official role on D-Day. That was scrapped because we never did get to that point.

James Earl Rudder, Lieutenant Colonel, 2nd/5th Rangers:

Of course, there was great apprehension among everyone as to what might be expected the next day. Some of us actually slept during the crossing.

Donald Chance, Staff Sergeant, F Company, 5th Rangers:

Everyone was re-checking equipment guns, ammo, gas mask, etc. We had trained hard for a definite mission, yet the enemy was still distant and the war not yet a 'personal affair'. We were handled completely by the British Navy including landing craft personnel. We were briefed thoroughly on our mission and what intelligence had found – I recall a division (German) was conducting exercises in our area – this would increase the size and reduce the time of counterattack. This worried most of us.

We lowered away from the mother ship about 4am and had 10 miles to shore.

The overall feeling conveyed by the Rangers of this period was one of quiet contemplation. Some men passed the time with nervous games of cards, going over plans and equipment or reading books, while others just tried to keep busy

High winds and rough seas awaited the Rangers on the Normandy coast, as seen here on Grandcamp beach.

– cleaning and re-cleaning weapons seemed to be a good way of spending the time. The larger ships hid the real weather conditions well as they were more balanced in the water. This did give the Rangers onboard a crossing which was for the most part relatively calm. The trip in the LCAs was a different matter however as their lightweight wooden frames and flat bottoms made them very difficult to manoeuvre and in some cases – keep afloat.

John Hodgson, F Company, 5th Rangers:

The order came through to get into equipment and into assigned boats. We were given food and ammunition for 24 hours only. We were also issued a Mae West and a puke bag. Men were very seasick, but as many things were happening you didn't seem to notice or think much about it. As far as the eye could see, anything that could float was heading for the French coast; planes overhead and destroyers firing on the beach. Nothing much in the way of conversation unless we saw a plane get hit. Our boat took on too much water so an LST picked us up and we went the remainder of the way with him. Some fellows sat in a daze, others prayed and one joked about the fact the he was losing the press in his trousers.

We heard that it would be impossible to get a ship into the beach because of logs with teller mines on the end, driven into the sand and all kinds of steel entanglement plus six German divisions and their 88 guns. We had also heard that they had flooded many acres of land and had driven logs into the fields so the airborne and glider troops could not land.

Regis McCloskey, F Company, 2nd Rangers:

All the boys just kept looking at the water and saying, 'Ike has goofed ['Eisenhower has messed up'], the Channel is too rough to get our small boats in.' This talk sure proved right … these boats got tossed around the Channel like corks, and with a full load rode so low in the water that the big waves just rolled over the sides and into the boats. We had to keep bailing with our helmets all the way in, and the boys were so damn tired or sick by the time we hit the beach, most of them just didn't care to much one way or the other.

Playing cards on deck of the mother ship during training.

Boarding the wooden LCA.

All Ranger groups were to leave their mother ships and rendezvous at sea. Once they were all in position the assault waves would go in together – at least that was the plan. The weather made that a difficult proposition and the differing speeds and variety of problems being encountered by the various craft made many of the detailed plans unravel – before they had even been put into operation.

Jack Burke, A Company, 5th Rangers:

When we started our ride to the rendezvous positions the seas got very rough and the seasickness took its toll on many guys in our boat. Fortunately I was not one of them. I was in the rear of the craft so I got up on the back next to the coxswain to see what was going on and to my amazement, and I didn't know it at the time, but I was watching a historic moment.

Emil Nelson:

At 0400hr we were ordered to man boats in which we got into the LCAs and headed for the beach. It was about a 2-hour and 15-minute ride in from the mother ship and we had to work our way in for the Channel was rough and the waves came over the LCA. Of course some of the fellows got seasick but, as for me, I guess I was too busy throwing out water in order that our LCA could get in. As fast as we threw it out there was more water coming in. At 0615 we hit beach obstacles – Element C.

And then the order of 'ramps down' came and most of us were ready to take off for the cliffs to get out of enemy fire and re-organise. Before the order came, I saw a couple of boats alongside of us blown sky high and a fellow in the water trying to get ashore, but we were helpless for our main job was too important and we knew what depended on us – so we went forward and just hoped and prayed that they got ashore all right.

James Gabaree:

It seemed the assault craft was in a great hole surrounded by water. We were seated on low benches on each side facing each other, and straddling a low bench in the center facing the exit ramp, while a British officer and a seaman directed the craft from the front. This boat was an English design used for commando raids. It presented a low profile, unlike the American landing craft, and produced very little wake in the water; therefore its presence was hard to detect. When briefed for the invasion, we were told that the Air Force would bomb all the German fortifications, there would be minimum opposition and bomb craters on the beach would give us shelter from enemy fire. I was 19 years old and was about to take part in an event that would affect the course of history ...

John Raaen, Captain, HQ Company, 5th Rangers:

As we circled into a double column to head for our objective, we again heard the loudspeakers blast out. This time it was the Prince Baudouin's Captain, Lieutenant Commander Gelling, wishing us well, 'Goodbye Rangers and God bless you'.

We were crammed into three rows, no shoulder room, no knee room and the sea was rough. Waves of 6 to 8ft battered the tiny LCA. Drenched and miserable, some of the men began to get seasick ... we had 2 more hours to go! The boat began to reek of vomit and any spare 'puke bags' were soon used up. Sunrise was at 0558. So many boats, so many ships at first ... then we were clear of the marshalling area and it almost seemed we were alone at sea. Much of the coast to the front was burning with smoke drifting to the left. Suddenly there was a tremendous crash, roar, blast. I jumped up, but the officer-in-charge, Sub Lieutenant Ernest Pallent calmly said, 'Sirs, that is the Battleship Texas opening the bombardment of the coast'.

Francis Coughlin, Private First Class, HQ, 5th Rangers:

I carried a M1 Garrand and a .45 in holster. They wanted to give us a different rifle but the first day I came into the service I wanted a M1. I was on the boat with Snyder and the priest, when we were coming in towards the cliffs we were slowly coming in to make the landing and seeing the men getting blown off the ladders. We got within maybe 100yd and he slowed the boats down. What's going on here ... we got no word ... he said you have 2 minutes to make up your minds and that's when we turned along the coast and I landed at Vierville.

Loring Wadsworth:

After we started in we had to bail with our hats – I think that we had the first man hit – John J. Sillmon (E Company, 2nd Rangers).

On his run in towards the coast, perhaps some 5 miles out, Captain Raaen spotted one of F Company's boats, LCA 578. It was Lieutenant John Reville and his first platoon of 5th Rangers. The boat began sinking and despite bailing with helmets, the boat pumps could not cope with the deluge. Later they were picked up by a Landing Craft Tank and taken under tow until the engines could be restarted. The men from Reville's platoon eventually put down on Omaha at 0900. Reville remembers the incident well.

John Reville:

Our boat started to take in water right way and finally it got ridiculous – a Landing Ship Tank was nearby so we transferred our people onto it. We went up the front of the boat and I was on top of the ramp looking at the shore where we were going to land, when a shell went right over us – it blew another little assault craft to pieces.

The Commander of the USS *Bayfield* wrote the following in his After Action Report:

During the landing of assault waves, three LCVPs which had been assigned to BARNET were swamped on discharging their troops and had to be left on the beach, their crews returning to the ship in other boats. According to reports made by the coxswains, their craft were heavily loaded, and they were compelled to run at high speeds in order to reach the rendezvous area on time. As a result, they took on water beyond the capacity of the pumps and grounded 20 to 30yd farther off the beach than other boats in the wave. When the ramps were lowered, the boats filled with water, engines were inundated, and the crews had no choice other than to abandon their boats. Troops waded ashore without mishap, although they started out chest deep in water.

Frank Needham:

Something like H + 240 minutes I remember passing the odd destroyer and rocket boat, but not seeing the masses of assault boats I expected. Eyes were fixed on the approaching shoreline. I remember clearly seeing two tanks trying to get up a path which led diagonally from the beach towards the top of the bluffs.... German incendiary bullets set fire to the canvas on the tank. This meant the tank men had to jump through a wall of flame and the few I saw achieve this landed on the ground not to rise again.

Then our LST was shelled but not hit. The captain reversed away from the beach and made out to sea. We sailed back towards the line of warships out of harm's way and then sailed slowly up and down in front of the line. We were almost under HMS Glasgow when she fired a broadside. The concussion was terrible, even moving our LCT sideways, the great smoke rings, ever widening, followed the shells towards the beach. The rocket ships started up again and one could easily see the plumes of smoke and soil rising from the top of the bluffs – presumably by then they were aware that the landing was in trouble and that no troops had reached the top.

We settled in for the night, some slept upright in the truck seats and I slept on one blanket on the riveted iron deck of the ship.

Frank's unit was attached to the American forces, but as his was a non-assault unit their landing was delayed and they were turned away from the beach until the assault troops could clear them. Frank was to land at Omaha Beach the next morning, in very different circumstances to the Rangers on the 6th.

Jack Burke:

It was approaching daylight, the sky was absolutely loaded with planes, and then to my right the battleship USS Texas fired a broadside and the flash from those 15in guns was frightening – the battleship heaved over from the blast and then righted itself.

You could see the huge smoke rings go out and also see the shell in flight on its way to the beach. I said to myself that no one could survive this shelling and we were going 'for a cake walk' when we hit the beach ... WRONG, WRONG, WRONG.

Carl Weast, B Company, 5th Rangers:

The small British LCAs were heavily loaded, the Channel rough and plenty of water was coming in over the sides. We took turns working the hand-operated bilge pump. Bailed with the bags and helmets, barely managing to keep afloat. I recall one of the boys suggesting an interesting place where the King might stick the Royal Navy. However, he and the others changed their attitude later when these British sailors got us through the beach obstacles to a dry touch down.

Frank Needham.

Nelson Noyes, Private First Class, C Company, 2nd Rangers:

We were about 2,000yd off the beach when the Germans started throwing artillery at us and then the Navy opened up with a big barrage. Destroyers and rocket ships were covering us. We kept going in. The Germans were shooting at us when we were 300yd off the beach.

Lee Brown:

Rangers climbing into their LCA.

We were told to keep our heads down, but I did peak up and the 'zip, zip, zip' of machine-gun fire had us ducking back down quickly.

Lieutenant Colonel Schneider, and I think Captain Heffelfinger were in my LCA – the British LCA driver did a great job getting us into the beach, I did not even step into any water – I was up onto dry beach. When the ramp went down on our LCA the lead officer off hesitated and because of that hesitation it saved many lives. The reason was because in the time of the hesitation a machine gun strafed right in front of the LCA ramp and would have cut down many of us coming right off – I was 5th, 6th or 7th off and likely would have been cut down. The officer who hesitated and didn't charge right off, like they had been told to do was Schneider. He had paused to take off his Mae West and toss it down on the beach. The delay likely saved my life.

I ran all the way to the sea wall as fast as I could with my M1 rifle, there really wasn't anything to hide behind until you got there. Many men fell around me on the run in to the wall. Getting to the sea wall I looked back and saw an LST get hit and blow up. There were bodies flying in the air – I turned to the radio man next to me and I said, 'This is war!'

I remember General Cota approaching us and him specifically talking to Captain John Raaen first and asking if he was Jack Raaen's son. He was then speaking with Schneider and I remember him exhorting them to lead the way on the beach. I was in awe of Cota's bravery in standing upright over them all hunkered down behind the wall and being impervious to fire.

Francis 'Bull' Dawson blew the barbed wire with Bangalore torpedoes nearby and then led the charge through.

For the rest of the day we were combined with other companies out of necessity. I did not settle into HQ company duties, it was just fighting.

Robert Edlin:

Our LCA hit a sandbar. We were 75yd from the shore, and the ramp went down. We went off the sides in case the craft was swept onto us by a wave. A boat carrying B Company took a direct hit on the ramp from a mortar or mine and I saw men sinking all around me. I tried to grab a couple of them. There were bodies from the 116th floating everywhere. They were facedown in the water with packs still on their backs. They had inflated their life jackets and turned upside down and drowned. I went across the beach to try to get to the sea wall.

John Perry:

We all talked about who would get hit first. I recall one of our platoon runners who always talked about being afraid of the water, and while coming in on the beach he jumped off the boat in the water and was dragged under the boat by the under-tow. We all had our full field equipment on and that weighed him down some. He was only a kid – about 19 years old. I was hit in my left arm by shrapnel, I felt no pain except it was numbed. I didn't realise that I was hit until the blood dripped down into the palm of my hand.

Charles H. Parker, A Company, 5th Rangers:

We were lowered down into the wild water of the English Channel in our LCAs. About 10 or 12 miles away from Omaha Beach. The waves were coming in so fiercely that the LCAs were going up and down, like crazy. Explosives were going off on the beach ahead of us – enormous sheets of fire from artillery guns, rifle fire and mortar fire.

The small wooden LCA vessels were manned by men of the Royal Navy and could in theory reach a top speed of 8 knots (9mph). These heavily overloaded craft rarely reached that sort of speed and the weather conditions did nothing to help. They were originally designed in 1939 to carry thirty to thirty-five men as low in the water as possible and take them as close in shore as practicable. It was thought that this design would make the wooden hulled craft a much harder target to hit due of its low profile on the surface. Another advantage of the flat plywood bottom was that it was able to land on a beach in much shallower waters than other vessels – therefore getting the soldiers closer to their objective. The reality on 6 June was more complex.

Charles H. Parker.

Indeed, the Rangers did get in further up the beaches, but their light wooden LCAs were swamped and burdened by water and spray due to the rough seas on the way in. The intake of water made them much more difficult to steer. The British coxswains had to avoid beach obstacles, get over sand bars and try to maintain a sensible course to the beach – all while being fired upon by an unseen enemy. Trying to make the LCAs respond to their changes of course and not drop the ramp too soon were all issues for the coxswains. The Rangers had only admiration and respect for the Royal Navy men carrying out the job under such conditions. Each LCA had a crew of four men and the design of the vessel meant that the boat had to hit the beach before the ramp was lowered. As a consequence, many men were 'landed' early on sandbanks and subsequently had to wade through varying depths of water. Some drowned as a result of their equipment carrying them under. Some watched as their friends were taken under the fronts of the boats and were crushed by the rise and fall of the heavy ramps. Others found themselves being 'chased' by the vessel as it got lighter when the men left. As the thirty-six men left the boat it would bob upwards and often closer to the beach, making it a more dangerous proposition for the men disembarking last. But leave they did.

Jack Snyder:

Coming into the beach our battalion commander ordered all boats to change course, violating orders from above – however, it saved the battalion. We landed without a casualty due to this ... another unit continued on to be almost annihilated.

Colonel Max Schneider, Battalion Commander, gave the order to form up into single file and the group of wave-battered LCAs carrying the 2nd and 5th Rangers lurched towards the shore. The Rangers and all other first-wave troops were designated to land on the beach which had been organised into sections: Dog Green, Dog White, Dog Red, Easy Green, Easy Red, Fox Green, Fox Red, etc. The idea was that everyone had their allotted landing spot and an individual set of obstacles to overcome on the beach. After this a global rendezvous inland would take place and the relief column for Pointe du Hoc would advance along the coast. This was quite feasible on paper, but there were so many factors working against this running smoothly.

James Gabaree:

One thing that helped the Rangers fighting ability on D-Day was the Commando training we received prior to invasion. We were tuned up and ready to fight ... I was not

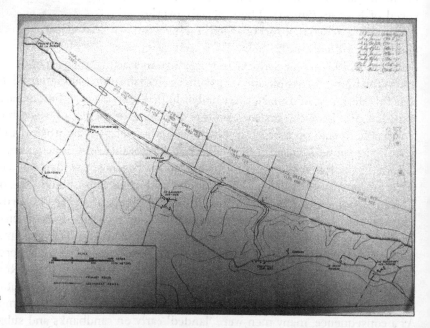

Map showing the lengths of the various landing sectors on Omaha Beach.

frightened. We had boarded the landing craft 10 or 12 miles from the beach, making us vulnerable to enemy fire from the big guns on Pointe du Hoc.

Charles H. Parker:

There were bodies laying all over the beach. There were bodies still alive in the water washing back and forth with the tide's waves.

John Martino, 81st Chemical Weapons Battalion:

Approximately 15 miles from shore the larger craft hove to, and at 0430hr all companies transferred their men and mortars to LCVPs [a Landing Craft for a single Vehicle or Personnel]. As the men clambered down the cargo nets in the murky, false dawn, the Navy wished them Godspeed, and the craft shoved off from the mother ships into a choppy sea for the rendezvous areas several hundred yards offshore. Here they circled, endlessly it seemed, causing the boat teams to be wet to the skin and, in many cases, violently seasick. We had to put our life preservers on and it was raining as we approached the beach. My buddy right beside me was killed as the ramp went down and we were all scared.

One of the many groynes which extend out from the road into the sand at Omaha Beach.

81st's B Company mission was to land on Dog Green Beach and provide direct support for the 1st Battalion, 116th Infantry. The water obstacles had not been cleared and the beach was under heavy mortar, small arms, and artillery fire. The control boat ordered the wave to land instead on Easy Green, the left flank of Omaha Beach. As the boats were running along parallel to the beach, about 1,000yd, offshore, two of the LCVPs were hit and disabled by artillery. Despite an extremely heavy sea and the continual harassing fire from enemy machine guns and other direct-fire weapons, all personnel and equipment were safely transferred to an empty LCT. At approximately 0930hr the

The 81st Chemical Mortar Battalion plaque in Vierville.

entire wave was safely beached. Here the company was reorganised and moved inland about 100yd. At this time only a small section of the beach was held by American troops, and enemy fire was still inflicting heavy casualties.

0710hr Rangers on the beach reported by radio to USS *Ancon*:

Two landing craft knocked out by enemy battery back of centre of Beach – Dog Green.

Glen Erickson:

I was with the brigade HQ on a LST and we had the DUCKS which were loaded with the heavy artillery that we had with the 116th Inf. I think they were 105mm and 75mm. The DUCKS would make one turn around and then head for shore. The DUCKS went around the LST and a lot went to the bottom because they were overloaded. So we lost the artillery for the combat teams and infantry. As a result of losing the artillery, there was no need for us to go in on the assault at H-hour. There were not a lot of troops on our LST so they waved us off.

Alex Barber:

Approaching the beach, it was plain to see that the Germans did not desire our social call. The beach was protected by numerous underwater obstacles consisting of element 'C', hedgehogs and tetrahedra, many with teller mines attached. Mortar and artillery shells continually burst in the area of these obstacles, and a heavy concentration of machine-gun and small arms fire swept the beach. About 75yd from the water's edge, a 4ft sea wall ran laterally along the beach. Our naval bombardment had set fire to the vegetation above the beach, and a pall of smoke obscured that area.

Charles Parker's LCA hit a sandbar and he and his men of A Company fixed the task ahead: get to Pointe du Hoc some miles away and leave the fighting on the beach to the 29th Infantry Division. Parker and his men were not alone – the first wave to hit the beach consisted of half of the Battalion HQ, Companies A, B and E landing on a strip of the beach designated as Omaha Dog White. Actually the landing point for these Rangers was Dog Green, but Lieutenant Colonel Schneider, seeing the fantastic volume of fire that covered Dog Green Beach, ordered the flotilla commander to touch down his craft east of the intended landing point. This wave crossed the beach in good order with few casualties, halted temporarily in the rear of the sea wall and immediately re-organised. The second wave, consisting of half of HQ, Companies C and D and one platoon of F Company repeated the performance of the first wave. The other platoon of F Company with John Reville which had shipped too much water into its LCA dropped out of formation and landed near the Laurent sur Mer exit at 0900hrs.

At 0824hr the USS *Ancon* receives a report:

Batteries at Maisy still in commission. Being kept under fire.

Frank Kennard:

Just before H-hour the naval and aerial bombardment produced balls of fire and explosions which extended from horizon to horizon. I personally thought nothing could survive and sort of danced a 'jig'. This attitude held until on the run-in to the beach from

10 miles off-shore (we were scheduled to land at about 0930). Our LC was bracketed by some shore battery shell-fire and some shrapnel 'rattled around'. But otherwise there was no damage.

The tide changes rapidly (1ft every 10 minutes). Thus bomb craters were hidden and our craft made three run-ins before we could drop the ramp in water shallow enough to permit unloading the vehicles. Also we were much further east closer to Les Moulins than Vierville. Our assigned exit was Vierville. There were 'Beach Masters' on the shore with flags, etc. – everything was rather orderly and there was only intermittent resistance evident.

The beach was 'chock-a-block' with bodies, groups of men and equipment. There were absolutely no communications functioning and it was impossible to move towards Vierville exit. We blew a gap in the concertina wire alongside the gravel road between the low beach wall and the anti-tank ditch. In attempting to get over the beach wall to the roadway with the halftracks we burned out the clutch on one vehicle and the other was hit by some kind of explosive and burned up. I lost two Rangers to intermittent enemy fire.

The problems encountered by Frank Kennard and his halftracks were well documented in US Army reports. He continues:

Landing craft being tossed about in the heavy swell. Note the beach obstacles sticking up from the surf.

Troops hit the beach amongst the obstacles and smoke.

Landing Craft approach the obstacles on Omaha Beach.

Smoke covering Omaha Beach.

There is a strip of shingle, about 15yd wide, extending along the entire beach near the high-water mark. It is composed of stones about 2in in diameter and forms a ridge with a gradient on the lower side of 1/8 to 1/10.

Infantrymen landing from a larger landing ship amidst the floating bodies of earlier waves of troops.

On Omaha I encountered part of a 5th Ranger platoon, including one Lt, early AM 6 June and we 'assaulted' the position on the top and inside the high ground there. Eventually I led my remaining men about halfway up the escarpment – visualise a large concrete bunker on which about 40 per cent of the side has been cut away. Then place it in the face of the Normandy escarpment with the opening facing the water. This would describe the form of the empty gun fortification. Can't estimate the dimensions, but it wouldn't hold a wheeled artillery piece. I don't know how one would get an artillery piece in unless you had a crane above it. More likely heavy mortar and the opening afforded a wide lateral range of fire. Only a direct hit from naval fire from miles off shore could have destroyed it. We saw neither a German plane nor naval vessel. We suffered no casulties and captured a few prisoners.

Francis Coughlin, Private First Class, HQ, 5th Rangers:

We landed with part of A Company, some guys from C Company – the boats got swamped and we lost a lot of personnel. Once we hit the beach my initial job was to make sure that the priest got off the landing craft and up off the beach to where we were going to congregate. But being a priest he had a job to do, so the first thing he did was to leave me and run over the beach to where people were either deceased, drowned or killed by shells coming in and that is where he spent his time. Finally the colonel hollered for me to bring him in, but I eventually left him there. I said he to me, 'I have a mind of my own and I have a job to do'. He told me to get out of here.

The guys I saw were Rangers and we all just got together a gang of us. I remember going up the back of a path into a house and it was through a mine field. That was the way the Germans got up the cliffs and the fields and that's how Rangers did it.

John Raaen:

For us in the second wave, still on the water and less than 5 minutes behind, the noise had now become deafening. An LCM or LCT to our right front was hit by artillery fire and burst into flames. Other artillery shells were detonating all around us, with small arms adding to the inferno. The scene was one from hell. Another vessel 50 to 100yd to our right was hit by artillery, fires on the bluff, fires from burning vessels, dust and flying debris everywhere.

We hit the bottom with a jolt, the ramp dropped and Sullivan dashed out to the left. I was second, chose the right and shouted, 'Headquarters over here'. Ten yards of the damnest racket in the world. You could hear the bullets screaming by ... I was now on the beach. It wasn't sand, more like gravel or small rocks, sloping upwards. Machine-gun bullets chewed the water. I dashed into the splashes and yelled for the men behind me to keep moving… Another 50ft was the sea wall. It was packed with men two and three deep. They couldn't dig in because the rocks were 6 to 8in in diameter layered deeply.

On D-Day there were stone breakwaters stretching out into the sea every 70ft or so. These gave some lateral protection to the troops landing from flanking fire, but only from one direction. From ahead and from the exposed side the Rangers were vulnerable to a sniper's bullet or the blast from an artillery round.

The sea wall about which all the Rangers speak was documented by the **US Army**:

A seawall 8 foot in height extends from the exit at 649917 to a point 500yd to the southeast at 654914. At the latter point there is a break of 200yd and then a wall 2 foot, six inches high (reduced to this height by drifting sands) extended 2,000yd to the southeast to 673902. A series of low wooden groynes extend at right angles to the sea wall between 658912 – 661909.

John Raaen:

Artillery was falling at the waters edge, bodies were strewn all over the beach from the water's edge to the sea wall. LCI touched down. As I watched, men started down the side ramps. Wham! An artillery round caught the starboard ramp. Must have hit the flame-thrower there, for the whole side of the ship burst into flames that spread to the deck.

A deadly obstacle. Belgian gates with wooden stakes to impale the landing craft.

We landed within a series of breakwaters and they were made of large stones and offered us a degree of protection.

The bluffs in front of us were covered in smoke and fire and had pushed the Germans inland and blinded others. As a result did not receive fire from above from the people who were placed there to stop us. We only suffered about 5 casualties in 450 men which was good.

Some of the many beach defences – these long poles lying almost horizontally were designed to turn over a landing craft as it floated over it. They were also often fitted with large anti-tank mines which exploded on contact with the small boats. The men seen landing amongst them have a long way to go to reach the base of the bluffs and the fires started by the bombardment can been seen quite vividly.

Cecil Gray, 2nd Platoon, E Company, 5th Rangers:

I was 19 years of age and scared to death. The ramp went down and I went into water up to my knees and I started running across the beach. I remember watching tidal pools with machine-gun bullets kicking across them and then they stopped ... they were reloading ready to fire again so I kept running. We had to get off the beach as fast as we could. We got to the sea wall – it was a wooden wall about 3 or 4ft high and we hunkered there for a while. I was one scared cookie ... I guess we all were.

Emil Nelson Jr:

We had trained for months to hit the beach and run like mad for cover – and when we landed we were loaded down with much more weight. When I got out of the LCA it was all I could do to crawl out of the water. Then we cut all the equipment off. I guess the idea was to get as much stuff on the beach right away.

John Raaen:

For the first time I began to take in the terrain in front of us rather than what was happening on the beach and at the sea wall. The terrain was different from the maps and models.... The sea wall in front of me was made of logs, 3 or 4ft high, yet, our designated landing beach had a stone sea wall – not a log one. Where were we? We couldn't be to the right of Vierville because there would be cliffs in front of us and the Pointe et Raz de la Percée beyond that ... therefore we must be to the left.

Using the code word 'Tallyho', the Rangers began to proceed through the gaps in the wire and make their way to their pre-arranged rendezvous points in Vierville. General Cota was spotted by **Captain John Raaen:**

casually wandering down the beach towards us ... it was clear he was someone with authority, for he was shouting orders and encouragement to the troops huddled against the sea wall ... I jumped up and ran over to him, saluted and reported ... he said, 'I'm General Cota. What's the situation here?' 'Sir the 5th Rangers have landed intact here and to the east about 200yd. The battalion commander has ordered us to proceed by platoon infiltration to our rendezvous points.' [General Cota turned to the troops in his vicinity and said] 'You men are Rangers ... I know you won't let me down', and with that he was off to see Colonel Schneider.

A pre-D-Day Allied reconnaissance plane took this photograph of the Omaha Beach defences at low tide. Just visible at the edge of the beach are the low breakwaters which offered the Rangers a little protection from lateral German fire.

Burton Ranney:

I remember the first shell burst near me after I landed. There were quite a few shell burst in the water as we were coming in, but they had no frightening effect on me, in fact, it was fun to watch them and the machine-gun shells churning up the water.

Digging in on Omaha for protection. Some Rangers had to dig a hole to stay hidden from the German rifle fire.

I was lying behind a dirt bank about 2½ft high and a shell landed on top of the bank within several feet of me. The bank sheltered me from shrapnel and concussion, but threw dirt all over me and the smell of powder was very heavy. I layed there with a million things going through my mind in a matter of seconds. That is when I really realised that I was in combat and everything was for real. From then on, the shell bursts and small arms fire became a matter of routine and after each if you could still move, fine – you would move on.

A German 88 shell exploded and caught three of us. A small piece of shrapnel hit the point of my left shoulder from behind and dropped down inside my fatigue jacket and lay against my bare stomach. When I got hit I was trying to dig a little by throwing these 3 and 4in rocks out. I was so scared that I turned around about three times before I realised what had happened. My shoulder hurt and I was afraid to look at it. I also had to bend over to keep hot pieces of shrapnel from burning my stomach.

Robert Edlin:

Sgt Klaus, one of the section sergeants, was showing me pictures of his wife and children on the way in – he was hit and about to give up to the tide near the water's edge – when I reminded him of our conversation – it brought him back.

Robert Fitzsimmons:

I recall resting for a short time at an amphibious tank on the beach road looking for an exit. I had lost my helmet and rifle. When I realised the tank was drawing mortar fire each time it stopped, I got off and went in close to the cliffs. I recall seeing a brigadier general standing up waving a pistol to show some men laying on the beach it would be best for them to move inland, not to stay on the beach.

The first-aid man that treated my head injury told me that my left eye was gone. It didn't disturb me as I felt fortunate to still be alive. He wanted to give me a shot of morphine to ease the pain, but I refused it as we had been taught not to use morphine in case of a head or stomach wound. I was unconscious for several hours and was left behind on our assault boat for dead. I was surprised at the lack of pain which didn't start until after dark.

Emil Nelson:

Our chaplain, a little Catholic priest about 5in tall and roly-poly, pulled some special service man out of the Channel twice his size and weight. He gave him the last rites before he died. After being pinned down for quite a while we made an attack on Vierville. Everything was confused and hectic.

Jack Burke:

As we got closer to the beach I got down in the landing craft and we began to get in range of the German artillery, and small arms firing. At times you could hear the pinging of bullets and the loud explosions from the shells. When we started for the landing on Omaha Beach the sounds could not be described. I can still hear them to this day as well as the odour of exploding shells [cordite], the engine sounds from the landing crafts, people yelling orders, and finally the ramp going down, and you begin to experience the 'worst day of your life' – D-Day.

I can still see the ugly sight in front of me of guys getting hit before I got off the craft, and much to my amazement the British naval officer standing up to his waist in the water wishing us good luck as we left the boat. 'Good luck Yank'.

Before I took four or five steps machine-gun bullets ripped just in front of me going from my right to left, not more than a foot from my chest and then a shell landed and the concussion knocked me down and I got up in knee-deep water. I heard a lot of screaming from the wounded, and then I saw a sight no one should ever see, of those killed, those who were still in the water wounded and couldn't move yelling for help, and the dead all over the obstacles on the beach, and the rest of us still trying to get out of the water on to the beach to reach the sea wall.

All this with Germans firing with their murderous machine guns – firing without stopping. The 88s, the 105s shelling the beach and the landing area. When I got to the sea wall for some reason I looked to my right and I saw a shell hit a large landing craft loaded with ammunition explode and I will never see anything like it again.... The flame shot sky high and the explosions continued.

Artillery shells have a whistling sound, you only hear it maybe 2 seconds before it explodes. It is a definite sound that anyone in combat recognises, and the general effect is to yell 'get down' or something similar. Incoming mortar shells have a 'whooshing' and you don't have much time to hit the dirt, possibly a second. If the mortar is firing close you can hear a 'thump' as the shell is dropped down the tube, but that is rare. The screaming Mini is a different animal, because it screams like a bunch of cats all screaming at the same time. It is not accurate, but it can unnerve some people.

Avery Thornhill:

We were behind the sea wall waiting for Rangers to blow the wire when two LSIs beached about 50ft from dry land, the ramps on each side of the bow were lowered and these soldiers started down the ramps when both ships were hit directly on the bow. Instead of jumping to the water the others waited, just frozen, I guess, from what they had seen and then the second and third shells hit the bow killing many fine young soldiers who never had a chance to fight. Every inch of that beach was zero'd in by the Germans and how anyone made it I will never know.

Captain Whittington ordered Lt Pepper to have a Bangalore torpedo placed under the double-apron barbed wire fence on the sea wall. Private Fred Rogers was then ordered to blow a hole through the fence and he did so in a few minutes. Scouts were sent through first, Captain Whittington following. The hill was covered with smoke, someone gave the order for gas masks and it was a rough climb up that hill with a gas mask on.

Rangers inside their LCA. Note some are carrying bangalore torpedoes attached to their rifles.

Parker called for 'Bangalores forward' and this call was taken up by James Gabaree and Richard Hathaway. They carefully added one piece to another to make the long strips of tubular explosive ready to go beneath the German wire. Parker noted later that the wire was rolled wire – concertina type and barbed.

James Gabaree:

The landing area was fortified with mines and metal barriers to repel invading forces, as well as many fortifications and concealed underground connecting tunnels. Artillery and machine-gun emplacements were strategically placed to kill men as they left their boats. Our Navy and Air Force were bombing the beach, creating smoke that concealed our landing area from us, causing much confusion. Casualties were heavy; American self-reliance came into play; plans were scrapped, and on-the-spot decisions were made by individuals who saved the day. Due to, wind, waves and currents, most of the landing craft failed to reach their assigned targets. Casualties were so heavy. The Allied air bombardment of the beach defences prior to the landing was largely ineffective, for most of the ordnance fell too far inland. The naval bombardment was allotted only 45 minutes, not enough time to subdue the German defences. The result was the German defences were largely intact, giving them an overlapping field of fire. We were like clay pigeons in a shooting gallery for the Germans. Due to the delay in landing schedule, the tide was lower; the gentle downward slope of the beach gave the Germans an excellent field of fire. We had to run a great distance from the low water mark to reach the shelter of a sea wall protected by barbed wire and land mines. The next obstacle was a steep bluff, it seemed impossible to climb.

James Gabaree was a Bangalore torpedo man. The two he carried comprised a long metal tube filled with dynamite and was fused at one end. It could be used on its own to clear wire entanglements such as the Rangers were encountering at the sea wall. In addition, it could be screwed to another one and pushed under wire to clear a wider stretch. This is what the Rangers did to the wire on the road at the back of the beach. The concertinaed wire at this point was blocking their advance and it was imperative that they blew it and got off the beach.

Gabaree continues:

My job was to precede the troops and blow up the land mines and barbed wire so the soldiers behind me could advance. I set the fuse, and I dived in the opposite direction. The subsequent explosion I felt lift me into the air and I landed on the ground in a dazed condition, but not for long, as my life and the lives of my fellow Rangers depended on me getting them off the beach.

The hole was just large enough for a man to clamber through and so began the exodus of A Company through the wire led by Parker. Other Ranger companies were doing the same along the sea wall at the same time and they inevitably presented the Germans with more and more targets ... once off the beach the Germans could not hit them all.

Jack Burke:

Lieutenant Parker was yelling for the Bangalore men to blow the barbed wire at the base of the hill. The hills were smoking and the word was passed when the wire was blown that we run for the opening to get up the hill. I heard the Bangalore men yell, 'Fire in the hole' and then the explosions ... and we took off.

Daniel Farley, A Company, 5th Rangers Battalion:

I was called 'Junior' in A Company. I was in good physical shape working in the coal fields and I was also a champion Golden Glove boxer. We landed at Dog White on Omaha and ran like hell to get off the beach and it seemed like forever with bullets zipping around us. Jim Gabaree blew the wire and then we went up the bluff.

The A Company men went quickly through the hole in the wire and across the road in a column.

Avery Thornhill:

On arriving on top of the hill we found a well-planned trench and tunnel system. This was cleared before we proceeded on. We had been pinned down about 500yd south of Vierville by snipers and two men had been killed. Captain Whittington and I were in a ditch behind a hedgerow when someone bellowed out from behind to get up and start moving forward as we would never win this war on our tail. Captain Whittington and I looked around to the street and there stood Brigadier General Cota. Captain Whittington hollered to the General that there were snipers in the trees and he should take cover. He said, 'there are no snipers up there' and about that time a bullet struck the ground next to the General and he turned with a passing remark, 'Well, there might be one.'

0859hr USS *Ancon* receives messages from Rangers:

Brit[ish] off[icer] reports on Dog Green Beach. Heavy machine-gun fire. Obstacles not cleared.

Nelson Noyes:

When my boat hit the beach it was sunk by three 88s and about eight or ten men were killed. We went onto the beach and the Germans had us zeroed in. We waded in about a foot of water and came to sand and then rocks which formed a shelf. All of us ran across the beach as fast as we could. I ran about 100ft before hitting the ground, then we ran into enemy cross-fire from the right and in front, which was coming from cliffs which were about 50 to 60ft high and which were sloped at 45 degrees. I was carrying about 75lbs and I crossed the shingle without stopping, hit the ground, got up to run again and then I was hit.

We should give the Navy a lot of credit as they saved our hides. During the naval bombardment very few of us were hit, not directly, but because some shells hit the cliff and knocked rocks down on us. The Navy flattened the town on the top of the cliffs with their fire.

We could see everything when we were lying wounded on the beach. When we hit the beach the 116th Inf. had not moved in. They were still in the water. Then three tanks came in, two of which were promptly knocked out. The beach was not cratered and there had been no bombs dropped at all, but the fighters were strafing all around us. The sea wall was a lot smaller than we were led to believe.

John Hodgson:

There were two of us in a hole on the beach with everything breaking loose. An officer from the 29th Division crawled over to us and asked if we knew where the Rangers were. I said we were Rangers. He then told us to go up the cliffs and knock out the German guns because his men couldn't move off the beach. I don't know if he thought we were supermen or not – just what 2 men from the Rangers could do that his whole battalion of 1,500 couldn't do ... We didn't go!

A shell hit about 6ft to my left, landing on top of a boy in my company and practically at the same instant, something hit me in the face and spun me around. I was afraid to feel my face because I thought I didn't have any left. I didn't have an opportunity to find out how badly I had been hit until I could get off the open field we were in. I didn't feel any pain, but a lot of blood was choking me. About ½ hour later when I found shelter, I found a piece of shrapnel in my chin which knocked out several teeth and was still lodged in my chin. Six days later it was removed in hospital.

0910hr USS *Ancon* receives message from Rangers:

Tide rising rapidly. Obstacles still on beach. Need demolition squad.

From a German defensive perspective chaos was the order of the day. The following report is a sombre relection on what was happening to their positions.

German Div Commander General Kraise to Commanding General Marcks:

The occupational troops in the defence works have fought gallantly. The defensive works 74–91 despite the losses they have suffered are still in full readiness to defend themselves.

At the time, the Pioneer Battalion 352nd together with the 7 company/gren Regt 916, is attacking from Formigny the defence works Nos 68–70.

The 6 company/Gren Regt 916 regained the defence work No. 65a but was then entirely covered by heavy enemy naval artillery fire. The 2 battalion/gren regt 915, in an energetic attack captured the defence works north of Colleville, but is now encircled near Colleville and is clamouring after ammunition. The defence works Nos 37 and 38 have been fighting gallantly and have shot altogether six tanks. On the left wing the counterattack by the 1st battalion Gren Regt 914 against the strongpoint Pointe du Hoc is still progressing. The Field Replacement Battalion and the March Battalion have been moved forward in order to defend Formigny and St Laurent against an enemy heading to the south. Almost all of the radio stations of advanced observation posts have been put out of action.

In Coleville and Vierville heavy local fights continued. In the 914th Gren Regt the enemy had broken through the ring of obstacles at Pointe du Hoc and has slightly pushed back towards the west.

All reserves available to me have already been moved up. Every inch of the ground has to be defended to the upmost capacity, until new reinforcements can be brought up.

Oliver Reed, Staff Sergeant, C Company, 2nd Rangers:

We landed a few minutes behind the 116th Regiment of the 29th Division which was at that time attached to the 1st Division. We were on the 116th's extreme right flank. The beach was not cratered and there had been no bombs dropped at all – but the fighters were still strafing around us. There was another pillbox on the cliff into which wounded were throwing grenades. Snipers were thick on the beach and the men took cover behind the rocks. Where we landed there were no obstacles and if I had landed in shallower water, I could have made it. There was supposed to be a sea wall and just to the right of it were a few obstacles not completely built up, but 50yd to the left they had been completely built up. Our boat could have been brought in further.

Some boys who had gone up the cliff to get the Germans attacked with grenades. Our guns and ammunition were so plugged up that the wounded had set to clean them so that they could be used. I heard from Captain Wysan, that 21 out of 67 men made the crossing and 52 per cent of the company was lost.

One of the deadliest positions the Germans occupied. It was sighted to fire directly down horizontally along the beach where the Rangers landed.

Glen Erickson:

We stayed on the beach and worked the beach – everything from unloading landing craft, protecting ourselves and punching holes in the barbed fire on the beach. You relied on the

Roy Larrison, Jessie Kelly and Joe Smith – 6th Engineering Special Brigade being rescued from their assault dinghy.

ingenuity of individual men and you looked after yourself, your buddies and that was all you could see. Early on there was a lot of artillery fire. You couldn't swim with a lot of this gear and you couldn't fight the water. One of our men punched a hole using a tractor with the blade and after he was shot another guy manned the tractor and let our men through. He was awarded the medal of honour by Bradley for that. It was something you would never forget. We had three battalions which made up the 6th Engineer Special Brigade and we were very good at mine work and demolition. The infantry units were not equipped to do this so clearing the beach obstacles was our responsibility. We were taught to dismantle, blow up and then allow the landing craft to get in.

Walter Rosenblum served in the Army Signal Corps and later the Army Pictorial Service – he took this photograph of 6th Engineering Special Brigade men being treated by their 5th ESB colleagues. A moment well remembered by Glen Erickson who watched his men being dragged from the surf. They had been bringing in ammunition and explosives in their dinghy when German artillery hit them. Despite the best efforts of members of the 5th ESB Medical team they died on the beach.

James Gabaree:

The command came to drop the ramp, and in an instant I knew we were entering a killing zone. The German defences were practically intact; the beach was semi-circular in shape, and we were heading into the centre of a death trap. With enemy guns firing at us from both sides and along the full width of the beach, I jumped into the water, knee deep and red with blood. Although soaking wet and loaded down with equipment, I think I broke the Olympic speed record. To stop to seek shelter meant death. The bullets, mortar and artillery fire were intense. Explosives were going off on the beach ahead of us, and enormous sheets of fire from artillery guns, rifle and mortar fire blanketed the beach. Machine-gun

Not all the men being dragged ashore made it!

bullets were hitting the water with such force, it looked like it was raining. The German 88 artillery gun was a deadly and accurate weapon that sank many craft and killed a great number of our men. The enemy targeted the ramp openings on the landing craft, killing men before they could get off the boat. It was a slaughter; men were dying all around me.

John Hodgson:

When we hit the beach the tide was in. About an hour later the tide went out and you could see about 100yd of sand to reach the beach. I don't know which outfit it was – probably the engineers from the 29th – whose job it was to blow up all the entanglements and mines on the beach so the remainder of the convoys could land. We watched these fellows running out to the obstacles – none carrying any weapons – to blow up the obstacles. Eight or ten men would run to one spot and you could see them being hit. Maybe one or two would come back safely. They kept this up until they had cleared a section of the beach. I couldn't begin to tell you how many of these men were wounded or killed, but the number was high. To me, this was sheer bravery.

0928 USS *Ancon* receives message from Rangers:

Enemy gunfire on Exit D-G and enemy battery behind Dog Green hindering landing.

Dan Schopp, T/5, F Company, 5th Rangers:

We were so cold and miserable that when an artillery shell hit the rear of our LCA and somebody hollered, 'We're sinking", ... the rest of us yelled, 'The hell with it, let it sink', the boat hit a mine which didn't explode, but we were damaged. The British commander and his crew came ashore with their Lewis and made like soldiers.

Robert Gary:

Going in everyone was a bit nervous – some seasick and that was a mess. We were on a British LCA – I remember specifically our training being so realistic. It seemed just like another training mission. The weapons firing and the terrain were so realistic. The weather was so bad that it attracted your attention. Approaching the beach we had trained and been rehearsed so thoroughly that we knew exactly what to do and how to do it. The only thing that changed was that originally we were going to follow in with D and F Companies and attack the Pointe, but it took them so long to get in and up that we went to land on Dog Green Beach.

They lowered the ramp and we landed in water up to our necks. It saved our lives because even though bullets were splashing around they lost a lot of their velocity. I remember looking around – it looked like it was raining on us with so much fire. And the guys were getting hit left and right. I went forward until I was up to my ankles in water – almost on the beach when a round hit my leg. It hit my bone and then it went up and hit my calf. It knocked me down and I lost my radio, etc. I had a carbine and it went flying. I was carrying a little radio and a sergeant from our platoon came by – so I told him I was hit and he took the radio.

I was still in the water and tested my leg. I was able to stand and see if I had a broken bone – I was indeed able to stand at the waterline and I looked down and there was a man dead ... he was the man I had given the radio to. The first thing we did was get rid of our gas masks. We were wearing impregnated clothing and it was awful. We also had the inflatable life vests. We got rid of those in a hurry. The battalion halftracks were not near us to give us support ... there were too many obstacles where we were so we as individuals were just taking care of ourselves and taking care of each other. There were a lot of people getting killed all around us. We just focused on our mission and nothing else.

Boy they were ready for us there ... in fact they must have known we were coming because there was no delay in the getting men into their firing positions. They started firing the moment they saw us coming. Fortunately at that time they didn't have too many big-calibre, direct-fire weapons – it was bad enough as it was.

I picked up a rifle from another dead man and his ammunition bandolier. I got up the hill eventually – it was pretty steep. When I opened the receiver of the rifle it was full of sand. I sat down and took the clip out and cleaned it, then put it back together again. I was sitting on the ground and decided to try and see if the rifle would fire when a man approached from the SFCP [Shore Fire Control Party] and he was looking for other men from his unit. He couldn't find his radio operator with the same markings on his helmet as he had. About the same time as this the Germans were firing traversing fire across the top of the bluffs towards us. He was a few feet away and a round hit him and he started hollering, 'I am hit'. He came over and he had a hole in his jacket about the size of pencil eraser. I sent him down to the beach and later on when I tried to stand up I found I couldn't straighten up my leg – and I asked someone if they had seen him later and they told me that he had died. That little hole in his jacket must have been significant enough to kill him.

Edgar LeRoy Arnold:

After reaching the edge of the water and while running across the beach, I suddenly found myself on the sand as if knocked down by some unknown force. I realised that my carbine had been knocked out of my hands and was about 10ft away lying on the sand. My first thought was to get across the beach and to reach cover at the base of the cliff. I jumped up. Picked up my carbine and raced across the beach. At the base of the cliff, I found that the forearm stock of my carbine had been knocked off. This I could not understand. I found two bullets in an ammo pouch which was strapped to my right side and also one bullet which had stuck in my first-aid packet. Apparently I had been hit with a burst of long-range MG first which knocked the stock from my carbine, two bullets hitting my right hip and sticking in the ammo pouch (twenty-one 1lb blocks of TNT were smashed), and one bullet striking my first-aid packet. No other damage.

The thing that struck me was the complete chaos on the beach. Dead men seemed to be everywhere. I began to get visions of being pushed back into the sea. The fate of the first two waves to hit the beach was not hard to determine because of the dead. One thing that did appear stupid, although I didn't give it much thought at the time, was a white flag waving on a rifle in the water about 20ft from the edge of the water.

Max Coleman:

I remember Cpl Boyington, walking slowly from the surf to the safety of the sea wall with machine-gun bullets falling around him. He was dragging a bag of ammo with his head down. He was unhurt and when asked after why he did not run he said that he was seasick.

We wore assault gas masks that had the canister on the face-piece. A rubber plug was installed on the breather to keep the water out, it had to be removed before one could breathe. I donned my mask and began to run up the steep hill from the beach. Halfway up and just before I was asphyxiated, I remembered to remove the plug. I found out later that the same thing had happened to other people.

Tec 3 Alexander Barber, a medic, confiscated a horse and cart and made numerous trips through 88 fire to carry wounded down to the beach to await evacuation.

1st Lieutenant Moody, killed in action later, lost his helmet on the trip in. His first attempt to replace it on the beach resulted in him picking up one that had a part of someone's head in it. The next helmet he reached for the owner *'came to life'* and claimed it.

Kenneth Bladorn, T/5, A Company, 2nd Rangers:

I landed on the beach about 2 miles to the left of C Company at D + one hour. We landed at extremely low tide. It would have been better if we had left at high tide. There were many obstacles and the water was up to my neck. We were the first in. No one had cleared the obstacles – which were just beach obstacles and a few mines. We just walked between them. I did not notice any trigger wires. We had about 200yd to go after I got out of the water and after about 100yd an 88 hit me in the back (shrapnel) and knocked me out for a minute or two. There was a sea wall to the left about 300 or 400yd away.

Bodies and debris on the beach.

A beached landing craft floates amongst the bodies.

USS *Ancon* receives message from the Air Force:

One squadron armed with 2,000lb bombs attacking Maisy Battery.

Gail Hamilton Belmont:

I had an argument after I was struck in the shoulder from a German machine gun, it was with the medic who came up to help me. I kept insisting that I had been hit in the back, he kept insisting that I had been hit in the front of the shoulder. All the time this argument was going on, we were pinned down by heavy machine-gun fire. Of course, neither of us realised at the time that the bullet had gone through my shoulder and I was bleeding from both sides!

At 0945hr USS *Ancon* receives message:

Batteries at Maisy completely destroyed.

At 0945hr radio report, USS *Chase*:

Last report from plane was that batteries at Maisy were completely destroyed have been unable to verify from SFCP Number 1. One batterie[s] have not fired at anytime during night.

At 0947hr USS *Ancon* receives message from the Rangers:

Tanks off Exit Dog 1 held up [by] crossfire from MGs reported by control vessel Dog Green. Machine gun on right side of Dog Green left side of DOLLY(?) Mortar fire on 2 Dog White coming from bluff.

Albert Nyland, 5th Rangers:

We were all trained to climb the cliffs ... we didn't get the message so we went into the beach ... Schneider said, 'we're not sitting here like sitting ducks' – so he took us in. We landed on Dog White Beach ... instead of Green and the tide was coming in – the obstacles were close to the landing craft. It was about the length of a football field that we had to run to get off the beach to the sea wall. The sea wall was like a big mound of dirt and the sea grass was all across the top of it. When we landed I had six rounds of ammunition for the 81mm mortar and I had to take them out of the wrapping to get them into the box.

I didn't realise that if they had hit me I would have been blown to pieces. I had my life preserver so tightly wrapped around me that I had to stop – not realising that they were still shooting at us – to get the CO_2 cartridge to break it to get it off. Our intelligence officer Captain Burns said it is going to be like a football field – when you get the ball RUN – if there are footsteps in front of you – follow them! Because if there is a big crater then someone hit a mine, but the Air Force did a lousy job. When the ramp went down we hit the sandbar that a shell had made and we all jumped in. We went down and all had condoms on the tops of our rifles – for a moment that was all you could see.

When I got onto the beach I had to pull that off and get to my ammunition and regular pack. As I was running a German shell hit further away from us – but it hit a railroad sleeper and a big piece of its shrapnel hit me in the rear end. Our Doc Captain Petrick came to me and he put sulphur on it. He said, 'No sense in staying here and dying.'

Wallace Wayne Young, Private First Class, 2nd Rangers:

One thing in particular (I remember) – Father Lacy (Ranger Chaplin) was giving plasma, last words and in general helping everyone although shells were falling all over the area. Many of our men at that moment come to realise God helps them that help themselves, a good fox hole was first on the agenda and then the prayer that you would not get hit!

At 1006hr the USS *Texas* reports:

Fighter bombers reported Maisy Batteries destroyed.

At 1037hr the USS *Ancon* receives message:

Rangers landed.

Jack Burke:

I was just getting on the Vierville black top road when they fired the 'screamers' and I dove behind the hedgerow. Later in the day I was up against a hedgerow and took out my cantine to drink some water … to my surprise … no water. I had a hole in my canteen from either shrapnel or a bullet … it was a close call.

Burke and other Rangers were ordered to dig into the field next to the Vierville church. The Germans sent probes and counterattacks into this area from the fields and trees, but each time they were mown down by the Rangers. Jack Burke went after two Rangers from B Company who had gone on a patrol, but then did not return.

Jack Burke:

Captain Whittington of B Company told me to go over the wall and try to find the two men from B Company that had not returned from a short patrol to check the area. He said they heard some firing just as they went out – I climbed over the wall and I went about 30yd along a drainage ditch and found them both dead. It was getting dark and I was out there by myself. I never felt so alone in my life. I crawled back over the wall and told Captain Whittington about them. He wanted to know why I didn't bring them back! … it was now dark so he said, 'We will get them tomorrow.'

Jack Burke dug in with his comrades in a field looking south west. Vierville church was to their left and the Germans came advancing through the wooded area undertaking a number of counterattacks.

Before D-Day **Lieutenant Colonel Robert F. Evans** of the 1st Infantry Division wrote an evaluation of the activity of the evening of 6 June – it turned out to be very accurate:

Probable Enemy Action ... Strong defence of beach 46 by one battalion of the 726th Infantry Regiment. Company sized counterattacks to re-establish beach defences. Rocket and artillery fire on our forces on the beaches from units not yet identified in the area with air bombing. A battalion-sized counterattack against the 116th in the Longueville area and a battalion-sized counterattack north of Treviers, both taking place about midday of D-Day. Minor infiltration of our positions during the night following D-Day.

His prediction of what might take place was indeed accurate as the Germans continued small-unit actions throughout the evening as darkness fell and they continued these probes against the Rangers late into the night.

Jack Burke:

But still they kept coming ... it was the Longest – Worst day of my life.

German report:

Around 2200hr the 916th Gren Regt reported that the Pioneer Bn 352nd was in hand to hand fighting in Vierville and had taken from a fallen American officer an extensive order of the (American) 5th Army Corps.

Paul Louis Medeiros:

Private First Class Bill Roberts told us one about T/5 Albert Uronis. The two of them came upon an abandoned Jerry machine-gun in the midst of a hot fire-fight. We were short of bullets and had practically no automatic weapons, but had been taught to use theirs in just such a situation. Bill grabbed the Jerry machine-gun set it up and began to raise hell with it. 'AJ' (Uronis' nickname) suddenly let out a yell, 'I'm hit, Roberts, I'm hit', and fell to the ground. Bill stopped firing and tried to assist AJ. 'Where are you hit?' he asked. 'Here,' said Uronis, pointing to his chest. Bill looked and could find no wound, meanwhile AJ continued to groan loudly. Finally, Roberts said, 'AJ, your alright, I can't find any wound.' Then he realised that the ejected shells had bounced off Uronis' chest with great rapidity and some force, but of course he was unhurt. AJ very sheepishly arose, picked up his rifle and once again the two of them made Jerry pretty uncomfortable. Poor Uronis never did quite live this down.

The Rangers were ordered by Colonel Canham of the 116th Infantry Division to guard his right flank. At that point Canham did not know what had happened to the task force sent to Pointe du Hoc, and he did not have sufficient men ashore from the beach to guarantee the safety of the landings if the Germans counterattacked in force. By retaining the Rangers in Vierville as a

The Vierville church and graveyard, which were devastated by naval gunfire on 6 June.

defensive line, he actually contributed (in advertently) to the problems of the Rangers at Pointe du Hoc and ensured that they were not relieved until the 8th.

German radio report stated:

In Colleville and Vierville heavy local fights continued. In the 914th Gren Regt the enemy had broken through the ring of obstacles at Pointe du Hoc and had slightly pushed back towards the west.

Ralph Goranson, Captain, C Company, 2nd Rangers:

Looking down from what remained of Vierville church.

After we had crossed the beach and we lay flat under the cliff overhangs I heard this voice hollering, 'Captain, mashed potatoes, mashed potatoes.' It was Mike Gargas, the messenger from the second platoon warning me that there was a potato-masher grenade between my legs and I managed to creep ahead enough so when it went off it did not hurt me. The name 'mashed potatoes' stuck with Mike the rest of the war. So many things happened that seemed normal then, but heroic later, that it is hard to single out one thing. Otto Stephens who led the climbing party up the cliff by pulling himself up with a bayonet to anchor a rope for the rest of us to climb, or the aid man Corporal Rinker who made trip after trip back out on the beach to bring in and treat wounded under the cliff overhangs, Lieutenant Moody who died cleaning out the trenches topside and Sergeant Belcher who single-handedly dispatched all the occupants of several dugouts. It is hard to recall individual happenings because the unit was so small and crippled, but did such a wonderful job as a team in accomplishing its objectives. In the face of direct small-arms fire and under artillery these men were across the beach and topside of the cliffs in a matter of minutes and had begun to accomplish pre-planned objectives practically single-handed, because the units on our left were still on the beach. They had planned their training on fighting in line at the waters edge where they died. We had trained to cross the beach one by one as quickly as possible to the safety of the overhanging cliffs.

Maynard J. Priesman:

I was wounded, it was like a bee sting – until afterwards when I got the pain. A thermite hand grenade came over the cliffs at us and Mike Gargas hollered, 'Mashed potatoes' instead of potato mashers like the Germans called the hand grenades. I remember one of my buddies hair turning white from black. We had twenty-two killed and eighteen wounded out of my company.

At 1146hr USS *Ancon* received the following flying message from the Rangers:

> Commander reported Germans leaving prepared positions and surrendering. Still need gunfire behind Dog and Easy Green Beaches.

Raymond Herlihy, 1st Sergeant, D Company, 5th Rangers.

> The water was rather choppy and the obstacles we encountered [on the beach] were similar to what we suspected and had actually been laid. Hedgehogs, teller mines, etc.

John Bellows, A Company, 5th Rangers:

> I was shot through the arm on the beach, I was trying to get through a mine field when the man in front of me was shot dead at the top of the hill. He hit the dirt and I was lying on a bag of grenades when suddenly one was hit by rifle fire. It hit the smoke grenades in my bag and I quickly threw them away. I was also shot

Vierville church was heavily targeted by the Navy when it was realised that spotters were directing artillery fire onto the beachhead from its spire.

Vierville church today.

through the arm with a flesh wound. I crawled after Lieutenant Parker and I remember what I thought was a dead officer shot through the head – amazingly he lived. We eventually made it to Pointe du Hoc on D-Day.

Alvin Rustebakke, HQ., 2nd Rangers:

I was wounded while still in the water after leaving the landing craft. I remember laying at the edge of the beach, pulling myself out of the water, little by little with each wave, but I was unconscious much of that day.

The 81st Chemical Weapons Unit history records:

At 0720, D Company's craft beached on Easy Green in support of the 3rd Battalion, 116th Infantry, under an incessant hail of machine gun, mortar, and artillery fire. Of necessity the boat teams were landed in water up to their waists, and the precaution that had been taken to attach inflated life belts to the carts proved a wise one. Machine-gun bullets ripped into the belts on several of the carts, deflating them and causing the carts to sink. Sgt Raymond Nicoli, T/R Felice Savino, Pvt McLaren, and Pvt Benton L. Porter were wounded while rescuing this equipment and refused medical aid until this was accomplished. These men were justly awarded the Distinguished Service Cross for their bravery. The preceding wave of infantry was lying only a few yards from the water, pinned down by the fire raking the beach. Lt Mohrfeld, platoon leader, 2nd platoon, was hit within a few minutes by machine-gun fire and died shortly thereafter. Lt Costello assumed command of the platoon and, knowing that too much longer on the beach was certain death, reorganised the squads and infiltrated them off the beach amidst the heavy fire impacting there.

Lt Costello later received the Silver Star for his gallantry. Captain Gaffney, company commander, was instantly killed when the craft in which he was riding struck a mine. Lt Marshall, platoon leader, 1st platoon, took over command. The bravery of the medics in taking care of the wounded under fire was again proven by T/5s White and Marrin.

81mm mortar on its cart ready to go.

The 4.2in mortars of the 81st were capable of instantly firing shells up to a range of 4,400yd and normally the mortars were transported in mortar carts. B Company was unfortunate enough to have one of the vehicle personnel killed and two others plus an officer wounded. Only one B Company jeep was landed, although another was later salvaged; all other vehicles were lost. This was to hamper severely the company's movements for the first few days. The sheer size and weight of the mortar components and ammunition meant that they needed transport to be an effective 'artillery platform' for the Rangers when called upon.

Charlie Ryan:

When we got to the beach our job was to head for Percée up the cliff. You could see the big shells landing on the beach from inland. They were few and far between – but regular. They were a bigger calibre than 88s.

Dan Schopp:

I hit the dirt [sand] halfway across the beach to catch my breath and took a blast of MG fire. Behind my shelter [a steel tetrahedron obstacle] was a GI I first thought dead. He pushed a scared face next to mine and shouted, 'I am supposed to be blowing up these obstacles, but those sons-o-bitches won't let me.' Another burst of fire and I jumped up and headed inland for the comparative safety of the sea wall.

An LCI with a flamethrower armed man was hit by artillery. Much fire and smoke. I saw a man being half carried across the beach. I thought he had on long white evening gloves, nearly removed and hanging inside out. It was his skin shredding off from burns.

Robert Edlin:

I felt a hot poker hit my left leg – I remember falling forward and my M1 flying out of my hand. I thought this is like a grade 8 Westerly – then the thought came – well, I'm out of it already with a Purple Heart. I found out within seconds that they don't stop shooting when you are down. The second time the pain and shock of both legs seem to come to me at once. I got the morphine needle out of my kit and Klaus gave me the shot. I asked him to get another one for my right leg – it seemed funny even then that a fellow would not realise that one shot (of morphine) would numb both legs.

I talked with Sergeant Richard James – after I was wounded the second time – we talked about trying to get some of the wounded dug in and organised at the beach wall. I told Sergeant James to move inland with Sergeant White – he was back in 10 minutes with the fingers shot off both hands.

This sort of thing was happening all along Omaha Beach. When General Cota reached Colonel Schneider's position some 50yd to the left of Captain Raaen the following conversation was overheard by **Ranger Lieutenant Shea:**

Cota asked, 'Are you the Colonel Schneider of the Rangers?' 'Yes, Sir!' Schneider replied. Cota then told him, 'Colonel, you are going to have to lead the way. We are bogged down. We've got to get these men off this God-damned beach.'

The Ranger battalion was now being ordered to lead the way off the beach and it was to attack straight up the bluffs by platoon. This was not easy as men were spread across the beach and some were out of earshot. Others saw movement and made their own decisions. Trained as Rangers, they were taught to move and fire, standing still or staying put meant death – they had to move.

Albert Nyland:

The Lieutenant sent the first Bangalores through and blew the wire. We were told to put on our gas masks because all the sea grass was burning. The guys were throwing phosphorous grenades to give us some cover. I never put my gas mask on and we got away without using them.

Cecil Gray:

We heard that someone had blown the wire and we went up the bluff quickly ... and it was mined. I don't think we lost anyone getting up the bluff – so we sent out patrols and they didn't get very far. I went on one patrol with Lieutenant Dee Anderson and went through 2 hedgerows – he put his head up and he got shot right between the eyes.

The German gun position at the Vierville exit. Sighted to fire down the beach, this position caused huge problems for the Rangers landing in front of its gun.

Albert Nyland:

The machine-gun nest way up top to our left was stopping us getting off the beach. We were trying to get closer to the village because they had an observer in the church and there was a local boy (French) giving the Germans information – we called for the battleship Texas to help us and they were supposed to hit the steeple and destroy it, but it looked pretty good to me.

Donald Chance:

There appeared to be a jam up on the beach at least in our section of Omaha. A 4ft sea wall, barbed wire fence and a steep hill. No one seemed to be moving, General Cota, a one-star General of 1st Division, was on the beach with us. He shouted, 'Lead the way Rangers.' This was the spark needed. The wire was blown up and we stormed the heights. The Germans threw everything our way – rockets, 88s, mortars, machine guns, but they were meant for anyone in the way. I was in charge of two machine-gun sections. They may have been the first to fire on the Germans in this area. On the way in my 1st gunner Darell Hancock (Methodist) was sick and leaning over the boat – he lost his helmet and tripod. My 2nd gunner Goldberry (Jewish) carried a light .30 air-cooled gun with a sling and fired from the hip. He was wounded in the stomach on D-Day. I only point out religion for I am a Catholic. At that time no one gave it a thought.

Richard P. Sullivan:

[I watched] the approach of [my] LCI to the beach, with troops all lined up to run down the gangway to the beach, when an artillery shell containing liquid fire (napalm?) exploded on the deck covering all with flame, causing most of the men to jump into the sea. This happened only a few yards from shore and was probably the man seen by other Rangers. He was carrying a flamethrower and took a direct hit from an artillery shell and was vaporised along with his equipment.

The activities of Brigadier General Dan Cota seemed to be stupid at the time, but it was actually nothing but the sheer heroism and dedication of a professional soldier and fine officer that prompted him to walk up and down the landing beach urging the men forward. I remember his aide-de-camp being a nervous wreck trying to get the General to stop his activities.

Edgar LeRoy Arnold:

I remember having lost about one half of my company crossing the beach and how the other half climbed the cliff and cleaned out and killed or captured the machine guns of the enemy fighting from trenches at the top of the cliff.

John Reville:

The American army were not quite truthful. As infantry we thought that there would be a lot of shell fire on the beach and they let us think that on the beach or a little bit beyond the beach there would be holes for us to jump into as we made our attack. When we finally did land we lay there for hours (in the shingle). My sergeant (I got him a battlefield commission later on), Jeffers, said to me – to make me feel good, 'If you had been in charge we would have attacked the moment we hit the beach.'

The reason he said that was that the company commander was in my boat and the company 1st sergeant was in another boat that stayed with the battalion around Vierville when they landed there. The other men in my boat had layed down with all these hundreds of others – we lay there for hours and hours. The shells were coming in and we were in the place with all the shingle and I remember trying to push them away. I remember the shells would land and I would have to push the shingle away again and again.

A couple of hours later and I remember kneeling up on the ground – as I looked at the ground where I had just been I saw a bullet hit the ground besides me. He had me in his sights and it hit where I had been. All the Navy firepower was directed inland and perhaps they knew better. They let us think that there would be plenty of shell holes – they didn't exist at all and Romell wanted to fight us right on the beach.

John Reville and his men started through the barbed wire and began moving up the bluffs but were stopped near the top:

More time went by and finally the word came to move out. There was nobody left by now where we had been on the beach and I remember stopping on our way off the beach for a moment. There was a soldier with his whole buttocks blown away. I gave him my morphine and then we carried on upwards – but didn't get right to the top – we came upon a place where a house had been levelled – near the top, but not on the top.

Out of the corner of my eye I saw two Germans sitting on a bench at the entrance of their fortification, just where it went down, and I hollered out, 'Crout' and we all got down out of sight. Then I did a foolish thing. I had Jeffers with me and Captain Runge and I pulled back, these guys had left the seat where they had fired a few shots at us from. I called for one man to come with me and we went around and it was a huge bunker. I caught the two Germans backing away from the place where we first saw them.

I dropped to my knee and I shot one of them and he was a seasoned [old] guy. The other guy immediately put the Schmeiser machine pistol above his head as he didn't know what was behind him and fired it. We dropped back down and returned to where the whole platoon was as it was getting dark. We had run out of ammunition and I remember getting a couple of the Schmeisers and using them. You had to be careful as someone 100ft way would hear the distinctive noise of the Schmeiser and he wouldn't know if it was an American or a German using it. I saw one German plane on D–Day at 11pm at night. It came right over our position – we were hardly off the beach at all and it turned right and dropped its bombs along the activity in that area.

Glen Erickson:

I think it was a LSI I saw – it took a direct hit with our men onboard and it became a marker on the beach which we used to indicate north or south on the beach. The men below the deck were fried. The company commander who was a friend of mine was blown off. That was B Company of the 149th and they took heavy casualties right off.

A helmet belonging to a captain in HQ Company, 6th Engineer Special Brigade.

The American aircraft were supposed to have dropped bombs, but they missed the beaches by several miles, so everything that could go wrong did go wrong. There were no holes on the beaches. When we got up on top of the hill at night there was very little in the way of German aircraft. The snipers used to let the men through and then target the officers, so we removed our stripes from the helmets quickly. On my helmet there was a stripe on the back before D–Day – but we removed them quickly after that. We didn't have it quite as rough as the Rangers. But I lost a lot of men on the beach.

Chapter 3

Rangers Lead the Way

James Gabaree:

There was thick vegetation in an earthen embankment 3 to 5ft tall and deep, it was almost impossible to penetrate – the farmers of Normandy have bordered their fields in this way for hundreds of years, with small sunken lanes running alongside. The hedges formed a canopy over the lanes that were perfect hiding places for enemy snipers and machine guns. Looking down at the incoming forces I saw the horrible sight of men being blown to pieces. I threw away all my gear except my gun and ammunition.

Daniel Farley:

We came up to a drainage ditch and kept low – following it along with the others we went up to a chateau and there was nobody there. All the way we were getting shot at by snipers.

It was at about 2pm in the afternoon when Parker and his men reached their first rendezvous point and began to search it. It is estimated that they had taken twelve prisoners and killed as many in that short distance.

1710hr German report from 2nd Battalion Grenadier Regiment 915:

Battalion has been bypassed by the enemy in the rear near Chateau Coleville, he has broken through to the south. Wounded cannot be brought back any longer.

Parker's group had in effect cut off the German rear positions from the front. Their engaging of units approaching towards the coast will have added to the German perception that the whole of that area had been captured, rather than in reality only a small set of buildings.

James Gabaree:

At the rendezvous point near a French farmhouse we were shocked to find that we only had twenty-six men in our group, having started at the beach with seventy-two men in A Company.

Working their way along hedgerows and ditches, the A Company men kept low and crawled much of the way towards their rendezvous point. At one point a couple of men went into some woods in search of a German sniper, but they were never seen again.

The Rangers' objective: Chateau de Vaumicel, marked by a dark circle. Later research indicates that it is perhaps the similar looking Chateau L'ormel, marked by a square, which A Company reached. The speed at which they reached their objective and that perhaps it was the wrong building are two factors that might have led to them thinking they were all alone.

The Chateau Vaumicel as it is today. When questioned A Company men have expressed doubts as to whether this is the chateau they arrived at on 6 June.

The Rangers had not had anything to eat or drink by the time they entered the chateau grounds and began to search the various barns and outbuildings. The farm had, in fact, been a fully working dairy farm until the previous day. Parker was surprised that there was nobody else there and said that he assumed that the rest of the battalion had been there and gone. He made the decision to move out quickly.

The US War Department official history states:

> *A platoon of A Company 5th Rangers – 1st Lt. Charles H. Parker Jnr., commanding, on reaching the bluff crest had seen no other troops, and immediately started southwest*

Chateau L'ormel as it stands rebuilt today.

Chateau L'ormel destroyed during the bombardment. It is possibly the actual chateau reached by the A Company men.

to get around Vierville and reach the battalion assembly area. After making a half-mile without meeting opposition, the platoon was stopped by enemy fire from hedgerows near the Chateau de Vaumicel, just south of Vierville. They spent the rest of the morning working past this fire toward the chateau grounds.

James Gabaree:

The combined forces should have equalled 560 men. We had a problem. Were we the only ones that got off the beach? Did the invasion fail? There was no time to ponder. Our mission was to destroy the big guns at the Pointe, so we took off at a run.

In reality what happened was that Parker ordered his men to blow the wire at the wall and Rangers Gabaree and Hathaway fired their Bangalore torpedoes. The A Company men had left the beach ahead of the main group, rushed across the brush straight up the bluff climbing hand over hand or using small paths. Wearing gas masks to combat the smoke, some men were confused and the contact between platoons and sections was lost when elements came under fire.

One of the many German machine-gun tobruks. These were sited to fire across the tops of the bluffs. You can see the sea some distance away and the beach is below the edge. When the Rangers arrived on the top they were confronted by withering fire from these positions and the trenches that surrounded them.

Parker was leading his company, which at that stage was virtually intact, across the fields above the bluffs and they continually came under enemy machine-gun and sniper fire. Parker felt snipers' bullets cutting into his pack as he lay in the open field and watched horrified as 1st Lieutenant W. Moody was hit in the head and seriously hurt by a bullet and William Fox was mortally wounded by another bullet which entered his shoulder and severed his spine. Parker was wearing an invasion vest – a jacket specifically designed to carry extra ammunition and supplies. Although it was useful, it was difficult to remove in a combat situation and he fought with the jacket as bullets cut into it. After struggling on the ground, he eventually succeeded in removing it and left it along with all his equipment still attached to it in the field. He was now left with only a pistol to defend himself.

Staying low and skirting the fields through drainage ditches, A Company advanced into Vierville in single file. However, unknown to Parker, an incident halfway down his column of men stopped the rear party from keeping up. One of his platoon leaders, Lieutenant Suchier had been hit, some say in the hand and others in the ankle – perhaps both, but whichever it was – as a result the column stopped behind him. Lieutenant Parker was now leading twenty-six men and not his whole company – something he did not realise until they entered the village.

James Gabaree was with Lieutenant Parker in the lead group:

The dirt country roads were lined with hedgerows, making them seem like tunnels affording cover for the enemy, so we took to the open countryside. There were many firefights, and in the process we captured about twenty prisoners. Our fighting force practically equalled the number of captives, so what should we do, take them with us, kill them or turn them loose? We disarmed them and chose the latter. At one point we were ambushed on a road between two hedgerows. The Germans were throwing hand grenades at us from behind the bushes, but Rangers grabbed the German's grenades before they went off and threw them back before they could explode on our side of the bushes. Their own weapons killed them.

The top of the bluffs seen from the German perspective. The houses and gardens were not there during the war and in many places beyond the sea wall there was a stretch of marshy ground to be covered before climbing almost vertically up the bluff.

Secret pre-D-Day papers described the conditions now being faced by the Rangers:

Although not listed as obstacles, the hindering effects of hedges and walls should not be overlooked. The cultivated fields which lie inland from the coastal cliffs are bordered by low hedges and earth banks. In the more fertile lowland those banks are several feet high and are frequently crowned with beach or hawthorn hedges. Almost all roads leading from Beach 46 (Omaha) are bordered by low tree-hedges and banks and in some places stone walls. These hedges and banks are fairly old and probably sufficiently resistant to constitute definite obstacles to deployment and cross country movement of motor vehicles and tanks.

With this type of thick brush it is easy to see why the Rangers became disorientated by the smoke and the shelling. The brush easily caught fire with the bombardment and it also aided the Germans as it helped to obscure their gun positions from the vigilant Navy spotters. The Germans could fire at a very short distance against the Rangers without risk of being noticed by the ships' observers out at sea.

James Gabaree:

At one point, in the dash to the Pointe, a German soldier appeared from nowhere. He had a weapon pointed at me … instinctively, I shot him in the chest. A surprised look appeared on his face, then he turned sort of blue and dropped to the ground. I was 19 years old and already killed a man. What a way to spend one's youth!

Daniel Farley:

We found we were fighting all the way – small firefights with the Germans and we collected about twenty prisoners. We kept getting into these firefights and the prisoners were not helping the situation. So finally Ace says, 'What the hell are we going to do?' And I said, 'Let's turn them loose.' We had destroyed everything they had, so we turned them loose and took off in the opposite direction. This might have been a factor in a lot of other Germans surrendering because maybe the word got around that we weren't going to hurt anybody.

Richard Hathaway, T/5 Sergeant, A Company, 5th Rangers:

Lieutenant Parker showed me the map and pointed out the direction we were to take. We took a dirt road that angled off toward a blacktop highway that went through the village of Englesqueville and then to Au Guay and Pointe du Hoc.

After checking the men they realised that they were three men short, Staff Sergeant William Scott, Private First Class Henry Santos and Private First Class George Chiatello. The group was now approximately 1½ miles inland, 10 miles from their target and down to twenty-three men.

Richard Hathaway:

When we eventually came to the village of Englesqueville there was a bend and two Germans appeared on bicycles. We didn't shoot them as it was all so sudden. I threw a grenade inside a house where one of them ran, but nothing came of it.

The Ranger group advanced along the lanes beyond Englesqueville and as they became narrower they were more open to opportunist attack from hidden Germans. Parker re-inforced the front of his column and the group came under attack again. He then decided to release the prisoners that were slowing them down and after a brief exchange of gunfire, which wounded Kalar, the Rangers set off at a run. A group of Germans had been trying to out-flank the Rangers through adjoining fields and Parker's move was a shrewd one. By releasing the un-armed prisoners in a farm and then setting off in another direction the Rangers maintained the advantage of speed and distance.

At the beach, given all the chaos surrounding the battle there, it is easy to forget that someone had to direct the fire on behalf of the battle fleet at sea. They were not just firing blindly, when fire was not directed by spotter planes, it was done by men on the ground.

Specialist units called Naval Shore Fire Control Parties acted as liaison for the men on the ground and were able to call upon the Navy to deliver shells where needed. Shore Fire Control Parties and fire-control ships were to use the Shore Fire Control Code which was standard operating procedure as outlined in the Allied Expeditionary Force Signal Book.

The SFCPs used SCR609 and SCR284 radios for gunfire support communications and all support ships. The exceptions were Hunt Class destroyers, *Soemba*, *Ellyson*, *Hambleton*, *Rodman*, *Emmons*, *Barton*, *Walke*, *Laffey*, *Meredith* and *O'Brien*, which were equipped with SCR608 sets.

The various call signs allocated to gunfire support ships were as follows:

The SCR609 portable radio set as used by Shore Fire Control Parties.

Nevada	DVN	*Shubrick*	BHS
Texas	SXT	*Nelson*	SLN
Arkansas	NKR	*Murphy*	PRM
Rebus	SBR	*Glennon*	NLG
Quincy	CNQ	*Jeffers*	FJF
Tuscaloosa	SUT	*Plunkett*	KLN
Augusta	TSG	*Tanatside*	TNT
Hawkins	KWH	*Melbreak*	BLM
Glasgow	SLG	*Talybont*	YLT
Georges Leygues	GRG	*Barton*	TRB
Montcalm	TNM	*Walke*	LAW
Enterprise	NTR	*Laffey*	FAL
Bellona	LBL	*Meredith*	DRM
Black Prince	CLB	*O'Brien*	RBO
Soemba	BMS	*Jouett*	TUJ
Frankford	ARF	*Somers*	MOS
Carmick	MRC	*Harding*	RAH
Doyle	LYD	*Satterlee*	TAS
Endicott	CDN	*Thompson*	MHT
McCook	CMC	*Forrest*	RFR
Baldwin	DLB	*Fitch*	TIF
Corry	RCR	*Davis*	VAD
Hobson	BOH	*Ellyson*	LEL
Butler	LTB	*Hambleton*	MAH
Gherardi	RHG	*Rodman*	MDR
Herndon	NRH	*Emmons*	MEM

Shore Fire Control Party No. 1 was attached to the 2nd Ranger Battalion – call sign DJX.

Shore Fire Control Party No. 2 was attached to the 5th Ranger Battalion – call sign FGH.

Shore Fire Control Party No. 3 was attached to the 1st Battalion 116th – call sign KRD. Naval Shore Fire Control Party No. 3 was composed of two officers and twelve enlisted men and was tasked with providing support for 1st Battalion 116th Infantry Regimental Combat Team on D-Day.

Lieutenant Coit Coker, USNR was in SFCP No. 3:

We landed with Captain Hawks of C Company at about 0740, approximately 1 mile east of the scheduled landing place (opposite D1 Exit). The ramp of the LCVP went down a foot and then stuck. Some C Company men were stuck in it and I do not know if they were ever extricated. Another man had his leg crushed between our craft and an adjacent one. Captain Hawks jumped over the side and was nearly crushed between our craft and one on the other side, but finally was pulled back in without injury.

Coker's craft was sinking and the ramp was indeed stuck halfway open. The only way off it was jumping over the side, but that was not without problems. To their right only 30yd away a boat received a direct hit and burst into flames. Struggling with all their equipment, his unit swam to the shallow water and eventually made it to the sea wall without further injuries.

Coit Coker:

We set up on the beach (about 0830) and contacted the destroyer McCook, *telling her to stand by. I then took Kelly with me on a scouting party up the beach towards D1 in an effort to locate the 1st Battalion, but we were unsuccessful. On this trip an 88 burst nearby and a small piece of shrapnel struck my right kneecap causing a superficial wound. About 0930hr all of us crossed over the remainder of the beach and worked up the slope, under enemy observation and fire, to the edge of the plateau on top.*

Here we were joined by Captain Vavruska (NGFO of 5th Ranger Battalion) and all of us joined with Lieutenant Vandervoort (1st Battalion) and his platoon and commenced working toward the D1 Exit.

On the plateau was a field of grass (650903) with numerous foxholes containing Germans. It was decided about noon to bring naval fire on this field by spotting in deflection from well to the right (to avoid hitting ourselves) crossing D1 Exit. All of us were close to death on many occasions and I can attribute our safety only to the Lord, luck and the fine sprit and level headedness of the men.

A great many prisoners from the 352nd Infantry Division were captured during the initial phases of the landings. Intelligence gathered from them along with a map found in a pillbox on the E-3 Exit gave detailed locations of all the 352nd Infantry Division positions. The exact placement of artillery units, regimental, divisional command posts gave the Allied commanders valuable intelligence.

Allied bombardments became more accurate and this helped to reduce the effectiveness of the German artillery. It is undoubtedly the case that the guns at Maisy came under more intense and accurate fire from that time, and this will have relieved the fire on the beaches when their guns were damaged.

Lieutentant Shea, General Cota's aide-de-camp, reported that Cota ordered Schneider to blow the wire and lead the 5th Rangers against the enemy fortifications at Pointe et Raz de la Percée. It was these forts lying between Vierville and the Pointe et Raz de la Percée that were shelling the assault boats as they landed on Omaha Beach. This was no light proposition for the Rangers. The positions between the Vierville exit up to and including Pointe du Hoc were listed in intelligence reports as follows:

648916 (defended locality). Infantry position on the coast in Vierville-sur-Mer: two pillboxes; one shelter; anti-tank gun, possibly 75mm reported; one AAMG; anti-tank ditch is reported across road at approximately 648916; this is not confirmed by air photographs; position is surrounded by wire on flanks and rear mine belt on south and east. Garrison is approximately one platoon.

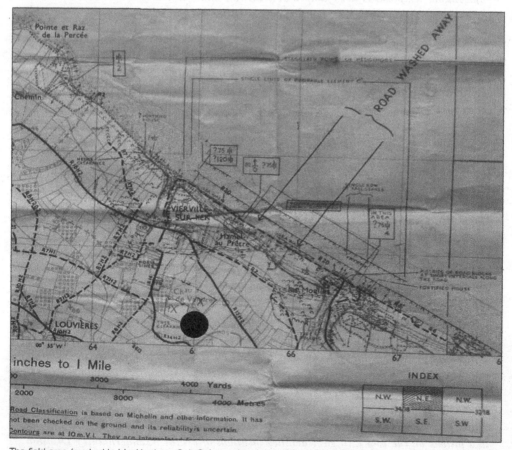

The field area (marked in black) where Coit Coker ordered the USS *McCook* to fire at. It was also very close to the rendezvous point for the Rangers, just south of the chateau.

645918 (Defended Locality). Infantry position on coast immediately west of Vierville-sur-Mer: one pillbox; one gun casemate for light gun; position is surrounded by wire. Garrison is approximately one squad.

655913 (Defended Locality). Infantry position on coast near Vierville-sur-Mer: two shelters; one pillbox; one 81mm mortar; one AAMG; possibly one 75mm infantry gun; position is surrounded by wire. Garrision is approximately one squad.

St. Pierre du Mont. 622935 (Defended Locality). Radar station on coast defended by infantry weapons: one pillbox; seven shelters; two under construction; wire to flanks and rear. Garrison is approximately one platoon.

611927 (Defended Post). Probably a company headquarters is located at the Chateau D'Englesqueville in the wood: three pillboxes are reported here; four large huts; this position is probably defended by light automatic weapons, although details cannot be seen on air photographs.

602937 (Defended Locality). Infantry position on the coast north of St. Pierre du Mont; probably not permanently occupied.

586939 Pointe du Hoc (Battery Position).

Each position offered the potential to be a heavily defended outpost and one that must be taken using all the skills learned by the Rangers in training.

Taken from the archives of the 16th Infantry Division for D-Day, the following passage gives an indication of what the Rangers were up against. Not only were they tasked with taking the various beach and inland positions, but they had to be aware of the increasing number of Germans infiltrating the area as D-Day progressed. Along with these extra reinforcements came intelligence that the Allies could use against the Germans.

Hundreds of German reinforcements had been sent into the beach villages on D-Day and many arrived by bicycle and on foot. In the Colleville area many were later captured from the 726th, 915th and 916th Inf. Regiments.

The advance continues – this photograph was taken from further inland looking towards the beach.

On the beach, General Cota's actions were quite possibly the catalyst for the Rangers' advance inland. His motivation at the right moment sent the troops away from the enfilading and artillery fire on the beaches. After briefing Schneider, General Cota turned around to a Ranger nearby and said, 'Rangers! Lead the way!'

The Rangers were coming under attack at Pointe du Hoc beneath the cliffs and on Omaha Beach with a ferocity which would have caused many lesser men to falter. The 'can do' mentality and strength of training kicked in and many of the Rangers like James Gabaree and Daniel Farley admit that they 'ran like hell' to get off the beach – and off the beach they went. While other units hid behind obstacles and the sea wall to avoid the gunfire, the Rangers famously did 'lead the way' and slowly made headway up the bluffs. In small

Souvenirs taken from German prisoners on the beach by F Company's John Reville. Now on display in Weymouth D-Day Museum.

groups, singly and in pairs, they blew Bangalore torpedoes to clear the wire and went over the shingle wall. Some looked to follow others up well-worn German tracks and others literally climbed hand over hand using knives and tree roots as supports.

At H-hour USS *Carmick* was stationed off Omaha Beach and was firing at targets of opportunity all along the beach. Initially its assigned target was an area some 1,500yd back from the beach which required them to fire air-burst shells into German positions. However, because of the extreme range it was decided that as American troops were advancing inland there was a possibility of hitting their own men and the plan was changed.

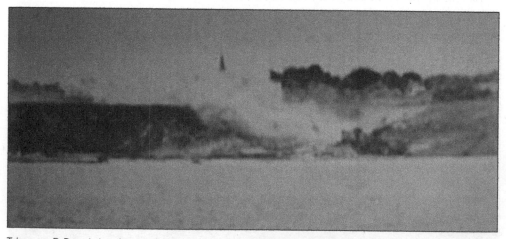

Taken on D-Day during the naval bombardment, this photograph of Vierville exit shows one of the problems encountered by the Navy. The exit is being taken under fire and is also obscured by clouds of smoke. The church tower is still visible behind the smoke, so it must have been taken early in the morning.

The SFCP was contacted only twice during the morning. Despite USS *Carmick* firing on areas ranging from Pointe et Raz de la Percée to Exit No. 1 on Fox Red Beach in the period from H-hour until 12 noon, most of its targets were on Dog and Charlie beaches. *Carmick* developed a novel way of knocking out German positions in conjunction with the ground forces. Troops on the ground would, in many cases, open fire on unseen Germans guns and their fire would alert the watchmen on the *Carmick*. The *Carmick* would then in turn also fire several salvos at the same spot. As the tanks and infantry advanced so did the ships gunfire. In one instance a group of American infantrymen were held down behind a house in the Dog Green area. The *Carmick* opened fire at a point above where they were directing their rifle fire and the soldiers were able to advance upwards again.

At 0810hr USS *Carmick* was called upon by its SFCP to fire on target T5 – Maisy Battery, Les Perruques. It fired one ranging salvo at Maisy at a range of 17,000yd and then it was unable to re-contact the SFCP because of transmitter trouble on the ground. It was later discovered that the SFCP had left their transmitter key open, thus making further contact impossible. However, the ship could hear the conversations and machine-gun fire coming from the open microphone.

At the same time USS *Franford* fired at an emplacement located at the side of the valley near D1 Exit. This position seemed to be holding up the ground troops' advance. The *Franford* literally covered the whole of the side of the valley with fire and the inland advance was able to continue. Some twenty prisoners were brought from the area half an hour later and the position was taken thanks to accurate gunnery.

Carmick, along with USS *Texas*, set about destroying the sea wall and demolished all buildings along the beach. *Carmick* also engaged the caves and stone emplacements set into the cliffs on the Vierville side of Pointe et Raz de la Percée ahead of the Rangers' advance and also any and all gun emplacements along the bluffs.

During the period H-hour – 40 minutes to 5pm on D-Day *Carmick* expended 1,127 rounds of ammunition. Throughout this time the ship's After Action Report recorded:

The ship operated as close to the beach as safe navigation and traffic would allow. This varied from 900 to 3,000yd. During this time medium calibre artillery and/or mortar projectiles fell around the ship, never seriously endangering it, however. The enemy fire seemed to be concentrated at the water's edge where numerous landing craft were beached. Several of these, including two LCIs and one PC were observed to be hit and burning.

As this modern-day photograph clearly demonstrates, one of the other obstacles to be overcome by the Rangers were the bunkers set into the bluffs. These were not ones that faced out to sea but were positioned to fire horizontally down onto the Vierville exit and presented a very difficult target for the Navy to see and destroy.

Alex Barber:

On the signal of the battalion commander, the leading troops scrambled over the wall, blew gaps in the protective barbed wire, and protected by the rising smoke advanced to a point near the top of the hill. Where the smoke had cleared and the hill was being swept by enemy automatic fire. First Lieutenant Dawson of D Company led his platoon over the top and eliminated an enemy strongpoint, enabling the entire battalion to advance. Here mine fields became as prevalent as bees on a honeycomb and the battalion had to change into a column formation, winding in and out of those formidable, hidden defences. B Company, the leading unit, reached the St Laurent-sur-Mer–Vierville-sur-Mer road at a point approximately 1km east of Vierville-sur-Mer. In the course of this advance, many Germans well concealed in weapons pits constructed in the hedgerows were killed. The battalion advanced towards Vierville-sur-Mer, B and E Companies, at attempting a penetration to the south, were stopped by intense machine-gun fire. C Company fired an 81mm mortar concentration, knocking out several of the positions, but they were replaced so quickly that E Company was forced to abandon its southern attack. Several direct artillery hits on the area of the battalion column caused many casualties.

T/5 Steven Oboryshko enlisted in the Army on 22 October 1942 in Camden, New Jersey and was originally from Delaware. Previously employed by the railroad, he joined C Company of the 5th Battalion. He had served in the Army for one year and seven months when he became one of the many killed in action during the advance from the beach.

The sea wall ran along the front of the beach and in this aerial photograph you can see the substantial groundworks undertaken by the Germans. Behind the sea wall they had built a large anti-tank ditch – visible as long zigzag lines across the photograph.

The village of Vierville-sur-Mer from above today. The Rangers landed on this stretch of beach and had to climb the steep bluffs to get to the high ground.

The exit from the beach taken by Ranger Jack Burke and many of his fellow Rangers. Although it looks flat in this aerial photograph, in reality it is not.

The same valley slopes sharply upwards.

Once off the road and into the bushes the Rangers found a small track made by the German soldiers. By following this track alongside the concrete fence posts they made it to the top clear of any mines.

Even halfway up the bluff exit the view of the beach is superb. One thing that worked in the Rangers' favour was the amount of fire and smoke created by burning bracken. This and the constant shelling made it difficult for the Germans to concentrate their fire on the Rangers leaving the beach area.

The top of the bluff. It is little wonder the Germans could fire immediately into the Rangers as they left the valley. The ground expands out towards Vierville village and offers little or no cover from German machine guns. The Rangers were forced to stick to the hedgerows and field edges. These fields were also all marked with 'Achtung Minen' signs. It is not clear if all the fields were actually mined, but there were plenty of instances of men falling foul of them.

Avery Thornhill:

About noon time we arrived east of Vierville and were engaged by the enemy. The enemy was in a retreat to the east and we did not attempt to engage them further as we had orders to get to Pointe du Hoc with all speed. We then passed through Vierville with no contact with the enemy. About 300yd south of Vierville we were engaged by machine guns and sniper fire. As we had made a fast move through the town it was decided that we would send a couple of squads of men back to check the area to our immediate rear, sure enough, they found a dozen Germans hiding in the hedgerows.

Here, we lost our first two men killed in action. One of the group had been pinned down in front of a hedgerow and it was believed he was hit as we could hear someone moaning, this boy jumped up, said 'They can't do that' and he leaped to the top of the hedgerow and was immediately hit in the heart. Needless to say, he died immediately. After giving his life for his friend, it was life given up for nothing as we were able to relieve the man on the other side without casualty and his friend was not hurt. A German that had been hit by a hand grenade was doing the moaning.

Alex Barber:

All pressure was exerted to take Vierville-sur-Mer, and after overcoming considerable sniper fire, the battalion advanced through the town to its western outskirts where heavy resistance was encountered. Dusk was all too quickly turning into darkness, and the battalion together with three companies of the 2nd Rangers – part of the first battalion of the 116th infantry and the 743rd tank battalion – set up a perimeter defence for the night. One platoon of A Company which had been separated from the battalion during the crossing of the sea wall proceeded through the town to the rally point SW of the town, arriving with twelve prisoners and killing at least that many more Germans. The platoon from F Company, which landed near St Laurent sur Mer, encountered heavy artillery and machine-gun fire. Numerous patrols were sent out in an attempt to contact the battalion, but failed. This unit then attempted to move along the beach towards Vierville-sur-Mer, but after advancing 600yd, receiving artillery fire which inflicted eight casualties, found themselves pinned down by a far superior force and darkness found the platoon in this position. I cared for the wounded as a medic. My first wounded case made me frightened, for I had to run to the soldier through the machine-gun and artillery fire. When I arrived at the injured soldier's side I felt relieved and administered medical attention and carried him to safety without being hit myself. From then on I felt I was leading a charmed life and defied all dangers in my efforts to save lives. I saw one soldier holding his best friend, not realising the friend was dead!

Captain Raaen was ordered by Major Sullivan to skirt around a field in order to draw fire from the enemy. This was essential to identify the enemy's machine-gun positions and to allow the rest of the battalion to spread out onto the plateau. This he did successfully and after zigzagging 75 to 100yd across a field he then jumped into a ditch with a dead German.

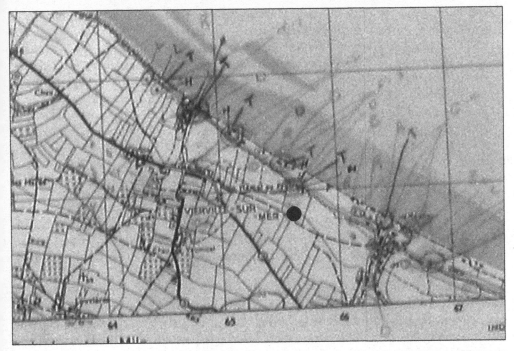

Grid reference 65559081 marked with a black circle where Captain Raaen ended up in a ditch with a dead German.

John Raaen:

From there we proceeded to the main road and got involved with a series of German police and German machine guns and we wasted a great deal of time trying to envelop them and every time we tried to take one, another one would pop up on our flank.

Colonel Schneider finally abandoned these efforts to envelop these machine guns and pass south of Vierville and we moved down the coastal road through Vierville and were ordered by the 116th Infantry (to whom we were attached) to undertake positions for the night – protecting Vierville on its west and its south.

Other Rangers joined up and examined empty trenches. A pair of men from A Company watched as the Germans came out of dugouts and manned their positions after the bombardment. Working in twos and threes, the Rangers mopped up each position one after another, taking six prisoners and killing as many more.

Carl Weast:

Captain G. Whittington was one of the lead men in our advance off the beach and up the bluffs. Near the top of the bluff a grass fire was burning giving us smoke cover, a very happy accident. 'Whit' came upon a German machine-gun position from their rear, unnoticed. When one of the three Germans turned and saw 'Whit', a fierce-looking fellow, he repeated the words 'Bitte, bitte, bitte'. 'Whit' shot the three of them, turned and asked, 'I wonder what bitte means?'

Shortly before we of 2nd platoon discovered Colonel Canham's isolated command post, we were hit by a heavy artillery barrage. As a result of it Elmo Banning was killed instantly, and Sergeant Walker McIlwain had a badly shattered left forearm. Mac continued to work with us for several hours, finally we almost had to fight him to get him to go back to the medics. As I recall about seven of us – a major, a captain and several enlisted men, found the 116th regimental Combat Team Command Post properly established according to plan while most of Colonel Canham's troops were still down on the beaches being blown to bits. We were indeed 'impressed as his CP guard', in fact as far as Colonel Canham knew, we were the only troops in the ETO. A regimental commander facing the coming night with an enemy counterattack likely along his 7,000yd front and the larger part of his available forces consisted of the 5th Rangers, not part of his command! We should have been on our way to Pointe du Hoc.

And so the die was cast for many of the 5th and 2nd Rangers who landed on the beach. Colonel Canham was facing an unknown and hostile counterattacking force and he had nobody else to provide his defence other than the Rangers. He told them to dig in where they stood.

C Company, 2nd Rangers, had a separate mission of its own at Omaha Beach. It was ordered to land with the first assault wave of the 116th and knock out German strongpoints near Pointe et Raz de la Percée, immediately flanking the Omaha Vierville sector landing beaches. This was a vital German position as it had unrestricted observation and firing positions for the length of the beach and had to be neutralised.

On its approach C Company watched one of six LCAs carrying A Company of the 116th Regiment ahead of them floundering. They witnessed men jumping over into the sea and being dragging underneath by their loads. Their own craft was suddenly covered in highly accurate and intense machine-gun and rifle fire. Chaos ensued as men attempted to dive overboard to escape the withering gunfire. They dropped into the surf just as accurate mortar fire 'disintegrated' one LCA.

About thirty of the C Company men got across the sand and they found shelter at the base of the cliff just west of the Vierville exit. Leaving the shelter was dangerous, but it was a necessity, it was an impossible 90ft vertical climb at this spot – so an alternative route had to be found to their objective above. As a result, three men went off westward looking for a likely spot from which to make the climb and by using bayonets, knives and pulling each other along they advanced upwards. 1st Lieutenant William Moody was in charge of the group and by using four toggle ropes attached to minefield stakes the group made it up the cliff.

Ranger Captain Goranson put his men into trenches just west of the house and sent them towards the enemy positions. A firefight ensued at a fortified farmhouse over some hours and a maze of trenches allowed the Germans to continue to reinforce the position despite heavy losses. Each time the Rangers had the upper hand the Germans would send reinforcements. The Rangers did, however, put out of action a mortar that was firing on the Vierville exit and a machine-gun nest. Both of these positions were sighted to fire along the Vierville exit approaching beach area and the actions of these troops during the vital period of the landings will have contributed significantly to the safe landing of the rest of the 5th Battalion – men who had been landing less than ¼ mile away under full view and fire from this position.

Although they had only suffered two casualties, an American burial party later reported the Rangers had killed sixty-nine Germans in this one action alone. There can be no doubt that they saved many lives by preventing the Germans from re-manning their weapons at this position.

William Runge:

I remember Lieutenant John Reville and I walked into a German position at dusk – Reville walked point blank into a German – pointed his gun, pulled the trigger and the gun failed to fire, he jumped back yelling, 'They're in there' – he threw a grenade in and forgot to pull the pin!

Robert Gary:

We had an aid station set up by the sea wall and when things had quietened down they put sulfur on my wounds. I didn't seem to need morphine so they tied it up. After that I started helping pull those guys off the beach. My wound took out a large chunk of flesh on my leg – it felt like a hot poker going into the back part of my leg. That night they took a bunch of us off the beach to a support vessel and they had a lot of wounded people on there before we were evacuated. There were two German planes that hit the beach. They were the only two German aircraft left in the area. Of course they were flying in against balloons … it was quite a sight to see these guys flying in. But all these weapons firing up at them. You can't imagine all the tracer rounds going off.

Frank Kennard:

I did see one German fighter make one pass over the Vierville section of Omaha Beach late in the afternoon of D-Day.

Raymond Herlihy:

I remember one incident during a German attack on the evening of 6 June – and with complete amazement – the incredible actions of an old French woman milking her cows during a real sharp small-arms fight.

George Miller also remembers the same thing:

One incident which was amusing at the time was during our attack on a strongly defended farmhouse near Vierville-sur-Mer. During the heaviest part of the skirmish, a small elderly woman sat out in the middle of the barnyard and milked her cow and ignored us completely. As far as I know she was not hurt!

Lee Brown:

Later that evening when things had quietened down some of the guys and I were messing around throwing a ball about. Suddenly there was a click and all I remember is 'running like hell' to get away from it … I had tripped on a 'S' mine which went up in the air – but luckily it didn't explode!!

As darkness fell Lieutenant Stan Askin was requested for a briefing by Executive Officer Major Richard P. Sullivan, who told him to take a patrol from HQ Company and return to the beach in search of ammunition. Commandeering a French horse and cart, he headed back through the dark to the beach.

Stan Askin, 1st Lieutenant, A and B Companies, 5th Battalion:

The night air felt oppressive against my face. My breathing was easy, but there was a tenseness in my legs.

Askin and his band of men were challenged on the way by an MP hiding in the darkness and when cleared, they continued towards the beach. Bodies stretched as far as they could see into the darkness – washing up and down as the waves made them move in a macabre way in the comparative quiet. Anti-aircraft searchlights scanned the sky and the dim glow from burning landing craft illuminated their way along the beach. Cries for water and morphine came from wounded and dying men lying in dark areas. Comforting where possible as they went the Rangers began the grim task of searching their own dead comrades for ammunition and supplies.

John Hodgson:

Many of my friends were killed or wounded – we were such a small outfit of 565 men and you knew just about everyone in the outfit. My company, sixty-five men, lost one-third of its strength on D-Day.

Hodgson kept a daily log of F Company casualties and those killed in action in a pocket book. For D-Day it reads as follows:

Killed in Action
PFC Robert T. Miller 36564311 killed in Vierville-sur-Mer.
PFC Howard J. Gardner 32587514 killed in Vierville-sur-Mer.
PFC Bernard J. Laboda 33359431 killed in Vierville-sur-Mer.

Wounded in Action:
1st Sgt Howard A. MacDonald 11117444.
Sgt Cinton L. Fogel 39308984.
Staff Sgt Orvylle A. Rosenblad 20722145.
PFC Stephen W. Minor 34153831.
PFC Louis Smerlick 39464061 [*sic*].
T/5 Roy Rand 35608613.
PFC Clark Baker 33573107.
PFC Robert Ovington 36313114.
PFC Richard T. Sorenson 31154675.

On the evening of 6 June 1944, Francis Coughlin recalled:

We got off the beach and went up through Vieville draw. We went through the town and that night we were bombed, so we took cover in some of the German emplacements.

John Martino:

It was not until late in the afternoon that part of the company was able to move to a bluff overlooking the beach and fire its first mission. The first round was fired by Sergeant Florio's squad at 1700hrs at a machine-gun nest in the woods near St Laurent-sur-Mer. The company was mainly intact, but that evening they found out that nine men and two officers were missing. They later learned that Lieutenant Walton, Corporal Grob, and Private Skaeski had also died of wounds received on the beach.

The company had to advance through uncleared mine fields and lost Private First Class Rone who was injured by an anti-personnel mine. He died later from his wounds.

John Perry:

When we dug in for the night on D-Day we were all told to stay in our holes, because the Germans were close by, and if anything moved to use hand grenades instead of shooting our weapons, so as not to give our position away. We were inside a hedgerow and during the night a number of moves were made and of course the boys threw a few hand grenades over the hedgerow, the next morning we found out that the moves during the night were made by a few horses and cows which were grazing and we had killed a number of them with the grenades.

Frank Kennard:

We encountered a 5th Ranger Lieutenant and about 15–20 men and spent the night of 6 June all together 'hunkered down' figuring we would be safe from shellfire as we were on a 'reverse slope'.

William Runge:

On the evening of 6 June I was on the edge of a German strongpoint behind Omaha Beach having lost thirteen of my thirty-five men.

Jack A. Snyder:

I spent the evening of 6 June in the village of Vierville with my men.

Robert Gary:

I spent the evening of 6 June being evacuated back to England. I went all the way back to England for two months. I was pretty lucky I guess.

Kenneth Bladorn:

I spent the night of 6 June on the beach – there were about fifteen of us wounded, lying under the rocks in a 25yd stretch. I was on the rocks all night and the next day until about 7 or 8 o'clock at night.

Gail Hamilton Belmont:

On the evening of 6 June I was in a 'perimeter – defence' on a coastal road approximately ½ mile from the beach.

Max Schneider:

On the evening of 6 June I was a few hedgerows beyond the town of Vierville in a shallow foxhole ... not asleep!

Burton Ranney:

[On the evening of D-Day] *I was in a half-completed pillbox just off the beach.*

Emil Nelson:

On the evening of 6 June I was in an open field outside of Vierville – wide awake!

Jack Burke:

I spent the night of 6 June dug into a small foxhole in the field in front of Vierville church.

Lee Brown:

The evening of 6 June we were in a barn with a lot of other troops – we weren't set up do HQ duties yet –still too involved in fighting to have time.

Cecil Gray:

On the evening of 6 June we did outpost duties for the beach just west of Vierville. We were worried about snipers.

Raymond Herlihy:

I spent the evening of 6 June on the western part of Vierville-sur-Mer.

Alvin Rustebakke:

In the evening of 6 June along with other wounded men from the beach we were loaded on an LST and returned to England. I spent the next six months at a hospital between Birmingham and Coventry.

Dan Schopp:

On the evening of 6 June I was in a farmyard on the outskirts of Vierville.

Robert Edlin:

By midnight on 6 June I was lying in a bunk on an LCT converted into a hospital shop – just off Vierville-sur-Mer. We stayed off the beach for several days.

Regis McCloskey:

I returned to the mother ship about 1100hr on the 6th with a boat load of casualties.

Albert Nyland:

I spent the night of 6 June in Vierville.

Richard P. Sullivan:

I spent the evening of 6 June in a farmhouse in Vierville-sur-Mer.

Edgar Arnold:

I spent the evening of D-Day on the outskirts of Vierville just off Omaha Beach.

Donald Chance:

On the evening of 6 June I was a few hundred yard past Vierville-sur-Mer waiting for counterattacks. The order for the first night was to 'shoot anything that moves'!

Coit Coker:

I spent the evening of 6 June on the NW outskirts of Vierville-sur-Mer.

So ended D-Day for the surviving Rangers on the beach.

Chapter 4

The Close of D-Day

On 7 June John Raaen recalled:

On D+1 I took a patrol out – four men to sweep through the area north of the coastal road. I had the Battalion Sergeant Major and the Battalion Supply Sergeant and a rifle man. We uncovered a couple of Germans and we chased them out of the area – at which time I continued down the Vierville exit road to the 29th Division HQ, and the two master sergeants proceeded back up the road to the column of Rangers and 116th and 734rd tank people who were headed to PdH. I reported in to General Gerherdt of our situation. He was very interested in our position and he asked me if there was anything we needed. I told him that we needed ammo and food. Gerherdt turned to Lieutenant Shay and he told him to take us down to the beach and load us up a truck with ammunition.

With the help of an engineering sergeant, we de-waterproofed a jeep – took it over to the ammo and loaded it up with mortar and machine-gun ammunition. We figured we could strip the machine-gun belts down and use the rounds singly if we needed rifle ammunition.

We loaded up and started up the road to Vierville. It was spooky, no sounds of rifle or machine-gun fire. The place was empty. Corporal Sharp, my driver, turned right and headed in the direction of PdH. Unfortunately, we reached a junction and we didn't know if we were to go right or left. As it happens we could have taken either route to PdH. I got out of the jeep and found lots of tank and small-arms ammunition cases showing there had been a firefight down both routes. I did a mental flip of a coin and chose the right-hand fork in the road.

We proceeded down the road and were taken under fire by snipers a couple of times. I had my helmet hit and knocked off my head into my lap. Several times it was close enough to make me aware we were under small-arms fire. At one point the protecting hedgerows were strangely missing for 50 or 60yd and we didn't know how we were going to get the jeep past the gap – we were by now under machine-gun fire.

We noticed a small hedgerow – 3 or 4ft high at the side and that's not enough for people in a jeep. Then we figured that if we lay down on the floor and then let the jeep run over our heads then perhaps the Germans wouldn't even see the jeep going by.

We did this and literally pulled the jeep along out of sight of the German machine gun for about 30yd over our heads ... until which time the hedges got taller.

It wasn't long then until we reached the end of the 5th Ranger column and we gave some walking wounded a ride and distributed ammunition and food to the rest of the troops.

About that time we ran out of gas. A jeep does not normally run out of gas on a 5-mile trip. Clearly our gas tank had been punctured by the small-arms fire during the firefight – so we took the jeep and pushed it into a farmyard in St Pierre du Mont.

Then Sharp and I walked out into the Ranger column, all on foot, and I approached Major Sullivan and was informed that all the plans we had made the night before had changed – as a result of a German counterattack that had hit the column just as it was moving out. The tree-burst artillery fire appeared to me (with hindsight) to have come from Maisy – there was no intervening artillery units between us and there and it seemed to me that it could only have come from Maisy.

The German counterattack had been approximately a company size force and I had seen it when I got up there and noticed that the 743rd tanks were just sitting there and paying no attention to the counterattack. I climbed up on the tank and banged on the tank lid with my rifle on the turret and got the commander's attention. I pointed out this counterattack some 200yd to the south of us and that he ought to take it under fire. He radioed his other tanks and they all turned their turrets around and took the German attack under machine-gun fire. I said why not cannon fire and he told me it was too indescriminate and we might hurt some friendlies that way. They actually beat off the German attack with their machine guns. That whole incident had some serious consequences because the Ranger force was about to move out at that time as the 'point' for the 116th Infantry in the relief of PdH and the assault on Grandcamp.

The overall result of that was that Colonel Schneider had to make a decision – did he stop the advance or did he let the portion that had already passed go and bring the others back? He decided to let the ones that had already gone forwards go on and the rest of the force was brought back.

On 7 June, once back on station, USS *Glennon* had a busy time. As the troops were advancing off Utah as well as Omaha Beaches, USS *Glennon* was given a number of targets. Even though Maisy was in the Omaha bombardment sector, the battery No. 16, La Martiniere, was busily firing at the shipping landing on Utah Beach. *Glennon*'s After Action Report reads:

At about 0900hrs SFCP 34 commenced designating targets, firing on target No. 5 (4 gun 155mm battery). SGCP 34 claimed all targets were demolished, approximately 200 rounds of AA common expended. About 1600hrs splashes were noted falling close to the USS Butler (CDD34) the source could not be found. The Butler backed down as splashes approached, finally turning away when she was straddled. Not hits were observed.

The *Butler*'s After Action Report reads:

In the afternoon, the protective fortifications for Target No. 3 were holding up the advance of our troops as they tried to capture it. The shore fire control party made a call for area fire at a high rate. As this target was in almost full view, BUTLER was able to cover area very effectively. The strength of the fortifications can be measured by the fact that this fire mission lasted for two and one half hours with an expenditure of 430 rounds of ammunition. The SFCP reported this bombardment as 'excellent'. While delivering this call fire on Target No. 3 BUTLER was under heavy fire from an unknown three gun 155mm Battery. The ship was straddled at least three times and there were several near misses. The accuracy of this battery demanded manoeuvring at high power in restricted water to prevent damage. (BUTLER had been under sporadic and more or less accurate fire during entire day, but apparently the enemy made no concentrated effort against the ship until he found it essential to relieve pressure on Target No. 3).

There is little doubt that the shelling would have come from Maisy Battery. The ship would have been in full view of the observers there and such accurate fire upon the *Butler* is unlikely to have come from any other field guns in the area. There were indeed no other 155mm guns that would have had observed fire on that area at that time.

This position was destroyed by the Navy later that day and in his war department notes Lieutenant Colonel Taylor discusses Ranger Goranson of C Company, 2nd Battalion who took a patrol from the fortified house towards Pointe et Raz de la Percée, and reached a site where they could see all the enemy positions on the Pointe et Raz de la Percée. He watched an American destroyer opening up on the gun emplacements which were built into the face of the cliffs. These were the ones that had caused so much trouble on the western end of Omaha Beach. As Goranson saw them smashed with direct hits, he knew they were 'out' and 'wrote off the mission'. C Company was spared what could have been a dangerous mission by the accuracy of the naval bombardment.

John Raaen:

So I was in St Pierre du Mont – I found I was most surprised to see that we had one company of the 116th plus a group of some other survivors made into another company of the 116th. We had two Ranger companies plus the survivors of the 2nd Battalion which we made into a provisional Ranger company under Captain Arnold.

We had three Ranger companies essentially and one infantry company, commanded by Lieutenant Colonel Metcalf of the 29th Infantry Division. He was in charge and Major Sullivan was his Executive Officer for this particular mission. The situation was very scary. With this one company sized counterattack and a couple of platoon-size attacks in Vierville and here we were 5 miles away from Vierville and well away from our main force. We began to worry – we were surrounded and wondered if we were going to be counterattacked again and this was starting to get the morale of the men a little bit. We had the equivalent of a battalion in St Pierre du Mont.

We pushed on the [Grandcamp] road – there was a huge crater across the road which I think was from a mine. That crater (I was told) blocked the road for the tanks and stopped them getting through. The tanks were therefore scattered around the town.

Sullivan was very worried about a counterattack so he told me to go around the village and check the positions of the tanks in St Pierre du Mont and see if they were in good defensive positions for the night.

I was pretty familiar with the way tanks set up for the night and found the tanks were all in good positions and returned to the crater. I was intending to cross the crater when a tremendous amount of artillery fire came down – about 200yd away in trees. Artillery fire in trees is very bad because the deadly tree fragments are very dangerous.

I could see the troops ahead of me starting to make their way back in panic and as they passed through the crater I started to shout out to the men (I didn't know) from the 116th and then I saw some Rangers who I knew and I called them by name. I told them to slow down and pretty soon I had managed to slow down and stop them. I had a couple of company officers who had panicked and I had them put the two companies back into the line – they moved back across the crater and took up defensive positions again. Some distance short of the artillery landing they took up positions.

At that particular moment Major Sullivan came over to me and said that the division was worried about the maintenance of the beachhead and about an armoured counterattack. We had come to expect it at that point.

All the tanks were therefore ordered back to Vierville – they were taking our seven tanks back to Vierville and he and Metcalf were also ordered back to Vierville.

Sullivan told me that 'I had the monkey on my back' and I had to continue with this particular operation.

I asked what the mission was. He told me to dig in for the night and hope to continue and maintain the roadblock.

Frank Kennard, back on the beach:

The morning of the 7th we assaulted the top of the escarpment and the MG position with my cannon platoon men (8+/-) and the 1/2 platoon from 5th Battalion – in so doing we captured a dozen or so Germans by going through the underground tunnels that covered the area.

John Reville:

The next morning ... and we attacked them again through a little gully and got into their trench system on the very top of the bluff. They started to come out and surrendered and we took all their valuables and threw them on a blanket. That was about 9 or 10 in the morning when we got into the trenches and Jeff was with me. We were determined we were going to attack and they had thrown all this barbed wire down there and we wanted to get into their trenches. Finally they started to surrender and Jeff said let them come out ... and after we had taken these prisoners we took all their guns – I took my first Luger. That was a sign that you were a good infantryman –you faced the German and you took his pistol away from him. All of a sudden from off to the left by approximately 100ft come ten or fifteen soldiers from the 116th Infantry and they are going to take over our prisoners. They had been sitting there and doing nothing while we were fighting and watching us ... they came over and wanted to take over our prisoners ... so one of my men said, 'What are you talking about? There's an officer here,' pointing to me, 'go find your unit ... what are you doing here?' We took all the German papers and collected them for intelligence. I asked one of the Germans to show me how to get down into there – meaning the tunnel – as it just looked like an embankment with a hole. It was about 100yd back from the cliff edge and he went back with us. That is where we found some money. The money that I saw was banded with a thin stripe of metal around it and we took it. Right behind the beach on the top of the bluffs was where they had built stairs down. If any artillery was going to fire into those positions they had 100yd of cliff defence to hit first – so they were pretty well dug in.

We took about forty prisoners – we were firing, they were firing, but we didn't have real tough combat. We were fairly safe. We were in one trench and they were in the other. We were firing back and forth and eventually they finally surrendered. When we took the prisoners back to the beach and an American officer heard who we were (Rangers) he got an assault craft for us and ordered us Rangers in the craft to go along the water in the LCA to the Pointe.

Later that day and with very little ammunition left, USS *Glennon* was in the process of being relieved by the USS *Jeffers*. During this handover period three salvo splashes were spotted landing 500–1,000yd short of the *Glennon*, but still this battery could not be seen by the ship's observers and the splashes ceased without actually getting any closer. It was not necessary for the *Glennon* to take any further manoeuvres to avoid it. It is likely that the guns firing ceased due to *Glennon* moving out of maximum range.

German 352nd Infantry Division Log, 7 June:

After the telephone conversation with Corps HQ several fighter bomber squadrons attacked the division command post with bombs and aircraft armament. The buildings around the church of Littry occupied by a few sub groups of the tactical group of general staff sections were destroyed and casualties resulted. As G-3 echelon was located 500m away; it remained fit for work. This attack was probably the result of the data found on the map taken from the fallen commander of the 915th Gren Regiment.

Towards 1600hrs I drove in the general purpose car to the C.P. of the 916th Gren Regt (centre) and from there on the side road to the pocket of resistance 76 (Pointe et Raz de la Percée). The trip, which usually takes 30 minutes, consumed 5 hours. The fighter bombers forced us to take cover. The view from the pocket of resistance 76 will remain in my memory forever. The sea was like the picture of a 'Kiel review of the fleet'. Ships of all sorts stood almost close together on the beach and in the water broadly echeloned in depth. And the entire agglomeration remained there intact without any real interference from the German side. I clearly understood the mood of the German soldier who was missing the German Air Force. That the German soldiers fought here hard and stubbornly is, and remains, a wonder.

81st Chemical Weapons After Action Report:

On the morning of June 7, D Company fired its second mission near St. Laurent-sur-Mer at a machine gun nest only 800yd from the gun position. A concentration of HE completely neutralized the installation. The company then moved northwest, cross-country over difficult terrain, subject to intermittent sniper and machine gun fire, and arrived at Vierville-sur-Mer at 1600hr, where the commanding officer of the 116th Infantry, 29th Division, assigned it the task of providing security fire.

This is where elements of the 81st became 'attached' to the Rangers and in the words of Captain John Raaen, *'they effectively became the Rangers Artillery unit'.*

John Reville:

When we got up on the LCA on the way to Pointe du Hoc from the beach, one of the sailors offered me 100 dollars for my Luger.

Francis Coughlin:

The next morning we took off and we were fighting towards Grandcamp. Our job was to get the information back to our battalion about what was going on. I went on three patrols in four days and managed to bring back some information, but they [the Rangers] were leaving the area so fast that our information was out of date by the time we got back. A lot of our people went towards the beach to see how the 2nd Battalion were doing and when it all seemed ok we took off.

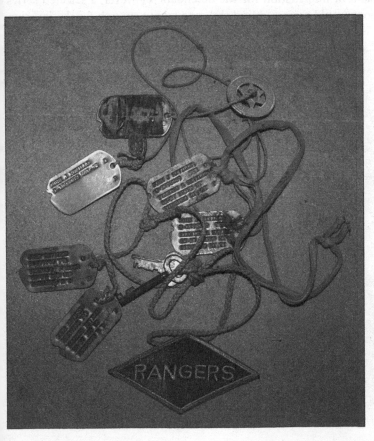

RANGERS patch and a number of pairs of dog tags belonging to John Reville of F Company 5th Battalion. They include the pair of tags he wore on D-day and note his original army locker key is still attached to one of them. Photograph courtesy of Weymouth D-day Museum.

Chapter 5

The Assault on Pointe du Hoc

The Germans had installed a Würzburg radar station just west of Pointe et Raz de la Percée. The whole position was cleverly disguised as a house on the cliff top with its surrounding command bunkers buried to the rear. It was part of the German defence system for the region and this station was linked into a network of other facilities via telephone cables. As can be seen from the planning maps, it was heavily fortified and therefore was bombed before D-Day.

In fact, the Germans had installed radar stations all along the Western Front from Norway down to the Spanish border, thus covering any possible approach being made by air or sea. There was a major station every 10 miles between Ostend and Cherbourg and the whole system was further enhanced by inland smaller stations and numerous mobile positions. It was considered virtually impossible to attack enough of these positions to create a complete blackout of information for the defenders. However, a selected series of attacks on key positions would serve to blind the enemy long enough for the invasion

This aerial photograph, dated 27 June 1944, shows the position after the battle and the damage done by the bombers.

to take place. This was also done by jamming them and where they could not be effectively jammed they were to be destroyed. Any sites giving good observation which would be useful to coastal gun batteries were also to be destroyed.

In addition, two radar targets outside the assault area were to be attacked for every one attacked in the area on 18 May. Installations used for night-fighter control and the control of coastal guns, such as those at Pointe et Raz de la Percée, were attacked. Three days before D-Day attacks were made on the twelve most important sites; six were chosen by the naval authorities and six by the air authorities. The RAF report states:

The Giant Würzburg dish at Pointe et Raz de la Percée. Note the Allied ships in the background.

These twelve sites, containing thirty-nine installations, were all attacked in the three days prior to D-Day. Up to D-Day, 1,668 sorties were flown by aircraft of A.E.A.F. in attacks on Radar installations. Typhoons in low level attacks flew 694 sorties and fired 4,517 x 60-lb. R.Ps. Typhoons and Spitfires made 759 divebombing sorties, dropping 1,258 x 50-lb. bombs and light and medium bombers dropped 217 tons of bombs.

In addition, the sites and equipment were attacked with many thousands of rounds of cannon and machine-gun fire.

The only known photograph of the radar control building at Pointe et Raz de la Percée. This was taken by the French landowner who still worked the fields around the site while the Germans were in occupation.

Listed under 'Radar Installations', intelligence papers stated the following:

Only one enemy radar station is located between Port-en-Bessen and Isigny. This is a coast watching station 1,500yd west of Pointe et Raz de la Percée. It contains one frame, two Giant Wurzburgs and possibly one standard Wurzburg. The range of this station is from 10 to 35 miles.

The RAF report continues:

The nearest defences either side of Pointe du Hoc are 1 mile on the west side and 2 miles to the east. Special attention was given the Pointe du Hoc Battery in the preparatory air

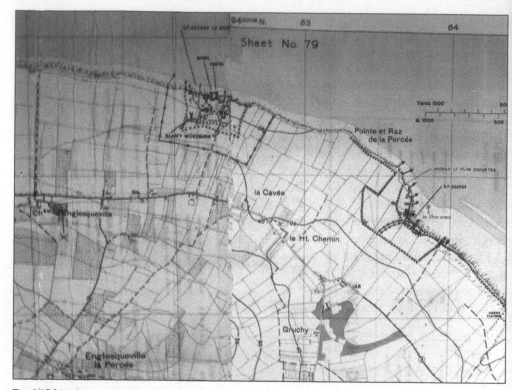

The GSGS inteligence map covering the radar station at Pointe et Raz de la Percée.

and naval bombardments. As early as the 15th April, medium bombers of the Ninth Air Force had begun attacks to soften up the position and to slow enemy efforts to construct further casemates. In order not to tip off the invasion plans, these early attacks could not be made too often and were combined with wide-ranging missions directed at other points on the French coast from Brittany to Belgium. On 22 May and 4 June, Ninth Air Force bombers struck again and on the night of 5/6 June RAF heavies included the Pointe in a major attack on batteries along the whole invasion coast. Naval bombardment of the Omaha sector and its flanks began at 0550hr, on 6 June; particular attention, especially by the main batteries of the battleship Texas *(14-inch guns), was paid to Pointe du Hoc in this time. At H-20 minutes (0610), 18 medium bombers of the Ninth Air Force made a last strike on the Pointe.*

At H Hour, 0630, the three companies of the 2nd Rangers, led by Colonel Rudder, were scheduled to touch down at the foot of the cliffs and deliver their assault. They totalled about 225 men, including a HQ detachment.

The Assault

The companies undertaking the assault at Pointe du Hoc were given detailed and extensive training and they were given specialised equipment for the mission. They had become accustomed to free-climbing ropes and they had done a lot of cliff climbing on the coast of England alongside beach assault exercises. Their training was organised by British Commandos who had experience of cliff-scaling. The use of rockets to fire the grapnels up the cliffs was also a new idea and had to be practised. The use of rockets firing from LCAs and the use of extension ladders was also a first and something that took a long time to perfect as the Rangers worked alongside the British naval crews.

It was thought that ten LCAs would be enough to carry the three Ranger companies and HQ group – which included signal and medical personnel – 21 to 25 men per craft. Each LCA had three pairs of rocket mounts at the bow, amid ship and stern and the ropes were coiled inside a box behind the rocket. Each rocket had a grapnel head and additionally each boat carried a pair of small, hand-projector type rockets with normal ropes.

Rangers training with the extendable ladders in England.

Sections of tubular steel ladders, 4ft in length, were partially assembled in readiness. They were fitted together in 16ft lengths and then one section could be fastened to another upwards as required. As the Ranger climbed section on section, he was supplied with new sections from the man behind him. Four DUKWs would come in close behind the first wave and they were each fitted with a 100ft ladder from the London Fire Brigade. Each ladder was fitted with two Vickers guns and the idea was that these ladders would have a dual purpose. They would be able to give some covering fire from level with the Rangers on the cliff top and also, after the assault had moved from the cliff edge, they would be useful for

The ladders being put away after the training session – the two Vickers K guns mounted on the top are just visible. The ladders are being covered to maintain the secrecy of the mission.

The Rangers landing at the bottom of the cliffs at Pointe du Hoc, taken from the film *The Longest Day*. It is one of the best films ever made covering the attack on Pointe du Hoc. The equipment was real, the location was real and many of the actors featured originally took part in the invasion. Despite it becoming a Hollywood epic, which is often the kiss of death for reality, Cornelius Ryan's attention to detail and factual representation means that if you see it, it is 99 per cent certain it actually happened on the day. All his research was done with people who were there and he did not seek to embellish their stories, just to tell it as it was.

transferring men and supplies to the top quickly.

Each Ranger carried a D-bar for rations, two grenades, and his weapon, normally the M1 rifle. A few of the men selected to go up the ropes first carried pistols or carbines. Heavier weapons were limited to four BARs and two light mortars per company. Ten thermite grenades, for demolition, were distributed within each company. Two supply boats (LCAs) would come in a few minutes after the assault wave, with packs, extra rations and ammunition, two 81mm mortars, demolitions, and equipment for hauling supplies up the cliff.

Right: Testing an assault ladder.

The plan was that E and F Companies were to attack the east side of the Pointe and D Company simultaneously the west. The first objective thereafter was the destruction of the guns and once this was accomplished the remainder of the force was to go immediately south to hold and control the main Vierville–Grandcamp road.

If all went according to schedule, the 116th Infantry would be at Pointe du Hoc before noon. Either way, it was expected that the other Rangers from the remaining eight companies from the 2nd and 5th battalions would have arrived on the beach behind them as reinforcements. The Rangers also had fire support from patrolling naval vessels, and as soon as available from the artillery units landing on the beach at Vierville. To this end, a NSFCP consisting of twelve men and also a forward observer of the 58th Armoured Field Artillery Battalion were attached to Colonel Rudder's headquarters. These men were distributed among the landing craft at the Pointe.

A clip from *The Longest Day* film (see p. 88) illustrates how easily the Germans could control the approaches to the Pointe. Accurate rifle and machine-gun fire accounted for many of the Rangers before they could climb the cliffs. Although a number of the German troops were older and conscripted from occupied countries, they fought hard against the Rangers.

The Landing

The weather was appalling as the Rangers approached Pointe du Hoc in their small vessels. The visibility was not good and the tidal flows were causing navigational difficulties for the Royal Navy crews. LCA 860 was swamped and twenty men of D Company had to be rescued by the Navy. The small boats were not designed for this type of weather and one supply craft sank losing all but one man onboard. Others were slowly sinking on the run in and had to resort to throwing equipment and weapons overboard in an attempt to get inshore. Others found the Rangers were bailing out the incoming water with their helmets while being sick and shivering with cold.

On the nine remaining boats the cold water was getting into everything, the men's equipment on their backs, their boots, their clothing. It all added to their misery and obviously had an effect on their ability to perform even simple tasks without great difficulty. The climbing ropes were also soaked and in a number of cases the rockets firing them were unable to lift them high enough up the cliff to be useable. They simply weighed too much and this was something that had not been considered during planning. A simple set of covers for the rope would have cured the problem instantly, but it was overlooked.

The LCAs in the flotilla were heading towards the shore, but due to a combination of poor visibility, navigation issues and the similarity of sections of the coastline they were heading for the wrong place. They were moving towards Pointe et Raz de la Percée and not directly towards Pointe du Hoc, some distance to the west. They realised the mistake, but not before they had committed to the run in towards the cliffs. Now the only course of action was to sail alongside the coastline towards the correct position. However, they were in range and full view of the Germans along the cliff tops. In total

Scaling the original cliffs at Pointe du Hoc. This photograph is from the film *The Longest Day* and is as lifelike as it was on the day, but without the enemy firing.

they were 38 minutes late in landing on the correct beach and thus were delayed in making their signals to the following waves of transports.

In their original orders they were to signal to the rest of the Ranger force by 0700hrs that all was well. If the other group did not receive such a signal, they were to assume that it had gone badly and they were to initiate their own landing at Vierville on Omaha Beach. Once they had landed there they were to proceed along the coast to the Pointe on foot. Theoretically they could then complete the mission with a landward assault. But in doing so they left Colonel Rudder's force to fend for itself at the Pointe.

During this change of direction five men were hit by German 20mm gunfire and some of the Rangers took it upon themselves to return fire at the cliff tops. The naval bombardment of the Pointe was organised to stop at a designated time. Therefore, the delay in reaching the beach meant that the shelling had stopped some time before and the Germans were coming out to re-occupy their positions. It was not looking good for the Rangers landing below them.

The LCAs landed at the base of the Pointe du Hoc cliffs side by side on the eastern beach. They were sitting right under the German machine guns and grenades could easily be thrown down at them. They landed 40 minutes later than scheduled and the first LCAs hit the beach at 0710hr and radio silence was broken to send Colonel Schneider the code word TILT – this instructed him to land with his force on Omaha Beach.

1st Lieutenant Amos Potts Jr, who was 30 years old, landed with the 2nd Rangers at Pointe du Hoc and had a very different mission to that of the Rangers around him:

I commanded a small unit that suffered 60 per cent casualties [1 KIA, 1 missing, 1 wounded in the first hours of the Normandy invasion], 60 per cent of this group of five, who were unique in that we did not volunteer for Ranger duty, also came out of it with individual decorations.

We were a Photographic Assignment Unit of a Signal Service Battalion borrowed to reinforce the Signal Photographic Company assigned to the First US Army. Around 15 May 1944 we received teletype orders to report to the Second Ranger Battalion. Upon arrival at the Headquarters of the Provisional Ranger Group we learned that we would have the opportunity to obtain some of the best pictures of the coming invasion of fortress Europe. The Rangers had been training for months while we had been photographing supply activities and we were untrained in cliff-scaling. But the Army had an answer for that; one of the scaling means was fireman's ladders mounted on DUKWs.

At the provisional headquarters, we spent most of our time shaking down equipment to the barest minimum – even the number of handkerchiefs in our assault packs was limited. One afternoon we had a practice session, scaling cliffs in England similar to those on the invasion coast. After that, the outfit was sealed in a marshalling area. Here, we were adequately and thoroughly briefed on the invasion plan. The briefing was so complete that long before it was over, any one of us could have conducted it.

In addition to the briefing, training consisted of climbing up one ladder and down another when two DWKS were placed near each other – with the ladders extended, elevated, and touching – forming an inverted 'V'. The period in the marshalling area afforded time for us to assimilate

We checked equipment again and again while waiting sailing time – H-hour – 24 hours as I recall. I was assigned to accompany the DWKS with the mounted ladders. The four DWKS were to cross the Channel on an LCT to five thousand yards off shore and then splash off down the ramp and complete the trip under their own power.

The following extract is taken from the US Government War Department Historical Division account of the Omaha Beach landings. It was written on 20 September 1945 and gives a very good insight into the background of this part of the Rangers' operation.

At Pointe du Hoe [sic], four miles west of Omaha Beach, the Germans had constructed a fortified position for a coastal battery of six 155-mm howitzers of French make; four guns were in open emplacements and two were casemated, with further construction work on casemates reported under way in April and May. This battery was one of the most dangerous elements in the German coastal defenses of the assault area. With a 25,000-yard range, the 155's could put fire on the approaches to Omaha Beach and on the transport area of V Corps; in addition they could reach the transport area from which VII Corps, to the west, would unload for assault at the base of the Cotentin Peninsula ('Utah' Beach).

It was considered a difficult position to attack by the Germans. After all the cliffs were around 100 ft tall and the climb is almost vertical with a difficult overhang to negotiate before reaching the top. With this in mind the Germans set up a series of rear defensive positions to defend the site from an inland attack. It was mined and wired on the landward side with the emphasis on an attack coming from the interior. Either side of it was protected by machine gun positions designed to give flanking fire onto the beaches and under the Pointe and a 20mm AA cannon was installed near the edge over to the west.

The number of troops at Pointe du Hoc was an estimated figure: 125 infantry and 85 artillerymen, but Allied intelligence considered these troops to be of 'limited fighting value'. Troops from the 726th Infantry Regiment held the sector from Vierville to Grandcamp and the strongpoints were widely spaced out at this point simply because it was thought that the cliffs would be difficult to scale. They held a 30-mile stretch of shoreline, but the allies believed the nearest unit available for re-inforcement was the 352nd, thought to be some 10–12 hours away. In fact, they were already in place near the beaches and had arrived sooner than Allied intelligence had thought. Or so it is said. Recent documentation found in the American archives suggests that Allied intelligence knew of the arrival of the 352nd Infantry Division in Normandy, but did not alert the commanders of the invasion troops. If this is true, one can only speculate as to the reason why. The most obvious reason is that they wanted the troops to stay focused on their missions and they had all been told to expect light resistance and hardly any defence in depth once they landed. The effect of any announcement of the 352nd being in place may perhaps have reduced morale within some units and lead them to be more cautious than was needed for the invasion to advance.

The Navy was engaged in taking out German positions that might have had the ability to fire on the approaching Rangers and subsequent waves of troops. Each vessel has its own distinct set of targets to attack.

USS *Herndon* proceeded towards the French coast ahead of the assault waves. Its mission was to bombard and destroy coastal targets, primarily situated between Grandcamp and the Carentan Estuary. All the targets were classified as being defended localities and either contained field guns, AA guns, troop concentrations and or command and control structures for the German Army. *Herndon*'s particular targets were the beach-front positions, and unknown to the *Herndon* one was the forward beach observation position for the batteries at Maisy. With this brief it was most successful and the positions it bombarded were not able or capable of engaging the first assault waves as they landed. In this mission alone they expended 212 rounds of 5in shells during a 40-minute bombardment.

Arriving in her designated position, HMS *Glasgow* opened fire on pre-arranged targets with the help of air spotters flying low over the coast. She was in touch by radio with her SFCP and was off station 3.1 miles north of Vierville church.

At 0540hr HMS *Talybont*, a Type III escort destroyer, moved down the fire-support channel to take up position to bombard another series of land targets. It was situated midway between USS *Saterlee* and USS *Thompson* and at 0550hr she opened fire at a range of less than ½ a mile on pillboxes or machine-gun emplacements which could not be seen. It was decided to cover the top of the cliff in the target area as thoroughly as possible prior to the Ranger landings.

At 0550hr (H-40) USS *Texas* commenced its main battery bombardment of the German coastal defences – which it thought was a battery of 6 x 155mm guns on Pointe du Hoc (target number 586939 – the observation area at the Pointe). This opening barrage was witnessed by many of the Rangers who were by now in their individual LCAs on their way into the shore.

One of the three horizontally aligned gun positions designed to cover the Grandcamp harbour. The other two positions seen in the next photograph (p. 94) taken from the end of the harbour show their location more graphically.

0600hr the Rangers aboard a landing craft passed HMS *Talybont*. It was not realised at the time that they were heading for the wrong position and instead of Pointe du Hoc they were going east towards Pointe et Raz de la Percée.

HNLMS *Soemba* was a Dutch gunboat fitted with 3 x 5.9in guns and equipped with a sophisticated fire and control system which allowed very accurate gun targeting. At 0610hr the *Soemba* opened fire on target 30 – in the centre of Grandcamp village. It was actually the water tower, which was being used for artillery observation.

Soemba then opened fire on its target number 32 (538934 – a group of bunkers and German positions at the end of the beach road, just at the sea wall at Grandcamp). This is the moment that Jean Marion, mayor of Grandcamp, referred to as he watched a ship destroy the guns in the beach emplacements.

A 0615 HMS *Talybont* ceased fire – yet within less than a minute it opened fire on other targets again. At 0625 she stopped shelling the Pointe and moved fire along some 1,000yd to the west to a strongpoint on the cliffs (575939 – machine gun on the cliffs).

At 0630hr HMS *Talybont* noted that the Rangers in landing craft ML204 were making for the wrong location. They also then recorded seeing the small craft as they changed course and headed for Pointe du Hoc. At 0630hr HMS *Talybont* fired on targets 81 and 82.

At 0632 having been released from escort duties, *Soemba* proceeded towards the landing areas. She then undertook a mission in support of the spotter planes for 3 minutes, attacking an anti-aircraft battery that was firing at planes from east of Pointe du Hoc (probably the position marked as 19 on the naval target map). The position was hidden in trees, but it was neutralised and the AA battery ceased firing permanently.

At 0640hr HMS *Talybont* noted that fire was opened up on the Rangers from the Germans onshore who were firing two light machine guns. Three rear DUKWs were being fired on and taking casualties and the *Talybont*'s fire was shifted to the cliff face

Despite being hundreds of metres apart these casements were designed to allow multiple guns to cover the entrance to the harbour. These were the positions engaged by the *Soemba* and as you can see it was done successfully – the furthest one being almost blown into the sea.

and top in the area where the guns were thought to be firing from. At 0645 she opened fire with her 2-pounder pompoms and the return fire from the shore was spasmodic. Two of the Rangers DUKWs were hit, one badly. Shortly thereafter a further two light machine guns opened fire from the shore and another DUKW was put out of action.

At 0646 HMS *Talybont*'s fire was maintained in the vicinity of targets 81, 82 and the Rangers sustained no more casualties from these areas.

At 0655 USS *Herndon* reported that one of the Maisy defensive AA batteries near Mr Maudelonde's home was firing. It was observed and taken under fire. The *Herndon*'s Action Report reads: '*At 0655 an active AA shore battery in the town of Maisy (Target 103) was observed and taken under fire. Ceased firing at 0703 having expended 42 rounds of 5" AA common ammunition. Battery was silenced.*' The battery was located near the farmhouse belonging to Gerrard Maudelonde, and where

The entrance to Gerrard Maudelonde's farm.

generations of his family had lived. It was occupied by the Germans, who lived alongside the family – something that had become common practice. The Germans operated an anti-aircraft battery of 3 x 88mm guns from a field behind this house on D-Day. They were destroyed by USS *Herndon*.

Another battery of 3 x 88mm anti-aircraft guns was one of the three units controlled by German officer Captain Kapusta. It was located at grid reference 539927 (in Maisy village) and was also completely destroyed during the attack.

At 0700hr HMS *Talybont* ceased firing at targets 81 and 82. However, the Rangers were still under small-arms fire from Pointe du Hoc. USS *Saterlee* was already giving gunfire support against these positions, so by 0703 *Talybont* engaged other targets and by 0710hr it withdrew from the Fire Support Area.

HMS *Talybont*'s After Action Report reads:

The position of one of the sets of AA guns in Mr Montagne's fields marked with a black circle.

Targets 67, 77 were evidently completely neutralised or destroyed. Targets 81, 82 though engaged for 25 minutes prior to 'H' hour were only 60% neutralised. It is considered that up to four LMG's were in action against the Rangers.

In the opinion of the lieutenant commander of HMS *Talybont*:

The mistake in identification of the target by [Landing Craft] ML 204 is difficult to understand as Texas *fall of shot was obvious. Their course from Raz de la Percée along the shore to Pointe du Hoc was suicidal.*

The Montagne farm, which stands high in the fields and has commanding views of the coastline.

At 0742 USS *Texas* opened fire with its main battery, expending seventeen rounds of HE ammunition. Again at 0810hr it opened fire on a howitzer battery, expending twenty rounds of HE ammunition (586932 – the wooded area in front of the Chateau du St Marie du Mont).

The Main Cliff Assault – Pointe du Hoc

Frank South, Medic, 2nd Rangers:

We went into the strict training programme. We were Rangers first and medics second, but we rarely carried arms. There was the one thing about the Rangers' training. I carried a Ranger army M3 fighting knife, but some of us used the Fairburne Sykes knife which came from the Commandos. We would get them second hand, but they were few and far between. We were never issued the 'Rangers' knife that people say we were given. We did use First World War trench-fighting knives in some cases with the round knuckle dusters on them occasionally. I bought mine in New York before we went overseas. (The thing was I bought it, but the FFE [Free French] guys took it out of my duffle bag and it was stolen at Brest later on in the war).

I wore paratrooper boots on D-Day at Pointe du Hoc. We got them some time before D-Day and I got them in England. We did not wear spats over the boots. We wore our trousers tucked into them. Almost all the guys in the 2nd wore them – some guys didn't wear them on D-Day in case they damaged them. The 1st battalion wore the smaller boots with spats. They used to cut their leggings to go over them, to make long-distance hiking easier. So from that day on we all cut down our leggings and that caused some confusion as some were not wearing boots. Nobody stood around taking photographs on D-Day we were too busy ...

We were called on deck and told, 'Rangers, man your boats' – we loaded. I went in with F Company and we were scattered about. Being a medic I was in the later part of the boat – I had never been seasick, but I got the full blast of the diesel fumes and it hit me badly. I had spent several days before putting together a huge pack for a number 2 aid station. It was about 80lb+ – everything I could imagine or thought about – everything from plasma to instruments, bandages, drugs, etc. It got to be pretty huge. So, I still had my regular pack and I don't remember if I carried a side arm. We were down to just what equipment we needed. All our surplus equipment was on another boat. We had our weapons, ammunition and D-bars (they were harder than concrete). I got on board with my pack and we were lowered away. We did the circling around and then we were off.

The seas were running high. We took the wrong heading because of the navigation error and the lead boat went wrong. Rudder corrected it – the only problem was that we were running lateral to the cliffs and picking up small-arms fire. On our boat was a RN sailor Tolyhurst – he took out a Lewis gun and started firing back with it and he was firing while holding the barrel with his left hand and he got terribly burnt.

Before D-Day when we were getting our briefings – there had been a series of photographs taken by a P38 – along the cliffs – parallel to the cliffs – and on those photographs dangling on them was a series of shells. But I think what happened was that the shelling from the Navy and the bombing had cleared them. We were very much aware of them as we had been spooked in advance by them, but I don't remember any of them going off during the assault.

All the officers had a map of the Pointe which marked the mine fields. They had all gone off from the concussion so we didn't have to worry about land mines. I think the same thing happened with the shells dangling on the cliff tops.

For our climbing each LCA had six grapnel rockets. Two of them were straight lines, two had toggle lines which had toggles intermittently along them and the remaining two had rope ladders which was a line with a rope ladder trailing behind it. We also had steel extension ladders in 4ft lengths which connected together and you got to the top – we used those when it settled down. They were no good for assaults. We used straight lines to get up.

There was a steel leader cable attached to the rocket. Attached to that were the rope ladders to follow them up. The fire-brigade ladders were spectacular – the guy on the ladders couldn't get close to the cliff face. He was up on the top with a Vickers gun trying to fire them at the Germans. He was a moving target for the Germans. I didn't have a red cross painted on my helmet. Nobody wanted to go out on patrol with someone with a red cross painted on his helmet, so we left them off. I wore a medic's armband when unarmed. We were meticulous about that sort of thing. It was a matter of pride to be unarmed when being a medic. We were in regular line companies and trained as infantrymen – it was basic training and then also medics' training.

The Rangers landed on a short 25yd-deep strip of beach directly under the cliffs – the shellfire had damaged the beach floor, but unlike Omaha Beach where the troops wanted shelter, the bombing had caused the opposite problem. The DUKWs could not cross the beach area to allow the Rangers to climb their ladders because of the shell holes. Whole sections of the cliff had simply been blown away and fallen onto the tiny beach giving it an uneven surface.

The fallen debris was, however, a help as it afforded Rangers some shelter from the withering machine-gun fire from the cliff edge. Some grenades were rolled down on them, but in general the Germans were reluctant to look over the edge for fear of exposing themselves to accurate fire from below. USS *Slaterlee*'s observers watched the enemy firing down on the Rangers and they fired her 5in guns and 40mm guns at the the cliff tops to try and dislodge the Germans from the edge. Colonel Rudder was nearly hit by falling debris from this bombardment. Although just missing the Rangers below, the gunfire kept many of the Germans from venturing towards the cliff top. Instead, many stayed in their bunkers thinking that the bombardment must end soon. This was vital as it gave the Rangers a much-needed chance to climb without being shot at.

Not all the Germans were inside bunkers, however. LCA 861 was carrying men from E Company, which was commanded by 1st Lieutenant Theodore E. Lapres Jr, when it grounded about 25yd from the bottom of the cliff. They found that three or four Germans were standing on the cliff edge, shooting down at the craft and they were in a very vulnerable position. The Rangers on this boat quickly returned fire and the Germans went from the cliff edge to seek shelter. But things were not going well, especially when the LCA fired its pair of rear rockets and their ropes fell short of their intended target – the cliff top. The ropes had become saturated with water and this added hugely to the weight of the ropes – the rockets simply did not have the power to send the heavy ropes upwards enough. Barely half of the necessary rope had left the craft and the grapnels fell back down.

The Germans were intermittently throwing grenades at the men below and this caused two casualties. However, the Rangers continued to fire their rocket grapnels, some of which reached the top and thus enabled them to begin their advance off the narrow beach. Other Rangers free climbed the ropes and in some cases the Germans cut the ropes away as the Rangers climbed them. But by now enough men were getting to the top to assist their comrades and keep the Germans back from areas of the cliff edge.

Amos Potts:

The DUKWs all got off the LCTs without incident, but as we approached the coast it was obvious that the pathfinders were leading too far to the east. We altered our course paralleling the coast within the range of small arms and proceeded to Pointe du Hoc, our assigned sector. Even the exposure to small-arms fire did not bother me.

All our study of aerial photos, stereos, and models of the cliffs was for naught because the 4-hour aerial bombing and the 250 x 16in naval shells had completely changed the appearance of the cliffs and had covered the beach with so much debris that it was impossible to get the DWKS out of the water. In fact, to get ashore I had to swim, getting all of my extra film wet. After shooting what film I had in my camera I felt quite useless, but found myself a job tying supplies to ropes to be hoisted to the top of what was left of the cliff. When the supplies had been all hoisted an English soldier mechanic, who was to have operated the ladders, and I scaled the cliff using a rope ladder to join the Rangers at the Command Post.

Ranger Harry Roberts had two tries at climbing a rope, the first time his rope was cut by a German soldier and the second time as he reached the top it was cut again, but he made it. He then helped others behind him to get up and along with five other Rangers he then set out against his designated target, the heavily fortified observation post at the tip of the Pointe.

More men from LCA 861 followed behind this group, but they were suddenly half buried as a pile of earth descended on them from above. It is more than possible that one of the large German shells on the cliff top had been detonated and that was what had sent tons of earth downwards. They all survived that potential disaster and they too climbed up and followed the other Rangers towards the observation post.

LCA 862 landed under heavy machine-gun fire from the east. This one machine-gun position was causing huge problems for the men landing on the tiny beach below. Upon landing the craft immediately fired its rockets and the men took off up the ropes, however, one Ranger was killed and another one was injured by a German stick grenade which exploded between them. LCA 862 was occupied by fifteen Rangers and most importantly their NSFCP personnel. It was imperative that these men reached the top of the cliffs with their communication equipment intact, so that they could liaise with the ships bombarding the area.

LCA 888 contained six HQ men, Colonel Rudder and fifteen E Company men and they too had problems getting the tiny craft around the craters and rubble on the beach. They were aided by the huge mound of soil and stone that had been blown down and using 16ft ladders they were able to reach the top.

Once at the top, 1st Lieutenant Eikner had his radio set up and working. He sent the code word PRAISE THE LORD to the Navy, as this was the correct signal to inform them that the Rangers had left the beach. He did not get a response, so he had no way of knowing if the Navy had received his message.

LCA 722 had a mixed group of men onboard as it landed. A *Stars and Strips* photographer, a British Commando officer called Lieutenant Colonel Trevor (a man who had been involved with the Rangers during their climb training in England), fifteen men from E Company and five Rangers from HQ. They faired better than the others as their ropes attached immediately when the rockets fired. For some reason it appeared that their ropes were less wet and this allowed the grapnels to go up and grip first time. One Ranger, P. Smith, literally walked up the wall of the cliff and shot three Germans with his BAR when he reached the top. They had been throwing hand grenades down at the other men landing and as he emerged nearby he took them under fire. Some of the LCA 722 Rangers tried to set up a 60mm mortar on the beach, but its field of fire was limited to a few possible visible targets and it was quickly abandoned and the crew went up with the rest of the men.

LCA 668 containing D Company landed badly, having hit the debris and boulders that had been smashed from the cliffs above during the naval bombardment. They were some 20ft short of the beach and had to swim in to shore, which made their subsequent climb much harder. While carrying a rope to the cliff edge, 1st Sergeant Leonard Lomell was also shot, by a machine-gun bullet fired at the men leaving the LCA. He was wounded but kept going, disregarding the pain.

LCA 668's set of rockets managed to hit the cliff edge and the men began to make their way up the ropes. Once at the top, twelve men along with Sergeant Lomell and 1st Lieutenant Kerchner moved inland.

1st Sergeant Len Lomell, 2nd Rangers:

Fortunately, Rudder was in the first boat – I was in the second and we all realised we were going to the wrong Pointe. Luckily, we got to the right Pointe, but we were late arriving at Pointe du Hoc. We wasted no time climbing the cliffs. I was one of the first ones to get up the cliff via a ladder. I was wounded through the fleshy part over my right hip. It just burned like hell. I was up near the top with my submachine gun with my radio man and we were struggling on the ropes, exhausted. My radio man Bob Fruhling said, 'Hey, Len, can you help me I am exhausted, my strength is going I am going to fall' … I said I was exhausted also and didn't know if I could continue. One of our guys Leonard Rubin – I called him over – he came over and grabbed Bob and tossed him over onto the top of the cliff and I jumped up with my machine gun to protect them. Lenny saved both of us that day.

LCA 858 had its own problems and was sinking on the way in. It managed to keep up with the other LCAs, but it was touch and go. In the end it landed only minutes behind the other craft and despite the ingress of water most of its equipment was intact. One launcher was disabled, but everything else was OK as their fired their rockets. Again, the machine gun to the east fired at them and it cost them three wounded. However, within 15 minutes all the men had left the cliff top and started inland toward their various individual objectives.

LCA 887 landed close to the beach and was not affected by the craters as the others had been. The men fired their rockets from the beach and they left the shore with only two men wounded.

LCA 884 was targeted for a while as it sailed toward the Pointe. They had fired back using a Lewis gun and the Rangers BARS and three Rangers were hit by fire from the east when they landed. They fired their rockets, but their ropes lay in positions open to direct enemy fire. They were struggling. They were covered in mud from landing on the beach debris and the Rangers could not practically climb the plain ropes. They tried without success and moved to the left and used the ladders left by LCA 883's men.

LCA 883 was the last boat to reach the shore. It was 300yd east of its intended landing position and way beyond the main Pointe du Hoc defensive position. It was dry and a perfect rocket/rope landing was made on the cliff top. The men used every rope and 1st Lieutenant Wintz said he was 'never so tired in his life'. He gathered six men together and set out across the cratered ground.

By now the Rangers had all landed and gone about their various missions, but any one of a million things could have gone wrong. It is obvious to think, for example, that the beaches would be cratered by the naval shelling once it has happened, but the Rangers' training had involved landing on flat beaches with the DUKWs, which were inappropriate for the reality of the beach at Pointe du Hoc. The naval bombardment and the subsequent destruction of part of the cliff certainly aided the Rangers, first giving them a step up the cliffs, but also offering at least some shelter from the machine guns to the east. Within approximately 30 minutes all the Rangers had reached the top and with a few exceptions, the injured, some HQ personnel and a few mortar men, the rest had gone into the German strongpoint.

The damage done by the naval bombardment is obvious today. In places half the cliff was literally blown away – it helped the height of the climb.

George Kerchner, Lieutenant, D Company, 2nd Rangers:

I lost my two superior officers when we landed and as I ran off the LCA I went into water above my head. I had forgotten to inflate my life belt so I swam ashore and helped as many men as I could out of the water. My radio wouldn't work so I threw it on the beach. I found a rifle and tried to locate the machine gun, but I couldn't. I immediately headed for Colonel Rudder and he told me to climb the cliff. I went back to the men and we started to go up the cliff and we were put under fire from a machine gun on the left.

I remember that some of my men were hit – Pacyga, Cruz and Harris, and I started up the cliffs. We could see Jerries running around the top of the cliffs and they were shooting at us and tossing grenades. I was too wet and miserable to mind. I know we felt pretty disappointed when we got there and there were no guns. I came across one of my men who was very seriously wounded. While we were there with him he raised up, then collapsed and died in our arms.

Taken from the cliff tops in the 1970s by veteran Jack Burke, this photograph is not far from the position occupied by the machine gun which Frank South remembered. The machine gun was located in such a position that it could fire directly down onto the beach below the Pointe and proved to be a real issue for the Rangers. It alone accounted for many Ranger lives as they left their LCAs. It was eventually destroyed by well-directed naval gunfire.

Taken in 2009, the same photo shows the level of coastal erosion that has taken place of the years.

Pointe du Hoc, 1977.

An aerial photograph from 1977 of Pointe du Hoc showing the actual 'pointe' still very much attached to the mainland.

Frank South:

We did the run in and our boat was the second one on the left flank and we started getting enfilading fire from the left from the cliff tops when our rockets went off – no problem. They were supposed to hit the cliff tops. We unloaded rapidly – I was the last person off with my heavy pack.

Of course, while unloading the boat was shifting around a lot and in and out – I finally got ashore and I made it to a shell hole when the first call went up for a medic. It was a man with a chest wound. I got to him against the cliff face and worked on him and we were taking a fair number of wounded. Grenades and small arms were hitting against us. Under the circumstances you have a narrow field of vision. You did what you had to do. Eventually, we were able to get the wounded up against the cliff – we were getting hammered from a machine-gun position on the top of the cliffs. The guys who were up on top made a decision and Walter Block our medical officer asked me to stay on the beach and take care of the wounded. I was down there for about 20 minutes and then I was able to bring the pack up to the cliffs with me. One of the sergeants from F Company landed and they were too close to be able to fire their rockets properly and so he unloaded them onto the beach. In spite of the machine-gun fire, he hot wired them and ignited them by hand. He aimed them so they would get up to the top and he came back to where I was with Block and his face was pockmarked with burnt powder. He had just got these things planted and aimed by sight – I commented on what a terrible complexion he had and a few other wise cracks.

The guys wounded on the beach stayed on the beach. The guys wounded up top stayed there. We had a provision for getting men down if they were wounded. We had a couple of poles set at an angle and a line brought over to bring them down with … but we didn't use it. There was enough fallen cliff to allow us to drag people upwards with ropes and ladders to get them up. It was not too difficult to get them up. We were able then to get them into shelter. The shell holes provided us with very good protection. You could hear the naval shells coming and when they hit. After a while it was so regularly that it was not a problem – so long as they didn't hit us. I was worried about them hitting the face of the cliff above me as they would cover the wounded with rocks – but it didn't happen.

It was a big help that half of the cliff was already smashed away because we used it to climb up. I would guess that 30– 40 per cent of it was gone. We still had to use ropes, but some parts were better than others to get up. I went on top when they decided that I should take the aid station to Rudders CP which was a shell crater seaward of an AA bunker. It had been a bomb crater and was pretty well protected or we could use the AA bunker – which we used as an aid station. It was a two-roomed bunker, so we used one for the aid station for the wounded and the other as a morgue and to store spare ammo. At first it was very difficult working in there because we only had flashlights – then we remembered that the supply boats had gasoline lanterns on them – one of them had foundered and the other did make it – so we were able to get a couple of litres of gasoline which allowed us to see what we were doing.

They kept bringing in the wounded and they kept coming. Sergeant Thomas from F Company … we had been good friends and he had been shot in belly and he said, 'It's OK, I can make it. He started getting a bit woozy – we made him lie down – he started getting contractions and huge pains and he had peritonitis – so we filled him with as much morphine as we dared. He died aboard ship – he was a friend. That happened time after time – as much of 70 per cent of my time was spent tending to people. It was the only thing I could do. Then at one point there was supposed to be a breakthrough and there were Germans, so I went into the line with a captured Schmeiser and then back into the bunker. Guys were able to move about from one shell hole to the next using them for cover.

William Stivison, Staff Sergeant, F Company, 2nd Rangers:

I was on an LCT with four DUKWs with power ladders. The Channel was very choppy. Conversation was not exciting – the men were very calm. I watched what was probably the greatest display of fireworks ever to be seen. I was to give Captain Harold Slatter the words 'Splash' when the DWKS hit the water from the LCT, which I did, over the radio. I was then to give him (Erase 1, 2, 3, etc.) when and if any DUKWs were put out of action, one was hit and as I stared to say 'Erase 1', his operator was saying, 'We're sinking, we're sinking, we're sinking, we're sunk'. (They too were in a landing craft.) Most incidents that day were heroic – as far as the men were concerned. The men going in sat and watched machine-gun slugs hit the water a few feet from the DUKWs and a couple of 20mms hit the ladders above their heads. All were as calm as if they would have been just running another problem.

Ralph E. Davis, Corporal, 2nd Rangers:

I landed with the first assault wave on H-hour D-Day morning. It was cold and foggy. Rain was drizzling down the back of my neck and running down my legs. We were all miserable and cramped from being in the little assault boats for more than two hours. Some of the boys were seasick, and the doctor passed around pills to keep us from vomiting. We also had paper bags to keep from messing the boat. Spray was coming in over the bow of the boat and getting everyone wet. There were boats on either side of us as far as we could see. We did not hear anything, but the steady drone of the motors and the squawk of a terrified seagull. An occasional squadron of planes would pass overhead on their way back to England after bombing the coast, the communications and main avenues of supplies for the Bosch army.

All of a sudden the battleships opened up on the coastal emplacements. We could see the blinding flash from their guns. Geysers of smoke arose off the ground, and we could hear the 16in shells whizz overhead, as they projected on their mission of deliverance, death and destruction.

The first machine-gun bullets hit our LCA when we were about 15 minutes off shore. As we drew nearer, the machine-gun bullets ripped along the sides of our boat and sprayed the water like raindrops all around us. Then the order came – 'Down with the ramps'. I jumped out in the water up to my neck, and half ran and half swam to the protection of the cliff's edge. The beach was strewn with rocks and boulders. Some were very sharp and were partially covered by the rising tide and the swelling sea. The bank was wet and slippery. In some places there was only 30ft of beach, before it ran into the ugly, jutting cliff. My legs were a dead weight, my body was numb and cold, and my hands were chilled blue, so that I could hardly grab the rope to climb the cliff. As I climbed the rope, bullets were hitting on either side of me, and potato-masher grenades exploded beneath me. When I got to the top, I dived into the nearest bomb crater to get my bearings, and survey the field of battle.

My platoon sergeant followed me up the cliff and jumped in the hole beside me. We decided to go to the first hedgerow and clean out some snipers who were making things hot for us. We ran from shell hole to shell hole – thank god for the butterflies and the bombs that put them there – until we reached the hedge. There, I bagged my first game. We captured three snipers within the next half hour. One of them was just a kid. The others were old enough to be my grandfather. 88 shells were zeroing in on us, and shrapnel was falling everywhere, and dead Jerries were lying everywhere.

Regis McCloskey:

When we hit the beach and were unloading the ammunition we had to carry the stuff across about 40yd of beach ... And this under machine-gun and small-arms fire. We would grab a box of stuff, run across the beach drop it back far enough so the high tide coming in would not touch it, and then dash back to the boat and get another box. On the return trip John [Madison] Cobb said, 'Give me that one and you get another one'. So I handed him the box and he turned and took about three or four steps and I then heard him scream ... he was lay on the beach.

Three bullets fired from the machine gun in the cliffs above had hit Cobb in the left arm right under the shoulder. His arm was hanging limply by his side loosely inside his shirt, but the same machine gun was still firing at the Ranger group. Bullets hit the water around the boat and the sergeant next to him was hit in the stomach by a burst. As Cobb was helped back into the boat he urged the Royal Navy men to take the boat out. As it pulled away he could see the sergeant lying dead on the shore – he had died instantly.

Madison Cobb:

I couldn't fall or I would have drowned.

Carl Bombardier:

With my buddy Leon Otto, I remember he was the first to fire at the enemy, he was our BAR man, and was returning the fire from the German machine gun on the cliffs as we were going in to the beach. He was always joking and I remember he was kidding and happy about being the first to fire at the enemy. Once we landed we were leaving the LCA in water to our waist, Red Ryan was trailing a section of ladder.

No signals back to the fleet had been received so the *Ancon* sent the following messages via radio: '*Have all Rangers landed on Pointe du Hoc?*'

The gun battery at Pointe du Hoc was a mess. There were shell holes everywhere and the Rangers found it difficult to navigate and negotiate their way around. Paths and trenches had disappeared and their briefing notes and maps bore little resemblance with the shell and bomb-ravaged landscape. Staying hidden was easy because there were so many places to hide, but moving from one place to another was difficult and communication was very limited when they did. Small groups of Rangers had been fanning out across the site for half and hour and many were separated and working alone.

This was not necessarily a bad thing. The Germans were also dazed and confused. Their working landscape as they knew it had changed and for them there was possible danger at every turn. By now they did not know which direction the Rangers would appear from and when they did how they could counterattack over the same terrain. Rudder's men had a clear set of objectives. First, the destruction of the gun emplacements and the observation post at

Huge pieces of the gun emplacements were dislodged by the bombing.

The devastation is still visible to the open pits today.

the end of the Pointe. E Company had the observation post and gun position 3. D Company was tasked with gun emplacements 4, 5 and 6. F Company guns 1 and 2 and the machine-gun position to the east which had caused so much trouble on the way in to the beach.

The Rangers were joined at the Pointe by three 101st Airborne paratroopers who had dropped disastrously off course. They should have been some 15 miles away, but landed near Pointe du Hoc instead and one was fished out of the water by the Rangers. (An Airborne lieutenant had landed earlier as well, but he had been taken away by the Germans for interrogation.)

Carl Bombardier:

Once topside of the cliff I first caught up with my CO. He had a prisoner which he turned over to me and told me to take him to the beach. I started off, but missed the spot where I came up the cliff. I was walking into a German machine gun down on our flank, so we ended up going from shell hole to shell hole.

John Gilhooly, Private First Class, F Company, 2nd Rangers:

We found out later these cliffs which we had taken were honeycombed with tunnels and the Germans could pop up anywhere at anytime!

The plan was that after these objectives had been neutralised the group would assemble near the southern area of the site. Following that D, F and most of E Companies would advance inland southwards to the main Grandcamp–Vierville road and create a roadblock to stop the Germans advancing eastwards toward the beaches. A platoon of E Company was to stay at the Pointe with HQ and arrange defence of the captured position. That was the plan, but inevitably things went wrong. Rangers failed to make their rendezvous points and others were simply held down by enemy action to the extent that they could not physically move without being shot at. F Company was involved in a firefight which lasted nearly all day and yet other companies were able to move around with little problem – except for the obvious navigational ones.

The casements were heavily damaged, but as each group arrived at their allotted gun position the discovery was the same: the guns were not installed and there was no sign of any artillery equipment. It was clear that the 155mm guns had been removed from the gun pits and some of the pits contained dummies made of wood, but the common misconception was that the 155s were also removed from inside the casements. This was not so. The

The mountings inside the two unfinished casements confirm that the steel rings and mounting pins are not fitted to enable a deck-mounted naval gun to be installed. It is estimated that the site would have been operational again in two months – obviously subject to these model of guns being available to be installed.

casements were in the process of being built and the new casements were for 10.5cm deck-mounted guns (guns without wheels and legs that mount to the floor) and were not big enough to house a 155mm cannon.

Charlie Ryan, 2nd Rangers:

We knew there were rumours going around that the big guns had been removed from Pointe du Hoc. We even had an officer removed from the unit for saying it publicly.

Clearly the site at Pointe du Hoc was being re-built when it was attacked and was not finished. The guns had been removed. The Rangers were not to know this at that time and they still sought to complete their mission. The logical assumption was that the guns had been removed and were local, after all why would the Germans have a battery without weapons? The observation post at the tip of the Pointe was essentially undamaged so the Rangers approached it and they threw grenades into the slits – the machine gun inside stopped firing. Following up with a bazooka round through the aperture, the Rangers from LCA 861 were able to contain the Germans inside. If they came out Corporal Aguzzi was watching the main entrance/exit and was ready for them. Ranger Cleaves was wounded by a mine which had perhaps been disturbed by the Navy shelling and Thompson was close enough to hear the German radio talking inside the huge concrete position, so looking up he decided to shoot away the communications aerial off the top thus denying the German High Command vital local information. They left the position guarded, but decided to wait for demolition charges to deal with it properly later.

There had in fact been two groups of Rangers attacking the OP, but they had been unaware of each other's efforts simply because of the size of the building. It was a day later when eventually someone found some demolition charges. Although there had been no movement from inside the building, Ranger Aguzzi was amazed when eight unwounded Germans eventually came out with their hands up. Only one body was found inside.

The anti-aircraft position (a 20mm gun mounted in a concrete emplacement) would fire bursts of accurate automatic fire on any Rangers who showed themselves and it was devastating. Additionally, the Rangers were coming up against more and more intensive sniper fire. A party of Rangers set out to destroy the 20mm position, but they found it a difficult area to approach. But they were not only under sniper and 20mm fire – the Rangers were now also coming under artillery fire from the west. Rifle fire was coming from the direction of gun position 6 and anyone going towards gun position 4 was attracting more of the 20mm fire. Their advance was also slowed because of the risk of mines and they were reluctant to open fire for fear of giving away their positions before they could adequately deal with the gun. Crawling and crouching to avoid discovery the Rangers advanced towards the AA gun, but they must have been spotted as they became the subject of intense mortar and artillery fire. They were bunched together in shell holes and so the D Company group split up in all directions. It was the only way to ensure that someone got the job done without being lost as a group from an enemy shell all at once.

The Germans were becoming more aware of the Ranger positions. They were advancing in small groups and testing for weaknesses in the Ranger lines. The Germans were inside the very same trenches as the Rangers and nobody quite knew where anyone else was. German re-inforcements could be seen in the distance and it was getting harder for the Rangers to create a stable front from which to defend. Some Rangers were captured. Ranger Cruz crawled back towards Colonel Rudder's command post and saw a pile of American weapons just lying on the ground. Thompson machine guns, pistols and rifles which could only have been left by captured Rangers in the trench he had left some minutes beforehand. A total of ten Rangers had simply disappeared because the Germans had infiltrated the porous Ranger lines.

The underground bunkers also provided the Germans with shelter – when they emerged suddenly, groups of Rangers had passed them by and it was easy for some of them to attack the Rangers from behind, adding to the confusion. Some units, the ones that had gone inland, had to watch their backs. As the Rangers left the minefields and machine-gun positions to the rear of the battery they were also the subject of scattered fire from the west. Some artillery and mortar shells began to target them and there was small-arms fire ahead of them to the south which also slowed their progress.

They were not yet at the Grandcamp–Vierville road and small groups were beginning to form larger ones. All the companies reported that their gun positions had been empty. 1st Sergeant Robert Lang found gun position 3 and reported 'a junk-pile of broken steel and concrete' so he moved south. E Company had checked gun positions 4 and 5 and found them to be empty also. They left a few men near the empty position 6 to deal with a number of Germans who were still in the anti-aircraft gun position. Stragglers from D and E Companies had created a group of about thirty men and together they advanced along the exit road in single file. Artillery rounds were firing in their general direction and from their right (the west) they started to receive accurate machine-gun fire and small-arms weapons ahead of them. Within seconds seven Rangers were killed and wounded as these weapons opened up on them.

Their objective was to reach a group of ruined farm buildings halfway towards the Grandcamp road. Snipers had been using these buildings to target the Rangers, but they had left as the group advanced. Covering the open ground under machine-gun fire, miraculously there was only one casualty, a Ranger who fell on a comrade's bayonet as he jumped into a trench. Small amounts of German resistance continued from individuals and on one occasion from three Germans who came down the road towards them, but other than that the journey to the road was completed. The groups slowly formed a more substantial force and set about defending the roadway. Back at the Pointe F Company were being repeatedly fired on from the east – along the cliff tops and through the land behind the 20mm position. Germans were obviously not using the highway to approach the battery, but were cutting across the open land to the east and engaging the rearguard of the Rangers near the observation post.

Some of the F Company Rangers realised that they had been crossing areas marked as mine fields on their maps. However, no casualties were reported from mines, so it is just possible that the mine fields had either been detonated by naval gunfire or had not been as prolific as the '*achtung minen*' signs would have had them believe.

No Germans were found in the hamlet of Au Guay, but a machine gun engaged them from 100yd ahead. No men were hit and they worked their way around to the south to reach the gun position. Lieutenant Hill and four men were sent west to reach the highway. They were attracted to the noise of machine-gun fire to the west near the exit road and they started heading in that direction.

0805 report from the German Grenadier Regiment 916:

Weak enemy forces have penetrated into Pointe du Hoc. One platoon of the 9/Gren Regt 716 will be committed to launch a counterattack.

There were now about 50 men on the road and they were expecting to see the 116th Infantry and the 5th Rangers arriving shortly from Vierville. In the meantime, they set up positions in the many dugouts and fox holes already prepared by the Germans. Men from E and F Companies took advantage of this cover and spread themselves over four fields and some of these positions also gave them observation across the small valley down to a stream. Sergeant Lomell placed his D Company men on either side of the road with his most important position – the most westerly one – being supplied with a BAR man, six riflemen and a grenade launcher. It was positioned to cover the road and had good observation right out across the valley towards Grandcamp. The rest of his men would cover the north and south of the highway.

Once set up the D Company men went out on patrols from their positions trying to gauge where the enemy was and at about 0900hr a two-man patrol consisting of Lomell and Kuhn went down a lane running south from the highway at Au Guay. After walking 250yd along the lane Sergeant Lomell and Staff/Sergeant Kuhn literally walked into a camouflage position which contained five 155mm guns – ones they logically assumed to be the guns removed from the Pointe. There were piles of ammunition nearby and they had been fuzed to fire, but strangely there were no Germans with them. They had seen nothing of this position until they walked into it.

Len Lomell:

There were just telephone poles in the casements so we just moved on. We didn't waste 2 minutes, we were off. We had lost half of our men on the roadblock. So there were only a couple of us to go looking for them. I said to Jack that we had to go out looking for them. We didn't know the difference between any of the guns. We were just looking for guns. We didn't even have a picture of the guns in advance. We were leapfrogging through the hedgerows and I looked out right in front of me, there were the guns. They were by the hedgerows and they were camouflaged. Not too heavily camouflaged. I told Jack to keep watch.

Out of dumb luck we had stumbled upon them – there were 100 odd Germans not more than 75yd away – it was early in the morning and they were still organising. They were getting dressed and were in all states as we watched them getting sorted out. They never expected us to be there at that time in the morning I guess. We saw guns of all types in the trees and it was pure luck.

They couldn't fire I guess because E Company had their observers buttoned up in their bunker out on the Pointe, so they couldn't get firing orders – those men were in a non-firing position. Why they were in those positions – which couldn't fire at anything even if they got orders. We knew the Germans wouldn't get firing orders, but the thought I had was that the Germans were perhaps waiting for someone to give them instructions.

There was nobody near the guns – I didn't see anyone with them. The Germans were coming in all directions, but not next to the guns. So I told Jack, 'Keep your eyes on them and keep your eyes on me. If anyone sees me kill them.' Nobody saw me, so I put them out of action. The Germans never even knew we had damaged the guns.

We ran out of [thermite] grenades, so I said we have to go back to the roadblock and get some from the other guys. We all carried one or two to lessen our load as we had so much to carry. I only had two grenades and I took out two howitzers and made them unusable. The grenades just melted into the metal work around the mechanism and working parts. But then I took my submachine gun and wrapped it up in my field jacket and I smashed the sights on the guns so the sights could not be used – or if they were they would be inaccurate. We managed to destroy them – the first two and get away and as we were getting out of there the whole place went up – it was the ammunition depot in the other direction and Sergeant Ruplinki had been looking for guns and destroyed the ammunition. We had no plan of where everything was. The blast from the ammo was on the other side of the hedgerow and the blast blew up the whole area. So we went back to the roadblock at a run. We got the rest of the grenades and stuffed them in our blouses ready to go back if necessary.

Within minutes of Lomell and Kuhn damaging two guns, E Company men led by Staff Sergeant Frank Ruplinski found the same position, but from a different access point. They did more disabling work to all the remaining guns by dropping a thermite grenade down each barrel – effectively to melt the breach closed and render the barrel unusable, and they too also removed some of the sights. They caused further damage by throwing grenades into powder charges which started a fire and subsequent explosion. Colonel Rudder was informed by a runner that the guns from the Pointe had been destroyed and that that part of their mission was accomplished.

The After Action Report records the following:

Just why the German guns were thus left completely undefended and unused is still a mystery. One theory, based on the fact that some artillerymen were captured that day on the Pointe, was that bombardment caught them there in quarters, and they were unable to get back to their position. All that can be stated with assurance is that the Germans were put off balance and disorganized by the combined effects of bombardment and assault, to such an extent that they never used the most dangerous battery near the assault beaches, but left it in a condition to be destroyed by weak patrols.

Fighting at the Pointe developed into two main groups. Group one consisted of men fighting around the gun battery and observation post, and the second group was men fighting near the main road. The Germans were firing across flat, open fields from the east from St Marie du Mont and the Rangers were receiving sniper fire and occasional artillery rounds. The machine-gun position on the cliff edge to the east which had caused problems during landing was still firing, but its location was proving difficult to locate. It was also still engaging the Rangers left on the beach and had to be destroyed.

Lieutenant Wintz decided to try to attack it, and it was in fact the third attempt that had been made on the position. They used every piece of cover available and advanced towards it and on the beach Sergeant Wellage had set up a mortar ready to fire once its location had been established. One round directed accurately would end the problematical position for good, but they had to find it. Small groups of men were looking for ways to flank the position, but gaps in hedges and open stretches of land meant that many were being wounded well before they could get near to it.

Colonel Rudder made a decision to use naval gunfire to attack the position and he thought hopefully this would save his men risking their lives undertaking the attack over open country. Naval fire was targeted in the area of the machine gun and reduced the cliff edge to rubble. They literally 'blew away' the edge of the cliff and that particular machine gun was destroyed in the process.

At 1145hr USS *Barton* took over from USS *Herndon* on station No. 4 off Pointe du Hoc. Her own NSFCP could not be contacted and the *Barton* waited offshore for targets of opportunity.

Colonel Rudder had reached the top of the cliffs around 0745hr. His command post was in a crater between the cliff and a destroyed anti-aircraft emplacement and although technically in the centre of things, he was not able to observe any of the Rangers firefights or achievements directly. He was limited to information coming back to him and he could only use this to make decisions, so his options were restricted. Again, communication problems persisted. His orders were technically complete. Destroy the guns/gun positions and take and maintain the blockade of the road until relieved. All of this had been achieved, but the road blockade could change at any minute if they were not on guard. Lieutenant Johnson's fire-control activities were putting the Navy to good use and it was undoubtedly the saving grace for the poorly equipped Rangers. They were starting to run out of ammunition and in places had resorted to using German weapons. This was problematic because when other Rangers heard the change in sound between the weapons of the two nations, they automatically assumed that Germans were firing at

Rangers and not the other way around. As they had used up their reserves of ammunition, they had no choice and it was commonplace to find Rangers using captured German guns. There were moments of calm and then bursts of gunfire from every direction. Everyone had to be on their guard – the Germans were infiltrating through trenches that they knew existed. The 20mm AA gun on the western flank was a lingering problem and if the Rangers showed themselves above ground level they were attacked. Colonel Rudder was hit by fire during one of these exchanges and suffered a wound to the thigh.

James Rudder:

I was wounded twice. The first time was a bullet piercing my leg like something hot going through it. The second one was an artillery shell with great concussion.

USS *Ancon* asked via radio:

Request information whereabouts of Rangers?

Another group of men again went out after the AA gun position and hoped that along with the mortar section from LCA 722 they could destroy it. Ranger Masny led an assault group towards it down an old lane leading in its direction. After a few hundred yards they were taken under attack from rifle, machine-gun and mortar fire from their left – as well as from the 20mm position in front of them. Their own mortar section set up behind them to bombard the gun, but while doing so they saw a white flag appear above the gun position.

Two Rangers near gun position number 6 stood up and they were struck down by machine-gun fire – it had been a ruse to get them into the open. Ranger Otto Masny and his men then became the subject of an artillery barrage. It was obvious that the Germans were in touch with the Maisy gun battery inland and were relaying the coordinates of the Rangers' advance to those guns. Rounds were bracketing their position in the lane and were getting closer. Once on target they stayed on the position and the attack was doomed. They tried to withdraw from the bombardment, but

The 20mm gun position as it is today. From here there is a clear view across the whole of the site and it is easy to see why the Rangers had a problem moving in open ground.

The same position photographed from ground level. It was almost invisible across the debris and destroyed land at the Pointe.

four men were killed and another two were killed by snipers during the retreat. Their mortar ammunition was gone and so they left the weapon. Masny was wounded, and surprised at being knocked off this feet and '*got up mad as a hornet!*'

USS *Satterlee* expended a number of rounds trying to destroy the 20mm gun position, but it was heavily camouflaged, set into the ground to avoid being hit by direct fire and surrounded by concrete, too far inland for the cliff beneath it to be blown away. It was becoming a real problem. Colonel Rudder tried to contact the 116th on the beach asking for re-inforcements. And at 1500hr he received a reply saying they could not understand his message. The same message was relayed via the Navy to the beach and General Huebner replied, '*No reinforcements available*'.

Lieutenant Colonel Trevor of the British Commandos had been responsible for setting up an extension ladder on the beach and he had it working to move the wounded downwards and supplies up the cliff. This was also to prove a vital link when supplies did eventually reach the stranded Rangers.

At 1300hr USS *Barton* reported:

A party of the 2nd Ranger Battalion was seen sheltering from German fire at the bottom of the cliffs below Pointe du Hoc. They were sheltering on the eastern side of the Pointe and they had with them a number of German prisoners which they had managed to get to the beach. They were under guard and a series of signals were communicated between the beach and the ship by the flashing of lights.

The *Barton* sent this information to the command ship USS *Ancon*.

The Rangers were requesting a craft to evacuate their wounded and provide reinforcements so the *Herndon* sent in a small vessel. The boat commanded by a First Lieutenant was 20yd off the beach before it was forced to turn back. The severely concentrated fire from the German machine guns holed the boat several times, with sailors being wounded, and as the situation worsened, the small vessel was forced to sail away from the beach.

USS *Barton* opened fire on the German positions and the effectiveness of the shelling was relayed by the signal lamps of the NSFCPs of Lieutenants Norton and Johnson. Using this very effective method of spotting and then sending a signal to the *Barton* via lamp they were able to damage or destroy a number of the positions causing problems for the Rangers. The *Barton* continued to work in conjunction with the Rangers' SFCPs and this was undoubtedly of huge benefit to the stranded men.

USS *Ancon* received the following message via radio from USS *Satterlee*: '*Rangers position 586934*' (this was a position in the fields approaching the German roadblock at Au Guay).

Herman Stein, T/5, F Company, 2nd Rangers:

My most vivid and memorable experience came around 2 o'clock. Cloise Manning, my newly made assistant gunner, by mutual agreement and myself had just been going through a harrowing experience of playing cat and mouse with a German mortar and artillery bombardment for a solid hour, when we heard quite a clatter of small arms fire.

At 1420hr HMS *Glasgow* noted in her log that she shifted berth again to engage targets to her westward at Maisy.

During the afternoon two attacks were made against the Rangers, both of which came in from the south and the first lasting for over an hour. It was supported by artillery from Maisy and mortar fire, most of which was fired high into the main battery area. These attacks were draining the Rangers' ammunition and some positions, such as the F Company mortar section, held their fire. The Navy could not be called in for a fire mission because the Germans were so close and this could have resulted in friendly fire casualties.

The Germans were beaten back by well-aimed rifle fire and they were later seen to be going away in the direction they had come. It is likely that this was a depleted force as the main German strike directed from the south had been heavily hit by Navy fire crossing the open ground behind Cricqueville.

The second German effort was at 1600hr and more severe than the first. They came in from the west and moved fast towards the Pointe. It was thought that they had come from the 20mm gun position to the west. Their advance was spotted by a number of Rangers and Sergeant Stein opened fire on them at about 40yd with his BAR. He hit a couple of them and the rest withdrew.

The Rangers bolstered the western side of their lines just in time. The Germans had re-grouped and were coming back. F Company relayed its position to the mortar team

Seen from the air the small square indicates the bunker and position of the two aerial masts shown on intelligence maps. The large white circle indicates the position the German soldiers were taken under fire again.

and with Sergeant Elder relaying adjustments, the mortar fired at a range of only 60yd. The Germans were hit and dived for cover in the surrounding area. They were then hit where they sheltered and some ran into the open. Of the approximate seventy-five mortar rounds fired by Sergeant Elder at Pointe du Hoc none were more needed than at that moment. The German attack was finished and, as darkness fell, there were only small-unit actions with rifle fire across the fields. The main attack had been halted.

At 1645hr a German counterattack was spotted advancing along the road south-east of Grandcamp at grid reference 556912 (shown in white on the map below) and it was engaged by USS *Barton* using its 5in guns. It fired forty-five shells at the advancing Germans who were in open fields at the time. This attack was continued and the *Barton* then engaged the same Germans again ½ mile closer – still in open country at grid reference 567924 (shown in black on the map below). It is not known what happened to the Germans involved in this assault, but it was noted by the SFCP to have been '*Good shooting*'.

This type of naval bombardment must have been devastating for the German infantrymen. They could not move in open country in this area without being seen from the higher ground and this would inevitably create an untenable position for them. They

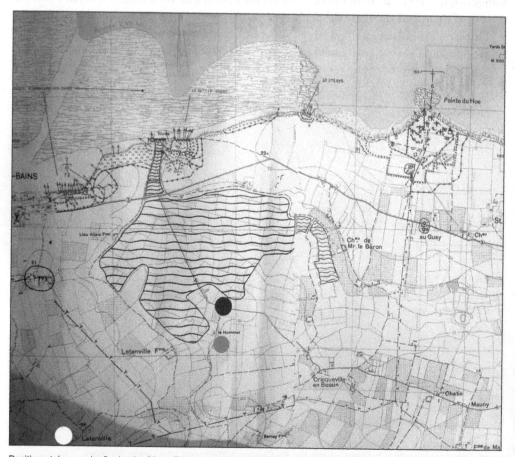

Positions taken under fire by the Navy. These consisted of bunkers, aerial masts and troop movement.

had to use cover and speed to advance safely across this wide, open terrain and this also left them open to observation from the aerial reconnaissance planes, the SFCP with the Rangers and when possible the Navy ships themselves. The position marked with a grey circle at 'Le Hommet' on the map on p. 114 was a signal or transmission centre. The small bunker and two aerial masts were not directly targeted at this time, but the route taken by the advancing Germans (white circle) must have led them right past this position.

1825hr German report:

The Commander of the Div from the command post of Gren Regt 916 to Ic. The 1 Battalion Gren Regt 914 has the order to clear up the situation at the strongpoint Pointe du Hoc by a counterattack. A counterattack from the East with detachments from the strongpoint le Guay has also been started.

At 1930hr the *Barton* was stationed off Port en Bessin and was awaiting another day of naval artillery support orders to help the advance inland.

The NSFCP officers were directing the ships to fire on targets inland and occasionally rounds fell short and close to the Rangers' positions. There was nothing that could be done as they were controlled from close to the cliff edge. They were little help to the men in positions near the road who were being stalked by the German patrols. At about 2100hr and still 2 hours before dark, a party of twenty-three men from A Company, 5th Ranger Battalion came through the fields to the east. They had made it across land fighting Germans all the way in small skirmishes.

James Gabaree:

We ran like hell, fighting and dodging battles through the fields, until we heard that sweet sound of an English-speaking voice, that demanded the password. We had arrived at Pointe du Hoc and joined the 2nd Ranger band.

Ace Parker heard an English-speaking voice challenging him and asking for the password. He replied, 'Tally-ho' and the small band joined the 2nd Rangers.

Daniel Farley:

We went on into Pointe du Hoc and Sergeant Hathaway and Ace went down and reported to Colonel Rudder in the command post, then we were assigned our defensive positions for the night. We joined up with two guys from the 101st Airborne that landed into the Channel. They came up – and they were with us on the Pointe there that night. Next day I was part of a patrol organised to be sent back to get the rest of the 5th men from the beach – but we had to give up after a while because of the mine fields and the German machine guns. Some of the other men in the group were Hathaway, Bellows, Pavey, Gabaree, Drodwell, Johnson and Ace Parker, he was the only officer from the 5th who made it with us to the Pointe on the 6th. Of course we ran across Lomell and some of the others, but everyone was busy. Taylor was there. The Navy sent us some jam sandwiches and water. I went down to the beach looking for supplies. We were out of ammunition so on the beach I collected ammunition from the bodies and the wounded and went back up using the ladders.

James Gabaree:

To our dismay, we learned that the big guns were not in place on the cliffs, but had been moved elsewhere. Telephone poles were put in place in the pillbox to deceive the Allied reconnaissance. Fortunately, members of the 2nd Rangers band found the hiding place of the big guns and destroyed their firing mechanisms.

At 2135hr USS *Ancon* received the following via radio: '*Rangers captured pillbox at 588939, request re-inforcements*'. This was the observation point on the cliff edge.

At 2135hr USS *Chase* received the following via radio from USS *Ancon*: '*Rangers captured pillbox at 588939 fifteen wounded x fifteen prisoners. Require re-inforcements. Come to beach portions to evacuate wounded and prisoners and have nearest beachmaster send necessary boats.*'

By now Colonel Rudder's force had lost over one-third of its men. There was no word other than the twenty-three men from A Company, 5th Battalion as to the whereabouts of the rest of the men, and ammunition and supplies were dwindling. But he was heartened to hear of the A Company men's arrival and the consensus was that the rest of the 5th Rangers were on their way. Germans were still evident to the east – ironically from where the A Company men had arrived by running through their lines.

Lieutenant Colonel Trevor commented that he was sure he was going to be a prisoner or a casualty by the morning and he was not wrong to be worried. The Germans knew full well by now where the Rangers were and it was not inconceivable that a heavy artillery barrage could dislodge the command post and the men at the Pointe. The Rangers tightened up their lines and reduced their exposure to a minimum and the men spread out again with a reduced frontage by changing positions. E Company had six men covering the eastern sector and found three German machine guns (one MG42 and two MG34s) which had ammunition with them.

The 5th Battalion men were split up into two's and three's and placed in the 2nd Battalion lines and the main defensive groups were positioned to defend attacks from the south and east. A much smaller group was placed to cover the approaches from the west as it was thought the relief column would come from that direction.

A period photograph of the surface conditions at Pointe du Hoc.

2201hr German report:

One battalion of the Mobile Brigade 30 in the middle sector is to be subordinated to the Gren Regt 916 as the situation near Grandcamp is uncertain. The parachutists there have joined with the terrorists [French Underground Movement].

James Gabaree:

Our men were deployed with the 2nd Battalion to secure the Pointe and block the German advance.

The moon was nearly full and there was only partial cloud cover, but the Rangers could not see downwards in the valley south-west of the road. The small orchards of trees and hedgerows obscured their vision. During daylight hours they had good visibility in this area and could watch the Germans approaching and when necessary they could call on the Navy to shell groups of them. However, once night fell they lost the advantage. There were hedgerows, farmyards and houses where the Germans could gather for an attack and at about 2330hr one such attack began.

The Rangers could not see what was happening as the ground to the south sloped downwards and the Germans could attack quickly and silently across the fields. Ranger Carty was killed by a grenade and Branley was wounded by a bullet and crawled away. All along the E Company front the Rangers returned fire. In places, the first they knew of the German attack was when the Germans literally walked into their positions. In places, E Company was firing at point-blank range at Germans emerging through the bushes. Some threw grenades and others fired at silhouettes of Germans as they were illuminated by an explosion from the area of the field guns found earlier. Its brief lighting up of the fields showed the Germans in open spaces and they were shot down. The Germans appeared disturbed by the large explosion and this attack was ended. No explanation is known for the large explosion, but possibly it was the ammunition from the burning guns nearby.

The Rangers again changed position fearing that the attack had been a probing mission designed to test the Ranger lines. A counterattack was considered, but in the dark with limited ammunition and intelligence it was eventually ruled unwise. Casualties for this action were also unknown at this time. Men could walk past others who would not speak in their foxholes, so there was no real continuity of command and structure. They were holding onto their pre-assigned positions on the whole and amendments to the lines were made locally. Indeed, two men arrived at the command post saying they had been told to withdraw, but no such order appeared to have been given. But, there was nobody with enough information to make an informed decision until daybreak.

On the east flank it was quiet. They could hear the other units firing, but could not influence it in any way without risking their own flank. At one point they heard what they thought to be animals in a farmyard in St Marie du Mont, but it later turned out to be a German machine gun setting up. It fired rounds in their general direction, but when they did not return fire it ceased. A group of German prisoners held near the command post were ordered to dig foxholes for their own protection – the Rangers were expecting more attacks and they did not have to wait long. At 0100hr the German infantry attacked again from the south and west again against E Company. The Germans' initial advance had again been a quiet one and they reached some 50yd from the Ranger lines.

James Gabaree:

The enemy attacked with vengeance and enormous firepower, shouting and blowing whistles. At one point they were within 50yd of us. To our men in the foxholes it was practically hand to hand combat; we were in a survival mode. Food or water had not passed our lips in days. Our ammunition supplies were very low.

Parker spotted that a few of his men were nearly walked upon by Germans who came around a hedgerow without warning. The Germans had been working their way towards the Rangers quietly and they started shouting out names and he assumed they were trying to intimidate the Rangers.

The Germans were trying to bluff the Rangers into thinking they were a big force and their shouting and whistles were accompanied by heavy machine-gun and rifle fire. They were firing tracer rounds which illuminated their positions. Much of their fire was high and it was going into the hedges, fields and over the Rangers, but not into the Rangers positions as such. The Rangers did not really know what was happening and each soldier reacted to the events in front of him. Some men did nothing as their position was not being attacked. Others found the Germans were almost upon their positions and they were again firing at point-blank range. Some could see the action from a distance and added their rifle fire towards the German advance.

Germans could be heard talking – as if discussing their next move, but it was all confused. Back at the command post, reports were coming in that the Ranger lines had been overrun and there were Germans within the defensive perimeter and many Rangers had been taken prisoner. It appeared that the Germans had indeed attacked at an angle where the Rangers had the least defences and defenders. An area only held by a rifle and a single Browning Automatic Rifle. By this stage of the battle ammunition was desperately low and orders were distributed to conserve ammunition.

At 0300hr the Germans attacked again. Whistles and names being shouted made it resemble the previous attack, but this was more intense with heavy machine-gun fire being directed into the hedgerows and mortar fire being accurately placed. The attack also encompassed the previously quieter area to the east and developed through the wheat fields towards St Marie du Mont. During daylight this would have been a difficult assault, but under cover of darkness the Germans were able to advance steadily without showing themselves.

Ranger Main heard Staff Sergeant Curtis being captured only 15ft from his position, but he could do nothing about it. The darkness meant he was not able to fire without fear of killing his comrade. Carl Bombardier was only 100yd inland from where he landed and had dug in with a Vickers machine gun, which he had taken from a landing craft. Other Rangers were using captured grenades to keep the Germans at bay and the Germans returned fire with heavy machine guns, spraying into the hedgerows. This gunfire allowed the Germans to move forward while the Rangers sheltered and they were, in places, able to advance into and through the Rangers lines. During one such exchange of gunfire Ranger Burnett heard Sergeant Ruplinski arguing with other Rangers about their chances. Moments later he was heard shouting, 'Kamerad' to enable them to surrender. The Germans quickly rounded up the Rangers, many of whom were badly wounded. About twenty Rangers were captured and later moved south about a mile to a German command post. The Rangers again altered their positions in order to adapt to the changing circumstances. More men were put into the north-east area of the battery to support that position. Riflemen from F Company, a BAR and a captured German machine gun were put into the hedgerow as the Germans advanced toward them. Using two BARs, the Rangers broke up an attack coming down a lane towards them and a German was killed by a Grenade thrown at him as he crawled under a hedge towards the Rangers near the command post. Rangers began arriving back at the road and as they were not being pursued by the Germans they set about re-organising themselves. Most of the men of F Company were still OK, but only a few men from E and none of D were present.

The men of the 5th Rangers made their way across the unfamiliar terrain in small groups, but they had a lack of understanding of the lie of the land. They had not seen it properly during daylight, as the 2nd Battalion men had.

At around 0400hr about fifty of the men who had been out near the road were put into a defensive line between gun position 5 and gun position 3.

By now a number of men from E Company had been killed or captured and some D Company Rangers had suffered the same fate. The remainder of D Company, comprising some twelve men, was still in concealed positions along the 250yd hedgerow. They did not know that the rest of the Rangers had withdrawn towards the command post and when they did realise, it was nearing dawn – any movement would have been exposed to fire from the Germans close by.

Amos Potts:

We were in a small crater when an artillery shell came close. A soldier was wounded in the foot and after I had him all bandaged, he said to me, 'Sir, you've been 'it'. So I had but hadn't noticed it. The left sleeve of my jacket had two holes in it and there was a little blood on my upper arm.

We finally linked up with the CP and since I was a signal officer, temporarily without portfolio, I assisted as best I could in the communication section. The radios were not working, but a lieutenant we called Ike – his name was Eikner or something like that, he always answered when you called 'Ike'

The Chateau de St Pierre du Mont was a good observation point for the Germans and for that reason the Navy undertook its destruction.

– had insisted on bringing a signal lamp with which to communicate to the Navy. The lamp was equipped with a 'scope' to aim it at the vessel intended to receive the message since it was rather narrow. I aimed the light.

When it came time to count noses and assign patrols for the night, I found that two of my boys had proved themselves in combat and the other two were missing. Duties were assigned on a two on, four off for the night. Our packs were to come with the battalion trucks that were to link up at H-hour + 6, but so far we had not seen hide nor hair of them. It was actually nearer H-hour + 66 when they finally made it. It was cold that night and no blankets – I used a gas cape [plastic bag large enough to crawl into] for cover and, had the ground been a little softer, I would have been quite snug. I did sleep well.

The 'score' for Photo Assignment Unit A, 850th Signal Service Battalion, attached to the Second Ranger Battalion was as follows:

Keghan Nigohosian – Killed in Action.
Irving Lomasky – Missing in Action.
Worden F. Lovell – Distinguished Service Cross.
Herbert J. Stark – Silver Star.
Amos Potts – Purple Heart.

The score for the Rangers was considerably higher.

On the morning of 7 June USS *Barton* was again assigned to work in Station No. 4 in conjunction with Lieutenants Johnson and Norton's SFCP. During the night the Rangers with Lieutenant Norton had worked their way inland and were effectively directing the USS *Texas* on fire missions to support them.

At 0600hr again the Rangers repeated their request to USS *Barton* for reinforcements and for a vessel to come inshore and take away their wounded. They still had German prisoners on the beach, but the beach was not a secure place to land. USS *Barton* undertook a number of fire missions and one such mission at 0700hr was directed at grid reference 592938 because of machine guns concentrated in that area. This was in actual fact an area east of the Pointe where the Germans were attempting to infiltrate in the direction that A Company of the 5th Battalion had arrived the day before. It was also the exact spot where Ranger James Gabaree would soon be left after being shot by machine-gun fire and his comrade Pavey killed.

At 0745hr the *Barton* fired at a chateau along the Grandcamp–Vierville road (592931) under direction of the SFCP. The Chateau de St Pierre du Mont was situated midway between the hamlet of Au Guay and St Pierre du Mont and its upper floors were an ideal German observation position overlooking Pointe du Hoc and the sea beyond. Also just in front of it to the north there was a small grove of trees with a machine-gun position. Both the chateau and the machine gun were hit repeatedly

From the upper floor of the Chateau de St Pierre du Mont the Germans could observe the whole of the invasion area and also engage the Rangers at the Pointe with sniper fire.

and a total of 185 x 5in shells were fired. The machine-gun position was also being strafed by a flight of Thunderbolts.

The SFCP reported friendly (Rangers) troops at ground level in this area, so after the machine-gun position was destroyed further shelling was directed at the second floor of the chateau.

Snipers were then seen so the Barton changed its shelling method and it recorded in its log, '[we] walked right through the grove of trees harboring snipers. A shell was seen to strike a branch and detonate, with evident shrapnel effect.' And so the Rangers advanced. Each target was identified and then its position called in. Another chateau was heavily damaged and rendered useless to the Germans.

USS *Barton* returned to its station off Port en Bessin having given a sterling account of itself. Its after After Action Report stated the following:

On some targets, such as the chateau, hitting was delayed in the interests of safety. As our own forces were immediately in front of the buildings. It was necessary to apply arbitrary out spots on the initial salvos. The spot was then reduced until the second storey of the building was hit.

On 7 June **Cecil Gray** was sent back into the village of Vierville:

We had to get the Germans who had infiltrated our positions overnight. We killed a few that day and then we got counterattacked, we repulsed it and we then were told to head for Pointe du Hoc. We walked down both sides of the main road towards Pointe du Hoc. We didn't get there that day because of enemy fire, but when we eventually got there it was all wrapped up. I had been separated from D Company and joined F Company. When we got to the sluice gates just beyond Pointe du Hoc I found the rest of E Company.

Glen Erickson:

The night of 7 June there was a lot of German sniper infiltration and we crawled back across the road where we had cleared the mines. I can remember crawling across the road and down the hill until the morning – we waited for daylight and then went back into the fields. The hedgerows were our cover.

There was not any heavy German fire after D+1 on the beach. They were possibly out of range and they were not coming in and they hadn't replaced any vacancies on the beach positions by then.

It's just you and the people that are right close to you … you don't see any plan and all the planning was necessary, but it didnt serve us well on D-Day – at least in the early hours. I stayed on the beach and we unloaded cargo and surplies working 24 hours per day in shifts. They were rough (those Rangers) and they had a very difficult time – getting up the cliff and down towards the village of Grandcamp. I saw them D+1 – quite early. I was across the road from Vierville exit at the church – 200yd or so down the road. I see these Rangers – filthy, tired and bog eyed like they had seen a ghost after their fighting. My motorpool sergeant Virgin Lucky was hit by shrapnel. He was a bloody mess – he was lying down on the beach and they took those big scissors and cut him up. They cut off one of his dog tags and it should have stayed with him.

Francis Coughlin:

Later that night we were behind a farmhouse which the Germans must have zeroed in somehow. They must have known exactly where it was, but only five shells landed that night. Our planes came over that evening and they bombed where the shells were coming from that day. They were flying at about 200ft and they were skimming the treetops right along. You could almost read the number on the engine when it went by it was so low.

Coit Coker, still in Vierville:

In the morning the battalion, joined by the 5th Rangers, proceeded in column down the highway to St Pierre du Mont, encountering minor resistance from snipers and machine guns. It was not definitely known whether the 2nd Rangers had been successful in capturing Pointe du Hoc and our mission was to effect or help effect the capture. At St Pierre enemy fire was directed several hundred yards ahead of us successfully interdicting the way to Pointe du Hoc. Intelligence from friendly natives indicated that the pre-arranged targets – (Maisy) No. 5 (Les Perruques) and No. 16 (La Martiniere) and target No. 87 might be delivering this fire.

I got the battleship Texas *to fire on any observed enemy gun emplacements in the Maisy area using air spot. This fire was delivered about 1300–1400 and the interdicting enemy fire ceased. I do not know how many rounds* Texas *fired, but I do know that on this occasion and on all subsequent occasions when we called on the* Texas *to fire for us with air spot, enemy fire was silenced.*

As Coker and the Rangers advanced towards Pointe du Hoc they encountered small enemy actions and it was deemed that these might develop into counterattacks on the column. **Coker continues:**

We withdrew and formed defensive positions for the night in two hedgerows which abound fields in St Pierre. The counterattack never developed further, but at about 2000hr the enemy began inaccurate intermittent artillery fire on the battalion position.

The church at St Pierre du Mont, as seen from the road. The field in front was marked as a mine field and snipers harassed the relief column as it approached Pointe du Hoc and Au Guay.

At 1315hr HMS *Glasgow* opened fire on Maisy Battery (target No. 5, Les Perruques) and discharged sixty-three rounds with aerial observation. Aircraft reported: 'Fire effective – several direct hits. Many within 50 yards.' At 1527hr she opened fire at Maisy Battery and expended forty-eight rounds. Aircraft reported: 'Hits obtained. Fire effective.'

At 2110hr *Glasgow* opened fire on a 'suspected gun battery' at grid reference 578918 – this was south of the Rangers' position at Pointe du Hoc and could have been responsible for some of the incoming fire they were receiving. After expending eighteen rounds the aircraft reported: 'No guns seen, but direct hits on farm house. Men ran out. Net results not known.' This may well have been a German mortar team.

At 1013hr USS *O'Brien* commenced firing on a German pillbox (coordinates 585934) as designated by SFCP 1 at Chateau de Mr le Baron. The *O'Brien* fired only one salvo at a range of 2,850yd.

At 1014hr after firing six rounds of 5in shells the Rangers continued to advance in this area (inland) and the *O'Brien* awaited new targets. Shortly after the bombardment of the pillbox German soldiers were seen running from this position also.

Frank South:

On D-Day + 1 we let the Navy know we were short of rations and they came in on a small boat and jetisoned over these cylindrical tubes used for shells and went back as they were picking up machine-gun fire.

We went down and picked them up – we had peanut-butter, jelly sandwiches of all things and we picked them up and gave them to the wounded. It was our survival rations.

Carl Bombardier:

On the second day our Sergeant William Petty took command … I remember we tried an attack and picked up one of the boys who were wounded, and had been playing dead with the Germans all about him for a day and a night. We thought he [Petty] should have had the Congressional Medal of Honour for his heroics (it took six months to get him a Silver Star).

John Raaen:

Had I been more mature and more experienced I would have pushed out immediately to relieve PdH and maintained the roadblock at St Pierre du Mont. I decided to obey my orders, so I called in the company commanders and got them in front of me.

Essentially we turned in for the night hoping we would not be counterattacked – unfortunately a major from the 29th Division came down the road from Vierville – he was all panicked and he told us that the Germans have broken through at Vierville and broken through the flanks at Le Moulin.

He told us that all of our forces have been forced to surrender and flee … and a German armoured column was right behind him.

As you can imagine, the morale when right down.

Captain Wise (C Company commander) flipped a coin to see if he or I would head back towards Vierville to check this information out. We didn't trust this major as he was too panicked.

I started out with Corporal Sharp down the road one on the left and one on the right back towards Vierville ... suddenly down the road comes another major from the 29th on a bicycle whistling – just as relaxed as anything.

I am only about 300yd from where I started and I asked him what the hell was happening at Vierville. He told me it was all going OK – everything is fine. The tank battalion is heading this way ... it was not Germans and it was the US Army tanks heading our way.

As a result we relaxed a bit more, but we still continued our night defences as we had done already. We were planning the night defences, but I did decide to send out a Ranger patrol consisting of Sergeant Moody and Corporal McKissick (both men from the 5th Battalion) to find out if PdH was still there and if the 2nd Battalion was still there.

It seemed silly to be sitting a thousand yards away and if I had been a more experienced officer I would have sent the whole battalion but I didn't.

Moody and McKissick (both men from the 5th Btn) went in at night, through the German lines, during a firefight and this was the second night the 2nd Rangers were there and they were counterattacked a number of times.

They overran the command post of Colonel Rudder on their first run in and then came back and found it. Moody told Colonel Rudder the situation as we knew it – including about the tanks. Moody being a mortar man found a reel of wire and ran it all along and back to our position. This gave us telephone communication with Rudder and my own position.

Moody and McKissick both received the DSC for the patrol action they went on – but mostly for their ingenuity for the laying of wire.

James Gabaree:

On D+1 our combined forces of the 5th and 2nd Ranger Battalions at the Pointe consisted of only ninety men able to bear arms. We held out. The situation was becoming desperate as we ran out of food, water and just about everything and the batteries in our radios died. Seven of us from A Company 5th battalion, led by Lieutenant Parker, volunteered to try to make contact with the main force on the beach. The advance was as a patrol eastwards but we stopped, only to discover we were in the middle of a mine field, in open ground, with 20yd to go before we could reach the shelter of a small mound on the cliff's edge. Enemy gunfire fire opened up on us before we could reach the mound, killing one man, my best friend [Ranger Pavey].

Richard Hathaway:

Denzil Johnson made a dash across a short open space and disappeared. Pavey jumped up and tried the same move. He was hit in the chest and he died almost immediately.

John Bellows:

> *Parker picked a number of us, Gabaree, Farley, Johnson and others to go back to the beach at Vierville to re-establish contact. Halfway back Gabaree was shot and we couldn't go any further.*

The Germans started strafing the ditch where the Rangers were sheltering and James Gabaree was hit and Johnson was missing.

Charles H. Parker:

> *We started our runs one person at a time.*

Sergeant Denzil Johnson went through the bushes and was not fired upon. Next Private First Class Paul Pavey followed, but instantly he was hit in the chest and killed by machine-gun fire from cover nearby. It was at this moment that Gabaree was shot in the buttocks as he too advanced. The other men pulled him back and tucked him into a crevice at the cliff edge. He was by now incapable of moving, so they gave him a canteen of water and told him to stay put.

It was assumed that Johnson had died in the chaos as he was thought to have been shot. However, Johnson re-appeared through a hedge and Daniel Farley remembers him demanding, '*Ace [Parker's nickname] – where the hell have you been – I have been looking for you for half an hour.*' Johnson had found a ditch in the field that allowed the men just enough cover below the field's surface and so they headed towards Omaha Beach along the cliff edge. Crawling along the field edges was slow going and mines were found and had to be avoided using bayonets to disengage them. It was hard work and as they rested for a few hours in heavy undergrowth on the cliff tops, John Bellows (using Parker's field glasses) noticed an LCVP coming in to the Pointe. They could see no further movement on the Pointe and after seeing the LCVP move back away they assumed that the position was being evacuated. They decided to return to the Pointe and Sergeant Bakos and John Bellows ran off at a crouch.

They returned to the Pointe without incident to find that the position had been reinforced and was still occupied by their fellow Rangers. They tucked into the bread, jam and spam that the LCA had delivered, for they had not eated for two days. James Gabaree was left at the cliff top alone with his rifle and the canteen of water, close to where he had been hit and to the body of his best friend Pavey.

John Bellows:

> *We returned to the Pointe climbing over trip wires and mines on the cliff top.*

Frank Kennard, was on the landing craft that the 5th Rangers had seen approaching Pointe du Hoc:

> *On the 7th, at the direction of a Major Street from the command ship ANCON, we commandeered an LC and our group which consisted of approx. eight guys from the*

2nd and twelve or more from the 5th Battalion motored up the coast towards the Pointe where we boarded the USS Satterlee. *We got some food and supplies and then went ashore to join the 2nd Rangers at PdH. The ride west (off-shore) was uneventful and I don't recall that the LC 'showed' any damage or blood from the previous landings.*

Naval records at the same time state:

At 0250hr one plane was observed to crash on the beach and at 0255hr, two more planes crashed. At 1405 sent two LCVPs in charge of Lieutenant R.C. Hill, U.S.N.R. to USS Texas *in connection with the supplying of ammunition to the Rangers at Pointe du Hoc, and the evacuation of casualties.*

John Reville:

When I went to Pointe du Hoc on the LCA. I had a Luger and I put that with my pack and I remember I went on patrol. I went back the next day and looked for my Luger and my pack – it was all gone. Someone had taken it.

James Gabaree:

While trying to make the run for shelter I was shot. My comrades pulled me into a crevice in the cliff, but had to leave me to continue on with their mission. I realised that my chance of coming out of this alive was practically nil. The primeval will to live kicked in. The cheek of my left buttock was blown open; it looked like a big red bowl of Jell-O. The army provided us with two first-aid kits to use in the event of being wounded, including sulphur drugs. I spread all of the drugs on the one wound and applied the bandage. After taking off my canteen belt, I found another wound where a bullet had entered my back. An unknown force told me to exchange the first bandage with the drugs on it and apply it to the newly discovered wound, thereby having the sulphur drug on both wounds. I also spit on the wounds for some reason. A decision had to be made. Do I stay here and hope they come back for me? Not very likely. It could not get any lonelier than this, not much chance of staying alive. There was no human being to ask for help or comfort. It would have been easier to end the pain, close my eyes, and give up the fight to live.

The spot close to where James Gabaree was left at the cliff edge. His comrades had no choice but to leave him and continue with their mission, but they did vow to return for him.

The thought of leaving Pavey's body caused me great anguish. I chose to start crawling back towards the Pointe. Sometimes I would try standing part way up until I could not stand the pain, then I would drop to my knees and crawl. At one point on my journey a bullet went by my ear. The nearest shell hole was my refuge. I put my helmet on the end of my rifle and raised it, hoping to draw fire – no shot. A sniper was in the tree and waved for me to surrender. I started towards him half-walking, half-crawling, but decided I would rather be dead than a prisoner, so dove into the bushes. The expected bullet never came; he let me get away. Not all Germans are bad guys.

Somehow I kept going and eventually came to an open field. I did not hear or see anyone or anything. A sixth sense told me to turn and fire my weapon. I killed a German lying in wait for me. He had fired his rifle, but missed his mark. By this time I was pretty well out of my head, having had no food or water and having lost lots of blood.

The German foxhole looked like a pretty safe place to be, so I crawled in. I lay next to the dead German, ate his black bread and promptly threw up. Until now, killing was a reflex action. A German would appear in front of me, I had seconds to pull the trigger or die. Now, the magnitude of killing a fellow human being weighed heavily on my mind. I then started to hallucinate, seeing Mickey Mouse and Goofy on a large screen in full colour. I decided to wait 4 hours, and then kill myself, as I did not relish a slow death. To ensure that I would not be captured, I placed the tip of my rifle barrel in my mouth. My finger was on the trigger. I was startled when I heard someone say, 'Son of a bitch'. Luck was on my side, a US patrol had stumbled upon me. In my delirious state of mind, I insisted on rejoining my platoon. I don't think I would have added anything to their fighting ability; I was half dead. The clothes on my left side were coated with dried blood, I was filthy and hadn't eaten, shaved or bathed since the landing.

The USS *Ancon* had no specific task in the ship to shore movements except to transfer various army units when they moved their headquarters ashore. She was the flagship of Rear Admiral J. Hall, Commander of Assault Force 'O'. During 6 June she lost a landing craft when it hit an underwater beach obstacle while landing First Division personnel and later it was hit by artillery fire. *Ancon* sent two LCVPs with supplies and ammunition for the Rangers at Pointe du Hoc and was no doubt a much-needed boost. It also facilitated the evacuation of casualties and prisoners of war from the beach.

James Gabaree:

The medics picked me up and carried me to a landing craft to evacuate me to a hospital ship. The hospital ship was a scene of blood, with maimed and dying men everywhere. The medics cleaned me up and stabilised my wounds until I could receive further treatment. I was passed out most of the time. I remember lying on a flat deck and looking into the face of another Ranger, I think he had just died. I did not receive any medical treatment prior to arriving at the hospital ship – Lieutenant Parker had offered me his morphine, but I didn't use it in case it put me to sleep.

When I woke up on the ship, I remember seeing the nurses' and doctors' clothing – it was covered with blood. I thought that I would probably be killed in the invasion, I accepted that. The adrenalin was high, but I was never frightened.

A US National Archives photograph showing wounded men in their LCVP arriving at a hospital ship.

When I arrived in England, they cleaned me up enough to get me to a hospital. I received a couple of major operations there. When I was examined they told me I was hit twice, once in the back at the belt line and I had to have been standing up. The second bullet ripped my left buttocks wide open. I had to be lying down when the second shot hit me. I think they were trying to finish me off!

At 2026hr USS *O'Brien* again commenced firing on a second German pillbox (coordinates 586931), as directed from Chateau de Mr le Baron by the Rangers. Opening fire at a range of 3,250yd, the *O'Brien* fired three ranging salvos and then changed to rapid continuous fire for 30 seconds, which was directed by NSFCPs.

USS *O'Brien* reported:

2033 Ceased firing on target as directed having expended fifty-four rounds of 5in/ 38-calibre AA Common ammunition. Results not observed by this ship, but Shore Fire Control Party reported 'target destroyed'.

The first chateau on the right going south down the road at the edge of the valley…towards Chateau de Mr le Baron. It was occupied by the Germans before D-Day and more specifically by the head of Organisation Todt for the area. He was in charge of the Todt workers at Pointe du Hoc and WN76. The chateau was occupied by the Germans who used it as a base on D-Day and as the counterattacks on the Rangers' positions developed. Then after shelling it the Rangers used it and the Chateau de Mr le Baron as observation positions for their SFCP, who could watch the Germans in the valley below. It was heavily shelled by the Navy before it changed hands.

The farmhouse and barn where the German artillery had a command post. There is a lane behind where this photograph was taken which leads up to the guns found by the Rangers and towards Pointe du Hoc. The Germans had their command post in a barn in the courtyard and it is certain that the German counterattacks on the Rangers would have started from here. It is literally 500m to the guns and approximately 500m beyond that to the roadblock at Au Guay.

At 2035hr the USS *O'Brien* again commenced firing on a German roadblock (coordinates 586931, at Au Guay). This roadblock was situated on the main Grandcamp–Vierville road and was holding up the advance of the Rangers. Again, it was a target designated by the US Army Ranger Fire Control Group at Chateau de Mr le Baron. *O'Brien* opened fire at a range 3,650yd and fired three ranging salvos, then as directed by a NSFCP, shifted to rapid continuous fire for a minute.

Further down the lane, past Chateau de Mr le Baron, also on the right backing onto the valley was the German command post for the guns found in the field. These were the ones destroyed by Len Lomell and the other 2nd Rangers.

At 2048hr USS *O'Brien* ceased firing after expending eighty-six rounds of 5in ammunition. The ship reported: '*Results of bombardment not observed*'. *But her SFCP reported: 'mission successful*'.

John Reville:

Rudder gave me the order that night D+1 to take a patrol from Pointe du Hoc – we were right on the Pointe – and go back towards Vierville to find the 5th Battalion and tell them what the score was at Pointe du Hoc ... and that is what we did. On the patrol I was with Muscatello. On the patrol two things happened. We waited until it was dark and Rudder told me to go. The point man told me that he thought we were in a mine field. I hadn't seen any evidence of it – there was no barbed wire with the triangles and the death's head saying 'ACHTUNG MINEN', I hadn't seen anything so I said keep going. It must have been several hours later, very dark in the sunken roads and all of a sudden an American voice cried out something. Halt or stop or something – and I called back ... What the Army had done for D-Day + 1, etc. was give us three sets of passwords – Thunder – Welcome, Thirsty – Victory and Weapon – Throat. This guy was a trained soldier, a machine-gunner, and we had walked right into his field of fire. He called out – I called back and then he came forward and identified himself. He said

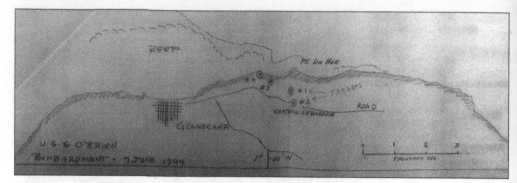

A map drawn by a gunnery officer on USS *O'Brien* to illustrate the positions it attacked.

*the whole group of men were a hundred yards or so to his rear and he said we would find
everyone there. Thank god this was a trained soldier from the 116th — he knew what to
do straight away as we were walking right into his machine gun. Sullivan and the others
were there and they were surprised to see us – they thought we had drowned.*

Later again at 2125hr the *O'Brien* began firing at or close to the observation post on the
Pointe, target number 576939, a machine-gun position. At 2128 firing was directed by
Rangers on German machine-gun nest, coordinates 579937, a gun position close to the
edge of the cliff west of the Pointe on top of the 100ft cliff.

It was was blocking the advance of Ranger patrols along the cliffs past WN76
towards WN77, the sluice gates located on the eastern side of Grandcamp. USS
O'Brien opened fire at a range of 2,550yd: '*Fired one ranging salvo which straddled
target, then shifted to rapid continuous fire for thirty seconds, as directed by SFCP.*' In
evaluation USS O'Brien reported: '*Two pillboxes, one roadblock and a fortified machine-
gun nest were completely neutralised. Target number 4 (machine-gun nest) was completely
destroyed in 2 minutes. The first salvo straddled and the subsequent 30 seconds of rapid fire
demolished the target.*'

There were four targets designated by the Army Ranger SFCP:

Target No. 1 – German pillbox (coordinates 585934).
Target No. 2 – German pillbox (coordinates 586931).
Target No. 3 – German roadblock (coordinates 579937).
Target No. 4 – German machine-gun nest (coordinates 576939).

Effectiveness as reported to the ship by the Rangers:

Target No. 1 – no report (it was an empty emplacement).
Target No. 2 – target destroyed (this was the roadblock).
Target No. 3 – mission successful (this was the machine gun on the cliff edge).
Target No. 4 – mission successful (this was also another machine-gun position on
    the cliff edge).

Working with spotter planes USS *Shubrick* engaged target 16A (the 4 x 150mm guns at
Foucher's Farm). These were the guns suggested to have been moved by the Germans

from positon 16 to the fields behind target 16A. This, however, was not the case as the guns at target 16 were still operational in that position later on the 9th; the two positions each had their own guns. This was the third Maisy Battery which was being engaged.

Jim Snakenberg was in the *Shubrik*'s combat information centre:

We were stationed right off the beach on 7 June. In the afternoon we got a call to fire on an ammo dump. The figures they gave us made us hit the top of a hill, if we depressed we went over the dump. The Ex (Executive officer) was an old fire-control man. He drew a hill and put in the hit we made. He gave me some figures that turned the guns almost straight up. This time we got the call back, 'On target, walk and talk'. After firing many times they said. 'Target destroyed'. A big black smoke came up from the other side of the hill. We knew we had him.

That was the end of target 16A.

HMS *Hawkins* had a problem with the Maisy Battery. It was designated as one of her primary targets on the morning of D-Day and in the Royal Naval History of the Second World War it states clearly that Maisy was *'completely destroyed'* on 6 June by *Hawkins*. However, its gunnery report has HMS *Hawkins* again firing at Maisy on 7 June, as were many other naval vessels. Reports received from spotter planes reported HMS *Hawkins* landed eighteen hits on target 5 and twenty-four hits on target 16 on 7 June. *Hawkins* again fired at Maisy target 5 and spotters reported *'silenced'*.

On 7 June the USS *Enterprise*'s aerial reconnaissance reported shots on target 5 'Shoot effective'.

The USS *Texas*'s log reported:

Word was received from destroyers close inshore at Pointe du Hoc that the Ranger Battalion which had landed there at H-hour on D-Day was still isolated from our own troops. They were running low on provisions and ammunition and had a number of prisoners and casualties to be evacuated. Two LCVPs were obtained and loaded with provisions and ammunition from the destroyers and the Texas and sent in to relieve the Rangers.

At 1730hr the LCVPs returned containing some 28 German prisoners (including one officer and several Italians from a labour battalion) and 34 wounded Rangers. The wounded Rangers were given medical attention and for the most part were suffering from minor wounds. One Ranger died during the night from very severe abdominal wounds.

German prisoners questioned by several officers proficient in German revealed that the attack had been entirely unexpected, at least in this area, and that no warning or alert had been sounded. The first real warning of the attack was the sight of the assault force covering the Baie de la Seine at daybreak on the 6th.

On the Pointe, the Ranger withdrawal, although over a short distance, had caused confusion, primarily because not everyone knew that is what they were doing. Rangers Theobold, Loring and Wadsworth were forced to hide from the Germans while left alone in their positions. Theobold was caught along with Wadsworth the next day and Ranger Main managed to get back to the command post after watching Germans from his concealed position in bushes.

Wadsworth was taken prisoner and was pushed into working with the German medics tending their wounded. He later convinced a German doctor to hide with him as the German Army fell back. Then he turned the doctor over as a prisoner to the first American patrol to come along and then rejoined the Rangers.

The remaining men of D Company lay hidden the next day beneath their hedgerows. The enemy did not come searching for them and only a few passing Germans were seen. They did not in fact know what had happened to the remaining Ranger force, so the prudent thing to do was to wait for the arrival of the 116th Infantry and/or the 5th Battalion.

Onboard USS *Harding* they reported at 1058hr that a machine gun on the beach opened fire on them as they approached Pointe du Hoc. At 1109hr the *Harding* despatched ammunition and food to the embattled Rangers using LCT 580 and at 1131hr the *Harding* opened fire with its 40mm guns at targets behind Pointe du Hoc – those positions being radioed by the SFCP with the Rangers. They fired 100 rounds and then ceased firing at 1310hr. However, shortly afterwards they began firing at a position behind target 90, again on the request of the Rangers.

At 1429 USS *Harding* hit an underwater obstacle about 1,500yd from the beach, but the ship managed to clear the obstruction 3 minutes later. However, during this episode the propellers and sound gear were damaged.

Gunner's Mate **Mike Stata** was working No. 1 gun at the time:

We were firing at enemy targets on the beach and our captain wanted to get a little closer so he could do a better job, that worked fine until we ran aground and got stuck. There we were near the base of the Pointe aground like a sitting duck. A diver was sent over the side to check for damage and discovered both our propellers were damaged. It wasn't long after that we were able to back off into deeper water. All of a sudden a huge enemy shell hit right where we had been.

According to the After Action Report at 1525hr: '*Enemy shore battery opened fire at* Harding. *No splashes came close enough to worry them.*' It is most likely that Maisy was firing at the *Harding* as it would have been visible to the observers in Grandcamp and Maisy churches. The peninsula sticks out so the *Harding* would have been in full view approaching the shoreline at that point and a large target of opportunity within visual range of the guns' observers.

At 1727hr the landing party returned from Pointe du Hoc to the *Harding* and she was soon back in action in support of the Rangers. Again targets were designated around German positions 90–1 at 2200hr – the SRFC reported that after forty-eight rounds expended the fire mission was successful. By then the crew of the *Harding* had spent 86 continuous hours at their battle stations. After that they returned to England for repairs and reassignment.

German report, 8 June:

Order was given to the 914th Gren Regt to use the personnel unit of the 3rd Bt of the 1716th Art Regt [about 300 men] which had lost its equipment, as reinforcement of the infantry forces of the 1st Bn 914th Gren Reg east of the Vire for this commitment, and the regiment was urged once more to hold the bridgehead east of Isigny by all means.

Lieutenant Colonel Ziegelmann:

As far as numbers are concerned, on 9 June there could be 'in the left sector – 914th Gren Regt: about 1,000 men' covering an area from Pointe du Hoc to the left of the Vire Estuary at Brevands – '12 light pieces of Artillery'.

In the final report of the day it was pointed out to the German General Staff of the LXXXIV Army Corps that the combat force of the 352nd Infantry Division had considerably diminished during 8 June and that *'there exists the danger of an enemy breakthrough on both wings of the division on the 9th June'*.

German shells came in close to the D Company positions, but they survived intact. The Rangers who had been stranded at Pointe du Hoc were relieved on the morning of 8 June by men of the 2nd and 5th Rangers and the 1st Battalion of the 116th Infantry. Their advance towards the Pointe was initially to include an assault on the radar station at Pointe et Raz de la Percée. However, the accurate naval gunfire on the morning of the 6th had indeed devastated the site, leaving it inoperable and thus it had all been abandoned by the Germans as the task force passed it.

The Ranger groups' advance had been supported by 123 rounds of ammunition fired by the 58th Armoured Field Artillery Battalion, firing from positions north of Longueville. Even though the relief force had only perhaps been 1,000yd away the night before, there were still Germans in the vicinity and it would not have been a simple advance onto the battery at night.

John Raaen:

We made plans for the early morning assault on PdH and the troops were moving into their positions for the attack. Then suddenly along came Colonel Schneider in a jeep at the head of the rest of the Ranger battalion and he then took over command and the assault using my original plan.

By 10am it was all over and we were sitting there swapping stories with the 2nd Battalion men when suddenly out of the brush come the tanks 743rd and they attacked us. We were sitting in the open when their 75mm guns opened up on us.

One of our officers ran out from cover and jumped on top of the tank, banged on the turret and eventually we stopped them firing.

We had about four killed and three more wounded from that incident.

We re-organised the battalion. We had lost two platoons, both of which had ended up at PdH before we got there ... one with A Company with Parker and another one with Captain Runge had got there D+1 and so they had to be integrated back into their companies.

Len Lomell:

I started out with 65 men and I wound up with about 15 – the rest were killed or not standing. That was the one shocking thing that I remembered was that I saw what was done to me medically – I had to walk down to the beach to get on a medical boat to get cleaned up ... it was a disturbing thing because I was by myself and I walked down the road ...

By D+3 the graves registration guys had got all my guys' bodies out. I never forgot that I could see my men dead on each side of the road. They were all my men and I lost control of my self – I wanted them to get up – it was a shocking sight. Death and horrors of war had not struck me before – it was at that moment when I realised the reality of war. Dick Rankin, 5th battalion was also badly wounded on D-Day and a French farmer buried him in the hay and then took him home to look after him until the Americans had advanced. I was one of the first guys shot. I was there D+2, after three days the wound on my side turned black with no medicine, so I had to go back to England to be operated on.

Coit Coker:

There was no opposition until we actually got out onto the Pointe and were dispersed in bomb-crater positions. Then quite a bit of hell broke loose in the way of mixed enemy and friendly mortar, small-arms and tank (friendly) gunfire, shrapnel was flying freely.

John Reville:

We waited until the next morning and then we started to come back up toward the Pointe du Hoc. A halftrack got in there and there was some friendly fire. We got organised and got back to the Pointe, but we didn't see any Germans by the time we got back.

It was confusing for everyone at the Pointe at this time. The incoming 116th Infantry and the 5th and 2nd Rangers who landed on the beach did not know where the enemy positions and trenches were. They could hear sporadic German gunfire and logically assumed this was coming from German defenders still at the Pointe. In fact, this was not the case and again it was 2nd and 5th Rangers using captured weapons.

Parker recalled that as the Ranger force approached the Pointe they were accompanied by tanks of the 743rd Tank Battalion. Unfortunately, the tank drivers were under the impression they were attacking Germans on the Pointe and they opened fire on the Rangers. It was a highly confused situation and it took many minutes to convince the tank crews and infantry that it was the Rangers they were firing at. The Ranger group from the beach had arrived to relieve Pointe du Hoc – three days late!

Coit Coker:

The remnants of the 2nd Ranger SFCP were still firing and being fired upon. Captain Harwood (FO) had been killed and Lieutenant Norton (NGLO) injured and evacuated. I volunteered our fire power to the 2nd Rangers, but they had no need for us.

The destroyer USS *Shubrick* located the battery at Maisy – La Martiniere firing from the eastern side of the Carentan Estuary at 0740hr. After opening fire the battery was duly silenced, only to recommence firing at 0820hr and land a pair of shells close to the hull of the *Shubrick*. USS *Shubrick* then bombarded Maisy again for a further 25 minutes and it was again silent.

It was common practice for the German gunners to take cover during such bombardments – just as Colonel Kistowski describes later – gunners would return to their weapons when it was safe to do so. It is likely that once the gunners were inside their shelters they were well protected from anything other than a direct hit.

USS *Harding* was off Pointe du Hoc with its crew at battle stations. Enemy planes were reported in the area and the ship patrolled at a slow speed. It was searching for targets of opportunity which might be spotted by its watch officers. At 0535hr USS *Ellyson* was ordered to relieve USS *Harding* in the bombarding force. She did so and at 0700hr she immediately established visual communications with Ranger SFCP and at 0800hr they made voice radio communications.

At 0918hr *Ellyson* was anchored 2¼ miles north of Pointe du Hoc to await orders of the SFCP and at 0929hr those orders came from a Rangers' observation post. The *Ellyson* was to bombard German light-gun positions in trees on the edge of cliffs about 800yd west of Pointe du Hoc (coordinates 579938). This machine gun was in a position to fire directly with enfilading fire onto the beach and along ground targets at the Pointe, so it was an important objective and one that needed to be neutralised quickly. By 0952hr, after expending 100 rounds, the SFCP reported mission successful. At 0953hr a German shore battery in vicinity of the target commenced firing at USS *Ellyson*. The shells were landing short and the *Ellyson* returned the fire and by 0959hr the enemy position had been swamped with shells.

At 1022hr the *Ellyson* fired sixteen rounds and then ceased firing on orders from the SFCP to allow army infantry and a tank to move in. The total ammunition expended was 124 rounds of 5in and at 1130hr the American flag was raised over the captured position.

The 81st Chemical Weapons Unit After Action Report reads:

B Company of the 81st had lost all but two of their vehicles during the landings, but they had acquired 2 x 2 and-a-half ton army cargo trucks from another artillery unit. On the morning of the 7th of June D Company arrived in Vierville and were subjected to one of the heaviest shellings it has ever experienced. Several batteries of enemy 150mm artillery were firing at us from the vicinity of Pointe du Hoc.

Maisy was the only battery in this direction of that calibre on the 7th. This incoming fire pounded the centre of the town (Vierville) and the road leading to the beach, covering a distance equal to the range of the 155mm howitzers at Les Perruques and a distance easily attainable for the Foucher's Farm guns. **The 81st Chemical Weapons Unit After Action Report continues:**

Heavy casualties were inflicted on the regimental OP group and on a field artillery battalion coming from the beach. An ammunition dump was blown up scattering small army ammunition in all directions. At 0530hr on June 8th D Company aided in the attack on Grandcamp and was credited with another enemy machine-gun nest.

An interesting footnote to the battle is this made by **Frank Needham,** of the British Army signals unit who landed on 7 June 1944 at Omaha Beach:

[7 June] Late in the afternoon we landed on the beach without even wetting our tyres, but we had been up down at the western end when we should have been put down at the other end – necessary in order to be in our radio beam. We pulled across the beach avoiding the few obstacles and ignoring the explosions along our part of the beach. At

the time I thought someone was blowing up mines, but later I realised that there was no one there to do that and therefore the explosions were from incoming German shells fired blindly at the beach – from the west.

Frank was quite specific about the direction of the shelling because

We watched the incoming shells making spouts on the sand when we landed. Our vehicle with the set aboard was in a sloping grass field near to the top of the cliffs. On a fence on this field was a large white German notice board having the skull and crossbones in black and white with the words 'ACHTUNG MINEN'.

Frank found some American soldiers with a mine detector and they said that there were no mines:

Why there were no mines I don't know, but afterwards I came to the conclusion that there had never been any and that signs were just to scare off the locals. The holes in the ground were from the bombardment in my opinion.

For a short period, of perhaps ten days, **Frank Needham** was stationed on a hastily created airstrip next to the site of the radar station at Pointe et Raz de la Percée. It was from here that he explored the surrounding area. His recollections of Pointe du Hoc are interesting and noteworthy:

Geoff and I explored along the coast and the local roads whenever we could. I was surprised at the number of German dead still lying around and not now in very good condition. Added to this were the dead cows in the fields with bloated bodies and all four legs in the air.

We walked around Pointe du Hoc some 2 miles further west than our site. Geoff and I decided to recover two of the rope ladders from the cliffs there and to carry it to a site nearer to our radio set. The rope ladders were made of two parallel ropes with 5in rope rungs. The cliffs were at this point about 100ft high, so we had to fasten the two ladders end to end. The cliff sloped down gently at first and then more steeply to the overhang,

A plaque marked as the first advanced landing strip in Normandy in 1944.

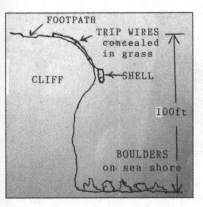

Frank Needham created an illustration showing the positioning of the bombs at the cliff edge. Rangers' accounts of the Pointe du Hoc assault make mention of the shells lying at the cliff edge with booby traps, and they were still there some days later when Frank went 'swimming'.

all this area being laced with steel trip wires leading to First World War shells hanging down along the cliff face. The shells were set to instant detonation so that the first attack to reach the top would trip a shell – which would explode to bring the overhang down onto the soldiers below.

German Lieutenant Colonel Fritz Ziegalmann:

We also assumed properly equipped enemy Commandos could scale the steep cliffs around St Pierre du Mont (area of Pointe du Hoc) and at Longues. Here, the Engineer Battalion prepared old 24cm shells, with an effective shrapnel range of 600m, to roll down on the beach and explode when triggered by a trip wire. By 1 June we had placed one of these shells every 100m on the cliffs.

The above extracts confirm two things. First, the Germans did indeed expect a 'commando' raid on the two cliff-top batteries, and, secondly, Frank Needham was correct about the existence of shells on the cliff tops. The Germans had prepared Pointe du Hoc for a cliff assault and were expecting it.

Frank Needham continues:

We had had enough of 'bathing' in a gallon of hot water and wished to have a swim in the sea. The spot we had chosen had trip wires, but they were less complicated and it was possible to thread your way carefully through them. We drove in an anchor away from the trip wires and very carefully lowered the ladders through the trip wires, and being unable to see the foot of the cliff, assumed the two length of rope ladder had reached the bottom.

Geoff set off first and we trod with care through the trip wires and then found getting onto the rope ladder was not easy because it was laying flat against the cliff face and I couldn't easily get my fingers through the rungs especially as Geoff's weight was still on the ladder. Then out into space which was not pleasant because the ladder, which should have been tied at the bottom was swinging round and progressively banged my body and then my head against the cliff face.

Another hazard halfway down, hanging in free space, was the

One of the trip-wired shells that Frank Needham had to avoid.

poor joint between the two sections such that the rungs on the lower section were 45 degrees horizontal. Reached the boulder-strewn bottom, undressed, clambered out to the sea and had a lovely splash around. The return trip was a nightmare for me. Climbing up the spinning rope ladder, I quickly realised that I was exhausted from presumably physical effort and nervous strain, and I doubted that I could get back up. However, the tide was now coming in and, in any case, it was impossible to walk the miles along the bottom of

The entrance to the Pointe du Hoc observation bunker after the battle. The devastation is clearly visible.

the cliffs to Omaha Beach. I just had to hook my arms and legs into the rungs and hang there until I could get my strength back, but it took a long time. After four or so of such rests I eventually reached the top; I didn't say anything to Geoff, but neither of us made the trip again.

I interviewed Frank Needham in England in 2007 and he could not emphasise enough the difficulty of climbing up the cliffs. He had not just endured a difficult sea journey, he was not carrying bags, wet weapons and equipment and above all he was not being shot at. His description of climbing while not in adverse circumstances says it all. The Rangers who scaled the cliffs did so under hugely difficult circumstances and that is a fact often left out of accounts.

Donald Fuesler, 95th Infantry Division, landed some days after D-Day and his recollections are interesting and add to the overall picture of the beachhead at that time:

The beach and surrounding area was cleared. There were no bodies in sight. I did see German prisoners and American wounded ready to be evacuated to England. I do not remember exactly the date that we came ashore. I do know that we came ashore with Patton's Third Army. It was quite late after D-Day. The beaches and surrounding areas were all secured, but debris and relics were still around.

I landed early in the morning. Had no watch, so I had no idea of

One of the casements at Pointe du Hoc – note the body in the foreground of a German soldier. This is as Frank Needham would have seen it.

the time. Besides, I was wet and cold and pissed off at the time – I only remember shucking off my equipment, bobbing up from the ocean floor, swimming toward the

A photograph of the same casement seen on p. 138 as it is today, but from a different angle.

beach, and then finally wading ashore, cold and wet. I don't remember anyone directing traffic. We just played follow the leader. There was no shelling at the time, but there were some US naval vessels in the area. I remember Vierville was a mess. Our orders when we landed were to go up the draw and assemble at the end of the draw. A Pfc is not given a lot of information from above, so we just mainly tried to save our asses. The roads were all rebuilt, and there was no rubble in the area. Beach obstacles were still there, as were Rommel's asparagus in the fields, also the barrage balloons were still flying. I clearly remember the crossed iron rails which the Germans had used for anti-tank and anti-vehicle obstacles.

I saw the remains of the church in Vierville, but we didn't get into the village. Vierville had been subjected to both bombing and naval shellfire. I remember seeing the ruined church as we came up the draw and French civilians were everywhere waving to us. They also flashed the 'Vee' sign. Our shoulder patch has a '9' and a 'V' for the 95th infantry division. I think they thought we were sent in to end the war and clean up the mess.

There was German equipment everywhere. Occasional booby traps and mines but most of the German forces had withdrawn. The minefields extended on both sides of the Vierville draw up to the pillboxes. One of our guys went outside the tapes to get a souvenir and was blown to bits. He was blown up by either a mine or a booby trap.

The Germans had large teller mines, shoe (shuh) mines, developed by the husband of the American screen actress Heddy Lamar and sold to the Germans. Also 'Bouncing Betties' which when stepped on would bounce waist high and then explode sending small ball bearings in all directions. Everyone ditched their gas masks on landing and we were later reissued them, when intelligence learned that the Germans planned on using nerve gas, probably when it became obvious that they were losing the war.

American troops inspecting the damaged Pointe du Hoc casements after the battle.

The 20mm anti-aircraft position which caused the Rangers so much trouble.

The heavily camouflaged observation bunker which is positioned at the top of the cliff just behind the Pointe.

One of the Pointe du Hoc 'mock' gun positions covered in debris.

The remains of the 20mm gun position.

Many of the German reserve units were equipped with bicycles. These became the local transport of choice for many of the US servicemen as the battle advanced inland.

Chapter 6

Starting from Zero

B y widening my area of study away from just the beach and Pointe du Hoc, I found plenty of things that occurred which had never been discussed before. My interviews with Rangers also provided information on actions and situations which add to the story.

To really bottom out the intelligence information available at the time I have only gone back to original sources. To repeat what has been written – or hypothesised about – before would be pointless, other than official reports. All the authors of previous post-war books did not know about the Maisy site, so I had to go back and start from zero. I then began with the German archives, although not many operational maps from the German side exist for Maisy. I have found no explanation for this, but it can only be assumed that after it was initially built Maisy was expanded, and with Rommel's increased influence in 1944, it expanded hugely again in preparation for D-Day.

When studying the Atlantic Wall as a whole I have often found that German weapons specifications simply state 15cm or 10cm, while in actual fact the size is 155mm or 105mm.

This map shows the German gun ranges as they recorded them for the Maisy Battery. It does not take into account the third heavier battery which arrived closer to D-Day. Unfortunately, I do not have a date for this, but interestingly the pages alongside this map do state that Les Perruques Battery has 6 x 15cm Fr (French) guns (as per the German specification).

This missing off of the 5mm was often done as a simplification and is quite relevant to the guns at La Martiniere.

During a search of the land some years ago I found 10.5cm steel German ammunition cases to the rear of the casements. I consulted an expert in ammunition of the period and he assured me that the Germans often bored out captured weapons to give their ammunition consistency of size along the Atlantic Wall. It makes more sense that weapons be standardised with 105mm and 155mm ammunition and if you look at the other defensive positions in the region this is understandable.

An early operational equipment request in the Organisation Todt records in Berlin dated 1942 includes an initial specification for weapons which lists batteries 8 and 9 of the 716th Artillery as having the following:

Maisy Südwest, Les Perruques WN 83 – weapons specification.

9/AR1716 (15.6.1943) [9th artillery battery of the 1716th Artillery Regiment – this was originally of the 716th Regiment).

6 x 155mm sFH 414(f) in R669 (not finished).

1 x 8.62cm KH 290 (r) in open emplacement

Barracks
Telephonshelter
Some shelters
1 x tobruk 58C

1 x SMG 257 (f)
1 x sMG 257 (f)
63 Gewehre
Main buildings

Barracks
1 – +Ringstand 58C

The document above describes the type of field howitzers installed. 155mm calibre (f) French-manufactured (First World War issue) guns were placed into R669 positions. These were a standard type of concrete emplacement which had a number to determine its construction type.

The Russian 7.65mm gun (r) would have been a standard Russian-issue field howitzer which in itself could have been able to reach the Rangers landing on Omaha Beach.

The SMG 257 (f) is French manufactured and then captured heavy machine gun – German positions using these captured weapons were commonplace after the capitulation of France.

Gewehre refers to rifles and this would be the number issued to the site on its first becoming operational.

Tobruk 58C is a type of below-ground emplacement which allows the soldier to fight with only his head above ground. These positions became widespread along the Atlantic Wall and there are a number of them at Maisy. They caused the Rangers a lot of problems during the run up to the assault of the site on 9 June and typically held a machine-gun position or in a variation might house a mortar position just above ground level.

The 622 is a standard shelter design for twenty men to allow them to eat, drink and sleep underground within a concrete bomb-proof bunker. The 622 was initially designed to create a self-contained defensive position which could allow its occupants to stay safely within the building even if their position had been overrun. In reality, the Germans tended to realise that they stood no chance once their positions were captured and they surrendered. F Company of the Rangers found that sometimes the Germans did not always want to give up without a fight from this type of position and they had to be 'coaxed out' using explosives.

The final building listed is a telephonshelter. This is an unusual building to find in the centre of a battery complex and it has come to light after research that the telephonshelter in question at Maisy was linked to the flak (anti-aircraft) units in the area. The radar information would come into the centre with regards to the height, speed, direction and distance of Allied planes and this would be transmitted to the anti-aircraft units in the vicinity. There is only one other of this type of building along the Atlantic Wall in Brittany.

Maisy – La Martiniere WN 84

8 / Artilerie Regiment 1716 (15.6.1943)
4 x H669 casemates
4 x 105mm LeFh 14/19 (t)
Barracks, Telephonshelter. Some shelters – 2 x 622
2 x tobruk

This was an early allocation of weapons and, as can be seen, it was not completely representative of the firepower installed on D-Day some time later, although it is a good starting point.

The artillery units 8 and 9, allocated for the defence of the sector between the battery at Longues-sur-Mer and the battery at St Marcouf (Crisbecq), were marked on maps and period paperwork as being stationed at Maisy on D-Day. The first German artillery units at Maisy arrived in 1940 and were stationed in the village in farms and private houses. I have interviewed many people who lived in the village at the time who remember the Germans well. Mr Montagne, for example, who still lives on his family farm in the locality, recalls the Germans arriving. They occupied his father's barns with their horses and horse-drawn artillery. They inscribed their unit number on the wall inside one of the barns and it is still visible today, the number 630 Rgt marked on the concrete post. The Germans used some local people to work at the site at Maisy in the early days, for example, excavating open pits for field guns, but nothing elaborate or particularly permanent.

4 x 100mm lFH 14/19 (t) (98hm) in R612 (Czech-manufactured howitzers). This is an actual one from La Martiniere.

2 x 75mm FK 16 n.A. in open emplacements. This is similar to those at Maisy, which were used for anti-aircraft defence. This is in a field position.

The 502 headquarters building at the centre of the Les Perruques complex.

The wall inside one of the barns on the Montagnes' farm. This building was used to stable horses from one of the first German units into Normandy, the 630 Regiment.

The 556 Infantry Division, of which the 630 Regiment was part, formed in February 1940 and after the invasion of France it advanced with the 7th Army. It was commanded by Generalleutnant Kurt von Berg between 12 February 1940 and 13 August 1940, and as part of this deployment the 630 Infantry Regiment were stationed at Maisy.

Mr Montagne's father was requisitioned to take milk up to the site every morning in 20-litre cans on this horse and cart. The Germans had installed large wooden crosses

American soldiers examine La Martiniere on 30 June after the battle.

The inscription inside the Montagnes' barn – the date 1940 at the top and R 630 underneath.

Mr Montagne senior.

with wire and concrete blocks halfway down the road (Route des Perruques) to stop anyone entering the site. The local farmers were ordered to clear off their land and leave immediately. Mr Montagne and all the other locals were ordered to hand in any metals, copper, steel, etc. to the Kommandantur in Maisy village to aid the German war effort. Soldiers would arrive at farms and demand a horse or a pig. Mr Montagne told me in his opinion no French were allowed to 'work on the important stuff' at Maisy. His father went to the site one day to ask what was happening there and he was turned away with a warning not to come back asking questions or he would be shot. On the morning of 6 June when he and his son were doing their normal milk delivery they arrived at the barrier just as the bombardment started.

The farm belonging to Mr Montagne. Its high tower gave it commanding views of the invasion as it happened. There were anti-aircraft guns stationed inside this field close to the house.

Mr Mongagne remembers his father looking at him and saying '*no milk for the Germans today*' and they quickly made their way home.

In time work started to be issued to people from the village and all men of working age were requisitioned to work on the local defences at least one day a week.

Gerard Maudelonde was 7 years old on D-Day and he remembers the period well: '*The Germans came and they were afraid of being sent to Russia so they were very well behaved. Well in the beginning – as they didn't want to have any problems with the local population. This changed later!*'

The Germans also took up positions in the open fields around Maisy and began clearing them. They set up the dummy positions in front of Les Perruques and they would train with machine guns in the local fields, which often scared the Maudelondes' horses. **Gerard Maudelonde** continues:

I remember when Rommel came to Maisy. We had to stay at home and there was no school. We were told it was for his security. Two rooms in our farm were occupied by the Germans and we were not paid for anything at all. They were repairing shoes and harnesses for their horses in our yard. They had many

The works building and Kommandantur where the daily workloads were distributed is now an unassuming building in the village close to the Maudelonde farm. It was once the hub of the German administration and construction management in the area.

horse-drawn vehicles and they brought their own horses, but we were expected to care for them.

On the day they first arrived my father hid his guns in a box and two years later a German looked in the box and reported this to the Komandantur. My father was spoken to by a German officer who said that if he was in the SS my father would have been sent to Germany ... it was a lucky escape. On another occasion my father cut through the telephone cables to the Komandantur and he quickly repaired the cables ... however, the next day two Wehrmacht policemen took him to the Komandantur and called him a terrorist. He had to explain that he had only cut the cable by accident and they let him go.

There were two barracks built on Rue du Hameau Bel and Chemin val Fonduval. The Germans put up a 144-acre exclusion zone around the batteries and worked in relative secrecy behind their mine fields. The position drew little local attention. It was, and always had been, an area made up of small parcels of land owned by a number of people.

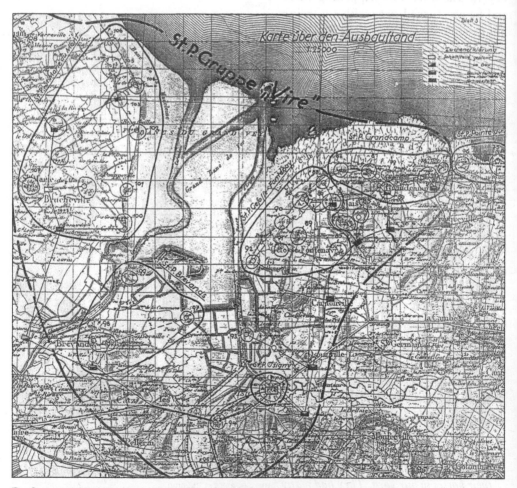

The German defence map for the Sector showing strong points and communication cables.

It was farmland with a good view of the sea, but on the reverse slopes it was sheltered from the possibility of direct naval fire. The Germans also built a lightweight set of buildings and rudimentary accommodation for daytime use. Little did the Germans realise that this site would be right in the centre of both the American landing beaches four years later.

At night anyone not on duty was billeted with families in the village or, as they did in the small village of Osmanville, the Germans removed the local people and took over every house for military use. Numerous villagers remember the Germans 'sharing' their homes – in some cases this was workable, but in others it was far from ideal. They also set up a roadblock at both ends of the Route des Perruques road, and this was manned 24 hours a day with an armed sentry. Another sentry post was built halfway down the lane and was large enough for one man to stand inside to shelter during bad weather.

The sentry post half way down the Route des Perruques. Despite the best efforts of the author the local farmer destroyed it the day after he was asked to preserve it. It stood on the road side almost directly behind the La Martiniere battery.

Long before the Germans 'invaded' Grandcamp-les-Bains and Maisy they were just small, provincial fishing villages. However, a small tourist industry had developed, formed predominantly from members of Parisian society, who built and owned villas near the waterfront. The construction of a harbour ensured a bustling fishing community and resulted in the construction of a number of small hotels.

From a military standpoint the harbour was not of any great significance as it is small. With the exception of fishing (oysters and mussels) and tourism, the area had no industry or manufacturing other than farming.

A view of the Maisy church and village before the war. These houses were completey flattened during the bombardment of the town and now there is a town square and parking in their place.

The main Grandcamp–Isigny road in the centre of Maisy. Trams were a regular form of transport along the busy coastal roads before the war.

The very rural setting of Maisy village – a typical French village surrounded by fields and cows. This field is the one which had to be crossed by the Rangers from F Company. The site at Les Perruques is behind where this photograph was taken.

In the fields behind the coastal positions at La Casino in the direction of the Maisy Batteries there lies the ruins of the Chateau Duguesclin. These ruins survived the bombardment and still remain much the same as this today.

Another view of Maisy church.

The inside of the Maisy church. Much of the gothic interior was destroyed by the shelling.

The beach front at Grandcamp. A real tourist destination for Parisian holidaymakers pre-war.

The aftermath of D-day. The same beach as it was only days after the invasion. Covered in debris, beach obstacles and equipment.

By placing the batteries at Maisy the Germans were 'plugging the gap' left between Longues-sur-Mer and St Marcouf, covering the small harbour and more importantly the estuary into Carentan. The disposition map on p. 146 shows the major German positions in that sector.

Equipment laid out ready for distribution into the local houses in Grandcamp.

It is clear that the Germans thought that a force would try and enter the Vire Estuary and also it is logical to have placed another battery either side of Longues-sur-Mer and St Marcouf to maintain the continuity of defence. The terrain at La Martiniere and Les Perruques also afforded the best views in the area. In the case of the Les Perruques (Maisy I) Battery, it has a sloping reverse to the land which allowed indirect fire from the battery onto Navy targets and also offered some protection back from the fire from ships at sea. The German 'occupation' that had begun around the fields in the village slowly began to spread. In 1940 the two local villages were called Maisy and Grandcamp-les-Bains, and it was only years later that it became known as Grandcamp-Maisy, so the site was on Maisy village land. The Germans set up military government and had the locals from both villages work on beach defences at Grandcamp.

By 1944 it was compulsory for all the able-bodied to work at least one day a week for the German Army. All aspects of civilian life changed in favour of the German occupation, although, on the whole, the Germans were courteous and polite and above all they paid their way in shops and bars. They were 'told' that they had to pay for everything they wanted and indeed they paid for their accommodation in many homes.

The intrusion into their lives was not always acceptable to French families, but nonetheless it went ahead. However, in some instances families became friendly with their German occupiers and sometimes this too created difficulties locally. Over time the Germans started to integrate into village life. With only a couple of exceptions, the Germans behaved themselves and the locals got on with their lives.

Life was good for the Germans in the village.

As this photograph clearly shows, the men of the 716th Infantry-Artillery were older and not considered front-line calibre. However, they were more than capable of making the guns work – something they did to good effect on D-Day.

Maisy village homes being occupied.

Two German officers enjoy a photo opportunity at the seafront.

School children were taught German in schools, signs started to appear in German and it was thought that in time France would become an annex of Germany and integrate fully. The Germans embarked on building more and more beach defences and they used local labour to do it. Pointe du Hoc was being constructed using French workers and these inevitably included Resistance operatives. There are numerous hand-drawn illustrations by Resistance workers that depict the construction of Pointe du Hoc reproduced in books, so there can be no doubt that these individuals were passing information back to London on the progress of the site.

But Maisy was very different. From the moment building work commenced the site was 'off limits' to the local population. There were a few exceptions to this, but it was accepted that nobody from the local community was allowed in.

The Germans brought in wagonloads of Czech, Polish and Russian workers to undertake the construction, which was overseen by the Organisation Todt. The site was far enough away from the road and any other available observation points to be seen by the Resistance during construction and it was surrounded by a well-signposted mine field. Maisy was certainly not somewhere that the local civilian population was going to be able to visit and draw maps of. Maisy developed steadily, close to, but far enough away from the village to remain secret.

It is difficult to put a time scale on the building works at Maisy. This is primarily because little first-hand evidence exists in terms of a building programme other than the Allied aerial photographic evaluations. But it is known that certain building types were produced at certain times. For example, a large number of lightweight concrete buildings were constructed in 1942–3. These were field-position buildings, but not effective combat buildings. Their construction was just not strong enough to withstand bombardment, but they were good enough for people to live and work in. The commander's office – his day office – was built in 1943 and when it was uncovered the date 1943 was still written on a wall. It must have been built before the 502 headquarters building, which is of the later 'bomb-proof' type.

The site developed with old and new buildings side by side. Maisy wartime resident **Brigitte Destores** remembers:

> *I went into part of the Les Perruques site a day or two after the battle and sat in a library with lots of books, there was a piano and there were guns still on their plates for turning. It was a village underground with an officers' mess with tables and chairs laid out and many covered trenches. I even went inside the hospital, but it was a mess with things thrown everywhere.*

Brigitte also remembers the piano being taken away to be used by her family for many years after the war.

There was the addition of the flak centre and a hospital. Other weaponry was added in the form of anti-aircraft guns and yet the site still retained its secrecy.

The Germans added a large anti-aircraft unit in and around the village of Maisy in 1942 which was commanded from the chateau of Mr Destores. The Germans occupied his house and set up guns in the local fields. This group was commanded by a Captain Kapusta, originally an architect from Hamburg, and Captain Wagner, who, when he was not working on the gun units, supervised the locals placing the anti-air landing defences in the fields. The other guns from the unit were stationed locally and they afforded the Maisy Battery a considerable additional anti-aircraft defence.

A poor photograph showing the badly damaged home of the Destores family.

The Germans lived in one half of the home of the Destores and the family occupied the rest. At one time it also became a temporary gaol. If any Germans in the village were imprisoned for crimes or misbehaviour they were brought to the home of the Destores where they would be locked in a room on the first floor until dealt with. The only problem for the family was that this was

The Destores family in their garden before the war.

the same room that they had previously hidden their rifles. This was a risky thing to have done at that time, but they were never discovered. The family's time with the Germans was not a bad one and they were treated with respect.

Inevitably the German presence meant that the chateau became a target for naval bombardment and on 6 June it was comprehensively damaged. However, the family had already decided to leave. On the evening of 5 June the family were in the house when it started to be attacked. All the windows were

Amazingly enough Captain Kapusta, the German Anti-aircraft commander stationed at the Destores' chateau, was an artist and he left behind some pictures he drew of the building during his stay.

blown out and the family quickly ran down the garden and sheltered in a hole until the bombardment stopped. Brigitte Destores remembers, '*We all stayed in a hole at the bottom of the garden. The noise was terrible and at some point our father decided that we would be safer if we went to our relatives in Colombier – luckily we were not at home during the 6th.*'

Brigitte's father, Marcel Destores, was helping with the funeral of a victim of the shelling on 6 June in Maisy cemetery when the Navy opened fire again on the village. The gunfire knocked some of the mourners into the grave where they were standing. Brigitte's then husband-to-be was wounded in the back and later sent to Vierville for treatment by American medics.

This illustration by Captain Kapusta gives an accurate impression of the Destores' chateau in 1944. Kapusta survived the battle and the war. He went back to Germany to live in Hamburg.

The Destores' house, which was rebuilt in 1954.

The Villa Mathieu was the headquarters of the Kriegsmarine in Grandcamp during 1944, but as a port Grandcamp was not considered a strategic one, so it was only lightly manned. As Jean Marion, the wartime Resistance mayor and chief, stated: '*On the 6th June there were only 20 Kriegsmarine men who had a couple of light guns and a line of trenches, there was nothing else in Grandcamp on the 6th.*' It is obvious that the Maisy Battery was not placed nearby just to protect a non-strategic harbour.

During their stay the Germans also experimented with mobile anti-aircraft positions mounted on rafts floating in the harbour, but due to the weather these were not operational on D-Day. It was possibly more useful as a training exercise for the men and for propaganda

The Germans have made a raft from dinghies and put a tripod-mounted machine gun onto them. Not a very practical weapon, but perhaps it was created more for propaganda purposes.

One of the few Kriegsmarine officers in Grandcamp.

The 88mm flak (anti-aircraft) gun was fitted with wheels and a number were used by Kistowski's battalion at Maisy.

purposes for the watching locals. After all, it would do no harm for the Allies to be told by the Resistance that the Germans had floating anti-aircraft positions.

These German Army machine guns are mounted on barges that appear to be made of aluminium. It would have been interesting to see what the local Kriegsmarine officer stood in the village made of it all.

Although the Maisy Battery and land were off limits to locals, some of them, for example, Mr Martin, were allowed onto the site. The Germans allowed him to supply them with meat from his cows. His daughter managed to take a photograph of the site at La Martiniere, which at the time was a dangerous thing to do, but it shows what that area looked like from ground level.

Another lady, Madame Lemoigne, used to tend her cows in the field next to the rear of the site. Normally this would not have been allowed but she was 'pretty – so they allowed me to be there!' Every morning she watched the Germans bring their wounded into the rear hospital by ambulances and the drivers would whistle at her as they passed down the lane.

One Battery in the fields of Mr Destores was indicated with the No. 1. The Germans set up an 88mm AA battery in the lane, marked No. 2. The other battery was in the field just behind the Maudelonde farm and was marked No. 3.

Two German officers standing at Fort Samson.

The fort before the Germans destroyed it. It is thought that it blocked the field of fire for their guns.

Fort Samson as it existed before German occupation.

The fort entrance.

German soldiers posing on the beachfront with Pointe du Hoc just visible in the distance.

The beachfront has changed very little today.

Taken from the end of the pier looking back into the harbour. Mr Montagne's fields are visible above the harbour-front houses. There was a group of AA guns in this field which could in theory have fired directly at the fleet had it attacked on the Grandcamp beaches. As it was, the fleet was further out, so they concentrated their attention on the aircraft flying overhead.

La Martiniere, early 1944. This picture shows a well-established and partially camouflaged site with a small roadway running around the casements. Telegraph poles and trenches are also evident. A Company later attacked from the left of this photograph and the Les Perruques Battery is in the distance.

The hospital facility built at the rear of the Les Perruques Battery was spilt into two. One part was a convalescent ward, almost 100m in length, and housed wounded soldiers who were sent to the area for rest and to take in the fresh coastal air. The other smaller facility housed an operating room and ancilliary treatment areas. On one occasion

Julius Karl Serzysko of the 8th Battery of Artillery Regiment 1716 was stationed at Maisy on D-Day and was captured on the 9th of June 1944 by the Rangers. He was stationed at La Martiniere battery and was promoted during his time there by the deputy battery commander to the rank of Oberkanonier. Serzysko died in 1972 in his native Poland aged 63.

Panzer crewmen were treated in the facility after their column was straffed by Allied aircraft. The hospital at Bayeux was full and the tank men were sent to Maisy for the 'sea air' to recover from their wounds.

The anti-aircraft control facility at the centre of the Les Perruques facility was also a hive of activity. While not in combat conditions, members of the Luftwaffe flak control unit were stationed in a large wooden roofed building, buried below ground level, but still vunerable to bombing. If a bombardment alert was sounded they withdrew to the bomb-proof 622 building

'When is the invasion coming?' would be a great title for this photograph, taken before D-Day under the cliffs at Pointe du Hoc. There is little doubt that the Germans knew that it was coming, but 'when' was the question.

next door for shelter. It was a standard building that had been specially adapted to house four antenaes and all their specialist equipment. The unit's job was to co-ordinate the information coming in from radar stations in the sector. Then disseminate height, distance, speed and other relevant information about approaching Allied plains to the Luftwaffe flak (anti-aircraft) companies in the surrounding area and to the Maisy AA guns on site.

In the area other gunners from the same artillery regiment, the 716th, regularly came from Merville Battery to Maisy to practise firing the 'big guns'. They used the empty island of St Marcouf in the bay as a target and areas of it were painted white to improve its visibility. Ironically, as the Allies were to do during the invasion, they also conducted

German soldiers are climbing with their weapons and walking up with a single rope.

The view downwards to the beach from the top of the cliff looking towards Pointe du Hoc observation bunker in 1944. You can just see the top of the bunker at the far end of the cliff near the Pointe. Obviously the German photographer was among the men who made it to the top, somewhere in the region of the Pointe du Hoc anti-aircraft gun position.

climbing 'excercises' at Pointe du Hable near Pointe du Hoc.

Another farmer who suffered the arbitary confiscation of his Maisy land was Roger Foucher. His farm, which went on to become Allied target number 16A, was built in 1934 and he was forced to leave it in 1940. His sister-in-law, who was 20 years old and lived in Cardonville at the time, remembers: 'The house was taken from him by artillerymen. He had to leave the house immediately and they placed mine fields everywhere. It was forbidden for anyone to enter the area and nobody saw the blockhouses. We never went back after the war.'

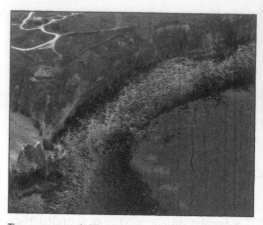

The same area of cliff at Pointe du Hoc, 2007. The effect of the sea on the Pointe can clearly be seen as the rock has been completely worn away creating an island.

These men are not all wearing helmets, they are not armed and most are wearing white fatigues, so this photograph was taken at a time when they felt comfortable to be in this area unarmed.

The same area as it looks today.

The Germans spent a lot of time planning for the invasion and undertook training along the coast from Grandcamp to Pointe du Hoc.

The harbour at the time of D-Day.

The harbour has changed little since the war.

Life was not generally too bad if you played by the occupier's rules, but inevitably as time went on the village atmosphere became more tense. The Germans in the region suffered regular attacks at the hands of the Resistance and curfews were then strictly enforced. Anyone caught outside after curfew could expect the strictest of punishments.

One Maisy resident, Maurice Lemoigne, got away lightly. On the evening of 9 February 1941 he was found to have been out after curfew and was caught by the Germans and taken to Bayeux. His wife recalls: '*My husband was captured by the Germans and put in gaol for one night for being out after curfew. We had to go to the Komandantur in Maisy to have him released.*' The German military court of Bayeux presided over by Major Hoffman fined him 3 reich marks/60 francs, and he was released the next day. He was lucky not to be sent to Germany as many able-bodied Frenchmen were 'exported' to work as slave labour. The local need for labour was also acute and it is quite possible that the deadlines for construction of the beach and air-landing obstacles were more important than the deportation of working men. Mr Lemoigne was allowed to go home with a warning and he was lucky.

Later in 1943 Mr Lemoigne was officially requisitioned by the German Army for work. Initially he was assigned to the 723rd Regiment in Isigny on 24, 25 and 26 January to clear weeds. Later this was expanded and by 19 November 1943 he had officially been requisitioned on a permanent basis to work for them. His 'Ordre de Réquisition

The entrance gate to Foucher's Farm from La Martiniere during the German occupation. The land had been cleared to create a wide field of fire for the machine guns.

A German requisition order for Mr Lemoigne meant he was to be placed under the control of a working party for the German Army. It is stamped with the German field post stamp for the Maisy mayor's office.

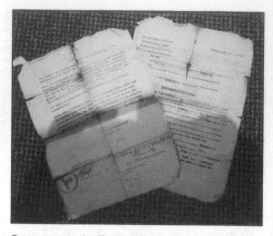

German papers detailing the offence Mr Lemoigne was charged with and his punishment for staying out beyond curfew. (Maisy Battery collection)

individuelle' issued by the Mairie de Maisy (seen above) indicates he was given an overnight travel pass to work for the 723rd Regiment Commander from 6pm to 8am in the Leson sector. Without such papers any local travel at night would have resulted in him again being arrested immediately.

Lieutenant Colonel Fritz Ziegalmann, Chief of Staff, 352nd Infantry Division, wrote the following in his history of the division:

> *Assuming these landings would only take place at high tide, obstacles of all kinds were erected on the tidal plate of the beach so that their upper parts projected just above the water surface at high tide. Pile driven stakes of metal and concrete as well as wooden trestles, and steel anti-tank obstacles called 'Tschechen' [Czechs] were installed, some armed with under-water or surface mines and high explosives.*
>
> *In the second half of May, the possibility of a landing at low tide was discussed. So work on additional obstacles out beyond the tidal flats was begun, but it was impossible to plant these obstacles at a proper depth.*

Mr Michel was a local man who worked in Grandcamp as a hairdresser. He was aged 19 in 1944 and saw at first hand the construction techniques used on the Atlantic Wall. He worked one day out of four for the Organisation Todt (the German construction division responsible for the construction of the Atlantic Wall). Then later he worked more:

> *The closer it got to June they would work us two days out of every four. I lived near Isigny, but I worked in Grandcamp for Mr Douceman as a hairdresser. We were instructed to meet up outside the farm in Maisy [now owned by Mr Legrande and close to the battery].*
>
> *A German Lieutenant called everyone by name from a balcony and we were marched off in tens with a sentry escort. I worked on the bunkers at the seafront – an area in front of Maisy called La Casino and later on I was put on to the beaches putting up obstacles.*

An Allied low-level aerial reconnaissance photograph of the landing beaches, You can clearly make out the Germans and their local working parties installing beach obstacles. Note the men to the left running away and the ones on the right lying down to avoid the aircraft above.

We had a special pneumatic hammer for doing that. We also put up the concrete triangles and the Germans requisitioned all the spare horses and trailors in the village for that.

I was working at Pointe du Hable (WN 76) one day when the machine guns of a Spitfire opened up on us … we dived for cover and it flew off.

We were kicked by a German Lieutenant if we stopped working and we were watched by others with binoculars. There was one officer at Pointe du Hable who jumped into a bush and we hid behind a wall during an air raid. The Americans were bombing Pointe du Hoc during daylight.

The German Todt officer always insisted that we build trenches exactly the same size … 175cm deep and 80cm wide. We built them all the way to Pointe du Hoc like that, but he always checked with his measure and if they were not correct, he would hit me across the back of the head with his stick.

The Organisation Todt official lived in Cricqueville and he was not well liked – he was simply called Todt by the locals. He met a sticky end on D-Day. He was found shot dead and thrown in a shell hole next to a dead cow – where he remained for some time for all to see. Another 'strange death' in the village at that time was that of Mr Garin. He was aged 34 when he was killed in the road on 6 June 1944. There was never an explanation given for his death, although there was speculation that he was involved in helping the Germans and was therefore later dealt with by the Resistance. His gravestone reads '*mort pour la France*', but strangely it carries no date.

Mr Michel continues:

My boss Mr Douceman was allowed into the site at Maisy to cut the hair of the workers. They were Czechs, Poles, Russians and Germans and as they were not allowed to leave the site – he was the only local allowed to see them. The site was treated as strictly off limits to outsiders and nobody could get in. I remember one day I was called into the farmyard of Legrande in Maisy to cut wood and I was stood talking to a German cook before role call. Suddenly everyone stood to attention. Feldmarshall Rommel had driven into the courtyard where we were stood. It was not long before D-Day and the local villagers had been told to stay indoors because of Rommel's impending visit. We were told if we were caught on the streets we would be considered to be Resistance and shot.

Thus began the approach to D-Day.

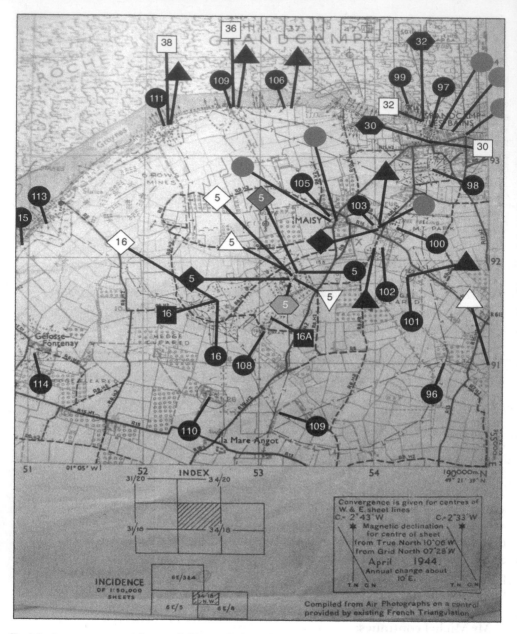

The following maps represent the recorded targets fired upon by each ship listed. These are targets with recorded and accurate six-digit grid references. However, when you take into account that the battle was fluid and the demands from the SFCPs and the airspotting as well, it becomes virtually impossible to have a full record of the targets – including targets of opportunity as they happened. One good example of this is USS *Carmick* which expended 1,127 rounds of ammunition at shore targets on D-Day. As the troops advanced across the beaches and up the bluffs, so its targets of opportunity expanded. USS *Texas* fired multiple times with at varying targets within the confines of the Pointe du Hoc battery. For ease of understanding it is only marked once.

The targets shown in red on these maps represent the pre-D-Day assigned targets, Maisy being targets number 5, 16 and 16A, for example. Where a ship was assigned to fire on a particular target – as opposed to a target of opportunity I have included the target number in the ship's colour. Hopefully this way it explains the initial targets as assigned in the UK (the red ones) and then the targets as they appeared from the air and SFCPs actions.

It was also impossible to plot the exact location of any vessel when engaging these targets, so for ease of understanding I have just placed the coloured ships indicator off-shore or close to the target – do not take these positions as being accurate as the firing position at that time. It is purely a way of conveying the ship's name and target location.

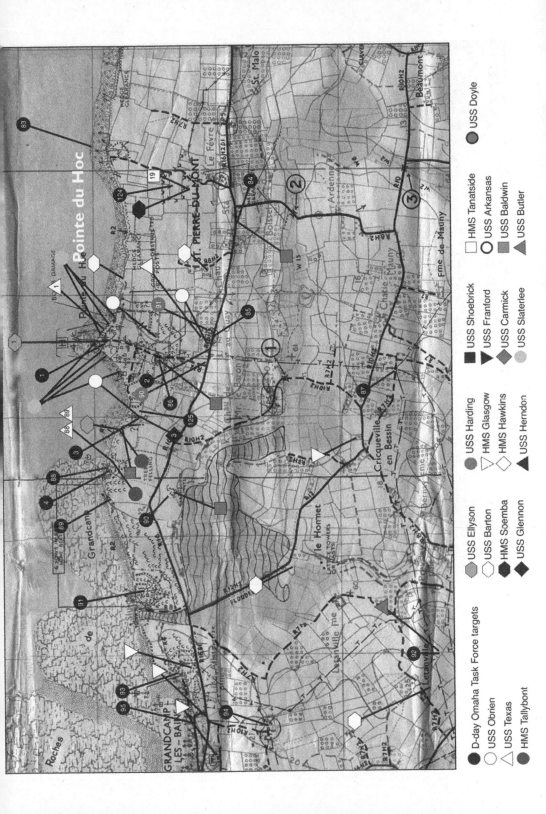

Pointe du Hoc

Legend:

D-day Omaha Task Force targets

⬤ USS Ellyson	⬤ USS Harding	■ USS Shoebrick
⚪ USS Obrien	⚪ HMS Glasgow	▼ USS Franford
△ USS Barton	◇ HMS Hawkins	◆ USS Carmick
△ USS Texas	⬤ HMS Soemba	⬤ USS Slaterlee
⬤ HMS Tallybont	◆ USS Glennon	▲ USS Herndon
⬤ HMS Tanatside	⬤ USS Doyle	
⚪ USS Arkansas		
■ USS Baldwin		
▲ USS Butler		

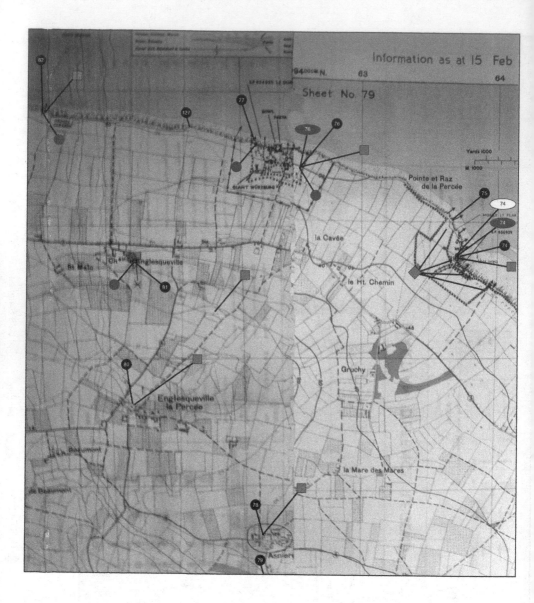

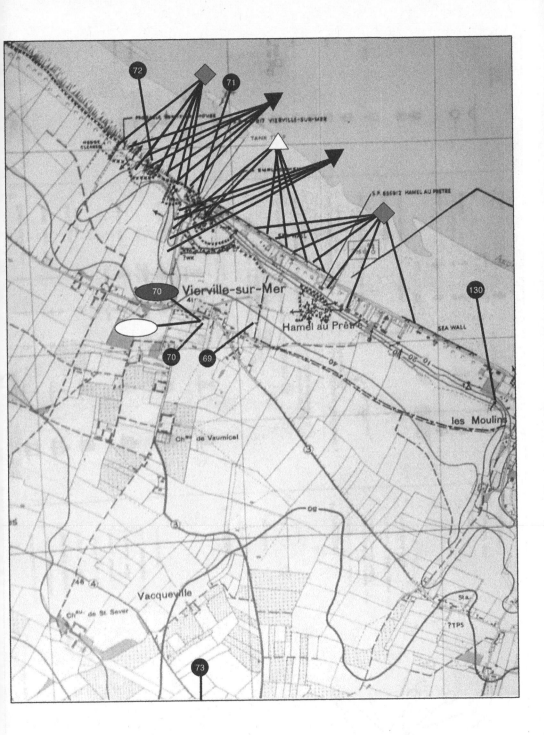

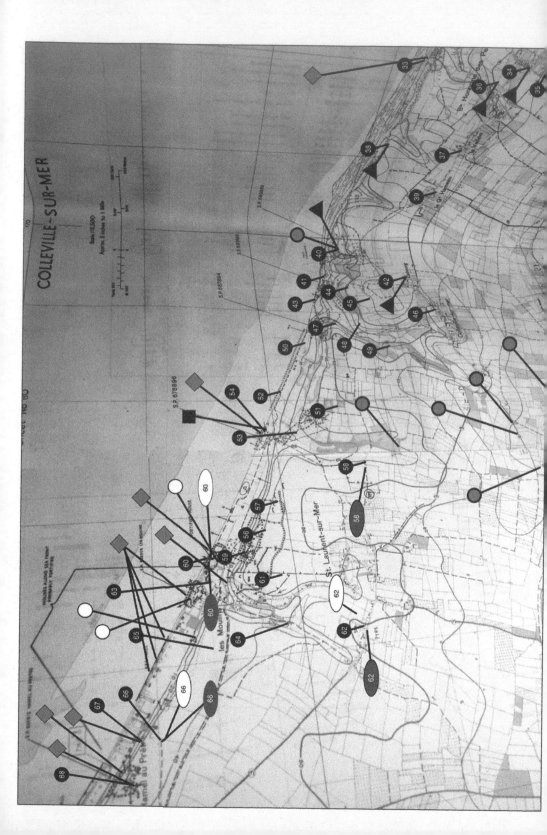

Initially designed in 1942, the US Navy used small boats designated LCS(S) and the larger Landing Ships – originally designed to carry tanks designated Landing Craft Tank – LCT(R) as rocket launching platforms.

These were to follow the first waves of troops and in the case of the LCT(R)s when the leading wave was 700yd from the sea wall, they were to open fire with an entire load of rockets.

The following LCT(R) numbers were designated targets numbers which are indicated on the maps with a ⬭ lozenge:

LCT (R) 368   Target 60
LCT (R) 425   Target 62
LCT (R) 439   Target 66
LCT (R) 448   Target 70
LCT (R) 481   Target 74

LCS(S): Landing Craft Suport (small). Their brief was to approach the beach until in range of the sea wall and deliver rocket fire on the beach area between targets 58 and 76. Firing after the LCT(R)s and when the troops were 600yd from the sea wall.

Indicated with a ⬬ lozenge one the maps the LCS targets were as follows:

LCS(S) 1   Target 58
LCS(S) 2 & 3   Target 60
LCS(S) 4 & 5   Target 62
LCS(S) 6 & 7   Target 66
LCS(S) 8 & 9   Target 70
LCS(S) 10 & 11   Target 74
LCS(S) 12   Target 76

The purpose of these fire missions was directly to assist the first waves of troops landing by destroying all enemy positions likely to give initial resistance. They were then to continue to support the landing waves by offering machine-gun fire at the sea-wall defences until they could see Green Star pyrotechnics – the signal to lift fire was given. After the green star signal, they were to move their machine-gun fire to the flanks and cover the advance of troops by firing at targets of opportunity.

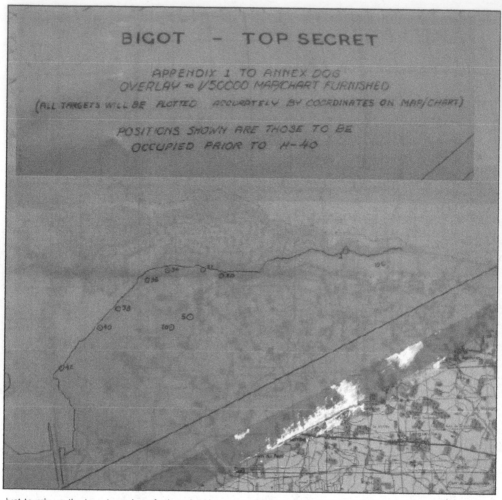

BIGOT – TOP SECRET

APPENDIX 1 TO ANNEX DOG
OVERLAY to 1/50000 MAPCHART FURNISHED
(ALL TARGETS WILL BE PLOTTED ACCURATELY BY COORDINATES ON MAP/CHART)

POSITIONS SHOWN ARE THOSE TO BE
OCCUPIED PRIOR TO H-40

Just to mix up the target numbers further, the above is a BIGOT marked TOP SECRET map giving target numbers for the seafront at Grandcamp. It clearly lists Maisy as targets 5 and 16 and Pointe du Hoc as target No. 1. Another target is 19 to the east of Pointe du Hoc somewhere to the east of St Pierre-du-Mont. Quite possibly the AA guns fired on by the navy... but this map shows target numbers 30, 32, 34, 36, 38, 40 and 42 along the coast. These are shown on Captain John Raaen's Ranger-issued maps as having target numbers 106, 109, 111, 113, 115 and 117. Very confusing if you are a SFCP officer surely?

Another variation is that USS *Doyle* gives targets 'assignment numbers', ergo priority numbered targets. For instance, its target No. 1 on D-Day was general target 40!

APPENDIX FOUR TO ANNEX "DOG" to
OPERATION ORDER
    NO. 3-44.

Serial: 00010

BEACH NEUTRALIZATION AND CLOSE SUPPORT PLAN

    4.   At H minus 40, HERNDON, CORRY, and FITCH, commence beach neutralization and target of opportunity fire as follows:

SHIP	TARGETS	ROUNDS PER MINUTE
HERNDON	34,36,38,40,42	8
CORRY	80,82,84,86,88,90,92,94	8
FITCH	96,98,100,102,104,106,108 110,112,114	8

    At H-hour discontinue fire except at targets of opportunity in sight or on call from Shore Fire Control Party.

    5.   TUSCALOOSA at H minus 40 commence fire with secondary battery to destroy installation (target '18) on Ile de Tatihou. Observe beach area from targets 122 to 134 inclusive, and take under fire any targets of opportunity. Use deliberate fire.

    6.   SOEMBA at H minus 40 commence direct fire at targets 30, and 32. Attempt to protect Ranger Party attacking POINTE DU HOE. Use deliberate fire.

    7.   LCG's when sweeping duties are completed, approach beach as closely as possible delivering fire ahead to beach area targets 56, 58, 60, 62, 74, 76, 78, 80, and then proceed along designated flanks abreast troop advance and take under fire any targets of opportunity. Fire may be commenced at any time after H minus 40.

Another document that further confuses the situation. It is primarily part of the Utah sector and refers to the *Herndon*, *Corry* and *Fitch*. Notice that the ships are given target numbers which conflict with the Omaha numbers... yet in paragraph six it refers to the *Soemba* firing at targets 30 and 32 (Grandcamp) in the Omaha sector. It also mentions targets 74, 76 – which are behind or close to Pointe du Hoc. So in effect we have ships firing on both sectors Utah and Omaha – but each sector has the same target numbers as the other – in some cases even those numbers are duplicated on action reports in the same sector but with different co-ordinates.

Chapter 7

German Operations

Reading through the radio traffic, telephone conversations and orders it is obvious that the Germans did not have a clear picture of what was happening in the run up to D-Day.

All across the Cherbourg peninsula there were reports of paratroopers landing and ships on the horizon, dummy paratroopers, continual bombings of strategic positions and hundreds of planes in the sky, not to mention gliders, all of which added to the lack of credible intelligence for the German chiefs of staff. Because of weather, heavy flak and navigational error many paratroopers were misdropped miles from their intended targets. This in itself created confusion as many of the American paratroopers took on targets of opportunity on their way to their intended destination. These groups of misdropped paratroopers also created further confusion for the Germans who could in some instances not understand the strategic importance of a particular village or road – of course, there was in some cases nothing strategic at all, it was simply where they had landed.

One thing was certain, the German Army generals trying to understand the situation were left in no doubt as to the severity of the landings.

The German Luftwaffe was almost non-existent over Omaha sector and a great many of the conventional methods of communications with forward positions were now inoperative. Shelling had destroyed phone lines, radios were buried and bunkers destroyed minute by minute. American naval gunfire was taking out observation points such as churches and cliff-top positions were being attacked from land one by one.

The German Army's defences were being worn down in an attritional way which meant that men, ammunition and supplies were not getting through. Roads were being blocked and held whilst German transport columns were being attacked by banks of Allied aircraft which were 'roaming' looking for targets.

Despite the lack of orders and in some cases a lack of ammunition, many Germans put up a strong defence of their positions. The battle was by no means won once the Rangers landed and the Germans had no intention of letting them stay on dry land.

The following are extracts from Seventh Army's telephone log conversations and conferences from 6 June 1944, particularly in relation to the Omaha sector. This sector was occupied by the 352nd Infantry Division and the 716th infantry positions with artillery batteries including those at Maisy. The huge number of non-area or non-relevant unit related reports and orders that show the larger scale of the confusion have been omitted.

If nothing else, the communications are jumbled with insufficient information getting through. It appears that the commanders on the ground were the ones making the decisions that affected the Rangers. Few specific orders other than general ones for counterattacks are initiated in the Omaha–Grandcamp-Maisy area by high command. Often there there were no communications at all, and when there were these were patchy and often inaccurate – opinions of people reporting their 'present' situation. As this was a relatively fluid battle once the Rangers had landed, some of the statements made by German generals were pure speculation. They certainly bear little connection with the actual events on the ground in some places.

6 June 1944

0130 – Chief of Staff, LXXXIV Corps reports: Since 0030 parachute jumps in area east and northwest of Caen, St. Marcouf, Montebourg, astride Vire and on East coast Cotentin. LXXXIV Corps has ordered Alert II.

Army headquarters alerted 0130.

0200 – CoS [Chief of Staff] LXXXIV Corps reports to CoS, Seventh Army: In sector of 716th Infantry Division further air landings. Area on the east coast Cotentin appears to be extending from St. Marie du Mont to Montebourg. Fighting at Le Ham. Very strong air units, east of Cherbourg and further west in the Channel area of Jersey, closing in. No reports on air landings on north and west coast Cotentin. Two main effort areas are shaping up: 716th Infantry Division and East Coast Cotentin, and clear through the middle of the 91st Airborne Division.

0215 – CoS briefs CoS Army Group B:

Fair size landings for the present from the air and mainly in the 716th Infantry Division sector, south portion east coast Cotentin and clear across the Cotentin at the narrows of Carentan. Small elements already destroyed. From out at sea engine noises can be heard on the east coast of the Cotentin. Astride Cherbourg and west coast Cotentin – so far no information.

Admiral Channel Coast reports ships tracking in the sea area Cherbourg. No details known.

CoS requests assignments of the 91st Airborne Division.

CoS Army Group B holds the view that the affair is still locally confined. CoS states that this is a larger operation.

0240 – G-3 Army Group B reports to CoS Seventh Army: It is the opinion of OB West that this is not a large scale operation. CoS replies that a number of American and British prisioners have been taken in the area of the LXXXIV Corps and in the narrows. In addition, landings in the depth of the corps area lead to the conclusion that this is a large operation.

0245 – Proposal by the Chief of Supply and Administration suggesting that Organisation Todt motor columns and OT workers be shipped out of the Cotentin Peninsula is turned down by CoS on the basis that the development of the situation on the Cotentin Peninsula is not clear.

0250 – CoS LXXXIV Corps briefs CoS Seventh Army: Further air landings near Azeville and to the west of the town. The 621st Artillery Group was committed on the east coast Cotentin.

Admiral Channel Coast reports: Sea targets 35 kilometres north of Jobourg have been tracked. The same also for the sector of the 716th Infantry Division. Details are not known, because the (radar) stations have technical trouble.

More Glider landings – ten planes – in a field south of Carentan.

Twelve planes southwest of Marais de Gorges.

0330 – CoS LXXXIV Corps to CoS Seventh Army: (1) Continuous, strong support landings since 0325 in area Breville, east of Orne estuary and Grandcamp.

Situation near Grandcamp on the Vire estuary still not clear. Assumption that there are landing craft.

0500 – G – 2 LXXXIV Corps reports:

Landings from the sea so far only Vire estuary and Port en Bessin.

0515 CoS gives the following estimate of the situation to Army Group B:

The depth of the enemy glider landings at the Orne up to 20 kilometres in the southeast portion of Cotentin peninsula, the occupation of crossings over the narrows of Carental – Pont L'Abée, in combination with tracked sea targets in front of the Orne estuary between Port en Bessin and Vire estuary, as well as north of Cherbourg and north of the Jobourg peninsula lead to the conclusion that this is an enemy large scale attack.

0535 – G-2 LXXXIV Corps reports:

1. *Landings Vire and Port en Bessin not confirmed. Up to now no British soldier has set foot on land in the Army area.*
2. *Off Island Marcouf and St. Vaast ships have been reported with course southeast. Near Marcouf about 15 big ships LCF, near St. Vaast 6 small ones ahead, followed by 3 big ones. Course southeast.*

   0600 – CoS LXXXIV Corpos reports to SoS Seventh Army:
3. *In front of the coastal sector Orne estuary – Bernieres sur Mer – Arromanches – Colleville – Grandcamp stronger ship formations have opened fire on the coast. Landing boats are approaching Bernieres sur Mer.*
4. *Situation at the narrows still not clear, at Carentan, however, contact has been established.*

0645 CoS submits to the army commander for approval the following.

Morning Report for Army Group B:

The depth of the enemy air landing area in area Orne and south portion Cotentin lead to the conclusion that this is a major attack. Intentions behind the bambardment of the coast are not clear yet. It is possible that this is a matter of holding attacks to be combined later with other attacks in a different sector.

Luftwaffe and Kriegsmarine reconnaissance have brought no new results since daybreak.

0700 – CoS informs CG LXXXIV Corps that 21st Panzer Division is assigned to the corps with the mission of eliminating the airborne emeny east of the Orne.

12th SS Panzer Division is being moved up to the area Lisieux. General Marcks reports that air landings have taken place from Carentan to the north to the area north of Valognes and that the 91st Airborne Division will be moved up to restore the situation.

0707 – Army submits to Army Group B the Morning Report that includes the counter measures initiated, air situation, and estimate of the over-all situation.

0900 LXXXIV Corps reports

Since 0715 stronger landings from the sea, astride, but especially on the west side of the Orne estuary, Bernieres, Asnelles, Meuvaines, Grandcamp, with infantry and armoured forces. Number of ships unconfirmed. Off Bernieres about 100, off Grandcamp about 60.

Total airborne divisions committed, about three divisions.

0925 CoS to CoS, LXXXIV Corps – CoS promises that a fighter and fighter-bomber group will be made available. LXXXIV Corps requests commitment in the danger area between Asnelles and Ver-sur-Mer. Time of commitment is at the present time still uncertain.

Battery Marcouf (Crisbecq) is at present not operational.

General Marcks states that the situation on the left Orne bank is critical and enemy tanks have already reached artillery positions.

LXXXIV Corps has no fast mobile reserves with anti-tank weapons.

General Marcks requests urgently the assignment of a mobile reserve west of Caen, the 21st Panzer Division is needed on the right of the Orne.

The 12 SS Panzer Division would be desired.

Penetrations occurred in the most forward lines of the 352nd Infantry Division; however, they are not as dangerous as those in the 716th Infantry Division sector.

1015 CoS, Enemy landing craft moving into Vire estuary.

11.00 – G -3 Seventh Army briefs CoS, Military Governor Southwest France, on our present situation and requests continuous reports on situation in the security area and the attitude of the civilian population. CoS, Military governor Southwest, reports that the attitude of the population so far is quiet.

11.45 – CoS LXXXIV Corps report to CoS Seventh Army:

1. *In the sector of 716th Infantry Division west of the Orne estuary the enemy has gained a bridgehead and has reached with advance elements, the line Colleville – Tailleville – Reviers – St. Croix-sur-Mer – Asnelle.*
2. *No new reports are available on the situation in the 352nd Infantry Division sector.*
3. *In the sector Madelaine, elements of the 1st Battalion, 919th Grenadier Regiment, having been encircled by Airborne troops.*
4. *Observations from east coast Cotentin reveal strong ship's formations off sector Calvados with carriers and transports continuously unloading under protection of powerful fighter cover.*

5. *No new reports on east coast because communications to that area are at present cut off.*

12.00 CoS Briefs Army Group B on situation within LXXXIV Corps sector.

CoS requests CoS Seventh Army for permission to commit the 30th Mobile Brigade in the sector of the 716th Infantry Division, since the situation there is markedly critical.

After a further proposal by the Commanding General, LXXXIV Corps, the Army Commander approves the request.

CoS points out that LXXXIV Corps can count on the assignment of the 12th SS Panzer Division for the sector of the 716th Infantry Division. The time cannot be determined at present.

General Marcks reports that landings from the sea have been completely repulsed, with the exception of the sector Madelaine, and that a critical situation exists only at the bridgehead west of the Orne estuary. To eliminate (this bridgehead) assistance by army is urgently required.

12.30 CoS requests at Army Group B that on the basis of the enemy penetration in the 716th Infantry Division sector the XXXXVII Panzer Corps assume command in this sector with the mission of eliminating the bridgehead. He requests, in addition, that the 711th Infantry Division be committed on the east bank of the Orne and that the 12th SS Panzer division be made available for commitment in the sector of the 716th Infantry Division.

1335 – G–3 352nd Infantry Division reports:

The Division has driven back into the sea the enemy that had penetrated; only near Colleville-sur-Mer a counterattack is at present still underway. CoS briefs Army Group B Headquarters on the situation of the 352nd Infantry Division, which is now clarified.

1620 – CoS reports to CoS, Army Group B the overall impression of the situation.

Strong enemy forces are in the penetration area. (The army) does not at present feel there is reason for fear in regard to a strategic crisis because (the enemy) has failed to force the east coast of the Cotentin, necessary to cut off the Normandy peninsula. The army assume that it will be possible to restore the situation with its own forces in the Cotentin. Attention is called to the fact that parachute troops have been committed there without direct support from the sea. There is a possibility that this is a preliminary operation designed to divert own forces. Owing to the weather situation, the commitment of the enemy air force is not so powerful as we expected. [This sentence was crossed out later.]

1640 – CoS LXXXIV Corps, reports strong additional landings from the sea in the sector Madelaine and in the Vire estuary, new air landings north of Valognes and near St. Mesnil.

Our own artillery is firing on landings at Madelaine from Grandcamp, but is not sufficient. [This was from Maisy Battery at La Martiniere.]

1800 – On the basis of reports from the G-3, 352nd Infantry Division, the CoS Seventh Army calls attention to the unfavourable developments in the sector of this division. The enemy has infiltrated between resistance points and has reached with advanced armoured spearheads the line Colleville-sur-Mer – Louvier – Asniers. It is becoming apparent that the enemy is planning attack on Bayeux from the sector 716th and 352nd Infantry Divisions.

1825 G-3 716th Infantry Division reports:- ... because of strong artillery fires and dropping of special bombs, mine fields have been largely rendered useless.

Enemy landed at low tide and was therefore in a position to bypass visible pre-shore obstacles. Very powerful naval artillery taking effect on every coast.

Application of new assault tactics by bypassing strongpoints, and infiltration of strong armoured units with infantry riding tanks, and bicyclists with subsequent attack against coastal positions from the rear.

CoS briefs CoC, Army Group B on situation of 716th Infantry Division and new assault tactics of the enemy:

Landing at low tide in order to bypass pre-shore obstacles.

Most powerful commitment of naval artillery. Mass commitment of tanks with infantry riding on top and bicyclists. Infiltration between strongpoints. Rapid advance and exploitation of success.

1825 Northwest of Vire esturary continuous new landings.

Battery Marcouf lies under heavy artillery fire by 360mm ship's artillery. Two guns knocked out by direct hits, one operational gun continues fire.

From the sea the enemy is employing successfully new type rocket artillery. Air landed enemy stands between battery and Ravenoville.

Off a line from Grandcamp to Barfleur 6 battleships and heavy cruisers as well as 20 destroyers and in addition 30–50 transports have been sighted.

2240 On the Cotentin, new air drops from Madelaine to Quineville. The hedgerow terrain makes it extremely difficult to restore the situation.

2400 CoS Seventh Army briefs G-3 of Army Group B on the report of the commanding General of the LXXXIV Corps: to the effect that the troops had especially high casualties, suffered from the preparatory fire of the naval artillery: further, that all anti-landing guns were knocked out by hits on the apertures. Counterattacks were initially successful, but later bogged down with high losses, on account of air superiority and naval artillery bombardment. CoS points out that the troops should be commended for their morale.

Telephone conversation between CoS with commanding generals 21st Panzer Division and 716th Infantry Division:

The 21st Panzer Division had already gained a narrow corridor all the way to the coast during the counterattack. Mass airlandings, however, forced the Division to fall back somewhat and, on orders of Headquarters LXXXIV Corps, go over to the defence.

The 716th Infantry Division is still defending its line in strongpoints. Contact between divisional headquarters and regimental and battalion headquarters has ceased to exist, so that losses as well as strongpoints still holding are not known.

CoS orders that the counterattack must by all means reach the coast on 7 June, since the defenders in strongpoints are entitled to expect to be relived.

0.'30 – The transmission of the attack order to the 1st SS Panzer Corps is interrupted by a break in the telephone line. It proves impossible to re-establish telephone contact with Falaise.

It is interesting to read this from the Comander in Chief's war diary, 1–5 June 1944:

Entry number 885 – OB WEST, weekly estimate of the situation.

All indications point to the fact that the enemy has reached an advanced stage of readiness to iump off. Probably invasion front is the area between Scheldt River and Normandy.

OB West war diaries note the following:

From 6–9th June 44, if situation permits, CinC West (Von Rundstedt) will make an inspection trip to area of Seventh Army (Southwest portion of Cotentin Peninsula, and north coast of Brittany including St. Brieue ... The trip will take place in motor car. Aides will be Major Ohrloff and Lt. Von Rundstedt. One additional staff car will accompany the Field Marshal. In the second car the body guard personnel, armed with submachine guns will travel.

The diary includes a full itinerary for the next few days, but by 2 June this had changed:

Telephone call of General Major Baron von Buttlar to OB West on 2nd June 44. Subject: Timing of emergency alert IMMINENT DANGER.

1. *CinC West has given careful consideration to declaring the emergency alert.*
2. *The measure would mainly affect rail transportation. Because of the well-known situation, preparations have been made in all other sectors of defense, although code word IMMINENT DANGER has not been declared.*
3. *Under normal traffic conditions – i.e. if the rail network were halfway intact – declaring the emergency would have had the effect of accumulating rolling stock required for movement of large units (division-size). Owing to the present traffic situation (it is very much disrupted) this is not possible. But locally rolling stock has been assembled. If the emergency were now declared the last reserves of means of transport needed for the supply of the population, economy, and war production, would be cut off. New problems would arise such as unemployment, strikes, and complete standstill of the war production plants, which are still operating, though in a much reduced scale. The result would be difficulty in supplying the large cities with food. The CinC West, therefore, believes that these dangers should be avoided for as long a time as possible.*

4. *On the other hand, consideration must be given to the alternative of applying the emergency alert to economically unimportant areas, which are centres of the Resistance, e.g. in the Massif Central. This form of blockade could possibly assist German anti-resistance operations. The SD [security police] will be heard in the matter.*

On 4 June Rommel comments:

Repeated landing excercises of enemy forces at low tide point to the fact that we must seriously reckon with the possibility of such a landing. Evidently the enemy is planning to land short of our strong beach obstacles that have been built mainly for conditions of high tide. Every possible effort will be made to complete existing obstacles to make a low-tide landing possible only at extreme cost to the enemy. Wherever the water only recedes 1,500 feet and the enemy thus finds favourable landing possibilities, construction of obstacles must be pushed forward with especial care. Completion is to be sought and reported to my headquarters by 20th June.

From this it is obvious that Rommel had a firm understanding of the Allied invasion strategy before D-Day, which as we know proved correct. He also shows no sign of letting up in the strengthening of the beach defences. It also tends to indicate that although he had aerial intelligence reports of 'excercises of enemy forces at low tide' (presumably the Slapton Sands excercise reconnaissance), he did not know specifically where such an invasion would actually take place in France.

The very fact that he was in possession of aerial intelligence information shows that despite a depleted Luftwaffe presence in April/May 1944 they were still spotting the landing craft (LCs) training and grouping on the south coast of England.

On 5 June Rommel comments:

Seventh Army, to accelerate completion of the programme of casemating of artillery batteries would require 8–10 trains with materials. For the power supply of the electronic power plant at Caen a daily shipment of 100 tons minimum of coal is needed.

These were requests of Seventh Army passed on to OB West by Army Group B. OB West replies:

Ten building material trains per day are at present just about the total capacity of the western theatre. Question will be considered, also whether it is possible to add 5–6 railroad cars, carrying coal, to the material trains of Seventh Army.

Given the date, 5 June, and the tone of the discussions, it is a fair assumption to say that they had no idea that D-Day was the next day. It is also obvious that Rommel's orders to continue fortifying the concrete defences were being implemented. The following report was despatched at 2150hr, 5 June:

5th June. Estimate of situation by OB West, 29th May–4th June.

Enemy situation:

West Coast Front: During largely favourable weather conditions very active enemy air activity. In comparison with the peak figures of sorties of the previous week, this week's figures on sorties were on an average 25% lower. For the first time strong commitment of the four-engine formations against the coast defence positions with main effort in area Calais, Boulogne, Dieppe–Fécamp, and Cherbourg. Low level (frequently dive-bombing) attacks against bridges and railroad installations with main effort in the Seine valley between Rouen and Paris (inclusive) caused considerable destruction to bridges and railroads and paralysed rail traffic between Paris and Le Havre. Crossing the Seine between Rouen and Paris (exclusive) is at present possible only with ferries. Construction of 'deception bridges' and temporary bridges (the latter at sites removed from the destroyed targets) has begun. Attacks on yards and air force ground installations did not exceed the usual intensity. A relative increase of attacks against radar installations, mainly in area Gravelines and Cherbourg was noticeable. On 2 June heavy air attack on harbour Boulogne caused damage to ship targets and other Navy installations. Rocket bombs were committed against Motor Boat bunker gates. Extensive air mining operation against sea area Calais, Le Havre, and St. Nazaire continued. Air supply operations – up to 100 planes – into the well known resistance area.

Activity of enemy naval forces remained low, convoy duty as usual. Photo reconnaissance of harbor of Dover on 30 May revealed increase of 20 LCT as compared to 24 May. Possible trans-shipment. Signal intelligence reports normal radio traffic, signal excercises, however, much reduced.

Visual reconnaissance and agents' report revealed no new data. The number of defense installations under attack mainly between Scheldt and Normandy rose to a total of 206 between 25 May and 4 June.

24 fortified structures were damaged a large number of these only slightly. 5 casemates were destroyed, while still under construction. Damaged 11 casemated gun positions, the majority only slightly damaged, 3 were still under construction, 25 reinforced field fortifications strong-points were destroyed, about 20 were damaged. 45 regular field fortification strong-points were destroyed, 31 were damaged.

Heavy weapons losses: 4 guns and 7 coast defense guns were destroyed 9 and 6, respectively, damaged temporarily. As a result of the tripling of attacks against strongpoints (as compared to the previous week) casualties rose to 150 killed in action, 48 missing in action, and 297 wounded. Defense effectiveness of the main line of resistance still largely unaffected. Losses in material and personnel are extremely low as compared to the enemy effort.

The Command in Chief West estimate of the situation is: the systematic continuation and distinct increase of enemy air attacks indicate that the enemy has reached a high degree of readiness. The probable main effort invasion front still remains the sector Scheldt–Normandy.

It is not impossible that the north front of Brittany including Brest might also be included. It is still not clear where the enemy will attempt invasion within this total area. The fact that enemy air concentrated attacks on coast defenses between Dunkirk and Dieppe and on the Seine–Oise bridges might mean that the Allied main invasion effort would be made here.

Imminence of the 'Invasion' is not yet recognizable.

The intensification of air attacks against coastal fortifications has resulted in a slight increase in losses of personnel and material, but these losses are still to be considered as very low.

The German meteorologist Dr Mueller, assigned to von Rundstedt's headquarters, produced his daily weather reports for OB West:

1730 5th June Weather forecast in regard to Enemy Operations, for the night 5–6 June 1944.

Air force: flights out of British staging area generally possible without difficulties. Only locally slightly impeded by stronger cloud formations. Air activity in area OB WEST largely possible during a period of clearing or broken over-cast ... in the Netherlands more difficult owing to solid over-cast.

Navy: in the Hofden and Channel medium to stiff breezes from Southwest to west, strength 3–5 and in instances 6; somewhat calmer towards morning. Sea 3–4 in instances 5; also somewhat calming toward morning. Mostly good visibility ...

High tide: Le Havre 2220 toward Ijmuiden 0415.

First light: 0521

OB West reports, 6 June 1944:

0325 Navy Group West reports landing craft near Port-en-Bessin and Grandcamp.

0330 Third Air Force reports:

Since 0240 six large four engine bomber formations are assembling over Southern England – large scale attack and landing not impossible. Air Force is going to reconnoitre in Southern England and especially in the Seine Bay.

0335 Navy Group West reports:

Landings have now spread also to Orne mouth – the British are supposed to have landed there. North of the Seine radar had been blacked out. Heavy bombings of Cherbourg.

0355 Army Group B reports:

According to reports from Fifteenth Army:

LXXXI Corps reports: ships targets picked up on radar in area Orne mouth.

The parachutists in the area of the 716th Infantry Division are probably a reinforced parachute regiment now assembling in area Blanville.

Some scattered parachutists in the area Le Havre. Part of these men have already been caught in mine fields and stuck. Demolition charges were found on a killed American.

0535 Check with Army Group B (on this report) reveals that they know nothing about it!

0545 Report G-2 (From LXXXIV Corps):

In the north part Cotentin peninsula Americans have jumped, have been pushed into the marsh area, they are signalling to planes.

0555 Report Navy Group West:

In the centre of a line running from Le Havre to Ouistreham strong enemy surface units in contact with our naval forces. In front of Port-en-Bessin our coastal batteries have opened fire on landing craft.

Radio intelligence reports a very great number of enemy units and ships in the western Channel at sea.

0600. Report for Air Liaison Officer:

Air reconnaissance reveals numerous landing craft in front of Orne mouth, about 80. In this area two of our batteries are supposedly encircled.

0605 Army Group B is informed.

0622 Report Navy Group West.

Off Cherbourg several hundred gliders. Enemy putting down black smoke screen in front of our batteries.

Message from Duty Officer OB West, Lieutenant Schneider, 5–6 June 1944:

0145 Army Group B, Lt. Col. Staufacher calls: At 0105 east of Caen and east coast Cotentin peninsula near Fontébourg and St. Marcouf parachute jumps, in part already engaged in battle. Corps Marcks (LXXXIV) has been alerted.

Air Force reports:

Near Caen and Cherbourg parachute drops. Flights of 50–60 two-engine planes coming in.

0130hr, Navy Group West, Duty Officer Lieutenant Huhn:

Many parachute drops in front of Army Coast Artillery Battery No. 1261 and in area 716th and 711th Infantry Divisions. LXXXIV Corps is on alert II.

0330hr, Third Air Force, Major Panitzki:

Since 0240 six large four-engine bomber formations in southern England assembling.

0345hr, Liaison Section Air Force:

Since 0315 assembly of four-engine bomber formations over southern England.

6 June 1944, morning situation reports, Army Group B:

Since 0000 enemy landings between Seine and Cherbourg. Since 0530 fire from the sea against coastal front in area Orne estuary, near Ver-sur-Mer, Arromanches and Corneville. Whether this is a grand diversionary attack or the main effort attack is not yet clearly distinguishable.

0930hr, G-3, 6 June 1944, report from Navy Group West:

Navy Commander Cherbourg radio message: Area Marcouf under heavy artillery fire. Between Vire and Orne, especially near Vierville and Colleville enemy tanks on land. Cliffs at Pointe du Hoc scaled by enemy with ladders, fighting in progress. From area Ravonoville to Vire mouth no reports. Near St. Vaast a large-scale landing supported by strong ships artillery fire seems under way. Battery Marcouf has sunk one enemy warship, destroyer or small cruiser. One ship (landing craft) blew up. Battery Marcouf lost one gun, which is out of operation.

1215hr, report from General of Artillery (OB West, T.), Colonel Lattmann, Artillery Commander Army Group B – 1716th (appears to be an artillery battalion) in enemy hands:

3rd Battery, 1716th Artillery Battalion, no communications [located near Sword Beach].

3rd Battery, 1260th Artillery Battalion destroyed its guns, hand-to-hand fighting in progress.

Unconfirmed reports say that Navy Battery Marcouf has lost one gun destroyed and two damaged by artillery fire from sea.

HQ (command):

Command became more difficult after further breakdown of means of communication. The sorties of enemy air force on the known division C.P. made it imperative for the future that subordinates be in ignorance of the location of all C.P.s. It was ordered that message centres be organised to check orders and reports (also callers) and forward them to the C.P.s. These measures had proved satisfactory in the East.

2.55 hours: Report from the Gren Regt 914: Approximately from eight to ten parachutists sighted near the 4 battery of the artillery Regt 352nd. Near Cardonville two parachutists with camouflage parachutes and in camouflage uniforms were taken prisoner. Apparently near Isigny landing of seventy paratroopers. Confirmation not yet on hand.

3.10 Hours: Enemy parachutists landing on either side of the Vire outlet.

3.35 Hours: Report from the Gren Regt 916. Strongest bombing attacks on Le Guay, Pointe du Hoc and Grandcamp.

4.34 Hours: Report from the Artillery Regt 352nd. Landing craft have not yet been slighted ahead of Grandcamp.

4.35 Hours: Report from Gren Regt 916.

An American 1/Lt taken prisoner near St. P le Guay testified that along with the parachute troops also dummy dolls were being deployed, which explode when contacting the ground.

05.20 Hours: Report from the Artillery Regt 352.

Advanced observers of the 2 and 4 battalions of Artillery Reg 352 have ascertained noises which probably originate from naval units, at an approximate distance of 2 km, heading towards the Vire outlet. Furthermore 29 ships, including four bigger type naval units (at least destroyer or cruiser class) are reported to be observed at a distance of from 6 to 10 km heading toward le Guay – Pointe du Hoc. Three or four aircraft have been shot down near Formigny, one pilot (a Pole) was taken prisoner.

Report from the Artillery Regt 352: The coast between the Defense works No 59 and 60 is held under the heaviest artillery fire. Large naval formations lie far away on the high sea. Heavy bombing attacks on battery emplacements of the 1716 some of the guns were buried by rubble, three of them have been set free again and emplaced anew. At the time the artillery regiment maintains good connection with the observer posts.

1235hr, G-3 report, 6 June:

Report from Army Group B, Lt. Tuemmler: According to a report from the Chief of Staff, Seventh Army a good-sized enemy bridgehead is shaping up along the following line: Riva-Bella – Colleville-sur-Orne – Tailleville – St. Croix-sur-Mer and Asnelles-sur-Mer. In all these places armoured spearheads. It is not known whether the enemy has formed a solid front yet.

Off Riva-Bella at sea – Calvados, according to report from Naval Commander Le Havre at 1225 there are the following units: 5 battle ships, 12 cruisers, 12 transports, 25 Tank Landing Ships, and very many small boats.

Carentan is in our hands. Near St. Marie du Mont still enemy forces. Near La Madeleine the enemy has a foothold. From there to the north our troops are holding firm.

1330hr, report Navy Liaison Officer:

As of 1225 Naval Commander Seine-Somme reports: According to report from signal station Cap de la Heve observed: 5 battle ships, 15 light and heavy cruisers, about 50 destroyers and Torpedo Boats, 12 troop transports, 25 Tank Landing Ships and innumerable landing craft. The force is continually growing. In the background there are still many ships that cannot be made out.

Evening 5th June – Starting 1940 flights coming in – once with 300 and once with many four engine formation with gliders, reported between Le Havre and Cherbourg. Highest concentration in the coastal sector.

2100 Area Isigny many gliders coming from area Barfleur.

OB West war diary, 5 June, 2145hr:

Report from radio monitor group regarding the reception of messages by Radio London at 2115. It is known that their meaning is to announce an imminent invasion. Although similar messages have occurred on several occasions since the beginning of the year, this transmission was accord special attention by OB WEST because at least part of the broadcast was meant for 'French Section'. [French section refers to the British

Intelligence Service and French Resistance.] Therefore all command headquarters that had to know were forewarned by telephone.

[0425hr, 6 June] OB West is fully aware of the fact that if this is actually a large-scale enemy operation it can only be met successfully if immediate action is taken. This involves above all the commitment, on this day, of the available strategic reserves that are located close-by. ... Under the circumstances OB West therefore requests OKW at 0445 in a first teletype report to release the OKW Panzer Reserves [which, of course, did not happen].

[0950hr, 6 June] Navy Group West reports that the enemy has landed tanks between Orne and Vire, has scaled the bluff near Pointe-du-Hoc with ships' ladders, and the landing attempt St. Vaast is evidently also on a large scale. Continued heavy ships' artillery fire on the coast and extremely powerful enemy air activity in the entire landing area. Determined resistance by our own batteries and sorties of available Navy surface craft directed against the enemy invasion fleet.

[1235hr, 6 June] The General of Artillery at OB WEST reports that several batteries have been knocked out. A message from Seventh Army of 1235 makes it clear that the enemy has already gained a bridgehead west of the Orne, marked approximately by Riva-Bella – Colleville – Tailleville – St. Croix – Asnelles ... e.g. on a width of 18 miles and slightly over one and a half miles deep.

Evening, 6 June:

The Commanding General LXXXIV Corps, with concurrence of the commander of Seventh Army, reports his personal impression of the day:

Our troops have fought very bravely, indeed. High rate of casualties. Weapons in field fortifications had to be first dug out, since they were buried by air bombings and ships' artillery. All weapons in concrete bunkers were put out of action by the extended preparatory fires of the naval artillery and by direct hits on the embrasures. Counterattacks were initially successful throughout, but foundered in the fires of the Naval Artillery and the bombings of the Air Force.

It was no different at Maisy. The following is based on an interview in 1954 with Colonel Werner von Kistowki. He was commander of Flak Assault Regiment No. 1 attached to the 3rd Flak Corps. It was fully motorised and it consisted of three artillery groups, the 497th, a mixed group, the 226th, also a mixed group, and the 90th, a light anti-aircraft group. The two mixed groups had five batteries in all, and the light group had three batteries. Each of the two mixed groups had three batteries apiece. These had in them four 88s, nine 37mm and twelve 20mm. The light battery had 37mm and 20mm guns.

The entire Flak Regiment had 2,500 men with approximately 600 men to each battery and 100 attached to headquarters and general duties, such as cooks and so on. Not all these men were gunners, of course. They were protective infantry which guarded the batteries. Flak Assault Regiment I arrived on 5 June in the morning at La Cambe, which was their headquarters, and it was to position at the mouth of the Vire at Grandcamp.

Colonel Kistowski:

> *The light group of batteries were placed at the mouth [of the Vire Estuary – at La Martiniere] and the mixed groups were placed at Maisy and stretched across to the outskirts of the town itself of Grandcamp.*

There had been no mention of the invasion, however. Kistowski was told his unit was being moved because of the continual bombing attacks and the planes seemed to be swinging over Grandcamp as they made their runs into and from the Continent. They dug in on the 5th, *'just foxholes and camouflaged tents'*.

On the evening of the 5th the Colonel drove to St Lo to the headquarters of the 84th Corps under the command of General Marcks. He went there for a specific reason. He had been warned that he should be ready to move again soon and since he had used up all his gasoline he needed new supplies. He saw the Chief of Staff, a Colonel Von Criegern and the Quartermaster General and requested gasoline. It was a requirement that he must always have 33,000 litres of gasoline – that was enough for a hundred kilometres and his motorised vehicles could not use synthetic gasoline.

It was about 2200hr when he got the okay on the supplies and then he set out for his headquarters at about 2300hr. It was as he was driving back towards La Cambe that he saw the 'Christmas Trees', the flares that had been dropped by aircraft and were hanging in the sky floating down to earth. He said to his engineering officer who was with him, a certain Lieutenant Colonel Busche, *'Busche, I think this mess is starting.'* The bunches of Christmas Trees hung all the way from Carentan to the mouth of the river at Grandcamp. They drove very slowly as they headed for his headquarters. Then he heard his guns firing and he could see the flashes in the distance.

At about 0145hr he sent out a pre-arranged signal to 84th Corps, 'LL', meaning that the invasion had begun. At 0148hr he received a telephone call from the 90th Artillery group (at Maisy) that the first POWs – paratroopers – had been taken. There were four prisoners and, *'This was immediately followed by another seventeen near Maisy ... These paratroopers fell on a battery between Maisy and GefosseFontenay'*. He wasn't sure whether they were paratroopers or bomber crews that had parachuted down to earth.

In fact George Rosie of the 101st Airborne and fellow paratroopers had landed near the Maisy Battery:

> *The plane came down low and fast and as my chute opened the ground was upon me. I came down a top a hedgerow, ran down a small hill and went through a wooden fence headfirst – knocking loose my 2 front teeth. I gathered together some other troopers – seventeen in total and almost immediately we were engaged by a large force of Germans. When we surrendered five paratroopers had been killed. But we had shot some of them including an officer, whom we had to pick up and then carry away.*

Rosie was taken to a farmhouse by Russians or Poles, interrogated and then he was later paraded through Paris in a cage where residents spat on him. He was then sent to a POW camp.

Meanwhile, Colonel Kistowski decided that he had time to write to his wife Ruth, who lived near Bonne. He had taken a room in a nearby farmhouse so he wasn't living in a tent. As he wrote he heard the pounding of the waves of bombers as they flew over and it began to get louder and louder to such an extent that halfway through the letter he wrote: '*Darling, I must stop now because the bombs are coming too close.*'

There were more reports of paratroopers landing so Kistowski drove to Maisy to see for himself what was going on. He described the bombing as '*absolutely hideous – it was just murder*'. His men cowered in foxholes and the bombs laid pattern after pattern across their positions. He and his men did not think they could possibly survive the pounding. When they climbed out of these holes, they were absolutely shivering but every time they thought it was going to stop, another wave of planes would come in and no sooner had the air bombardment ceased then the naval bombardment, which was much worse, began.

All the time in his foxhole Kistowski was able to follow the path of the gliders as they were towed in over the mouth of the River Vire passing over Grandcamp. All the time he thought to himself, '*If only this foxhole was smaller*'. The foxhole itself seemed to him much too wide and he felt that every shell, every bomb that fell was aimed at him.

Instinctively Kistowski tried to make himself as small as possible. In fact as he put it, he was trying to duck and crawl inside his helmet. The moment it let up he lifted his head out of the foxhole and yelled to his communications officer, '*Schmidt, are you still there?*' Next he called his adjutant, 1st Lieutenant Gelaubrech, 'Are you still alive?' He was astonished to discover that they were. The bombs he remembered were dropped by the air force and were a special type that detonated just above the ground. This is substantiated by the Allied air force reports that they were dropping air-burst bombs on targets on D-Day to clear mine fields and wire emplacements – today they are known as 'Daisy Cutters'. He thought how much worse this was than the forty days of bombing night after night he had experienced in Berlin in 1943. Lieutenant Schmidt said to him afterwards, '*Colonel, now I know what my wife is going though in the Ruhr.*'

When it all stopped the air was filled with the acrid smell of cordite, both from his own guns and the explosives. Very slowly they came up from their foxholes and even more slowly looked around. The Colonel stood up and one by one he saw heads appearing. Everybody was black and covered with dust and everybody was trembling. Some looked around cautiously, some were braver than others and stood up and stretched. Then everybody got out of the foxholes and washed.

The entire Flak Regiment had lost only one man killed and three wounded at that time. He was absolutely amazed. He drove across to Grandcamp and there for the first time he realised the terrible bombardment they had just experienced because of the huge craters that covered the ground.

It was while Kistowski was at Grandcamp that he happened to look out to sea and there to his amazement he too saw the fleet on the horizon steadily steaming towards the coast. Quickly he drove back to his guns and just as he did the naval bombardment began again. Because he had been a former naval officer, he knew how devastating the naval bombardment could be. He knew that it was laid out in squares and that whole areas would automatically be covered, so he '*drove like hell*' back to his positions. During this naval bombardment, he had one 88mm gun destroyed and four or five other smaller ones, and there were terrific casualties among his men. He forgot what the casualties were, but he said it was more than a hundred.

Now Kistowski found that he had no communications except for one radio set. At the time he thought this was due to the 'Daisy Cutters', but the real damage was done by naval shelling. It was different from the air bombardment and was absolutely 'devastating'. Now he fully expected the invasion as he watched the fleet come in closer. He ordered his communications officers out on the coast with a small radio to act as an observation post for his 88mm guns.

This goes some way to providing an understanding of how the guns at Maisy were still able to operate. By this time many of the Germans' conventional observation posts had been destroyed. Kistowski's men would have had a clear view of the Utah and a partial view of the Omaha landing sectors from this area because of the high ground.

The terrible situation which the Colonel found himself in was one of being caught squarely in the middle, along the seam between both Utah and Omaha Beaches and his guns could not hit the beaches where the landings were taking place. He could not depress his guns sufficiently to reach these areas and anyway the boats were too far away for his guns to have any effect.

This is interesting because in 99 per cent of interviews with the Rangers they state that they were coming under fire from 88s when in most cases – for example on the beaches and the approaches – it would have been from heavier calibre guns. For example, the 75mms (Pak 40s) situated on Omaha Beach were designed to fire laterally to the beach and not out to sea, or on the beach approaches.

Kistowski was caught in the middle and he remembered saying to his communications officer, '*Damm it, if only we were a bit to the right, or the left we would show them*'. He never did finish his letter to his wife. He couldn't hear his own voice that morning because of the shelling that was taking place.

Kistowski's guns '*fired right, left and centre*' at the hundreds of planes that came over and by the end of that day he was able to record that his light battery had shot down the following:

01:38 a B–26.
01:42 a B–26.
06:10 Two Lightnings.
09:15 a Thunderbolt.
10:00 a Thunderbolt.
04:15 a Mustang.

To the Colonel it was, '*A very good day, a very good day indeed, one of the best.*' One of the planes came down near his headquarters quickly followed by a terrific fire as the plane's ammunition exploded. Throughout this morning and afternoon, the Colonel was absolutely on his own with no communications with the 3rd Flak Corps, his headquarters, and the 84th Corps. General Marcks and the 7th Army had nothing whatsoever to do with them so he did not receive any orders.

On the afternoon of the 6th he decided to move his headquarters to Littry. He had sent one of his officers to Le Mans to telephone to the 3rd Corps to get more instructions and set off himself to co-ordinate his activities with those of the 352nd Infantry Division. The night of 6 June Kistowski moved out the battery at Maisy.

There had been five batteries of guns in addition to the Maisy guns which could have been utilised against the invasion, yet these were guns that were under used and were acting without any co-ordination or orders. Basically shooting at anything flying over. The presence of this artillery in addition to the existing weapons at Maisy presented a massive obstacle to planes and gliders trying to land on the peninsula. That in itself may have added to the chaos experienced by pilots as them came over the coast.

It is also interesting to note Kistowski's annoyance on not being able to 'lower his guns' enough to fire at the beaches. It is a commonly heard expression, 'the 88s were firing at us on the beach', but it is quite possible that there were very few if any 88mm weapons firing directly on the beaches.

On the morning of 8 June two Georgian conscripts from the 439th Ost Battalion were patrolling the beach at Gefosse and they came upon the dead bodies of a US Army officer and a beachmaster in a damaged launch, which had been blown onto the beach. They were seen carrying the soaking bodies on a cart from the beach. The mayor of Gefosse asked them what they were doing and they told him that the bodies had maps and the invasion plans on them, so they were taking them to the 'HQ at Maisy'. It is not known if the bodies reached Maisy or if the information with the bodies was considered significant. However, there is no mention of this incident in the divisional records. It is equally possible that this was another opportunity lost by the German high command.

Chapter 8

Allied Air Force and Army Intelligence

What did the Allies and in particular the RAF know about the German defences before D-Day? Prior to 2004/5 a lot of the documentation relating to the RAF and missions of any kind were routinely subject to the Top Secrecy Act, which effectively meant that no documents were released for sixty years. At the time of finding Maisy, information was sketchy. However, one thing the Allies did record in great detail was the fortifications between Omaha and Maisy.

Typical of many small operations, it was vital for troops on the ground to have an up-to-date indication of what they were up against. Each photograph would be studied, marked, evaluated and then passed to the appropriate authorities prior to any operation. This whole process would have been a logistical nightmare. Mistakes on photographs would not be uncommon and interpretations could be subjective. In the case of the Maisy Battery, the interpretation was very good. Weapons calibres would turn out to be inaccurate and obviously the interpreters would have no idea of troop numbers, fields of fire and changes made after the photographs were taken. But on the whole the photographic interpretation was accurate.

During the 2 weeks prior to D-Day one RAF Mobile Field Photographic Section had demands for more than 120,000 prints alone. If this was expanded to cover every eventuality, then the task was enormous. Each target had to be located, analysed and evaluated as a threat. That information was passed to the relevant department for mapping. It was then, if considered dangerous, allocated a bombing mission. This then had to be re-photographed, analysed, evaluated and then the process started again. Each time the maps being drawn up would be changed to reflect the latest intelligence available. It was indeed a colossal task.

The reconnaissance of the coastal positions provided vital intelligence information on not just gun batteries in the invasion sectors, but enemy strengths and potential areas for command and control, AA positions, supply dumps and targets for the ground troops – so the whole mapping of an area could change overnight. Numbers of Mustang fighters were converted to medium and low altitude reconnaissance aircraft. Given their speed and ability to protect themselves, they were able to complete their missions and yet be fast enough to outpace the German fighters sent to intercept them. Once back their film runs would be evaluated immediately and the whole process above would begin again.

Photographic interpreters studying aerial photographs.
(Courtesy of Gerald W. Thomas, Airgroup4.com)

Did the RAF even know Maisy existed, did Allied intelligence just miss Maisy altogether? As Maisy Battery was not allocated 'special forces' to attack it on the morning of D-Day then it must logically have not been thought to be a big threat. This was an assumption that with hindsight was wrong and has possibly proved the most baffling of revelations. Having studied the documents released in Washington and Great Britain in 2005, I can conclusively prove that Allied intelligence knew what was at Maisy, but did virtually nothing about it prior to D-Day.

As far as it is known, all the information gleaned about Maisy up to D-Day was from aerial reconnaissance photographs. A Top Secret Nepture planning paper entitled 'Summary of the Enemy Situation' and dated 11 May 1944 states the following:

The Omaha beaches are defended by elements of the 716th Static Division. Entire sector defended by this division extends from Ouistreham west to the mouth of the River Douve. This division was formed in April 1941 in France and has never been out of that country. It was composed originally of older reserve personnel, but has been called upon frequently to furnish replacements for more active units. The equivalent of at least two battalions are Russian and Polish troops. Division is known to consist of the 726th and 736th Grenadier and 656 Artillery Regiments. A third infantry regiment probably does not exist, but certain divisional units as a reconnaissance and/or an anti-tank battalion are probably present. Division headquarters is located at CAEN. Defensive dispositions place the 726th Inf. Regiment in the immediate Omaha Beach area. Regimental headquarters is located at Bayeux. One battalion is believed to have its headquarters at Grandcamp-les-Bains, a second at Isigny, and the third at Bayeux. 726th Infantry is supported by four batteries of field artillery.

The significance of the above paragraph is obvious. The US Army G-2 Intelligence report states that they are aware of the German artillery units' HQ at Grandcamp-les-Bains (Maisy) and yet they did not seek to actively destroy it in advance. There are documents at the US National Archives which contain many references to Maisy that have now been released after sixty years have passed. However, there is virtually no mention of Maisy at all before that in any books. It simply did not exist.

The reports are at times quite random and sometimes speculative as to the size of weapons, etc. References to Maisy I and Maisy II distinguish between the left-hand (westerly) side of the site at La Martiniere and the right-hand (easterly) side at Les Perruques. Maisy III was where guns were added close to D-Day at 16A, Foucher's Farm to the south.

On D-Day naval targeting maps La Martiniere was target number 16, Les Perruques was target number 5 and 16A was an added battery at Foucher's Farm which seems to confuse in some of the reports below. They interpret this new addition – some weeks before D-Day (6 March) as being the temporary movement of the guns from 16 – something which we now know was incorrect. The battery at 16A was a wholly additional group of guns.

According to AIR 34/157, 'Interpretation Report No. Y.264, Coastal Battery List of the Isigny area', 4 April 1944, Maisy I was first reported (new battery) on 7 June 1942.

The site was occupied by a mobile artillery unit, but it was in 1942 when the earthworks were started for the fixed position, thus changing the position from a mobile one into a 'static battery'. On 9 June 1942 'Interpretation Report No. Y.264' notes (updated in April 1944), 'AIR 34/157, La Montagne battery [572935] (close to Pointe du Hable) probable battery position under construction. Two circular emplacements, approximately 30' in diameter.' This position was completely ignored by the bombers on and prior to D-Day. However, the Navy did fire upon it after noting activity on 6 June 1944.

Maisy: 17 April 1943 (B512):

Constructional activity is taking place at this battery. Four excavations are being dug, and a casemate/shelter approximately 35' x 45' is in early stages of construction in an excavation to the left of No. 3 gun. The four emplacements are occupied and are approximately 30' in diameter. (5006/7 of sortie RA/187, 13 April 1943, 1/8,500, quality fair)

5 November 1943 (B702):

The sunken casemate/shelter, reported as being in the early stages of construction in B512, appears complete and the excavation which was to the right of No. 2 gun now presents a similar appearance to the completed casemate/shelter. Two of the three long huts behind the battery have been removed [built to house construction workers]. The guns have been camouflaged and signs of the previously reported activity toned down. (1011/12 of sortie RA/867, 24 October 1943, 1/12,600, quality good)

5 November 1943 (B702):

A dummy battery [at GR 532923] for battery Maisy I, 600 yards in front of this battery and similar to it in layout. Emplacements are 25' in diameter and contain objects [in actual fact wooden mock guns]. (1011 of sortie RA/867, 24 October 1943, 1/12,600, quality good)

18 January 1944 (B758):

Four sunken casemates/shelters in all have been completed among the emplacements of this battery, three of them being approximately 35' x 30' and the fourth 55' x 30'. (2054/5 of sortie RB/41, 6 January 1944, 1/10,000, quality fair)

27 February 1944 (B798):

This is now considered to be a 4 gun light battery. (5004/5 of sortie AA/725, 24 February 1944, 1/16,000, quality good)

4 April 1944 (AIR 34/157, 'Interpretation Report No. Y.264, Coastal Battery List of the Isigny area):

Four gun medium or heavy battery. Circular emplacements 30' in diameter sited to fire NNW. Four sunken shelters, three approximately 35' x 30', one 55' x 30' have been built on the site. Guns are camouflaged. 600 yards in front there is a dummy battery. Now considered to be a 4-gun light battery. (5004/5 of AA/725 [no date])

On Tuesday 23 May 23 1944 the US 386th Bomb Group undertook Mission Number 177 to Maisy. Their briefing was underway at 1530hr for both the first and second box

Perhaps the best way to articulate the problem fully is to show both navy and army target numbers on the same maps. The pre-assigned Allied Naval Bombardment targets are shown in red on the maps and the ships assigned to them are marked. The additional targets often of opportunity are colour coded per ship.

But just what were the ships intending to destroy?

The following is the accompanying list of Naval Target Numbers along with target descriptions and was described in the Neptune papers as the Gunfire Support Plan – List of Targets, 20 May 1944.

Where possible I have omitted targets outside of the Omaha–Maisy sphere.

Target Number	Target Description
T1	6 guns, 155mm
T5	4 guns, 155mm, 5 concrete shelters, 3 MGs, 1 hut
T16	4 guns, 75mm, 2 MGs, 1 pillbox, 3 shelters
T32	3 MGs
T33	2 concrete shelters, 16 MGs, road blocks
T34	Houses
T35	Houses
T36	Houses
T37	Houses
T38	C/D Gun in concrete
T39	Houses
T40	5 pillboxes, 2 MGs, 2 concrete shelters
T41	3 pillboxes
T42	Houses
T43	3 pillboxes, 1 concrete shelter, 4 MGs, AT Ditch
T44	Beach exit
T45	Beach exit, 1 camouflaged position
T46	Troops in houses
T47	4 casemates, 3 concrete shelters, 5 MGs, 1 AT gun
T48	Beach exit
T49	Beach exit
T50	3 pillboxes, 1 med gun, 1 casemate u/c
T51	Construction activitiy
T52	AT ditch
T53	AA gun, 4 concrete shelters, 2 pillboxes, 5 MGs
T54	AA guns in concrete, 6 MGs, 4 inf. weapons
T55	Beach exit
T56	Troops
T57	4 emplacements unoccupied
T58	Troops
T59	1 AA/MG, 8 concrete shelters, concrete OP, 3 pillboxes 2 concrete shelters under construction.
T60	Fortified house, 1 pillbox, 2 concrete shelters
T61	11 MGs, 3 weapon emplacements, 3 pillboxes
T62	2 MGs, possible CP
T63	6 MGs, 1 pillbox
T64	Beach exit
T65	Radar station
T66	1 pillbox, 3 MGs
T67	Fortified house
T68	5 concrete shelters, 1 pillbox, 10 MGs, 1 AA gun
T69	3 MGs, 1 AT gun
T70	Possible AT gun, possible fortified house,
T71	4 pillboxes, 6 MGs, 3 concrete shelters, 1 AA/MG 1 AT gun

T72	2 pillboxes, 4 mortars, 2 emplacements, 11 MGs
T74	4 concrete shelters, 1 OP, 4 pillboxes, 14 MGs
T75	AT weapons, hutted camp
T76	13 MGs, 2 pillboxes, 10 concrete shelters
T77	6 concrete shelters u/c, Wurzburg, radar station, AA guns, 1 searchlight, 1 hutted camp
T78	Troops
T79	2 MGs, supply depot
T80	2 MGs, houses
T81	Strongpoint
T82	1 MG
T83	10 MGs, 2 concrete shelters
T84	Road junction, houses
T85	Troops in houses
T86	1 AT gun
T87	Possible CP, cable trench junction
T88	3 MGs, 2 pillboxes, 2 Shelters
T89	1 MG
T90	2 gun positions, troops
T91	12 MGs, 1 pillbox, 2 shelters
T92	Strongpoint, troops in houses, 7 MGs
T93	29 MGs, 3 pillboxes, 4 shelters, 2 flak guns
T94	Houses with troops
T95	Houses, 1 MG, 1 pillbox
T96	Cable trench junction, possible CP
T97	7 MGs, 1 pillbox, 1 flak gun, 4 road blocks
T98	Strongpoint with 9 MGs, possible CP
T99	1 light gun
T100	Houses with troops
T101	Houses with troops
T102	Strongpoint
T103	4 possible gun positions, troops in houses
T104	Road block, houses, 14 MGs, 3 pillboxes
T105	Houses
T106	2 MGs
T108	Houses with troops
T109	4 pillboxes, 4 MGs, 4 concrete shelters
T110	Troops in houses
T111	13 MGs, 2 concrete shelters
T13	11 MGs, 2 pillboxes
T114	Strongpount, 7 MGs

To further add confusion First Army Target Numbers for Enemy Beach Defences and Strong Points – Utah Sector have the following targets in or near Grandcamp (which also appear in the Omaha Sector!) Indicated on the maps ☐ ;

Target No 30. Defended Locality. Infantry position in the built-up area of Grandcamp. Two pillboxes. One light gun at the end of the Eastern mole. Three guns probably field, reported on the coast in this area. Elevation 12 yards.

Target No 32. Defended Locality. X Infantry position on the open coast West of Grandcamp. Three Pillboxes. One 37mm A/TL gun. One 47mm A/TK gun in a light turret. One shelter. 2 x 150mm guns reported in this area. Elevation 10 yards.

Target 34. 527934 Defended Locality. X Infantry position on coast in open country NW of Maisy. Three pillboxes. One casemate, three shelters. Position surrounded by wire. Elevation 10 yards.

Target 36. 521931. Wired and mined infantry position approx 770 yards wide and 220 yards deep. Elevation 10 yards.

False guns and dummy trenches in front of Les Perruques.

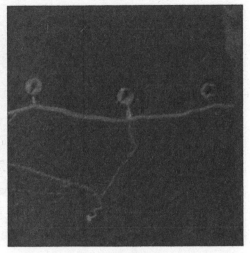

This dummy position was not occupied at all during the war. When I interviewed a local man from Maisy he told me that the Germans had built 'dummy guns' made of wood into this site and left them there.

of fifteen planes each, along with two extra ships. The first box would go out to their aircraft at 1610hr, while the second box crews would remain in the briefing room until 1630hr. Pathfinder (PFF) crews were flying directly ahead of the lead plane in each box and were to guide both boxes. Heavy cloud cover was anticipated and encountered in the general target area. The target for this mission was '*the coastal gun positions located at Maisy*'. RAF Spitfires provided area cover in the target zone and the formation was made up with three ships in each lead flight. The high flights and low flights had six planes each.

Lieutenant John R. Cheney was the station weather officer and he gave the following briefing on the weather situation concerning the mission:

At take off time 1655 hours; four to six-tenths cumulus with a base of 2,500 feet, tops to 4,000 feet. Altostratus clouds from six to eight-tenths with a base of 6,500 feet with tops of 8,000 feet. Visibility will be five miles in haze. The route out will have no low clouds, eight-tenths altostratus over south England. Nine to ten-tenths over the channel with tops to 8,000 feet – visibility above the clouds is eight to ten miles. Target

The earthworks in front of Les Perruques, clearly visible by the white disturbance to the soil (centre bottom).

There is no evidence to dispute that the dummy positions were never occupied. To my knowledge it was never targeted specifically, but it was hit collaterally. The reconnaissance information was 100 per cent correct. In the photograph above taken on 22 May 1944 you can see the leading edge of the Les Perruques Battery in the centre bottom. The dummy positions discussed are seen upper left of centre and far left – they look like white lines or track marks for trenches, etc. They even appeared on GSGS intelligence maps as being occupied on at least one occasion, see below. Note the 2 x [symbols in the centre of the map below with the number 4, which indicate two positions occupied with four guns each. The position at 16A on this map is marked 'in open earth emplacements', but without barbed wire and mine-field surround.

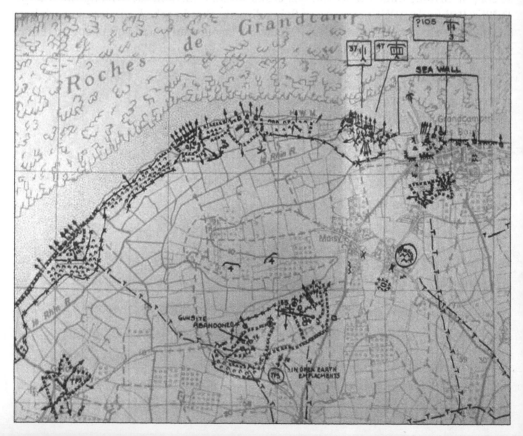

This photograph taken on the same 22 May 1944 mission shows the site in the opposite direction to the last one and is facing south. Les Perruques (Maisy I) is seen at the bottom, centre left and La Martiniere (Maisy II) is the white area of earthworks towards the centre right of the photograph.

An enlargement of the La Martiniere Battery. The earthworks in progress are clearly visible and they were still underway when the battery was attacked.

The battery at Maisy I, Les Perruques with all the earthworks, trenches and gun positions clearly visible. Also of note are the small white blobs in the fields, upper left. These were anti-airlanding posts put into the ground to stop gliders from landing near the site. The areas where the fields appear clear were actually covered with wire and were mined.

The Germans put in a new road through the site which went through Mr Foucher's farmyard. The road leads across the fields to the back of La Martiniere. Foucher's Farm was heavily damaged during the bombardment of the site and never rebuilt and there is little that remains of it now, only a set of gate posts and some concrete on the ground near a stream the Germans used to wash their clothes. There were a number of underground shelters in this area and you can see the guns in position 16A, one to the left and three to the right of the diagonal treeline running towards the farm. These guns arrived shortly before D-Day and were the subject of an artillery bombardment by the US Navy. If you look carefully you can even see a car on the road driving away from the site, no doubt worried about the air-raid warning triggered by the reconnaissance aircraft.

A 150mm cannon in a field position. This would have been identical to the position at Foucher's Farm, except that the weapons would have been covered with netting to try and avoid aerial reconnaissance.

area at 1830 hours, ten-tenths altocumulus tops to 8,000 feet – no low clouds, visibility above clouds will be good. The return route to base will remain unchanged.

The Group Operations Officer Lieutenant Colonel Hankey continued with the briefing:

The route out from base to Brighton to 49 Degrees 43 Minutes North – 00 Degrees 17 Minutes West to target. Turn Right off target to Brighton to base. Bomb load in all ships will be 2 x 2,000 pound general purpose demolition bombs. Fusing to be one-tenth nose and one-fortieth tail. Both Path Finder planes will each carry 4 x 600 pound general purpose demolition type bombs. Intervalometer setting is one hundred feet. Bomb run altitude will be 11,900 feet. Radio call sign for the first box is, Animal, second box will be, Bouncefoot. Briefing was concluded with a ten second count down to synchronize all watches at 1605 hours.

First box crews were delivered to their planes at 1610hr with engine start up following at 1620hr. The first box leader Hankey began to taxi out at 1650hr and was in the air at 1655hr with his three-plane lead flight. His high-flight leader was Lieutenant Colonel

Charles Lockhart flying his plane named 'Winnie' 131 617 RG-A. Low-flight leader was Lieutenant Colonel Thomas Ramsey flying a plane named 'Ye Olde Crocke'.

Soon all of the first box planes were in the air, circling the home aerodrome as they climbed for altitude over Great Dunmow, before striking out for the first checkpoint located at Brighton on the south coast of England. This was reached at 1800hr. From there it was off to the navigation point over the English Channel, as had been highlighted during their briefing procedure. Heavy clouds covered the area in all directions and visibility was very poor. Any serious navigation was based entirely upon the efforts of the Pathfinder PFF plane flown by Lieutenant Gilmore from the First Provisional Squadron.

The Martin B-26 Marauder formations were able to make incredibly steep turns after their 190mph bomb runs were executed. This was necessary on this mission because the target was so very close to the enemy coastline. It made no sense to meander over enemy territory with solid cloud cover hiding the German flak batteries. Bombs were dropped at 1829hr, and then the enemy coast was cleared a minute or so later. The second box of bombers led by Captain Aberson flying a ship called 'Hell's Angels' had followed the same course as the first box – unloading their bombs at 1850hr. His high-flight leader was Captain Gus Hoffman and the low-flight leader was Captain Robert Perkins flying 'Sexy Betsy'. All of the retuning bombers flew to Brighton, and then took up a course of 240 degrees to base.

The 386th had dispatched a total of thirty-two planes and succeeded in dropping sixty-four 2,000lb bombs on the target area, as well as eight 600lb bombs by the two Pathfinder planes. Results were unobserved due to ten-tenths cloud cover. However, the planes had carried strike photo cameras, although all that showed was three rolls of film of beautiful rolling clouds and some blue sky as the B-26s banked into their steep turn off the target! However, based on data from the Pathfinder ships and timing in the target area, an evaluation by **Captain R.W. Bushnell** stated:

> *Bombs hit in the target area straddling a road running in front of the battery, and extending southwest down the road toward Maisy 2. The 386th Bomb Group sustained no casualties, no losses, and no battle damage during the mission. In the target area at 12,000 feet the temperature was minus one degree Centigrade, the wind was from 350 degrees at 23 miles per hour.*

27 May 1944, Neptune Argus 30, Appendix A:

> *This medium howitzer battery was bombed on 23 May 1944. No damage was caused to the emplacements, all four of which are occupied. The road in front of the battery is cratered and one bomb hit in the wire perimeter. (5008-10 of sortie US17/75, 24 May 1944)*

29 May 1944, WO 205/172, 'Pre D-Day bombing of batteries – Neptune area' – consolidated report on results of bombing to 28 May 1944:

> *No damage to the battery. All emplacements occupied.*

31 May 1944, Neptune Argus 34, annex on 'Enemy artillery in the Neptune area':

> *Medium coastal battery, four 155mm (6.1") howitzers. Range 13,000yd. Practical rate of fire about 5 r.p.m. Weight of shell 95lbs. Wide staggered trapezoid layout.*

Guns mounted in open circular pits, 35' diameter, 65–120yd apart, probably with concrete beds. Battery faces VIRE estuary. Accommodation and storage: underground concrete shelters and magazines. Huts in rear. CP – underground concrete shelter centrally located in rear of emplacements. OP – unknown, presumably on the coast west of GRANDCAMP. Road serviced. Communications, buried cable. Secondary armament: two 20mm anti-aircraft guns and possibly three anti-aircraft machine guns. Identification: ? Army Static Coast Troop. Dummy at GR 532923. (Date of information 24 May 1944)

31 May 1944, WO 205/172, 'Summary of present situation of batteries which might affect Neptune beaches or their approaches':

Four open emplacements occupied.

Maisy II (GR 528915) [AKA Maisy la Martiniere]

12 February 1943: NEW BATTERY:

Four occupied emplacements measuring approximately 30' in diameter are seen on a single print 800 yards south-west of battery Maisy, 533918 (now to be known as Maisy I). This may be a new battery or a dummy, but further comment is impossible from this cover. The position is sited to fire north-west. (5118 of sortie RA/62, 8 February 1943, 1/8,000, quality poor)

10 April 1943:

Clear cover shows that this is in fact a four gun battery. The site has been surrounded by wire and a deep excavation approximately 70' square is being dug between Nos. 3 and 4 emplacements. (5097/8 of sortie RA/160, 5 April 1943, 1/9,000, quality fair to good)

17 April 1943:

Constructional activity previously reported in B505 of 15 April 1943 is continuing. (5006/7 of sortie RA/187, 13 April 1943, 1/8,500, quality fair)

5 November 1943:

A casemate/shelter is nearing completion in the excavation reported in B505. A casemate/shelter approximately 30' square is nearing completion in an excavation to the rear of No. 4 emplacement and a further excavation 50' x 40' is being made 70 yards to the rear of No. 3 emplacement. The guns have been camouflaged. (1010/11 of sortie RA/867, 24 October 1943, 1/12,600, quality good)

5 November 1943:

A probable dummy battery [at GR 527923] for battery Maisy II, 700 yards in front of this latter battery. There is slight track activity and the positions contain objects. (1010/11 of sortie RA/867, 24 October 1943, 1/12,600, quality good)

The assessment at this time was incorrect. Guns had been moved into position and only one was in a field awaiting the construction of its casement.

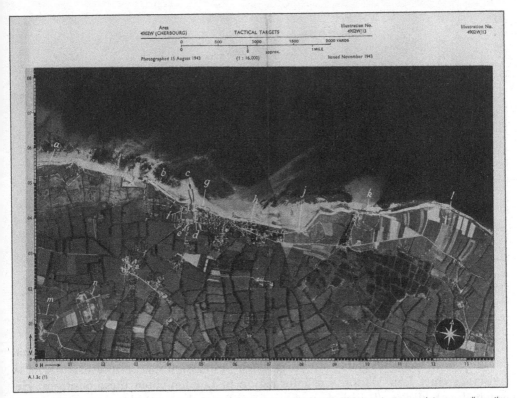

The following aerial reconnaissance photographs start to show other objectives and strongpoints as well as the Maisy Battery in the Grandcamp-les-Bains and Maisy area. They indicate defences in the Maisy port and along the coast edge, the heaviest being those positions marked 'd' and 'e' in front of the Maisy Battery at La Casino on the beachfront. These were destroyed by naval fire on the morning of D-Day.

The view from the bunker pointing towards Grandcamp harbour.

A present-day photograph of Maisy, La Casino bunker, from the opposite direction. The destruction or damage to the forward observation positions of Maisy could have caused the gunners problems with targeting, but it is likely they undertook their own observation and fire control after that.

The damage to these positions was quite intense and it is obvious that they did not continue to offer any resistance after that. Their destruction was assured after the local resistance chief Jean Marion sent information to London about these positions. He watched with glee as a British destroyer opened fire at the emplacement from its blind side on the afternoon of D-Day. He shouted, '*Give 'em hell!*'

Jean Marion continues: '*The Germans blockaded the streets and wouldn't let anyone down to the harbour – so I watched the proceedings from the top of a three-storey house … at about 11am [two men came walking down the street] in full daylight, one tall and one small – dressed in odd uniforms – armed with machine guns and grenades … They asked, 'Where is the port?'*

They were given directions and when they reached an intersection they came face to face with Kriegsmarine personnel. They stopped dead and opened fire:

Wartime photographs of these positions just after they were finished.

Before the Germans recovered they were gone back down the street. People didn't know what had happened. That evening on the square there was a trench and a bunch of Germans were walking along the street. Two machine guns opened fire – it was the same two paratroopers.

There are RAF reports of planes taking part in SAS operations to demoralise and disturb the enemy. From the description given of the paratroopers concerned it may well be that they were wearing British uniforms, which may be why they appeared to be different from American ones. Perhaps this will remain a mystery unless one of the men involved left an account of his own actions.

The area marked 'd' on the aerial photo is the forward observation and coastal defence position in front of Maisy. It was heavily shelled and bombed on the morning of 6 June, although it was not bombed at all during the run up to D-Day.

By now it was clear that the Germans were under attack.

As D-Day approached the development of the various sites was clear to see from the increasing amount of information appearing on the reconnaissance photographs. The more that was added on the ground to the area, the more was indicated on the photographs.

The following quotes are taken from RAF bombing reports.

8 November 1943:

A mine field approximately 75' wide is seen to surround this position. (? of sortie RA/873, 30 October 1943, 1/16,000, quality good)

19 January 1944:

This battery is now unoccupied; there is no sign of activity and the already reported excavation (50' x 40' approximately) on the site has not been recently worked on. (1004/5 of sortie RB/59, 14 January 1944, 1/9,500, quality good)

11 March 1944:

This battery is camouflaged and may be occupied. (3075/6 of sortie RB/380, 6 March 1944, 1/9,400, quality good)

To add to the confusion, in some reports only subtle changes appear and this does not really add anything especially useful to the overall picture. An example of this is 4 April 1944, AIR 34/157, 'Interpretation Report No. Y.264, Coastal Battery List of the Isigny area:

Four gun battery. Emplacements measuring 30' in diameter, sited to fire NW. Probable casemates are being constructed in rear of Nos. 3 and 4. Battery is camouflaged and may be occupied. A mine field approximately 70' wide surrounds the position. 700 yards in front there is an occupied dummy. (3075/6 of RB/380, 6 March 1944)

Detailed as these photographs are, many important targets have not been identified and this later caused the ground troops problems. To add to the confusion on the day, the letters used to identify various photographed positions vary.

Strongpoints, such as houses and crossroads, are identified and given target information. These details would develop into numbered target maps for the Navy and latterly for ground troops.

An aerial view of the Maisy Batteries (bottom right) showing the land all the way out to the coast at La Casino.

28 April 1944:

There are now four casemates under construction here; they are laid out in an arc facing north-west. (6068/9 of sortie 140/51, 25 April 1944, 1/14,000, quality good)

21 May 1944 (NCWTF Intelligence Bulletin No. 1, 'Supplementary Battery Summary'):

75mm guns, 13000. Casemate No. 3 complete. Nos. 2 and 4 lack only a roof as of 1 May. No. 1 in excavation stage. Guns still in temporary position at 531914 (target 16A).

27 May 1944:

Recent raids on this battery were without effect on the four gun casemates under construction. Some damage may have been caused to the light anti-aircraft guns in the vicinity, and at least 175 mines have been detonated between the two belts of perimeter wire at the rear of the battery. At least three guns of this battery are still in their temporary position at GR 531914. (5008/9 of sortie US15/75, 24 May 1944)

28 May 1944:

Casemates 3 and 4 are completed, No. 1 is almost complete and No. 2 is still surrounded with scaffolding and other constructional material. Spoil is not yet removed. (4044/5 of 106G/429, 19 May 1944, 1/12,500, quality fair)

On the earlier maps Maisy is marked as positions 'f, g and m' and yet on the map above it is marked as 'n, m and o'. This tends to indicate that the maps were all studied by different people and no one person co-ordinated the numbering or lettering of various targets.

29 May 1944, Neptune Argus 32, Appendix A:

At this four-gun light casemate battery, No. 1 casemate is almost complete, No. 2 well advanced, but still surrounded by scaffolding, and Nos. 3 and 4 are complete. Spoil has NOT been removed from the site. (4044/5 of 106G/429, 19 May 1944)

29 May 1944, WO 205/172, 'Pre D-Day bombing of batteries – Neptune area' – consolidated report on results of bombing to 28 May 1944:

No damage to casemates or guns. Guns still at 531914. All four casemates under construction at 528916.

31 May 1944, Neptune Argus 34, annex on 'Enemy artillery in the Neptune area':

Field troop. Temporarily unoccupied position for four ? 105mm (4.14") field gun howitzers. Range 13,000x. Practical rate of fire 6–8 r.p.m. Weight of shell 33lbs. Now being reconstructed as a CASEMATE battery. During the reconstruction, the guns are camouflaged in position at 531914. The original open circular emplacements have been demolished and four casemates, 35' x 40' are under construction, facing north-northwest; spaced 48x apart. No. 1 almost complete, No. 2 well advanced, Nos. 3 and 4 complete. Accommodation and storage; underground concrete shelters and magazines.

The interpretation of this photograph is correct. Although Maisy I and Maisy II had, in RAF terms, been hit, they were fully operational. It is indeed quite possible the anti-aircraft gun positioned at the bend in the Route de Perruques was damaged given the proximity to the crater. But it is unlikely any large-calibre guns were damaged.

Maisy I. The rear areas of trenches and the hospital were affected by the size and proximity of the bombs landing during this mission. Although not obvious in this photograph, the land slopes down left and right from the road running down the centre of the picture. As there were few emplacements to the left edge, it is the bombing of the right area that would have potentially caused the most damage.

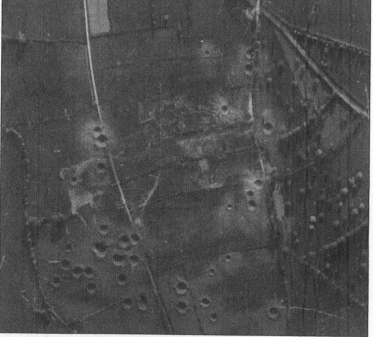

OP – unknown. Identification: ? Division field troop. Dummy at GR 527923. A mine field protects the rear of the battery. Secondary armament: two light anti-aircraft guns. Bomb damage: possible damage to anti-aircraft guns. At least 175 perimeter mines exploded. (Date of information: 24 May 1944)

Maisy II. The bomb landing in the field in front of the site with the crater, seen in the bottom left of the photograph below, right, did indeed destroy a row of mines as the intelligence operative points out. As the Rangers found out to their cost on 9 June, this field was fitted with S-mines which were linked to each other – when one went off then a series of ten or more would also go off and cover the area. Where it says 'OP – unknown' it was common practice for the Germans to use the church tower in Maisy village and the one in Grandcamp as observation posts. Additionally, the bunkers at La Casino (the beach in front of Maisy) contained an observation position.

The water tower in Maisy failed to be spotted by aerial observers on reconnaissance photos and it was manned for some time during D-Day. It is marked on targeting maps but only ones with numbers. The Germans had realised that the Allies were reluctant to destroy water towers because of the problems it would cause the local villagers. To this end the Germans then built a small concrete personnel bunker at the bottom of the water tower in Maisy village and continued observation from on top of the tower.

The Germans also had the observation position down at the beach at La Casino and on one of the GSGS maps there is a 'lattice tower' marked near the casements at La Martiniere. This could have been damaged by the bombing and because of its lightweight structure this could have rendered it unsafe.

31 May 1944, Neptune Argus 34, annex on 'Enemy artillery in the Neptune area': Maisy II(a):

Field troop. Four guns ? 105mm (4.14") field gun howitzers. Range 13,000x. Practical rate of fire 6–8 r.p.m. Weight of shell 33lbs. Centre line north-west. Staggered layout.

Maisy II. A close-up of the bombing around La Martiniere shows little damage. One large crater inside the perimeter of the site would have only caused damage to the wire at this point. There is no damage to Foucher's Farm and the guns close by at Maisy III (target 16A).

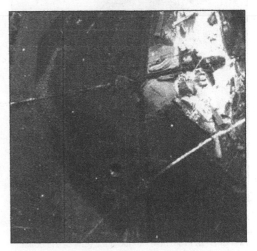

A close-up of the minefield in front of La Martiniere. The bombing exploded the mines in rows.

Now covered in graffiti, the forward observation bunker at La Casino.

The view from the Grandcamp church tower looking towards the modern-day Maisy church. The water tower is visible in the foreground.

A German soldier from the 716th Infantry Division Artillery standing guard on the church tower at Grandcamp. From here he had a full view of the coast. The balcony of the Grandcamp church provided an unrestricted view of the invasion coast.

The church as it is today – it has changed little over the last seventy years or so.

There was a French First World War 75mm field howitzer sited against the side wall of the entrance to the church. Its positioning there is a mystery, but it is most likely that it was placed in the village before the Maisy positions were developed. Once they were more established it fits with the specification at Le Perruques and could have been used as one of the anti-aircraft guns.

The same spot in the grounds of the churchyard today, unchanged except for the removal of the gun.

Looking to the right any German observer would clearly be able to see the ships and landing craft approaching the Omaha sector. From this vantage point it would not be difficult to direct the guns at Maisy onto their targets.

In the grounds of Grandcamp church today. A poignant reminder of the local cost – a plaque to a number of local French villagers killed during the invasion.

Rough open earthen emplacements 20–25' diameter; 32–35x apart, sited in an open field. Camouflaged. This is a temporary position for the battery at 528915. (Date of information: 24 May 1944)

31 May 1944, 'Summary of present situation of batteries which might affect the Neptune beaches or their approaches':

75mm guns or ? 105mm gun howitzers. Four guns in the open at 531914. Two casemates complete, two nearing completion at 528915. Presumably unoccupied.

The church has a commanding position over the town.

The water tower in Grandcamp which later became the target for naval bombardment was a German watchtower on D-Day. Its commanding position over the coast can be seen clearly here. Ironically, the monument in the foreground is in the wrong place. It commemorates the French heavy bomber groups' bombing of the Maisy batteries, not the bombing of the civilian town of Grandcamp where it is situated. It was erected at the waterfront because it was (at the time) thought that the Maisy Batteries were destroyed. A new smaller monument to these units has now been unveiled at Maisy – Les Perruques.

The Maisy water tower as it is today – nothing remains of the taller wartime tower.

Photograph taken from the spire of Grandcamp church. Looking to the west over the harbour at Grandcamp you can clearly see the sand of Utah Beach in the distance.

A photograph of La Martiniere under construction. The lattice tower is obvious in the centre of the photograph, but it is perhaps being used as a construction aid and not for observation. None of the Rangers I have interviewed remember a tower on D-Day, but it could easily have been destroyed during the initial bombardments due to its fragile nature.

As time went on these positions developed more and more. With each reconnaissance trip it was clear what had been added and a more detailed picture of the site was developing. That said, there was still no concrete evidence from intelligence or reconnaissance as to weapon sizes and therefore the Allies had a lack of accurate weapon capabilities. See the note above, '75mm guns or 105mm gun howitzers', something that could make a devastating difference on D-Day.

A 622 at La Martiniere with camouflage netting.

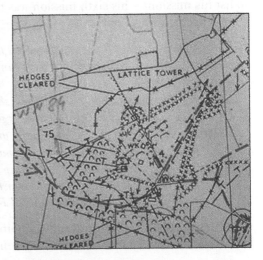

The map, bottom right (page 201) and on p. 211 show the three batteries at Maisy with their wire, machine-gun and other defences – presumably marked by a specialist intelligence officer in England. They also show the fields and direction of fire for the anti-tank guns and machine-gun positions. It is interesting to see the building that has gone into these positions was being accurately put down on paper. Some of the information provided alongside these photographs is not entirely accurate. At no point was La Martiniere 'unoccupied'. The arrival of the 3rd battery of guns on the subsequent photographs seems to have made the intelligence operatives think the guns had moved. They had not. However, at some point this idea must have changed as the rear position was given its own targeting number and the two batteries became three, targets No. 5, 16 and 16A.

There is some speculation as to the use of shelters. It states that the command post is at the rear of the site and yet in reality it is in the heart of it. The structure they indicate on the photograph is in actual fact one of the three hospitals at Maisy. It does indicate accurately the arrival of the four new guns to the rear of the complex at Foucher's Farm, but it states that they have probably come from a position at Maisy II. The plan does miss off some bunkers and buildings, but on the whole it is quite accurate.

Gerald William Ainsworth's sixteenth mission was to bomb Maisy Battery at 0330hr on 4 June 1944. The citation for his DFC records:

> This Air Bomber has taken part in 34 successful attacks on the enemy in which he has always displayed great keenness and set a fine example to his crew. His photographic plots have always been under 1,000yd on pin point targets, and he has also had excellent photographs on Schweinfurt, Aachen and Munich.
>
> His ability and devotion to duty have been exemplary on all occasions, and his experience has proved of great value to his colleagues. He is an outstanding Bomb Aimer who has set a very high standard in skill and keenness to the rest of the squadron.

William Walter Briggs F/O DFC, No. 77 Squadron won his Distinguished Flying Cross on 19 December 1944 when he had flown thirty-five sorties. His citation goes on to list his missions – his sixth mission was to bomb Maisy Battery at 0504hr on 5 June 1944. He citation also states:

> This Captain of aircraft has completed his first operational tour consisting of 35 sorties which have been carried out over a wide range of targets and performed during day and night raids.
>
> During his operational tour he has shown consistently good results and great determination in attacking his allotted target, resulting in a good photographic record being obtained and one which shows many aiming point photographs.
>
> Possessed of a likable and cheerful personality, Flying Office Briggs has set a splendid example to his crew and his fine leadership and sustained operational endeavour have contributed to a hightly successful tour which is considered worthy of recognition. He is strongly recommended for the Distinguised Flying Cross.

The Australian Air Force undertook a 'joint fire plan' for Operation Overlord which included Bomber Command attacking ten coastal batteries on the night 5/6 June.

Maisy Battery, which threatened both Utah and Omaha Beaches, was one of those batteries. No. 4 Group RAF, with 110 heavy bomber aircraft carrying 528 tonnes of bombs, commenced the attack on Maisy Battery at 0320hr on 6 June. Of the Halifax aircraft attacking Maisy Battery, twenty-eight had Australian pilots, including all thirteen Halifaxes from No. 466 Squadron Royal Australian Air Force (RAAF). Pilots reported that although there was broken cloud over the target, several near misses were scored near the casements. No losses of No. 4 Group aircraft were reported that night.

Hamilton Connolly DFC enlisted in the RAAF in September 1940. After operational training on heavy bombers in Britain, he completed his first operational tour in early 1943 in 78 Squadron RAF and was awarded the Distinguished Flying Cross for skillful flying on this tour. His citation reads:

> *On D-Day he was the Commanding Officer of 466 Squadron RAAF, which dispatched 13 Halifax bombers as part of an attack on an artillery battery at Maisy, which threatened the Utah and Omaha beaches where American troops were to land. The Squadron's aircraft experienced a number of near misses while helping to reduce heavy fires against American forces when they began landing.*

RAF records for 4/5 June 1944 state:

> *259 aircraft – 125 Lancasters, 118 Halifaxes, 16 Mosquitos of Nos 1, 4, 5, 6 and 8 Groups to bomb 4 gun positions, 3 of these were deception targets in the Pas de Calais, but the fourth battery at Maisy, was in Normandy between what would soon be known as Omaha and Utah Beaches, where American troops would land in less than 36 hours time. Unfortunately, Maisy was covered by cloud and could only be marked by Oboe skymarkers, but it was then bombed by 52 Lancasters of No. 5 Group. No aircraft were lost on these operations.*

On 5/6 June 1944 the following was recorded:

> *1,012 aircraft – 551 Lancasters, 412 Halifaxes, 49 Mosquitos – to bomb coastal batteries at Fontenay, Houlgate, La Pernelle, Longues, Maisy, Merville, Mont Fleury, Pointe du Hoc, Ouistreham and St. Martin de Varreville. 946 aircraft carried out their bombing tasks. Only two of the targets – La Pernelle and Ouistreham were free of cloud, all other bombing was entirely based on Oboe marking. At least 5,000 tons of bombs were dropped, the greatest tonnage in one night so far in the war.*

Wing Commander John Viney, DSC, DSO, commanded a Halifax Heavy Bomber on the Maisy mission.

Night Raid Report No. 624 RAF. Bomber Command. 4/5 June 1944, Calais, Maisy, Sangatte, Boulogne, Cologne:

Forces of 50–100 aircraft attacked the coastal defences at Calais, Maisy, Sangatte and Boulogne in bad weather. No aircraft lost.

Weather Forecast Bases:- Variable cloud, thickening after midnight.

Wing Commander Viney and his crew made fifty operational sorties during the Second World War.

Year		AIRCRAFT		Pilot, or 1st Pilot	2nd Pilot, Pupil or Passenger	DUTY (Including Results and Remarks)
Month	Date	Type	No.			
				—	—	— Totals Brought Forward
JUNE 1944	1.	MOSQUITO XVI	939 ML	SELF	F/L RIMMER.	N.F.T.
	1.	MOSQUITO XVI	939	SELF	F/L RIMMER.	OPERATIONS FERME D'URVILLE.
	2.	MOSQUITO XVI	ML939	SELF	F/L RIMMER.	BOMBING WHISTLESEA
	3.	MOSQUITO XVI	939	SELF	F/L RIMMER.	N.F.T.
	4.	MOSQUITO XVI	939	SELF	F/L RIMMER	N.F.T.
	4.	MOSQUITO XVI	ML 939	SELF	F/L RIMMER	OPERATIONS (M) MAISY COASTAL BATTERY
	5.	MOSQUITO XVI	ML 939	SELF.	F/L RIMMER.	N.F.T.
	6.	MOSQUITO XVI	ML 939	SELF	F/L RIMMER	OPERATIONS (M) 3T.4.R. I.T.4.B. MERVILLE COASTAL BATTERY D. DAY.

RAF logbook showing 4 June Halifax Bomber operation to Maisy.

Nose insignia on Halifax B Mark III, LV907 'NP-F "Friday the Thirteenth"', of No. 158 Squadron RAF. It was one of twenty-three aircraft from the 158 Squadron which took part in an attack on the Maisy Batteries on 5 June 1944.

Plans of Attack:
Maisy, Sangatte, Boulogne. OBOE groundmarking. On each target, 4 OBOE Mosquitoes were to drop reds and greens, and the main force were to aim at the centre of Target Indicators (T.I.) irrespective of colour. H=0110 Sangatte, 0140 Maisy, 0310 at Boulogne.
Narrative of Attacks
Only at Calais were the T.I. clearly visible. The reds fell in a tight group, with the greens scattered to the N. Most crews bombed the reds. At Maisy and Sangatte, crews bombed the glow of markers through the cloud.

Maisy

Bomb Group 5.	Sorties		Primary Area	Flak	Not attacked	Results HE Inc.
Lanc. I	24	24	1	-	206.5	0.9
Lanc. II	28	28	-	-		
Mosq. XVI	3	2	-	-	-	-
Mosq. IV	1		1	-	-	- -
MAISY TOTAL	56	55		1	-	

BOMBER COMMAND INTELLIGENCE NARRATIVE OF OPERATIONS no. 817
Covering period 1200 hrs. 4th June to 1200 hrs 5th June.

MAISY C.D.B. 52/52 Lancasters of 5 Group and 3/4 Mosquitoes of 8 (PF) Group attacked from above 10/10 cloud. Only the glow of Target Indicators could be seen. There was Heavy Flak from about 4 guns and slight fighter opposition at the coast.

Bomber Support. 5/6 Mosquitoes of 100 Group carried out patrols over the Low Countries in support of the bomber force. Enemy fighters were active. One Mosquito destroyed a Ju88 N. of Langeoog after a 15 minute chase, a short burst setting the port-engine on fire and flames approaching the fuselage. One of the crew of the Ju.88 was seen to bale out and the enemy aircraft went into a vertical dive and hit the sea in flames. Another Mosquito closed to 1000 ft on a Ju.88 when our aircraft had warning of another aircraft closing astern and had to break off.

June 1944: Op 4: Lancaster R2: F/O Bennett/Crew

Pilot's comments: Calais heavy gun batteries. Bombed through 10.10 cloud, Load 8000 lbs. Port outer started to ice-up.

Navigator's comments: Sangate: Bombed an 11" gun battery with 9000 lb of H.E. Bombed from above cloud – used radar. This was in the Cap de Gris-Nez near Calais. 3 hours 20 minutes duration.

Mid-Upper Gunner's comments: Sangatte, France – Target: coastal batteries – 11" guns. Bomb load 11– 1000 pounders. Bombed at 12000 through clouds with instruments. Engine cut-out on us but re-started. Flak was very light. Trip was 3 hrs 20 minutes. All A/C back.

Incidental: *259 aircraft – 125 Lancasters, 118 Halifaxes, 16 Mosquitos – of Nos 1, 4, 5, 6 and 8 Groups to bomb 4 gun positions; 3 of these were deception targets in the Pas de Calais, but the fourth battery, at Maisy, was in Normandy between what would soon be known as Omaha and Utah Beaches, where American troops would land in less than 36 hours' time. Unfortunately, Maisy was covered by cloud and could only be marked by Oboe skymarkers, but it was then bombed by 52 Lancasters of No. 5 Group. 2 of the 3 gun positions in the Pas de Calais were also affected by bad weather and could only be bombed through cloud but the position at Calais itself was clear and was accurately marked by the Mosquitos and well bombed by Halifaxes and Lancasters of No. 6 Group. No aircraft lost on these operations.*

One of the Pathfinder illumination bombs. Once dropped these would burn very brightly to light up a large area for the following bombers to aim at. This particular bomb casing was found at Maisy – Les Perruques during trench digging. The Pathfinder aircraft that dropped this would have followed two transmitted radio signals both sent from different locations in Britain and use their intersection point as the target. These were especially effective from within cloud cover or at night.

The British War Cabinet were given a 'Summary of Operations of Bomber Command for Four Weeks ending 18th June 1944' which states:

Results of Operations

The great bulk of operations carried out during this period were designed to assist either directly or indirectly the establishment and maintenance of our forces ashore in Normandy and the reduction and hampering of the enemy force opposed to them.

Gun Positions and Coastal Batteries in France.

Bomber Command took a highly successful part in the attack of gun positions and coastal batteries in France during the period. Very good results were obtained on Beaumont, Trouville, Eu, Le Clipon, Neufchatel and St. Vallery-en-Caux. On the eve of D-Day attacks were carried out by 1,136 aircraft on 10 coastal batteries to such good effect that, with the sole exception of the battery at Maisy, not a single battery was able to offer any serious resistance to the invading forces.

This is probably the most significant statement retrospectively relating to the Allied air force's involvement in the Maisy battle. At the War Cabinet meeting less than a month after D-Day it is stated that the only battery offering serious resistance was Maisy. Considering the battlefield at Maisy has been 'lost' and buried for sixty-two years this is quite a statement to have been ignored by other historians.

German aerial reconnaissance photographs were taken in August 1944 of the Maisy/ Grandcamp area at a time when the Germans were obviously trying to understand the details of the Allied invasion. It specifically shows the Maisy Battery. Although the photograph is not of very good quality, the extent of the devastation caused by the bombing and shelling from the Allied ships and planes is obvious. The white areas are land that has been turned upside down by shelling, revealing the lighter soil colour underneath. In the area marked A are the gun positions at La Martiniere, Target Number 16. Area B shows the gun positions at Foucher's Farm, Target Number 16A. Position C shows the gun positions at Les Perruques, Target Number 5.

The 3 x 88mm AA guns at the Destores' family farm are at the area marked E and the three in the lane (D) are shown as heavily shelled. The guns at Mr Montagne's farm were also shelled, but they are just beyond the scope of this photograph at the top of the picture. The shell and bomb holes visible are those made by large weapons. The smaller but equally deadly weapons fired or dropped on Maisy would not be visible on a photograph taken at this altitude.

Royal Canadian Air Force planes flying from RAF Pocklington, 5–6 June reported in their A Squadron Record: 'Maisy: Heavy Coastal Battery. 26 aircraft. All attacked the target through 3/10 cloud at 5000 ft. No night fighters but some light flak.'

A town report that was written in the post-war years looking into war reparations said it estimated that a bomb or shell landed at the ratio of one per every square foot in the village of Maisy during the period 6–9 June 1944. The village certainly suffered as a result of the batteries having been placed there some years before.

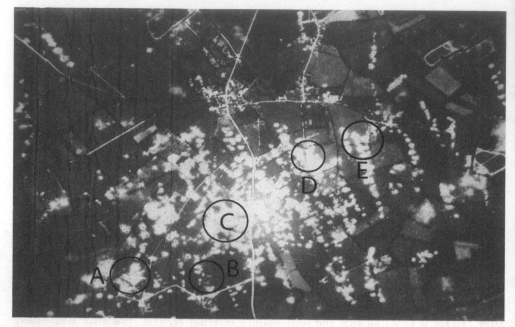

A German reconnaissance photograph taken in August 1944.

A B-26 of the 391st US Bomb Group bombed Maisy at 0625hr on 6 June; it was their eighty-fourth mission. Their group's official history reads:

> *The bombing of coastal defenses in northern France occupied the first five days of June 1944. On the morning of D-Day (6 June), the Group struck at coastal defenses commanding the beaches on which Allied Ground Forces were landing. At that time more than fifty aircraft were dispatched in a three-fold mission, striking simultaneously on Benerville, St. Pierre du Mont and Maisy, France.*

17 aircraft were dispatched, all dropping 31 x 2000 and 2 x 1000 GP on the primary target. Fifteen aircraft sustained flak battle damage, one crew member wounded. There were no losses.

One enemy aircraft is reported destroyed by a PPF ship when it was attacked by 20 FW190s in the clear – as the rest of the formation was making a second run on the target.

Box II –

1st 3. GOOD. Concentration fell in the target area about 500 feet SE of the desired M.P.I.

2nd 6. POOR. Bombs fell about 1200 feet SW of the desired M.P.I., across a road and open field.

3rd 6. GOOD. Bursts occurred about 500 feet NE of the desired M.P.I., having been released on the first flight...

S/Sgt George E Cochran, 36441881, of Decatur, Illinois, flying as waist gunner on the first raid of D-Day and he destroyed his second enemy fighter, a FW 190. His plane was a Pathfinder ship leading the formation, but it swung away from the other planes as the target area was reached because of the weather conditions. While the Pathfinder was on its way, alone, to join another formation in the area, a German fighter attacked, and Cochran picked him off at a range of approximately 200 yards.

Overleaf is part of a GSGS intelligence map, marked 'May 44' on the top. It shows the upgrading of the site and the increased intelligence information gathered in the area. The four guns have been added to the rear of the site at 16A and the chateau of the Destores family in the village has troop concentrations (TPS). It shows the water tower of Maisy village and its bunker as a box with barbed wire around it – an area that also contained 3 x 88mm AA guns. A note has been made to delete the dummy emplacements in front of Les Perruques. The AA guns in the village are now noted, although they have moved from the Montagne and Maudelande farms to a new position near the German office in Maisy village. The details of the weapons on the Grandcamp seafront have also been included with calibres, and more information has been given for the positions on the outskirts of Grandcamp itself.

The Germans were upgrading the area and the mine-field map (on p. 211) of the sector for D-Day shows various WN positions (strongpoints) as single blobs. The batteries at Maisy are clearly distinguished by the surrounding stretches of black. These

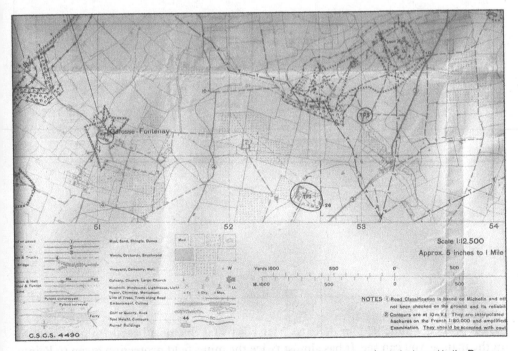

Above and overleaf: Two BIGOT (Top Secret) D-Day issue maps. These maps were going to be issued to the Rangers, but never were. The first of the two maps shows plainly that the position at 16A is not used, but it is clearly marked in on the second one (on p. 211). Again, this is evidence of the continual acquisition and interpretation of new information right up to D-Day.

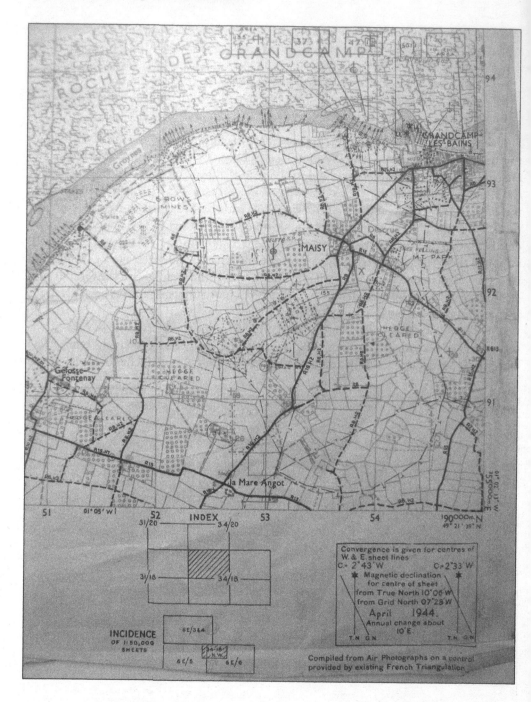

each represent a minefield for defence. Maisy is by far the most heavily mined position on the map, as you can see. It has almost twice the mine-field protection given to Pointe du Hoc and far more than was given to all other areas in this sector. It is worth noting that the Germans have placed minefields all the way along the coast in front of Maisy,

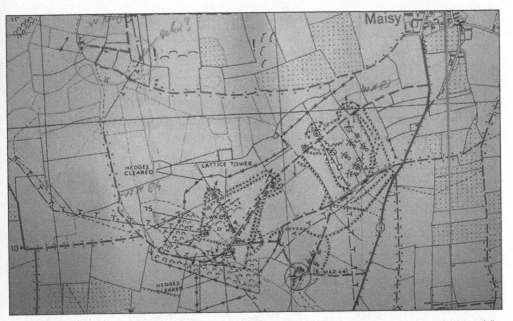

The third set of guns are clearly marked, dated 6 March 1944 the level of detail on the map has increased substantially.

shown by the continual black line. But along the beach areas of Omaha sector the mine-field coverage is patchy. This may reflect the fact that the mine fields were still being laid. Or that the mine fields in more important areas were strengthened and in others they were purely marked 'achtung minen' without actually having been laid.

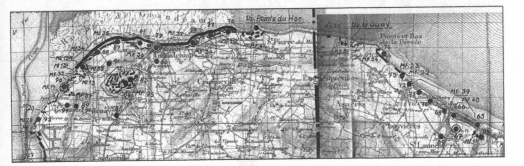

As soon as the destination of the landings was known – albeit to a select few, a number of secret missions to photograph and record the coast of Normandy began. Military intelligence studied the Omaha Beach coastline and concluded the following from photo interpretation:

The approximate total number of actual beach defence weapons on the beach are:

For Omaha Beach – length 7,500 yards.
8   Casemates occupied by 75mm or better.
35   Pillboxes occupied by guns smaller than 75mm.

4   *Open field positions 75mm or better.*
18   *Anti-tank – 37mm to 75mm.*
85   *Positions less than 37mm (MG).*
6   *Mortars (Infantry).*
38   *Rocket pits bearing on the beach. 4 x 32cm rockets per pit.*

The following series of photographs was taken of the approaches to Grandcamp and Maisy from the sea via a submarine in February 1944.

The elevation of the Maisy church made it an ideal observation point for the German artillery spotters. It had a great position as the overall landscape was much flatter and sloped quickly to the sea.

Maisy church, with its modern spire, almost invisible against the landscape today is marked here.

An interesting close-up. The water tower clearly stands above the town and almost beneath it marked SP (strongpoint) is grid reference 545933 – the Degusclin Hotel. This photograph was taken covertly by submarine.

Admiralty Chart 2073 stated the following:

The village of Grandcamp was completed in 1926 and is a small refuge port for fishing craft lying NE of Baie du Grand Vey. The port consists of an entrance channel protected by two diverging reinforced concrete jetties and a rectangular drying basin. Both channel and basin dry out at 8 to 10 ft. The eastern, western and southern sections of the basin are suitable for berthing. It is doubtful whether ships drawing more than 10 feet or more than 40 of beam can enter the port.

On 21 April 1944 a report reads:

Dumps and parks. There is no suitable area in the immediate vicinity of the harbour, or among the buildings of the village. To the south, there are pasture fields and small orchards where trucks might disperse and find cover.

The entrance to the channel is controlled by a double boom which, in turn, is covered by a light gun at the end of the eastern mole.

Port defences: 549933. Infantry position on coast in built-up area of town. 1 pillbox.

545932. Infantry position in built-up area of town. 2 pillboxes. 1 light gun at the end of eastern mole. 3 guns probably field-type report on coast in this area.

544932–543932. Wall approximately 6 feet thick and 6 feet high along south side of harbour.

543932–542932. Element 'C' continue line of wall above from west side of road. (Appears to follow outline of harbour). Possibly some hedgehogs.

543394. Further stretch of Elements 'C' running south from west mole.

543933. Road leading from quayside blocked, probably by knife-rests.

Neptune papers state:

Observation post: unknown, presumably on the coast west of Grandcamp. Communications: buried cable, presumably also radio. Secondary armaments: one (or two) 20mm AA guns.

The beaches in front of the Maisy Batteries. A landing here would have been considerably easier than the one at Omaha Beach. As one veteran said it would have been a 'cake walk by comparison'.

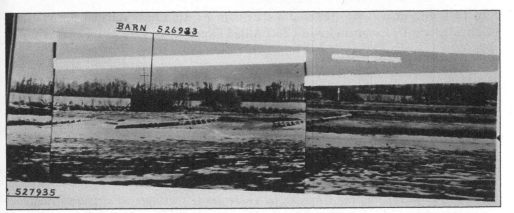

In this photograph the breakwaters are clearly seen sticking out onto the beach in front of the Maisy – La Casino positions. This area contained a number of small bunkers with machine guns and the artillery observation post.

On 1 May 1943 the Allied Inter-Service Topographical Department produced a 'Special report on the coast between Pointe et Raz de la Percée to Pointe du Hoc'. This was done as a covert operation from a submarine – it was basically a blueprint for what could and could not be possible for an assault on Pointe du Hoc.

> *Coast and beach … The coast between these two points consists of precipitous chalk cliffs from 80 to 100ft high. There are thin layers of flint in the cliff face, but these do not provide a handhold as they are likely to break away if any weight is placed on them. Similarly the nature of the chalk does not favour the use of climbing irons or steel spikes and these cliffs are unscalable over the length under report, except at the semaphore station, 1600 yards west of Pointe de la Percée, where the cliff has fallen and is accessible to specially trained and lightly equipped men. The beach is composed of drying rocky ledges with scattered boulders fallen from the cliffs.*

> *The beach is 5,500 yards long and about 50 yards wide.*

> *The beach is only suitable for small boats in calm weather. With these limitations a landing can be affected at any state of the tide. At low water the going over the beach will be rough and laborious. At high water springs the sea washes the foot of the cliffs.*

The evaluation highlights the two aspects of an assault on the cliffs that were thought to be significant: 'These cliffs are unscalable' and 'The beach is only suitable for small boats in calm weather'. However, neither point seems to have been taken into account. Obviously the Rangers landed in high swells and did indeed attempt to climb a cliff which was thought to be near impossible. If nothing else, it shows at what point the decision makers would ignore the inteligence reports in order to get the job done. As D-Day approached the Allies were clearly aware of the existence of the gun positions at Maisy – but what did they do about it? The RAF, USAF, AAF, RCAF all undertook bombing missions on Maisy. However, all but a couple of these missions took place after D-Day had actually begun! The site was not given the level of treatment that Pointe du Hoc had been subjected to for so many months.

In 1946 the Air Ministry released a statement by Air Chief Marshal Sir Trafford Leigh-Mallory, Air Commander-in-Chief Allied Expeditionary Air Force (AEAF):

Objects of Preparatory Bombing.

Preparatory bombing plans included attacks on coastal batteries, enemy naval and military targets and the Radar chain. It was necessary to remember when making these plans that the enemy should not be given any indication of the area selected for the assault. The principal effect of this on the preparatory air operations was that at least two attacks were made on each type of target outside of the projected assault area to one attack on a target within that area.

Estimation of German Air Force (G.A.F.) Capabilities.

I was confident that the German Air Force would constitute no serious threat to our operations on land, sea or in the air. However, I could not dismiss the possibility that the enemy was conserving his air forces for a maximum effort against the Allied assault forces. A bombing plan was therefore prepared which aimed at driving the G.A.F. fighters on to bases as far from the battle as were the Allied fighter forces, by destroying its bases within 130 miles radius of the assault area. Enemy bomber bases even further inland were also scheduled for attack.

Operations during the Assault

1. *To protect the cross-Channel movement of the assault forces against enemy air attack, and to assist the Allied naval forces to protect the assault craft and shipping from enemy naval forces.*
2. *To prepare the way for the assault by neutralising the coast and beach defences.*
3. *To protect the landing beaches and the shipping concentrations from enemy air attack.*
4. *To dislocate enemy communications and control during the assault.*

It was vital that the Allies obtained air superiority over the landing zones. German airfields were targeted heavily prior to and during D-Day to disrupt, and where possible, deny the Germans the possibility of an operational air defence. In reality, the Germans were somewhat taken aback by the scale of the D-Day operations and could not physically muster significant aircraft for some period of time. Many German squadrons had been sent to other locations well outside the operational range of the beaches and that was due in part to success of the deception programme designed to convince the German high command that the intended Allied invasion would be Calais. At 1 April 1944 the number of operationally available aircraft was as follows:

Type	Ninth Air Force	Royal Air Force
Medium Bombers	496	70
Light Bombers	96	38
Fighter and Fighter Bombers	607	1,764
Transport Aircraft	865	225
Gliders	782	351
Reconnaissance Aircraft	63	156
Artillery Observation Aircraft	—	164
	2,909	2,768

As the run up to D-Day gathered momentum the scale of Allied air operations increased significantly, reaching a peak in the last ten days. The operations were predominantly carried out by fighter bombers and medium bombers of the 9th Air Force, the US 8th Air Force and the Royal Air Force Second Tactical Air Force. As the infrastructure of the surrounding area was destroyed this would undoubtedly have had a knock-on effect on all aspects of the coastal defence. Bridges, canals, railway lines and all other types of communication were targeted.

Mr André Jacques was employed by the Germans to deliver ammunition to coastal batteries and gives the following account:

I had been sent by the Germans to Caen Railway station to collect ammunition with a horse and cart. The journey there was uneventful and the large calibre ammunition was collected and I completed a delivery to Longues-sur-Mer.

However, when I reached my final destination – the batteries at Maisy, the site came under heavy aerial attack from fighter bombers. The planes were attacking anything that moved on the road, so I had to seek shelter for my horse – the problem was that my wagon was half full of ammunition and would not move quickly ... I ended up tying the horse up beneath a tree and then running into a ditch a long way away. Luckily the planes did not see the wagon or it would have been destroyed and me along with it. I did not deliver the ammunition for some time because I could still hear the planes in the distance.

The ammunition wagon would have been a target of opportunity for the fighters, but it shows how the mere existence of ground-attack planes in the area was enough to stop the delivery of ammunition to coastal positions.

On D-Day twelve railway bridges and twelve road bridges were rendered impassable and this infrastructure decay would only get worse for the Germans. There were forty-nine coastal batteries capable of firing on the ships approaching the landing areas. This included the batteries under construction and the report goes on to say, 'it would clearly be impossible for the naval forces successfully to engage all the coastal batteries. They, therefore, had to be dealt with before the landing and the air forces undertook this task at the request of the Naval and Army Commanders.' The report doubts that bombing of completed, heavily fortified casemented batteries would be effective, but as the account above shows the presence of Allied aeroplanes did have logistical effects on the German preparations. Where direct hits were scored then the problems were increased. During the pre-D-Day preparation bombings it was also important not to give the German high command any sense of where the invasion was actually going to take place. To this end the air force continued throughout to attack batteries well beyond the assault area as far north as Ostend.

In a large number of cases the air force did actually neutralise or reduce the capabilities of the batteries. However, at Maisy and others such as Longues-sur-Mer and Crisbecq the casements, open emplacements and underground blockhouses prevented too much damage. At Maisy the site was operational again after a very short period of time when earth and rubble was cleared from the guns.

On the night of 5 June a series of countermeasures were also put into action which included a naval and air diversion against Cap d'Antifer, the same against Boulogne, a radio–jamming mission to cover the airborne landings, VHF radio jamming and air drops of paratrooper dummies, and there is no doubt at all that these countermeasures were effective. Across the Cotentin peninsula the German Army did not have a clear view of what was happening until its troops engaged the enemy – either by airborne troops landing in French villages or landing near key positions like the Orne River bridge. In some cases 'intelligence' was literally from a radio report from front-line soldiers of landing craft touching down on the beach, or by visual confirmation that troops were approaching the shore in boats. The element of surprise was almost total in some areas.

This lack of firm intelligence in advance effectively blinded the German high command. Their communications were so disrupted it is more than likely that decisions that would have made a vital tactical difference on the beaches were deferred due to lack of concrete information. Had, for example, tank units been sent to the front immediately the outcome in some sectors would have been significantly different. As it was, the 'wait and see' mentality – coupled with a lack of urgency in the Fürher's headquarters, all added to the problems encountered by the German troops on the ground.

This was no more evident than in the German radio reports which show a lack of detailed information reaching the command centres. Often a complete lack of communication with their forward positions was taken as a sign of communication and infrastructure failure, when in reality it was a sign that the position had been captured or destroyed.

A further extract from the statement written by **Air Chief Marshal Sir Trafford Leigh-Mallory**, Air Commander-in-Chief Allied Expeditionary Air Force (AEAF):

In the period 1st May to 5th June, 1944, the following effort was made on these targets. Sorties R.P.s. Fired Bombs dropped 423 282 x 60-lb. 152 tons 1,139 — 5,218 tons Force A.E.A.F R.A.F. Bomber Command ... 1,562 282 x 60-lb. 5,370 tons – great damage done to the enemy supply dumps, and the attacks must also have had considerable morale effect on enemy personnel in addition to the actual casualties inflicted.

RAF Flight Engineer Selwyn Morris 1861960 took part in the raids of 5 June. His log book calmly reads:

	Aircraft Type	Pilot	Duty	Time
5/6/44	Halifax 'G'.	Flying Officer Taylor.	Engineer	04.45

Remarks: *Operations to Gun Battery – Maisy, France.*

It is difficult to imagine that the average German soldier did not think that D-Day was coming, given the growing number of Allied planes over their positions. Although many captured Germans were glad to be out of the war, many others still gave a good account of themselves. German infantryman Franz Gockel is a good example of this at his WN (Wilderstand Nest) 62 position overlooking Omaha Beach. Despite a severe and continual bombardment of their position from H-hour, he and his surviving comrades from the 352nd Infantry Division continued to fire their machine guns and rifles into the waves of oncoming Americans. It is reported that they fired over 12,000 machine-gun and over 400 single-shot rifle rounds into the advancing troops. They accounted

Morris's log book showing his Flight Engineer's entry for 5 June 1944.

for many American lives and yet they must have known time was running out. Despite watching troops landing all around them and seeing these same forces moving inland, they continued to defend their position until it ultimately became impractical.

Air Chief Marshal Sir Trafford Leigh-Mallory continues:

Fifteen squadrons of fighters were allotted the task of protecting the shipping lanes. These squadrons flew 2,015 sorties during the course of D–Day and D + 1, the cover being maintained at six squadron strength [on] Coastal Batteries Crisbecq St. Martin de Varreville, Ouistreham, Maisy, Mont Fleury, La Parnelle, St. Pierre du Mont, Merville/Franceville ... Houlgate and Longues.

It is interesting to note that Pointe du Hoc was target number one in the invasion plans, but it is omitted from this list of important targets. Did the RAF not consider Pointe du Hoc worthy of continued attack, or was it the fact that Allied ground troops (Rangers) had possession of part of the site and there was a risk of friendly casualties? If that was the case, then why were the RAF still bombing Merville which was assaulted by the British Airborne and itself potentially in Allied hands?

As the aircraft of the RAF left the invasion area the US Eighth Air Force heavy bombers took over the bombardment role:

In the thirty minutes immediately preceding the touch-down hour, 1,365 heavy bombers attacked selected areas in the coastal defences, dropping 2,796 tons of bombs.

The result of these operations added to the previous air bombardment and combined with the naval shelling, neutralised wholly or in large part almost all of the shore batteries and the opposition to the landings was very much less than was expected.

In all, the Eighth Air Force flew 2,627 heavy bombers and 1,347 escort and offensive fighter sorties during the day.

In order effectively to destroy the heavy coastal batteries Bomber Command stated that the following tonnage of bombs were dropped:

Sorties	101	100	116	116	124	131	124	109	116	99 = 1,136
Tons of Bombs	598	613	645	592	585	668	698	382	468	604 = 5,853

It is unfortunate that at this point the report does not give sortie numbers which relate to Army/Navy Nepture target numbers. The report continues: 'The result was that on D-Day and subsequently, we were just able to meet the heavy calls for spotting for naval gunfire that were made on us.'

The spotter planes where possible consisted of two planes, one spotter and one escort and standby spotter, both on the same frequency 'over target area'. Each spotter plane was to remain over the area for 45 minutes and was briefed to spot on two targets per sortie. Initially, targets were pre-arranged, but as time went on aircraft spotters inevitably found targets of opportunity. In some cases more planes were used. Thus each ship had aerial reconnaissance at all times. On D-Day 394 sorties were flown and during 6–8 June a total of 1,318 sorties for the purposes of naval gunnery spotting were flown. This task was a dangerous one and not without a cost. A total of five Allied planes were destroyed undertaking these operations. From the information provided by German officer Colonel Kistowski it is clear that his anti-aircraft battalion at Maisy was responsible for some of these, although Allied intelligence did not record this unit being operational in the Maisy area beforehand.

In an Allied intelligence report, 'Flak Density in the "Overlord" Area', produced pre-D-Day, all anti-aircraft positions along the coast are listed:

Between Port en Bessin and Pointe et Raz de la Percée there are 5 AA/MGs, while about half a mile to the West of this point there are 3 light guns defending the RDF station. At Pointe du Hoc there are 3 light guns and a further 3 half a mile to the S.W. of Maisy. 2 AA/MGs are located on the coast at Grandcamp Les Bains.

There is no mention of the heavier anti-aircraft guns in Maisy village commanded to Kapusta and no mention of Kistowski's unit being in the area.

A chateau known to house German corps and division headquarters was heavily bombed and German Army telephone exchanges attacked on the evening of 5 June. These attacks continued into D-Day and beyond with bombs and rockets being used against these targets inland to further reduce the German command and control system.

346 Squadron and 347 Squadron were the only French Air Force heavy bomber squadrons of the Allied air force during the Second World War. They were based at RAF Elvington, York from June 1944 until October 1945 and on 16 May 1944, No. 346 'Guyenne' Squadron RAF was officially formed at Elvington, followed by No. 347 'Tunisie' Squadron RAF on 20 June 1944.

'Guyenne' was pronounced operational on 1 June 1944, and attacked the Maisy positions during the night of 5 June, prior to the D-Day invasion. **Jean Carmel**, then a captain with the unit, wrote the following account of the Maisy attack in his book *Night Pilot*.

Veterans at the Groupes Lourds memorial in Grandcamp. They are joined by family members, the author and Ian Reed from Elvington Air Museum. This impressive memorial to two French squadrons ('Guyenne' and 'Tunisie') of RAF Bomber Command stands near Grandcamp harbour's north-east corner. It was dedicated in 1988. These two French heavy bomber units participated in the D-Day bombing of the nearby Maisy gun battery.

A Groupes Lourds French heavy bomber squadron 346 log book showing (in the centre) 5 June 'bombardament MAISY'.

5th Elvington Air Base, York … That evening at Elvington base no one knew for certain of this operation – at least among the crews. Admittedly, at the general briefing the particular precautions which were taken for our flight over England rather surprised us. The intelligence officer had warned us that 50 square miles of the coast would be fringed with searchlights rising vertically half a mile apart. We were absolutely forbidden to enter this square.

As we learnt later this was the zone from which aircraft and gliders carrying parachutists took off. Moreover, the target that night was a special one. We were given orders to bombard a heavy German battery installed at the base of the Cotentin Peninsula.

One hundred and fifty bombers were specially detailed for this raid. The disparity between the means and the apparent end were

The Groupes Lourds memorial at Maisy Battery.

obvious. We easily understood the next day when we learnt that this battery, silenced by our mass raid, had allowed the fleet to sail close in to the shore.

The flight went without incident. England was covered with medium cloud which hid the searchlights. The markers were clearly spotted despite a light mist which made them less bright than usual. Brion took off in B for Baker. He had a full bombload because

Members of the French Groupes Lourds at their barracks in England.

the target was so near home. In actual fact we never had the pleasure of having an easy take-off with a lightly loaded aircraft. If the target was near then it was a full bomb-load, if it was a long way away it was a full load of petrol.

For the Frenchmen it was finally an opportunity to attack the Germans on French soil. This was something that up to this point had been avoided in case the Germans used it for propaganda purposes. Their bombing undoubtedly created mayhem on the ground and would have assisted the Allied approach to the beaches. For the Frenchmen it was the moment they had waited for – D-Day and the start of the liberation of France.

The headquarters at Maisy remained operational throughout the initial invasion and Allied push inland. It is interesting that RAF official reports make no reference to

Dated 17/7/1944, a certificate recognising the men of the Groupes Lourds with the French Military Medal with Bronze Star. Listing them by name and 'in particular they carried out on the night of the 6th of June 1944 a remarkably precise bombardment on an objective of great tactical importance'.

Maisy resisting the invasion at the time, but they talk up the operational successes of the Allied air force against German headquarters.

The pre-invasion activities of the RAF were not limited to just a ground-attack role. A limited number of SAS troops were dropped in selected areas before and after D-Day for special missions by aircraft of No. 38 Group 221. The airlift of all these forces was provided by the transport aircraft of AEAF and their missions were often ones of simple disruption of German supply routes and designed to draw vital German resources, such as men and vehicles, away from the invasion areas. One operation took place at Isigny sur Mer, 4 miles from Maisy. At 0255hr, German radio traffic reported: '*Apparently near Isigny landing of seventy paratroopers. Confirmation not yet on hand.*' It is likely this was a group of paratrooper dummies sent to distract the Germans in Isigny into thinking a large force was in their area.

Other ground troops tried to assist the bombers by marking targets with smoke signals where possible. This could be done by coloured smoke grenades when close to a target or by mortar and artillery fire using smoke from a greater distance. Once called in the position would normally be located and destroyed by the fighters. If the target was of significant size, often the Navy would be requested to shell the position until it was neutralised.

The use of mobile radar stations to locate low-flying German aeroplanes was also introduced once a foothold had been gained and a number of these British units were attached to the Americans in the Omaha sector.

A continuous fighting presence was maintained utilising nine squadrons over the whole of the assault area with Thunderbolt squadrons operating inland. Four squadrons of Lightnings patrolled the beaches and shipping lanes during daylight hours. During the D-Day planning it had been agreed that no anti-aircraft gunners were to fire at any aircraft unless they were given the green light by a qualified observer. To this end Royal Observer Corps personnel were provided on a number of vessels.

At 1500hr on 6 June enemy fighters and bombers appeared over the beachhead. By this time the assault had been underway for nearly 9 hours on land and some 15 hours if you include airborne transportation and air-bombardment groups. The Germans sent FW190 fighters and one group of twelve Ju88 bombers. This air activity increased by 7 June and approximately eighty-five German aircraft were active over the beachhead.

The truck used by British soldier Frank Needham with the specially adapted radar and communications system.

Air Chief Marshal Sir Trafford Leigh-Mallory continues:

The drawing up of the fire plan for the assault phase was rightly regarded as an inter-service and inter-Allied responsibility. There is a tendency on the part of the other Services to expect too much of the air forces from the point of view of the destruction of prepared gun emplacements, especially when completely concreted; their neutralisation for a critical and limited time is, of course, another matter.

This is no doubt true. The cessation of firing from a coastal artillery battery for only a few minutes would allow much-needed men and equipment to be landed safety. This will have aided the landings enormously at H-hour and beyond, when the battery firepower would have been at its most effective.

The demoralisation of the gun crews through the psychological reaction to bombing contributes as much towards the neutralisation of gun defences as damage by actual hits or shock effects does. Many of the guns crews left their positions during heavy attacks and often were more 'reluctant' to return to them. In a number of cases SS officers were on hand to 'assist' the gun crews back into their positions after a particularly bad attack.

The Fleet Air Arm was not given the full responsibility for spotting the fall of naval

This jacket is is marked on the shoulder with the title 'SEABORNE'. This was a designation given to a small number of Royal Observer Corps personnel who were permitted to sail on invasion craft. It was their task to ensure that any aircraft fired upon was in fact a German and not an Allied plane.

shells, rather this task was undertaken by the RAF fighter reconnaissance squadrons. The pilots of these squadrons were specially trained in naval procedure and had to be able to relay accurately the fall of shells to the ship, correct for effect and evaluate the damage, while maintaining an ever vigilant eye on their surroundings. As it turned out no German fighters were around to cause problems, however, had they been in the air it would have made sensible naval aerial reconnaissance virtually impossible while under potential attack.

The following passage illustrates the type of thinking being employed in the services on D-Day. Most of the Rangers landing on the beaches speak of there being a lack of suitable bomb craters to use as cover. However, it would appear that some air-force units did indeed bomb inland to reduce the risk of hitting their own men on the ground.

Air Chief Marshal Sir Trafford Leigh-Mallory continues:

Army Commanders in some instances insisted on the bomb line being pushed too far ahead of the line of our forward troops. This often proved a handicap to the effective use of tactical support aircraft. The land forces should accept a bomb line as close as possible to our front line, and be prepared to run some small risk of casualties in order to enable the air to give them the maximum close support.

The idea was that the units on the ground would have liaison officers with them who would work with the bombers, giving them targeting information and relaying results back to them. They came under the general heading of Combined Operations and would in theory work with the air force and remain with the ground troops to ensure their safety.

A classic example of this happened shortly after D-Day when the US General Lesley McNair was killed on the outskirts of St Lo. He had gone ahead and literally entered the target area during the bombardment. There is some speculation as to the accuracy of the bombing on that day and that it was perhaps 'off target' bombing that killed him, but either way he lost his life at the hands of his own planes on 25 July 1944 while in a foxhole. The heavy and medium bombers began attacking the coastal batteries, but were wholly unsuccessful in destroying the guns placed under thick concrete. An RAF report notes:

> *Thus, although the pre D-Day attacks on coastal batteries were unsuccessful in destroying, they not only stopped constructional work in 'half finished batteries', but also caused sufficient general damage to reduce critically by D-Day the efficiency of those which had been completed. In fact, opposition offered by the coastal defences was relatively slight that there was virtually little opportunity for the employment of the fighter bomber against enemy forces in the landing areas.*

This is said with an air of arrogance when certainly in the case of Maisy Battery the site put up a sterling resistance both directed towards the aircraft and gliders coming in from the Utah sector, but also in directing fire towards the shipping lanes and landing beaches of Omaha. The report continues:

> *From H-30 to H-5 minutes heavy bombers of the Eighth Air Force would strike enemy beach defenses in the assault area between the Vire and the Orne. In the V Corps' zone 480 B-24s were to attack 13 target areas with 1,285 tons of bombs. Of these targets, 11 were between Pointe et Raz de la Percée and the eastern end of the Omaha landing one, including every strongpoint in the system of beach defenses. The loading consisted for the most part of 100-pound fragmentation and high-explosive bombs, with some 500-pound high-explosive bombs for certain strongpoints. **All loads were fitted with instantaneous fuzes in order to prevent cratering of the beach and consequent delay in movement of traffic across it.** West of Omaha, the battery positions at Pointe du Hoc would receive a final attack by 18 medium bombers of the Ninth Air Force, delivered between H-20 and H-5 minutes. In the same period, mediums would deliver a blow of equal weight at Maisy, and the gun positions there and at Gefosse Fontenay were the targets of two squadrons of fighter-bombers.*

The significance of the paragraph highlighted in bold is obvious. Contrary to the opinion of virtually ALL the troops on the ground and every historian to date, the bombing of the beaches may well have taken place, but not for the reasons they assume. All the Rangers I have interviewed have commented on the lack of craters for shelter on the beach. It would appear from the statement above that the RAF was using specially selected ordnance to do completely the opposite. Was this simply a mistake in expectation between the two sections of the Allied troops – the army were expecting craters and the air force were trying to destroy wire and emplacements and not make craters? It's an interesting thought, and another alternative is that perhaps the two parties never actually discussed it.

There is a thought-provoking evaluation in the American Forces in Action Series Historical Division of the War Department entitled 'Omaha Beachhead (6 June–13 June 1944)':

The Omaha sector was not strongly defended by coastal batteries of heavier guns. But at Pointe du Hoe, some 5,000 yards to the west, there was a battery believed to consist of six 155-mm howitzers (French make), mounted partly in casemates. This position was regarded as the most dangerous in the American one, for guns of that caliber could cover not only the V and VII Corps landing beaches but also both transport areas. Further west, at Maisy, was a battery <u>estimated</u> at four 155-mm howitzers and near Gefosse-Fontenay were four 105-mm field gun-howitzers. Both of these batteries were later found to consist of mobile field guns.

It is of interest that even with the hindsight of D-Day phrases like 'believed to consist of six 155mm howitzers, mounted partly in casements' are used, as it is known that there were only two gun casements at Pointe du Hoc which were unfinished on D-Day. Also, if the 155mm 'howitzers' (in reality the guns originally at Pointe du Hoc were 155mm cannons) were 'the most dangerous', then the ones at Maisy were equally as dangerous. The assumption that 'the Omaha Sector was not strongly defended by coast batteries of heavier guns' was inaccurate as the fields of fire for the sector were continuous – as they were everywhere else along the coast, even without the battery at Pointe du Hoc being operational. It is also worth noting that the casements being built were too small to house a 155mm weapon.

A different view of Allied intelligence thinking is seen in the following extract taken from Ninth Air Force Operation Orders, dated 15 May 1944.

Prearranged missions. General priority for the first support program is given to the neutralization or destruction of batteries which might interfere with the approach of the Naval Forces. Batteries covering the sea approaches and the beaches are regarded as primary targets for the heavy night and medium Oboe bombers, while beach defences should normally be dealt with by daylight heavy and medium bombers.

Because of the prohibitive effort required to achieve destruction, the restricted number of AP bombs available, and the need, for security reasons, to include two batteries outside the Neptune area for each one within it, the number of targets to be engaged prior to D-Day has had to be restricted. With the exception of the batteries indicated below, which are specifically selected for neutralization in the assault phase attacks on batteries will be confirmed to those in open emplacement or under construction, with a view to harassing rather than destructive effect.

Pre-D-Day bombing targets have been assigned in the Western Task Force Area as follows:-

Pointe du Hoc   586937
Crisbecq   368044

All main enemy defences in the Omaha sector were on the beach or just behind it; there was no evidence that the Germans had prepared positions inland for a defence in depth. There were known to be a few mine fields in the fields just south of the bluffs, and some scattered emplacements at bivouac areas and assembly points. Defence beyond the beach would depend largely on the use of local reserves in counterattack.

B-26 Marauder Operations on 6 June 1944

Unit	Target	Take Off Time	Bomb Release Time
391st Bomb Group	Maisy	0445hr	0625hr

The bombing of coastal defences in northern France occupied the first five days of June 1944. On the morning of D-Day (6 June), the Group struck at coastal defenses commanding the beaches on which Allied ground forces were landing. At that time more than fifty aircraft were dispatched in a three-fold mission, striking simultaneously on Benerville, St Pierre du Mont and Maisy, France.

B-26 Marauder, 42-95902. 497BS, 344BG. MACR 5656. Shot down by AA fire on D-Day after attacking shore batteries.

1942095902, 42-95902 Martin B-26B-50-MA Marauder Fate: Shot down Unit: 344BG497BS

Remarks: 344BG497BS Silver Streaks Code: 7I-G named: The Bad Penny shot down by AAA Jun 6, 1944. MACR-5656. The Bad Penny was on its first mission of the day for the 344BG on D-Day, 6th June 1944, flying in the third box of the formation. The target was the coastal batteries at the Cherbourg Peninsula in France. The Bad Penny was hit by flak in the right engine and exploded into flames.

B-26 Marauder, 41-31961. 455BS, 323BG. MACR 5527. Shot down by AA fire on a mission to Caen, Normandy on D-Day.

Chapter 9

The Rangers' Advance on Maisy

From 8 June the next Ranger objective was the sluice-gates bridge near German position WN 76.

John Raaen:

When Pte de Hoc was cleared, the four companies with Schneider took a little time to reorganise. One platoon of A and one of F were already at the Pointe. These platoons had to be merged back into their companies. Because of losses, this was not a simple thing. After the re-organisation, Schneider sent D Company to reinforce B and E Companies. He then sent Sullivan with three companies to accompany Lieutenant Colonel Metcalf and the 1st Battalion, 116th Infantry, which was now the rear guard of the 116th task force. I do not know whether Schneider remained at Pointe du Hoc with Rudder or moved up to where B, D and E Companies were. When they reached the sluice gates their advance scouts were taken under fire from the opposite side of the valley. When they reached the causeway they had to withdraw back and take up defensive positions along the sluice-gate ridge. D Company had been in good shape under my command. After our re-organising I was never clear why but Colonel Schneider decided to stay in the vicinity of PdH with Rudder and he took command of B and E Companies.

Major Sullivan was given the mission to clear Grandcamp and then proceed towards Maisy. It included A, C and F plus a small HQ detachment that I was with – plus a cannon platoon of two (motorised) guns from the 2nd Battalion – plus the 81st Chemical Battalion (co B) with 4.2in mortars.

We had artillery liaison officers so we could have heavy artillery on call from the 58th armoured field artillery [the 58th were between Vierville and St Pierre du Mont].

The road leading south to Cricqueville was completely flooded and this presented the Rangers with a big problem. There only way across this area was the small bridge from where this photograph was taken and along the road that leads to Grandcamp.

The 5th Rangers were then split into two forces. Colonel Schneider stayed with his command post and three companies B, E and D, leaving B and E to attack the sluice-gate area east of Grandcamp les Bains. The idea was to mop up any enemy forces between Grandcamp and Pointe du Hoc. Originally only B and E Companies were on this mission, but they were later joined by D Company along with Schneider.

Cecil Gray:

E Company turned off the beach road away from the sluice gates and went past Cricqueville church. We then turned right towards Maisy and reached a chateau. We spent the night in the hedgerow behind it.

At 1455hr HMS *Glasgow* fired fifty-eight rounds from direct observation from its own deck at German troops crossing the land from Grandcamp towards Pointe du Hoc. This was at position 555932 which is open ground and the Germans stood little chance against the *Glasgow*'s guns (indicated in grey on the map below). This German counterattack would have been directed squarely at the Rangers and the 116th Infantry waiting to cross the small road bridge in the flooded area.

It is likely that the force of the initial bombardment by the Navy caused the Germans to retreat towards the gun positions on the west of the valley as they had no heavy weapons at the sluice-gate position. Although the 2 x 75mm guns in the emplacements above ground on the land to the right of Grandcamp (indicated in white below) had been destroyed, the underground bunkers at this position (along with a 50mm gun that faced Grandcamp harbour) had survived thus far. So had the farmhouse where the Germans lived before D-Day.

The access from the farmhouse for the gunners was via a series of trenches around the field edges and across the road towards the sea. From this house marked 'TPS' on the maps (meaning troop concentration) the Germans were fully able to see the advance of the Rangers on the valley opposite and prepare themselves.

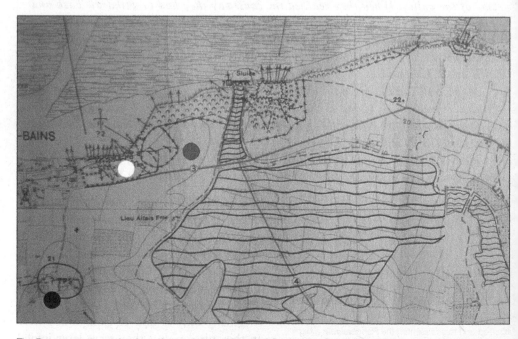

The Rangers were moving from right to left on this map following the Grandcamp–Vierville road. Here the ground dropped steeply as they approached the sluice gates leaving them open to direct enemy fire from the land opposite. They were expecting the Germans to defend the sluice gates heavily, but that was not the case when they arrived.

A modern-day aerial photograph of the 'other' sluice gates (black square) next to the seafront. Behind the circles indicated on the eastern side of the gates is a German position, strongpoint No. 76, which consists of a series of bunkers, machine-gun and mortar positions. Fortunately for the Rangers the Germans had abandoned these positions before they arrived.

A German 'tobruk' on the edge of the beach looking out towards Grandcamp Harbour.

One of the many small shelters and observation posts that look out towards Grandcamp harbour to the left and Pointe du Hoc (seen here) to the right.

The position was thankfully empty and in fact there are two sluice gates, one at the shore front – clearly marked 'sluice gates' on maps, and the other to the south, which was actually the Rangers' objective. The latter was a roadway over a watercourse and without it the tanks would have had difficulty crossing towards Grandcamp. The Germans had left the small bridge intact and this was a strategic error on their part.

John Raaen remembers crossing the valley towards Grandcamp:

It was late morning when Colonel Canham commanding officer of the 116th Infantry gave the Rangers the mission of securing the high ground west of the Sluice Gates. This order was given to his 'advance guard' of the 5th Rangers – B and E Companies. So the Rangers advanced towards Grandcamp, ignoring what we thought were empty German positions to the West of the valley as we went. After we passed the bunkers [marked in white on the map on p. 230] machine guns at the road ahead and to our right in the bypassed positions opened up on us – forcing us to retire pending the higher firepower of the 116th with accompanying tanks and artillery.

The area of the machine-gun position as seen from the beach. This position has command of the small beach below and just to its right is a much greater threat – a 50mm anti-tank gun that was mounted into a bunker facing Grandcamp harbour. Now virtually buried under local rubbish this position was set to cover the approach by any vessels into Grandcamp harbour to the west.

A photograph taken from the same position looking towards Grandcamp harbour.

The field of fire available to the 50mm gun position. It was deadly for anyone trying to attack the seafront of the town.

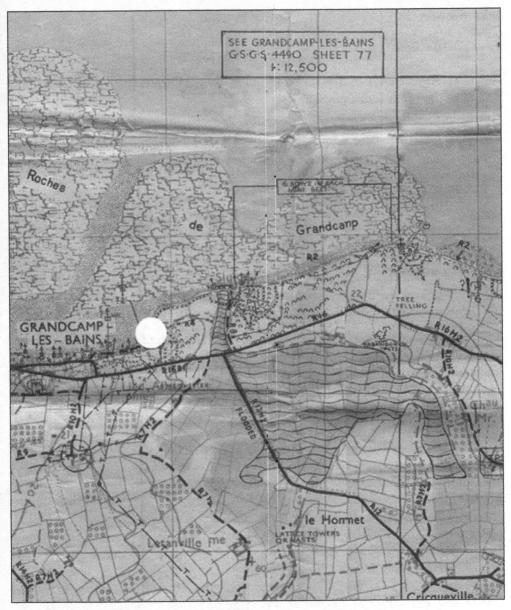

The white circle on this map indicates the position from where the Rangers were attacked.

German report, 8 June:

In the sector of the 914th Grenadier Regiment the enemy attacked the positions just east of Grandcamp, but was repelled.

This was a short-lived action for the 914th men – their report is accurate, but this situation did not last long.

John Raaen:

The 58th Armoured Field Artillery Battalion and the 4.2in mortars supporting their advance allowed the 116th to make short work of the German positions so we could advance.

American Forces in Action Series Historical Division, 20 September 1945 reviewed the actions of the 116th at this position:

Movement toward Grandcamp started at once. Taking that small resort town promised to be difficult, since the approach by the coastal highway led across a small valley with flooded areas on both sides of the road, and the enemy strongpoints west of the valley had extensive fields of fire from higher ground. The enemy had failed to destroy the bridge, but the 5th Rangers were checked at this crossing by machine-gun and mortar fire, and lacked heavy weapons to deal with the enemy resistance. The British cruiser Glasgow *rendered assistance by fire on the German strongpoints near Grandcamp, expending 113 rounds between 1455 and 1600. Late in the afternoon the 3rd Battalion of the 116th took over the job. Tanks of Company C, 743rd Tank Battalion, led across the bridge, losing one vehicle to a mine; then Companies K and L of the 3rd Battalion worked over to the west bank and attacked abreast on either side of the road, under covering fire by machine guns and BARs which displaced rapidly.*

The report goes on to detail the emplacements to the north of the highway, i.e. those passed by the Rangers which were subsequently engaged by the 116th, as well as snipers in the town that continued to engage the ground troops. I company of the 116th led by Lieutenant Norvin Nathan went through Grandcamp and forced the pillbox at the end of the beach to surrender. The Germans capitulated or ran. The American Forces in Action Series Historical Division, 20 September 1945 report continues:

During this attack along the coastal highway, the 1st Battalion of the 116th was making a wide sweep to the south, not only outflanking Grandcamp, but aiming at Maisy. Paced by Company A of the 743rd Tank Battalion, they moved south to Jucoville and then swung west through an area which was practically undefended. Heavy naval guns had torn Maisy to pieces, and the tanks were able to deal easily with resistance from enemy machine guns. Just west of the village an enemy strongpoint blocked the Isigny road and was supported by mortar and 88mm fire, including interdictory fire behind Maisy which prevented reinforcement of the leading infantry elements. Since the tanks were running short of fuel, advance was halted for the night.

Trenches led from this house and over to the right giving the Germans an elevated observation area looking towards Pointe du Hoc, yet at the same time allowing them to maintain covered access to their gun positions near the beach. The German infantry used this high ground to their advantage as they allowed the Ranger advance party to pass them.

The 58th Armoured Field Artillery Battalion was supporting the 116th on 8 June and their records reported that they fired '123 rounds from positions north of Longueville'.

Coit Coker closed up his communications and maintained limited contact with the ship. He continues:

> We proceeded to a point on the road about 1,000yd NW of Au Guay where all three 116th Battalions assembled in preparation for an advance toward Isigny, the Rangers and 2nd and 3rd Battalions planning to advance to the right and the 1st Battalion via Maisy to the left.

To go 'left' after the sluice-gates bridge the Rangers and the 1st 116th had to pass the Germans in the house along that road and luckily they had cleared out of the area and were occupying their positions at the seafront.

On 8 June 1944 the 3rd Battalion of the 116th Infantry was advancing on the strongly held German defences at Grandcamp when the leading elements were suddenly halted by decimating machine-gun fire from a firmly entrenched

Machine-gun position blocking entry into Grandcamp. This was the site of an attack of great courage undertaken by Technical Sergeant Frank Peregory of the 116th Infantry. He risked his life and single-handedly attacked this position killing a number of the Germans defending it and taking more than thirty prisoners. He later received the Medal of Honor for this action, but was unfortunately killed shortly afterwards in combat. His actions and those of the other men of the 116th allowed the Rangers to overcome the obstacles on the outskirts of Grandcamp.

enemy force on the high ground overlooking the town. After numerous attempts to neutralise the enemy position by supporting artillery and tank fire had proved ineffective, Technical Sergeant Peregory, on his own initiative, advanced up the hill under withering fire and worked his way to the crest where he discovered an entrenchment leading to the main enemy fortifications 200yd away. Without hesitating, he leaped into the trench and moved toward the emplacement. Encountering a squad of enemy riflemen, he fearlessly attacked them with hand grenades and bayonet, killing eight and forcing three to surrender. Continuing along the trench, he single-handedly forced the surrender of thirty-two more riflemen, captured the machine-gunners and opened the way for the leading elements of the battalion to advance and secure its objective. The extraordinary gallantry and aggressiveness displayed by Technical Sergeant Peregory are exemplary of the highest tradition of the armed forces.

Suspecting a German observation point in Grandcamp church (visible in the distance in the photograph at the top of p. 236), Coker suggested to Colonel Canham that they fire on the church at the east end of the town. Canham agreed so **Coker** proceeded on a Sherman tank to a point several hundred yards up the road:

> From here we delivered observed fire on the church (about sixteen rounds) and two 1-minute rapid fire barrages (about sixty-four rounds) traversing the waterfront. I then requested 2 minutes of unobserved rapid fire on the town of Maisy, SW of Grandcamp (sixty-four rounds).

On his return to the main group, Coker found that Captain Vavruska of the 5th Rangers had organised firing against the church for a second time as well. So both SFCP officers were working to the same end. **Coker** continues:

Both of our fire missions were undertaken by a ship [USS Harding*] with the call sign RAH.*

Lee Brown remembers the same incident:

We approached the open land in front of Grandcamp and came under sniper fire from Grandcamp church. I watched a lieutenant nearby calling it in and then him saying, 'It's on its way'… and then I saw the steeple blowing in one shot.

The monument to Frank Peregory today. It is made from the very bunker he attacked.

I didn't go into Grandcamp and we didn't see any more Germans that night, other than prisoners. I could hear the bombing and the shelling of Maisy, but I wasn't directly involved in the actual attack on Maisy as I was with HQ. I did get a German officer's dagger with scabbard. Beautiful orange handle with eagle and swastika. This dagger was taken off an officer that I and another Ranger captured when the officer was peeking out from a hedgerow with his binoculars. The other Ranger got his Luger.

The view from the Grandcamp church tower today, looking towards Pointe de Hoc. The German observer would have a clear view of the Ranger force leaving Pointe du Hoc. With the help of binoculars, he would have been able to give the Maisy gunners a very accurate picture of what was going on along the coast road. If you look to the very left of the photograph you can also see the Ranger monument on the top of the Pointe du Hoc observation bunker. It is safe to bet that Rudder and his men were observed at the Pointe by the Germans in the church tower. This may well explain why they were so accurately targeted by artillery when they were in the open ground above the trenches at Pointe du Hoc.

Just over an hour later USS *Harding* was in action again. Its spotters had seen a water tower in Grandcamp being used as an observation point, grid refeference 555932. They engaged it with forty-five rounds, but only registered several near misses. They also fired at the main road behind it using different coordinates (555930) in an attempt to destroy it. It was later discovered that the water tower had tripod legs and due to the surrounding woods and buildings it was a difficult target to hit. So the Germans maintained this as an observation position a little longer.

Major Sullivan, Captain Raaen and a small detachment of HQ personnel went into Grandcamp along with the 1st Battalion, 116th Infantry with Colonel Metcalf commanding. They were engaged in house to house fighting and succeeded in clearing the southern edge of the town of enemy stragglers.

John Raaen:

We went through each house with two men on the left and right sides of the road. I led the first team on the left. The team would enter a house. If the doors were locked I would stick a bayonet through the keyhole and fire one round and kick open the door. It worked! First man up the stairs to clean out the second floor. The second man was his back-up. Third and fourth men handled the main floor. Then the first two finished we would take the basement. The teams would leapfrog from house to house. Luckily we found nothing but frightened French families for our efforts.

By now the 1st Battalion had wheeled left with some of the Rangers and was on the way to Maisy, but they were encountering stiff resistance from incoming artillery. Colonel Canham agreed the following plan, as described by **Coit Coker**:

One hour's intermittent fire be placed on Maisy and he said that he would notify the 1st Battalion of this fire. I called for RAH to deliver unobserved intermittent fire of twelve rounds every 5 minutes on the Maisy area for a period of one hour, which they did from 1500–1600 (144 rounds). Our party caught up with the 1st Battalion outside of Maisy after hitching a ride with cannon company's vehicles.

One group advancing along the main road towards the Maisy square fired a bazooka rocket into the upstairs window at the rear of the tobacconist shop. They had seen movement upstairs and suspected the Germans were using it as an observation position. The rocket went straight through the open window, but did not explode so the Rangers concluded that there was nobody home. Two days later the owners of the building, who were hiding in their garden shelter, had to ask a passing American patrol to remove the live rocket from their bedroom wall!

At 1433hr NGLO 3 (Naval Gunnery Liaison Officer 3, part of the Rangers SFCP) again requested fire from USS *Harding* on the waterfront of Grandcamp. She duly obliged and fired 160 rounds into the normally sleepy seafront for an hour. It is unlikely that this fire was particularly effective, although some of the small machine-gun positions may have been hit. It is more likely that the shelling had a psychological effect on the defenders more than anything else. Although the GSGS maps indicate the presence of 3 x 105mm guns along the seafront, they are also accompanied by a question mark, suggesting that this was subject to verification.

At 1440hr NGLO 3 requested that *Harding* also open fire on the town of Maisy using intermittent fire for an hour. This move was to try and stem the flow of reinforcements moving in from Maisy through Cricqueville towards Pointe du Hoc. It will have also been aimed at the AA position and the battery in the village. Accurate as it was, the naval gunfire would not have guaranteed destruction of either group of positions, so it was probably used to 'soften up' the Maisy positions prior to the Rangers advance. In all *Harding* fired seventy-three rounds at Maisy village.

USS *Harding* ceased fire at 1900hr and by 1920hr NGLO 3 reported the firing on Maisy had been highly effective and that American troops were entering the village.

D Company 5th Rangers was already near Maisy along with E Company, which had come up by way of Criqueville past the old village church, advancing cautiously into the edge of the village. The remains of the church steeple that they could see ahead of them had been destroyed by naval gunfire. There had been German troops using it as another observation position.

The order to enter the village of Maisy was given by Schneider and members of D Company stopped in the ruins of Mr Destores' chateau on the eastern outskirts, ironically the same buildings recently vacated by Captain Kapusta and Lieutenant Weneger. The chateau was badly damaged and three of the anti-aircraft guns lay destroyed in the field next door. The shell-marked fields were not an ideal place to rest for the Rangers as the Germans were still around in great numbers, and members of the anti-aircraft unit that had survived the bombardment and destruction of their guns were coming out of hiding as it got dark. D Company posted guards and were mindful of a German counterattack which could come from any direction.

Francis Coughlin:

I went on a patrol looking for a colonel of the 29th division and we walked about 5 miles. Behind our lines and behind the German lines – there was nobody around. Finally the captain said, 'Let's turn back, God who knows where he is – maybe he's a prisoner of war ... there's nobody here – let's go' ... well then we had a little firefight for about half an hour with some Germans and then we took off running like heck – down around the turn away from the Germans where they were firing and we eventually got back to our unit. The Captain made his report and then that afternoon we took off and we started inland. I can remember

The entrance to the Destors' chateau where the Rangers found shelter at the rear of the destroyed buildings. The chateau had only recently been vacated by the German anti-aircraft men.

running across the fields and the machine-gun bullets were going over our heads. I remember a cow in the field and we were out of breath – we laid there looking at the cow as the machine gun was zipping about and shooting it. All the blood was running down the cow as we laid there. I remember saying it's a good job we were not 7ft tall or that would be us. We went across a field by crawling and got into the woods.

Cecil Gray:

We turned left off the beach road and went south towards Cricqueville and then went to our right ... then another right and down a small road to a large farmhouse/chateau. It had a farmhouse at the end of a square and a barn to the right and I did outpost duty that night.

Cecil Gray spent the night of the 8th 'half' sleeping in a ditch at the back of the Destores' destroyed house, as it was the safest place he could find.

A **German report** written at that time stated:

On 7th June the enemy succeeded in a deep assault in the right, open flank of the 352nd Inf. Div. Though it was not possible to fling back the enemy toward the sea, at least we managed to thwart his probable intentions of attack on the 7th June. A landing of other new fighting forces in the Grandcamp area on the 8th of June is also not out of the question.

When the division – towards 0000 hours, received the captured (US invasion) orders from Vierville the situation could be estimated in a much clearer way. In my opinion this extensive operation order disclosed that the invasion plan was far beyond the scope of the American 5th Army Corps. I admit that I, along with my division commander did not have time to study this operation order in detail. This order covered every minute item from D-Day.

Based on these reports an evaluation of the situation in the division C.P. showed that on D plus 2 days the enemy had almost reached the objectives established for D plus 1 day and that he will probably try to reach the objectives set for D plus 2 days with his armoured forces by the end of that day. Therefore, it was important to hold up the enemy throughout the day from positions held by German elements about noon, in order to make it possible to withdraw into a position more suitable for a weakened unit. The division was aware of the fact that this

The ditch at the back of the Destores' house where Cecil Gray sheltered on the evening of 8 June.

decision, to withdraw before the enemy was in contradiction with the Führer's order for the combat installations 'Hold out to the last shot!' The commanding General of the LXXXIV Army Corps had given notice that he would be at the division C.P. at 1500 hours in order to accept the decision.

In the left sector (914th Gren Regt) the situation was definitely more serious. Two points needed special attention. Firstly, it was imperative to succeed in leading the parts of the 1st Btn of the 914th Gren Regt as well as of the 1352nd Art Regt which were still fighting near Grandcamp, via Isigny to the south.

Working their way towards Maisy and halting about ½ mile to the north-east in the area of 541929 the Rangers settled into ditches and hedgerows for the night. The battalion food-distribution system had at least been able to supply them with some K rations to eat rather than just K ration bars, and for some this was the first food they had received in days.

John Raaen:

Lieutenant Colonel Metcalf ordered the task force to halt for the night. He called Sullivan and laid out a disposition of troops plan. Sully returned to his 'flying CP' and called us, the company commanders in and did the same for us. He assigned us to missions and positions for the night. F Company stayed in positions off the road to our left for continued flank protection against a night counterattack. C Company provided right flank protection, but most of the company would be next to the road. The 4.2s and I would slip inside of C Company's rear guard elements. I presume the HQ was formed around the half-tracks. I just know Sullivan, he was good and wouldn't allow his command to be ambushed at night or any other time, so he deployed us into night defensive positions.

We would generally cover 100yd by 100yd per company with perhaps a hundred between each. Our companies had less than sixty men by this time. That's two platoons of maybe twenty-five each with two Ranger sections of about ten, each with an M1919A4 machine gun. Each platoon had a mortar section of four or five. The BARs could have been with company or platoon.

Each company did it differently and they would have been fairly close together. I think that in Maisy the whole battalion position that night was perhaps 300 x 150yd.

The lane nearly opposite Gerrard Maudelonde's farm, where the Germans had situated anti-aircraft guns, was disguised with camouflage netting. Invasion target number 102

The lane leading past the water tower which contained 3 AA guns on D-Day.

Naval Target 100 was the German administrative headquarters where the official running of the village was organised by the military regime.

on John Raaen's map, these guns did not fair well on the morning of the 6th. They were destroyed by accurate fire, initially thought to have come from the Navy, but Gerrard Maudelonde remembers seeing a low-level bomber blasting them accurately and the bombs hit one after another.

Alongside the AA guns was the camouflage-painted water tower which served as an observation position for the Germans. In the field behind it the Germans had a small concrete underground building which was destroyed during the naval bombardment. It functioned as a shelter for the men while on duty, but it was literally blown away by the Navy guns.

Slowly the Rangers entered the buildings and barns recently vacated by the Germans. They all had to be searched and this was not a quick task. In places the Rangers could see evidence of clothing and equipment which had been left in a hurry. In other places fires were still burning and there were dead bodies in some of the gun positions.

Coit Coker:

Maisy village had been pretty well destroyed by the intermittent fire and had been evacuated with the exception of one machine gun emplaced in the church steeple; this nest was knocked out by Browning Automatic Rifles and rifle grenades. However, when the forward part of the battalion passed the church and reached the main crossroads of the town the Germans fired a two-gun artillery salvo onto their position. I happened to be with the forward element at the time and was cut off with forty men and a 2nd Lieutenant.

Coker quickly ran along a dirt road lined with evacuated trenches and emplacements – which ironically was within line of sight of the Maisy observers. His aim was to get away from the Germans who obviously had him under observation from somewhere high – but he did know where from. Wherever his small group ran the artillery followed them until the track ended in a meadow. They were fortunate because none of the shelling produced any casualties and then suddenly a German infantryman emerged from a

The Maisy village centre seen from the church tower. The main road with the bus shelter in the centre and the land in front of Les Perruques is visible at the top left. It was from here that Coit Coker and the advance party of Rangers were taken under fire.

This photo shows what is now a car park in the village square of Maisy from ground level. It is a similar photograph angle except that the area in front of the church is now a car park as all the houses that were in this area were demolished by the bombing and shelling – prior to the site being captured.

camouflaged position, hoping to lure them into the open and most probably a trap. **Coker** continues:

> *We motioned him toward us, but just at the edge of the field he decided to dive behind a hedge row, immediately receiving a burst from the Lieutenant's tommy gun. The Lieutenant and I had a record-quick joint Army–Navy conference and decided that we were in too small a force to continue further and that the only procedure open was to retrace our steps back to Maisy and attempt to find and rejoin the rest of the battalion. This we did, finding them on the road just south of the town. Enemy artillery shifted onto us again here, one heavy calibre probably firing from Isigny and the other light calibre short range (horse drawn?) probably from vicinity of targets No. 16 (La Martiniere) and No. 108 (Foucher's Farm) about 1500 S and SW of Maisy. Under this artillery fire the battalion dispersed to cover again.*

Re-setting up his radio set, Coker was unable to find ship call sign RAH (USS *Harding*) or the *Texas* – call sign SXT. He did, however, get in touch with a ship code named LBL, which he later discovered was the British cruiser *Bellona*, and asked for messages to be relayed to the *Texas*. This complicated method did prove successful and he called for aerial reconnaissance to fire on any artillery seen firing near Osmanville and Isigny. **Coker** continues:

Foucher's Farm after the bombardment. The roof of every building has literally been blown off.

> *We were working under combined difficulties at this point – exasperatingly we had radio communications problems; shrapnel from enemy fire falling about us, and isolated from the remainder of the battalion. Private Henson is to be commended for his courageous spirit and devotion to duty in sticking by me in a trying situation where nearly all others had taken cover.*
>
> *Finally we were forced to close down and return to the battalion which had reformed and taken defensive shelter in abandoned enemy entrenchments on the southern outskirts of town. When we reopened [communications] the* Bellona *was calling us direct and said they were now assigned to us, also that the* Texas *was going to fire a barrage on Isigny for us.*
>
> *In regard to the naval gunfire which we placed on Maisy, I believe that without it, the 1st Battalion would either have had extreme difficulty in taking the town and at worst might have fallen into a trap. This belief is based on several facts. The battalion encountered heavy opposition in its approach to Maisy, and there were many entrenchments in the vicinity of the town which had been evacuated, evidently very recently. The town itself had been completely evacuated with the exception of the one machine gun nest. Artillery pieces which had probably been in the area were no longer present, evidently moved to the south toward Isigny.*

Other Ranger units began entering the village and clearing houses one by one. It was evident that the Germans had all but left the village. For some it was the first time in three days that they had had the opportunity to sit and relax. For others it was the first time they had had anything to eat and for F Company's Private Sorensen it was the first chance he had had to take off his invasion vest since landing. These ill-fitting jackets were poorly designed over-jackets created to provide spaces for extra ammunition and equipment. But as A Company's 'Ace' Parker found on the bluffs, they were difficult to get out of once they were on. The Ranger's personal equipment strapped through the jacket onto the belts underneath and was difficult to get out of. Sorensen spent the night of the 8th in a barn at Gerrard Maudelonde's farm along with other Rangers amidst piles of German equipment. They tentatively picked through the equipment, ever wary of German booby traps. One such item found there was a device designed to replace the fuse of a large shell and turn it into a road-side boobytrap. Sorensen left that and took off his assault vest and he stuffed it into the rafters of the barn. There his jacket remained for sixty-three years, along with mortar carriers and empty ammunition tins and the booby-trap fuse.

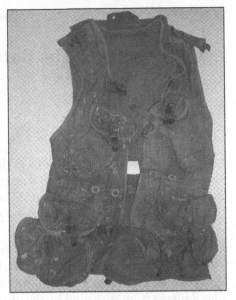

I found Sorensen's vest along with other Ranger kit when the barns were being cleared ready for sale in 2009. The jacket still had Sorensen's name written inside the back of it.

John Raaen:

It was late afternoon when we left the town and it was going dark, so we buttoned up for the night midway between Grandcamp-les-Bains and Maisy. We 'slept' in the hedgerows beside the road.

Francis Coughlin:

I didn't do actually much fighting as I wasn't supposed too – my job was to get information. If we had to fight to get information that was a different story. But we only had two little firefights and none of us got hurt. We took a long walk along the road to shorten the distance to where we were going. That's where the tank commander told us, 'We are going to stop here. We need to get organised and find the rest of our troops and get them gathered around.' Myself and the other guy who went on patrol with me. I said to him, 'Where are we going to find our guys – they could be spread all the way back to Vierville.' I said we just have to watch where we go and we'll be OK. We went out and found about three companies and they passed the word along that the companies were to fall back and hook up with headquarters because they wanted to talk about what they were to do the next day.

Chapter 10

The Battle for Maisy

Coit Coker:

At 0100 we called on the Bellona *to fire on target No. 16 about 1,500yd SW of our position where mobile artillery was suspected. This fire was spotted by sound and comprised about twenty-six rounds. To avoid placing the gun target line over our position the* Bellona *was requested to move to a position NE of the target before opening fire.*

As it grew light Major Sullivan briefed everyone on the coming assault. It was just before 0800hr and the weather had improved drastically from the torrential wind and rain of 6 June. Gone was the lack of visibility and rain, there was now a clear sky and sunshine. The Rangers were surprised by the change in the weather, but the improved visibility was both an aid and a hinderance to them. The Germans were set into positions that they had occupied for a number of years and the Rangers were walking into these areas on a bright, sunlit morning.

They were deployed by Major Sullivan as follows. C Company along with elements of the 116th Regiment left A and F Companies and travelled along with two halftracks from the 2nd Rangers heading south along the Grandcamp–Isigny road. Most of the 116th men continued their journey in the direction of Isigny and left the Rangers to deal with the batteries that were then to their right.

The Rangers were attempting to flank around Maisy Battery at Les Perruques and at the same time give the Germans the impression that they were being bypassed. In a co-ordinated attack they would attempt to bring fire to bear on the position from a southerly and south-easterly direction to cut off any enemy escape, while at the same attacking from the seaward north side with F and A Companies.

F Company was to hold a position in the hedgerows and sunken lane north and north-east of the Les Perruques Battery and engage the enemy in small-arms fire. Once the other units were in position and the main battle commenced, they were to attack up the field parallel to the Grandcamp–Isigny road and turn right into the site. The rest of F Company would go up the field directly from the sunken lane later in a south-westerly direction into the battery.

The men of A Company started alongside F by jumping off the Isigny road and going to their right. They left F Company in position and continued along the sunken road parallel to the Les Perruques and La Martiniere road (now called Route des Perruques). They were effectively crossing right in front of the German guns up to their left – but they were 300yd away, out of sight in the sunken lane. Their mission was to continue until they were in front of the La Martiniere Battery then wait for a signal (i.e. gunfire) and advance uphill and take the battery.

Major Sullivan took C Company and elements of D Company, along with some of his HQ men, and advanced down the Isigny road until they had passed the Les Perruques Battery. They came under heavy machine-gun fire from the battery as they did so. Sullivan ordered the halftracks to wheel right and go into the battery's lines from the rear. He directed the developing action from on top of one of the halftracks and he was initially alongside C and F Companies mortars which were set up in firing order 400yd away from the site on the road. The mortars had also gone past Les Perruques toward Isigny and then turned back – this gave them the sufficient distance required to lay fire on the site and maintain a safe operating distance from the Germans.

Since Sullivan's briefing, the guns of the 58th Armoured Field Gun Battery had already fired 123 rounds into the site, and so had the 81st Chemical Weapons Unit. All naval gunfire had now halted to allow the attack to begin.

Approaching the crossroads where the Ranger companies separated for the attack. This building was used by German officers as accommodation before D-Day. It was empty as the Rangers passed it, everyone was at the site and expecting the attack.

100yd further on. The cross roads on the Isigny–Maisy road where A and most of F Companies carried straight on down into the valley to engage the Germans to their left.

Looking towards Isigny from Maisy. The battery is ahead to the right.

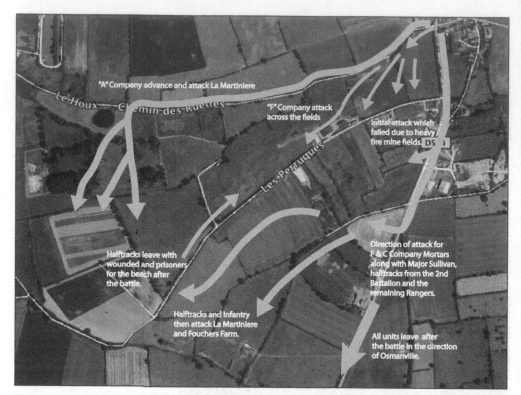

"A" Company advance and attack La Martiniere

"F" Company attack across the fields

Initial attack which failed due to heavy fire mine fields. D5

Halftracks leave with wounded and prisoners for the beach after the battle.

Direction of attack for F & C Company Mortars along with Major Sullivan, halftracks from the 2nd Battalion and the remaining Rangers.

Halftracks and infantry then attack La Martiniere and Fouchers Farm.

All units leave after the battle in the direction of Osmanville.

This image shows the direction in which the Rangers first advanced and then slowly enveloped the site. By engaging the Germans from the front using A and F Companies the Rangers will have drawn attention away from the encircling movement undertaken by the halftracks and the rest of the men from the rear.

The sun is rising and the mist lifts over the Route des Perruques road as it did on the morning of 9 June. The weather had finally cleared leaving a fine dry, sunny day.

The view from above at the Les Perruques road. The men of A and F company were able to stay in the valley out of site of the Germans long enough to find a good approach position. They then had to climb out of the valley and into the open.

Albert Nyland:

We had gone through Grandcamp fast, bypassing the village. We were with the 116th Infantry at that time. We had a couple of halftracks and mortars. We had mortars in C Company. With a mortar you had a gunner and I was a loader carrying the ammunition. I was a big guy and it was my job to carry the ammunition and follow with the rest of the crew. What we did was to go and make a reconnaissance before the Maisy attack. We put up stakes for firing – the Germans had dug it all out and there was a big hill – we fired into the site from a distance, but we only had six rounds left for each weapon. We had left the rest on the beach because we had no transport. We took them out of their containers to make them easier to carry.

Intelligence reports for the two positions reported: '*Minebelt 75 feet wide around the southern side of the battery position*'. However, the Rangers had no knowledge of this and they could not wait for other American troops with mine detectors. The report continues: '*The artillery positions southwest of Maisy are surrounded by double bands. Some of these bands are reported electrified.*'

The units in the southerly position with Sullivan, including some of E Company, advanced onto the fields after the brief C Company mortar attack. Small-arms fire came from the German trenches and it was difficult to see where the fire was coming from. Machine-gun fire was well aimed and well camouflaged and coming from multiple locations just above ground level.

It quickly became clear to them that the fields to the rear were mined, as were all the surrounding fields, but they continued regardless. Major Sullivan climbed off the halftrack and was working with his men, advancing on foot when he was caught by the blast from a triggered mine. It was set off by another Ranger and he was lightly wounded, but nonetheless he continued to lead the attack, this time slightly to the left of his original start position.

Each of the Ranger units operated separately. They could hear, but not see other companies and so they focused on their own area of the battery to assault.

Donald Chance:

We were lead company in the behind the lines attack on the Maisy Batteries.

John Reville:

After we left the (main) road – what we were supposed to do was go with A Company and as the thing developed it seemed that A Company just disappeared and my platoon was going into the fire again. We got going and as I recall when you look from the water inland we went to the right towards Grandcamp, the flooded area. There was a firefight and we took some prisoners. We continued from Grandcamp down to the left on a road. Quite a distance – about a 100yd and came under some sniper fire and we laid there for a while. We had gone through the flooded area to the left, there were American parachutes – multi-coloured and I remember cutting some and using it as a helmet cover. I put it on my helmet and I remember seeing dead paratroopers in the flooded area. Some of my men were falling asleep … we had had two or three days without sleep … when you lay down and nobody is firing directly at you then all of a sudden you fall asleep and the platoon moves off. After all how long can you go without sleep … that's what those first few days of combat were like. There was no help coming. A strange thing did happened – John Hodgson was laying down and he called out he was hit. I crawled over to him and said 'Where, John?' He said his chest. We were still wearing gas masks on our chests at that time and the bullet went through the gas mask and hit a grenade he had in his pocket. Because of the styrations on the grenade the bullet dropped into his pocket. Another one of my men was shot in the helmet – that was quite common in those days. Where you have those hedgerows only 100ft between them – it's no great thing to shoot someone in the helmet at that range. The bullet went through the steel helmet and between the steel helmet and the plastic helmet and came out of the back and into his shoulder.

Maybe we were not aggressive enough by keeping our heads down, but finally someone said, 'Get the hell out of here' and we started moving up the field. From there we were up on our feet and we started to run to where the fire was coming from. There were buildings there – before we knew it a German popped up – he was well in advance of the rest of his people, but he popped up and put his hands up and he was Polish. We had someone who spoke Polish so we told him to walk forwards in front of us with his hands up. We got him to go up towards the next pillbox and Muscatello was shot in the throat. I shot the guy who shot him and then we still had the prisoner we caught first. We were firing near his feet to get him to order the others to come out.

Richard Hathaway:

Our battalion commander Major Sullivan said we were going to take the battery and we set off around 8 o'clock in the morning. It was fairly good weather and it wasn't raining. We had the place well covered from all sides and we made sure there was no room for any of them to get out. The 75mm halftracks were quite a ways away. But we could only move so far with them. We were up against the swamp where we were. The swamp held us up and we couldn't cross the wet ground with the halftracks so they went along the road.

Corporal George W. Monks Jr, F Company, 5th Rangers:

It was clear and bright that day. Our company was in the lead and we moved up the road towards Isigny. I had a mortar section, I was a Squad Leader in F Company mortar section. Where my mortars were set-up firing, they had brought up a 75mm halftrack. I believe Sullivan was right behind us and he was conducting the attack at that time. I heard Sullivan talking to the Battalion Commander from the halftrack and our mortars were hitting the site. We were 300 or 400yd away from the battery – we had gone past it and turned back – attacking towards the sea. We fired on the site before the attack began. A lot of times you don't have a good orientation when you're a ground-pounder, but I remember we were facing the sea.

Staff Sergeant Anthony Muscatello was wounded. I wasn't directly there, but the story I heard was that when the Germans surrendered, and our troops came up from their firing positions and were walking up, the Germans were standing there with their hands up. One German grabbed his rifle and decided he'd take an American with him. He shot our Platoon Sergeant who was Muscatello at that time. As soon as he did – he went down from friendly gun-fire. I don't know if his people shot him, but our people shot the shit out of him.

John Reville:

I remember putting the German potato-masher grenades down the side of my boots just like the German had it. They were a joke – they were like a beer can on a stick. It was not a fragmentation grenade at all. Just a big boom that was all.

The men with Sullivan entered the trenches on the south side of Les Perruques and one of the halftracks engaged a German 622 personnel bunker with its 75mm gun. The gun was a direct-fire weapon meaning that it needed to point directly at whatever it wanted to shoot. This inevitably made positioning the vehicle vital and sometimes the halftracks would literally have to advance right towards the enemy. In this case the machine-gun position on top of the 622 building, which had been effective in keeping the Rangers heads down at short range, was deadly. This type of position was the same as the ones being attacked by F Company on the Route des Perruques road – a concrete circle that a man could pop his head up from and then retreat back down into after firing. Known as a 'Tobruk', they contained a German MG 34/42 machine gun which had a high rate of fire and in this case an accurate gunner. 2nd Ranger Lieutenant Conway Epperson commanded one of the halftracks and he ordered the advance straight towards the bunker with his 75mm gun firing as it went. A number of men of the 2nd Battalion fought alongside the halftracks using it as protection as they advanced. The machine-gun bullets bounced off the front of the halftrack and the 75mm gun returned fire with its main gun.

Kisselman's helmet still has his name inside.

One of the leading gun pits at Les Perruques assaulted by the F Company men. This is also the same gun pit shown with the man standing beside the destroyed gun after the battle (see p. 253).

Another view over another gun pit taken from above, showing how easily the emplacements sit into the fields. You can see the roofs of buildings built into the ground which would not have been visible to the Rangers.

The halftrack hit the front and top of the bunker more than seven times with its 75mm cannon and only after killing a number of fresh gunners did they succeed in taking the building. The Rangers on all sides of the site were now assaulting inside the enemy trenches and it was only a matter of time before the Germans were either captured or killed. Many chose the former in preference to dying for the cause, but others did kill themselves.

One of the German officers captured in the trenches was 37-year-old Unteroffizer Frederick Kisselman, who had joined the Heerkunsten Artillery Abt 315 (coastal artillery unit 315) and was attached to the 1716th Artillery 9th Battery stationed at Maisy. He was captured by the Rangers and later taken back to the beach – his helmet was taken as a souvenir by one of them. He was later sent to Medicine Hat POW Camp in Canada and repatriated to Germany in 1947. But he was only one of many Germans and conscripted soldiers still inside the site.

John Reville:

One of those that was captured there put his hands up – he had a fur hat on – he was a little short squat guy with slanty eyes and on his fur hat he had the hammer and syckle. He was one of those guys captured there, so he must have been from Russia some place and put into the German Army. The Normandy troops were much poorer quality – if you attacked them hard enough they would surrender.

As the battle continued, so did the problems for the Rangers. Inside the trenches it was a warren of unlit and dark places designed to confuse and disorientate an attacker. Narrow trenches with net coverings had in places collapsed from shelling and buried German soldiers. In other places the camouflage around each trench coupled with small entrances allowed the Germans to run off and disappear inside bunkers and in some areas shut the steel doors. In many situations they would simply fire a couple of rounds and then disappear – yet in others they were only too happy to surrender. The larger bunkers had blast doors fitted and they created a major problem as the Rangers did not

A Ranger looking through the Maisy 502 headquarters building periscope after the battle. Note he is still wearing the anti-gas brassard issued on D-Day to all the troops.

have heavy weapons to damage them. It was not safe for the halftracks to advance into the centre of the site because they could not guarantee they would not be attacked from behind. This problem had also been encountered earlier at Pointe du Hoc where the Germans would re-appear from sunken positions once bypassed. There was also the problem of traversing the dozens of trenches that intersected with others, often still very much 'alive' with Germans.

In the centre of the Les Perruques Battery the Germans had constructed a 502 Headquarters Building, designed with the same heavy concrete as other buildings, and it was from here that the commanding officer gave orders to his troops. The bunker was fitted with a large naval periscope set completely through the 3m-thick, bomb-proof roof. From here he and his men could watch the approach of the halftracks and try and effect a defence of the site. The 622 buildings had doors, which once closed could be sealed against small-arms fire and gas. They also included a machine gun that would fire upwards from inside against anyone approaching the building's entrance. F Company men devised a simple counteraction to the heavy steel doors – they tried once or twice using a Polish conscript as an interpretor to coax their fellow fighters out of building. He was 'pushed' out towards the entrance and instructed to tell the Germans officers to come out, and if they didn't come out – as one SS officer wouldn't – then the Rangers tied two satchel charge bags together and blew them out. The damage from the blast was considerable. Ranger John Reville remembered '*the steel blast doors were blown off their hinges*'. When the F Company men entered the smoking 502 headquarters building all the officers were dead from the concussion but '*their radios were all still talking to them*'.

While Sullivan and his men were busy attacking Les Perruques from the rear, A Company was approaching the La Martiniere Battery from the sunken road to the north of the battery, right in front of the guns above.

Jack Burke:

I do remember us skirting around the village of Grandcamp the night before and we were spread out with about 10yd between each guy. We marched until we came to a dirt road with woods on our right side and fields on our left. We stopped and got our orders to attack what we later knew as Maisy Battery. It seemed that as soon as we got into the field the Germans opened up with heavy firing with machine guns and mortars.

Jim Wilderson, F Company, 5th Rangers:

We waited to the north of the Maisy position. We were set up along the hedgerow with our backs to the village engaging in small-arms fire with the enemy for about ½ hour while the other units moved around and encircled the site. Suddenly we seemed to be moving forwards up the fields. The Germans would fire – we would fire and we split up and moved separately. They were positioned in bunkers with only their heads visible. They would pop up and shoot then go back again. Muscatello was wounded during this assault – he was shot in the neck.... We were leap-frogging German bunkers – shoot and scoot – then we would drop explosives into their position and blow them out. We were doing this and I remember the Germans surrendering at one position rather than being blown up. We gathered them up and had about 6–8 of them in front of us and we were pushing them for information. We were shooting at the floor near their feet, etc. Not at them, but just to get information when a big explosion went off behind us. Perhaps one of the big guns being destroyed or its ammunition ... either way it caused us all to turn around for a split second..It was enough for one of the Germans to bend down and pick up a rifle, he then shot Muscatello at virtually point-blank range in the throat and he instantly went down.

John Reville shot the German with his Thompson and we tended to Muscatello. The bullet had gone through his neck and out the other side without damaging him badly. In fact there were only two or three F Company guys who were wounded at Maisy. Muscatello was lucky that time, but he was killed in action shortly afterwards.

The men of F Company then crossed the road or entered the trenches from the Route des Perruques tunnels where they were engaged in firefights with individual Germans at close range. They overran one of the gun emplacements and the surrounding bunkers.

The first Maisy gun encountered was not now operational. The base of the concrete platform it sat on was cracked right across by an explosion which had thrown the gun upside down and rendered it useless. The camouflage netting above the trenches was shreaded and there was wooden trench lining and ammunition scattered around. Other guns had been variously covered in soil and buried by debris from the bombing over the three days. This was something that was reported to German high command as having been rectified for three

One of the tobruks attacked by F Company. Two in a row were destroyed before the men inside this one surrendered. This is where Ranger Muscatello was shot in the neck.

This photograph was taken shortly after the battle and shows the destruction to the first gun at Les Perruques. It was literally blown upside down by the naval blast and it can seen here facing backwards.

of the guns, and they were now operational again. However, their firepower was not in any way able to affect the Rangers' assault as the infantry was attacking below the line of fire of the heavy guns. They could now only use small-arms fire against them. Negotiating the trenches was proving difficult because of the amount of damage that the bombing had also caused to the trench walls. In addition, bodies had been blown into trenches and German equipment, mines and ammunition were all in disarray. In effect, everything was an obstacle for F Company.

Early on 9 June **Cecil Gray** left his trench at the back of the Destores' chateau and made his way towards the rendezvous point.

On the morning of the 9th we re-assembled and went down the road maybe 100 or 200yd then we went over a field to our left. Someone – about three men ahead of me stepped on a mine and I got a piece of it. I caught a fragment – worth a purple heart, a nothing bit and then we finally got to one of the batteries. I was injured in the leg. I was there – but not involved in the big fight ... All of E Company were there with me, but it had been captured when we got there. I do remember some German firing a gun after everyone had surrendered and someone took him out and shot him.

Jim Wilderson:

I didn't go into the main site, but I know some of the guys had some of the cash that was in there. When we hit Maisy we did three of the gun emplacements and when it was over we didn't make any big deal over it, we didn't think it was any great big deal. It was just part of the job – but we only saw a small part of the site as we were guarding prisoners. I was one of the youngest in the company. We used to wear jump boots ... we were issued them for possible cliff assaults or beach attacks and we were proud of them! I do remember Hodgson getting hit (for the second time) in the chest with a spent bullet

... he carried the bullet for years in his pocket and used to show everyone at reunions. He must have been at the extreme range of the weapon ... we had taken some champagne out of a pillbox and we were sitting there drinking this stuff and all of a sudden he was hit in the chest with a bullet ... it hit him in the chest and it fell down into his chest inside his shirt. I stopped in a pillbox to pick up a couple of Luger pistols – I put them in the back of my duffle bag and they disappeared later.

Alongside the Rangers' own firepower, the heavy mortars of the 81st Chemical Weapons Corps was also available to them. B Company was ordered on the morning of 9 June to support the 5th Rangers in their attack at Maisy and it is most likely that their mortars were the ones firing over A Company during their approach to La Martiniere.

Each company had twelve mortars and they were capable of laying down an extensive barrage of firepower in a short space of time, and the 81st later became known as the Rangers' artillery unit in other European actions. It is guaranteed that their heavy weapons would have been devastating at short range against the German positions at Maisy and they would have ensured that the Germans were kept underground while the Rangers got themselves into position.

Unfortunately the unit history does not go into the role of the 81st at Maisy in detail, but it is clear that their heavy mortar weapons were of great value to the Rangers as they prepared to attack. The 81st would have been part of the pre-assault 'softening up' called in by Captain Raaen's men of 5th HQ Company.

This bombardment would have eaten into the Germans' defences prior to the Rangers' ground assault and it is something that cannot be underestimated. By the morning of 9 June the Germans at Maisy knew full well that the Allies were coming and they would have seen their observation positions disappearing one by one. There would have been a continual and slow loss of personnel to bombing and shelling. They would also have had their contact with other units fail one after another towards their own positions and this lack of communication would normally mean the positions had been overrun – with their comrades captured or killed. By the morning of the 9th the Germans at Maisy would have been on a knife edge.

George Monks:

None of the guys from our company were killed – I think because we were outside the site and we stayed there. We picked up the prisoners and lined them up, we disarmed them and took them off to the beach. I don't recall how many. We just stayed on the edge of the site and didn't go in. There was a lot of money around after someone found the payroll – I got a bit of it, yeah, a couple of bucks, Francs, French Francs. I remember guys talking about a big hospital bunker and what a big place it was in there, but I didn't get to see it.

Cecil Gray:

I saw some of the rifle pits and machine-gun pits, but not much else from where we were and I heard about the halftracks and a cannon company from the 116th, but I didn't see Sullivan on the halftracks. We were too far away to see who was there.

Jack Burke:

We received artillery fire as we approched our line of departure with A Company to attack the front, coming through the swampy area with the beach to our back going up the hill with F Company attacking from the flank. As we started across the open field we encountered heavy mortar and machine-gun fire coming at us. We took some casualties.

John Perry:

We went into a flooded area and their mortars opened up on us. They were heavy and there was plenty of machine-gun fire. There were woods to our right as we went uphill and I remember Sullivan and Battice getting hit.

Lieutenant Parker gave the order to fix bayonets as the A Company Rangers left the swampy ground. The order to fix bayonets was an indication of what was to come. The Rangers would have to enter the trench system, go from bunker to bunker and fight the Germans face to face.

Jack Burke:

There were dead paratroopers in the Maisy area lying dead – some in the flooded area on the ground and still hanging in the trees.

The men of A Company tried to turn left into the flat field, but they encountered an unexpected obstacle. The ditches at the road edge had an excessive amount of water in them and in places it was 6 to 8ft deep. They had tried to walk across the ditches at the field edges just where they were at their deepest.

A couple of the men had to be dragged back out of the water, all whilst they were being fire upon by Germans in the positions above them. The Germans had seen the men advance out of the trees down the lane, into the open and then engaged them with a number of different weapons. The Rangers moved quickly further down the lane and within 50 or 60yd they found a section of the ground where the ditch was not present. They were now walking through water some 8in tall rather than a full–depth ditch.

They spread out and ran through the open field, water dragging at their feet as they went. Covering the first 100yd of open ground meant they had at least a little cover to allow them to approach the Germans battery. The small bushes and lightly wooded area offered some protection from the gaze of the Germans above and a group of men besides Jack Burke set up a 60mm mortar. They began firing up at the Germans – not with a specific target in mind, but to try and keep the defenders heads down to allow the advance to gain momentum. The other Rangers fired their Browning Automatic Rifles and .30 calibre machine guns into the German positions.

Using the same methods employed by their colleagues in F company the men of A Company ran up and quickly entered the trenches at La Martiniere. The barbed wire in front of the emplacements was designed to slow troops down – it was light as the Germans had wrongly assumed that the minefields would be a sufficient deterrent to any advancing infantry.

The forward bunkers reached initially included a mortar pit, set up with pre-arranged markings on the wall for distance and fall of shot. Had the Rangers stayed at the bottom of the valley they would quickly have been targeted by the mortars as their position was pre-calibrated. The fact that they advanced swiftly over this area meant that the mortars were unable to keep up with their changing positions.

They fired randomly at first and then as the gunners realised that the threat posed by the Rangers was a much more pressing one, they picked up rifles and machine pistols and engaged the Rangers individually with small arms.

The A Company men could not stop. It was in their training and it was in their mindset. They were taught to advance quickly and efficiently at the enemy and this is what they did. Unlike the Omaha Beach situation three days before, they had no sea wall to hide behind to take a rest. They had no bluff at which to stop and take stock of their surroundings. They were running in the open, up hill at their enemy and every second they were above ground they were a target for a German who only needed his head above ground for a few seconds to hit them.

Richard Hathaway:

Once we started our assault, we came in from one direction, but we couldn't cross that area, so we had to come out and come in from a different direction. The problem was the swamp. It was the depth of the water. There was just too much of it for us to get through in that one spot. So we pulled out and Parker ordered us to fix bayonets. It was too large an area to cross and too much open space to go up against a fortification. So we all split up. I went into one trench and there was a guy nearby called, I can only remember his nickname, it was Frenchy. I said, 'Frenchy, come out with me we're going in here.' I went in. We came around a corner. Three other guys had come up over the top. They had blown up one guy, a German, they had blown his face off. He had no face. I remember Taylor saying, 'Hey, this guy isn't dead', and he stuck him with a bayonet. We walked down many trenches and when we entered a trench going into one of the gun pits, it was covered with wood and steel slats, like one overpass over another road. It was pretty deep underground. At least 20 to 30ft in some places. I remember there were long barrelled guns. They were impressive looking, all camouflaged and it was a well-organised fortification. The position of the guns was good for defending and the troops were all pretty well disciplined. They put up a good fight in some sections and it went on for a while, but we got the better of them.

Gradually the Germans started surrendering at La Martiniere. It was a Polish gunner who put his hands up first and started advanced towards the Rangers in front of him. Others started to follow by putting down their weapons and standing up with their hands in the air. At this moment two SS officers simultaneously opened fire on their surrendering men and forced them to take cover. They shot one of the Polish gunners in the back and wounded another before anyone realised what was happening. Everyone hit the ground and then the battle began again in earnest. The German conscripts' surrender faltered and then stopped with them again returning fire at the Rangers. The Rangers hastily moved back down out of harms way. The battle resumed with both the Germans and the A Company men exchanging fire – but now over an even shorter distance.

Sullivan's force was progressing well, capturing the trenches and emplacements at Les Perruques. His halftracks led by Conway Epperson had successfully destroyed the main rear-facing machine gun position closest to the back lane at Les Perruques and it enabled the attached infantry to wind their way through the barbed wire, avoid the mines and enter the trenches.

By stopping their advance into Les Perruques Sullivan realised that the two halftracks would be vulnerable to German fire if they remained stationary.

He ordered Epperson to cut across the fields towards the back of La Martiniere where there was still heavy gunfire coming from the A Company assault.

The two halftracks wheeled to their left and advanced across in front of Foucher's Farm with their protective group of 2nd Battalion men on foot – firing as they went.

The field was zig-zagged with barbed wire fencing and they were mindful of mines. However, for some reason this field between the two batteries was not mined and the wire was not a great obstacle to the halftracks. This was the same field where so many paratroopers had mis-dropped and been captured on 6 June, only three days before.

The German officer commanding La Martiniere was presented by a very clear problem. He had Ranger infantry engaging his front and flanks but the Ranger group Conway Epperson was commanding would overrun his position from the rear if it they were not stopped. He ordered his three remaining casemented field pieces to be turned around in order to counter the imminent threat from behind.

The guns were heavy, but their eight-men crews quickly wheeled them around and they began to engage the halftracks from their rear as bullets were hitting the concrete around them.

The 2nd Ranger men took shelter behind the halftracks as the German 10.5cm guns fired at them. The Ranger 75mm gun was accurate when fired from a stationary position, but the group were advancing to avoid the German gunners who were getting more accurate. They fired at the casements using bazookas and light machine guns and the bullets rattled off the back of the building around the Germans. Ranger M1 rifles were also taking large chunks out of the back of the concrete structure as they advanced and a number of the German gun crews were injured.

The Germans did not have the ability adequately to defend the men operating the field guns because they were outside of the casements in the open. They were in effect easy targets being static and the closer the 2nd Ranger men approached, the more likely they would be hit. One by one the German gunners realised it was not going well.

One gun was hit and the crew wounded, another was unable to get ammunition to continue to fire and another was disabled simply because all of the gun crew were wounded.

Although this loss of their primary weapons was a blow, it did not effect the soldiers in the surrounding trenches from continuing to fight. They were not aware of the advancing halftracks to their rear and many of them were still concerned that the Rangers were coming up the hill towards them and – more acutely for some, that there were SS officers quite ready to fire into their backs if they did not maintain their positions.

For some it was obvious that sitting tight and waiting for the Americans was a better option – if the Americans gave up the assualt then they still had the advantage of being in a concealed position. Little did they realise that in reality they were not outnumbered by the men of A Company.

Had they known this, it would perhaps have stiffened their resolve to defend the position. As it was, they had been subject to intense bombardment for three days solidly and although they could shelter in the relative safety of their bomb-proof positions, once they surfaced they had to negotiate the ever decreasing number of accessible trenches. Life had simply got worse and worse for them over the last three days.

Many trenches had collapsed from bombing and equipment and netting was everywhere. Moving around was getting impossible and yet surrendering was equally as difficult for the reasons already stated. Many of the conscript gunners were happy to surrender – but they had to choose their moment carefully. If they were seen by the SS to be giving up it was certain death. If they appeared to be armed when the Rangers approached then surrender would not appear to be on their minds … and again they would likely perish.

Many took the gamble on the Rangers reaching them first and so they disarmed themselves. Standing in a non-threatening position in a trench was no guarantee of safety – but it was more likely that one would survive doing that than being armed and appearing dangerous.

The German position was by no means lost at La Martiniere. There were a good many forward postions to the right of the Ranger up-hill advance, which were not yet affected in any way by the assault. These infantrymen started to come in from outlying positons and were able to give effective flanking fire from the tree line to the right (west) of the A Company advance. This was a real problem as the Rangers could not spend long above ground. They were in the open and vulnerable from these men who were were laying down accurate machine-gun fire at ground level. The Rangers who had not already done so entered the trenches and emplacements quickly.

Leading back from one of the forward mortar positions was a concrete tunnel some 20ft long. It ran under the surface of the field and backwards into the German trenches. Many of the Rangers took the opportunity to enter the position using this route, but it was not without its dangers. The Germans were becoming aware that the A Company men were amongst them, and in some cases they lay in wait for them to come around corners and fired at close range.

Rangers countered this by throwing grenades over the top of trenches when they encountered a blind corner or bunker entrance. Often they did not have time to

One of the guns at La Martiniere just after the battle. The gun is facing backwards to defend the position from the advancing Ranger halftracks. Note the small-arms damage to the concrete.

go into the many doorways which led downwards. They simply threw in a grenade and continued. It was a risky strategy as Ranger Daniel Farley remembered. He passed a number of men who appeared to be dead only to see one of them move as he did so. He assumed they were pretending to be dead to allow the Rangers to pass. Trying to catch them from behind. The A Company men then adopted the policy they had learned back at the beach of 'double tapping' all bodies in case they were pretending to be dead. (In some bunkers at Vierville a number of 'dead' Germans had come alive and killed Allied men – the A Company men were learning that it paid to be thorough.)

With infantry supporting the halftracks, their 75mm guns firing as they went, the concrete positions of La Martiniere were becoming untenable for the Germans. The A Company assault to the front through their trenches and the advance on the position from the rear meant that surrender or death was inevitable. But the gunners still continued firing from the shelter of the casements.

Richard Hathaway:

They folded up pretty fast initially. But the battle took about 5 hours to complete from the time we started out. Simply because of the size of the site. I wasn't really scared. I was all hyped up. We were in a bayonet assault and there was no question we were taking the place. I had it on, but I didn't have to stick anybody. We did use some concussion grenades. I threw a couple. I was armed with an M1 rifle. I saw about six dead Germans I guess. The guys we came up against were German troops. I didn't go into the hospital area – that was in another section, but I did see the 155mm howitzers. They were French. I saw five and all of the gun positions were tunnelled into concrete. They were really deep down in the rock or concrete. I didn't see any horses or motorised transport of any type, but I did see a lot of 155 ammo, it was for the French guns. They had 155 howitzers in there and they could reach both Omaha and Utah Beaches. They did not fire to my knowledge any shots on Omaha Beach. They may have fired on Utah as you could see it. It took us I'd say about 5 hours of fighting to get the position. I think the only way we could get inside the place was on foot. When we took it we captured it complete and the Germans had a payroll for their men all in French currency. We were told the money was no good. I was a Tech Sergeant, T/5 and I moved over to HQ Company, but I was with A Company on the assault.

The Maisy guns at both La Martiniere and Les Perruques had not suffered from a lack of ammunition for their weapons at any time, so they were still operational at La Martiniere against the halftracks. Because they were a wheeled weapon they could be simply removed from the casements and turned around to fire across the fields at the halftracks of the 2nd Battalion. And this is what the Germans did. As they opened fire from the back of the three remaining casements the 2nd Battalion halftracks fired back and were successful in damaging both the guns and the casements in the process. A post-D-Day naval intelligence report written in July 1944 states rather quisically, '*the guns were turned around to fire backwards?*'

By now the anti-aircraft weapons at both batteries had been destroyed and they were no longer capable of being used as ground defence weapons. The naval and aerial bombardments of the days before had rendered their field positions useless. However, regular supplies of ammunition had been arriving at the site prior to the invasion and the lack of consistent and effective bombing of the batteries meant that stocks were good. Therefore, the guns continued to fire at the naval forces arrayed against them and amazingly, despite all that was capable of being done to them, they were still operational on the 9th. A post-battle naval evaluation reported that the Maisy ammunition storage bunkers were found to '*contain over 180 tonnes of ammunition*' after the battle and three of the La Martiniere weapons were still operational. One gun, however, had been placed in an open position while its casement was built and it was destroyed completely by naval gunfire on the 6th – well before the battle on land had started.

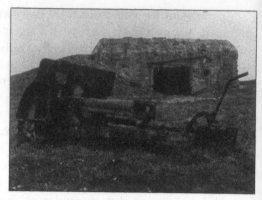

A cannon at La Martiniere post battle.

Jack Burke:

A Company had about forty-five men at this time for the assault because we had lost the remainder on the beach. Farley and Lieutenant Parker went into a pillbox from a tunnel and underground they had a complete medical dispensary – I did not see it. The Germans were well supplied with sausage and I ate some of that, and I remember the German doctor working with us on the wounded. There were four medics. A guy called Pete Mullins who was the head of the medical battalion. He was sergeant. I later took his place. There was Medic Bill Taylor from F Company and there may have been a guy named Knajdek – I'm not sure. I did not wear a red cross on my helmet as the Germans gave it no respect and still shot as us, but some of the other medics did. I wore the white armband with the red cross on it.

Rows of unfired 155mm shells in the Le Perruques ammunition bunker dispels the myth that the Germans had little or no ammunition on D-Day.

Veteran Ranger Jack Burke standing beside one of the 'Tobruks' at La Martiniere which was firing down on him as he and the other A Company men advanced up the hill.

We treated a lot of guys who were wounded up at the top of the hill. They mainly suffered gunshot wounds, you know, leg wounds and stuff like that.

I remember the big guns, but not the calibre. The mortar and artillery emplacements all had painted charts on the walls with firing objectives and the exact firing range for each place. That is why they were so accurate. There was absolutely no damage to the guns in there as a result of naval fire. To me they seemed in good condition. I recall the trenches and seeing the emplacements and I remember one of the officers telling someone to go out on patrol and see what's ahead of us and bring back some prisoners. There were some Polish guys up there – conscripts in the German Army. They were intermingling with our Polish guys and one of my buddies was a guy named Stan Bojara – he was talking to them.

I heard we hit a big payroll, but we were too tired to go looking for it. We hadn't really slept or eaten and we had very little water. We were just numb.

Richard Hathaway:

After the battle we only stayed long enough to collect all of the prisoners and then move out. We didn't stay too long. I did get some of the French money from the payroll though. I stuck a bunch of it in my shirt and many years later I finally donated it to the museum to display there. We even used some to heat up our rations at the time as we thought it was worthless. The Germans must have thought we were crazy burning the money and not caring, we were burning it to heat up our C-rations. It surprised everybody when we found out what it was and how big the site was. There was even another sector where they had a hospital, stores and barracks built way underground. They were really organised.

John Reville:

We eventually took about 40–50 prisoners in our section, but we just didn't see A Company. It was my platoon that took that area – we ended up taking part of the site on our own. The pillboxes that we saw there were really small. They were probably just to take shelter in. Not like the beach shelters.

As the fighting moved away from the front edges of La Martiniere it became more and more difficult for the Germans to maintain their positions. Lieutenant Parker was now confident that the Germans were done and he was also aware that he had left wounded men on the slope approaching the battery during the advance. He called over Jack Burke (A Company medic) to deal with them.

Burke recalls:

I was sent down to get the wounded – Jim Sullivan and Bob Battice from A Company – they had been wounded as the advance started and they were still down in the swampy area. I was standing at the top of the hill with some wounded guys, a couple of wounded Germans and a bunch of prisoners and Parker said, 'I've got two guys that are badly hurt. They are down at the base down there in that flooded area and we've got to get them out.' The Germans had flooded the lower area and it was all marshy. It was where Battice and Sullivan and a lot of other guys got hit.

Captain Petrick, who was a medical officer, said to me, 'Go down there and get them.' I kept saying to myself, 'How in the hell can one guy get two guys out of there?' Anyway being the dumb GI I went down there. They gave me support with a guy named Joe Virers – he was a BAR man. Looking left back down the hill there was a wooded area and they were shooting at us from there. He gave me cover from his BAR and I started to run down the hill – then all hell broke loose with machine-gun and rifle fire shooting at me from the left. I could hear the bullets hitting all around me and smashing into the swamp. Sullivan and Battice were together. I mean they were right together, side by side. I guess they got hit by at the same time. Battice got hit in the head and Sullivan got hit in the arm, the shoulder and the back. They were both badly wounded and still under fire, but slightly hidden at the base of the hill behind a small mound or hedgerow.

Richard Hathaway:

No Rangers were actually killed to my knowledge. I don't know of any men in our group who were killed. There were wounded, but nobody to my knowledge was killed.

The source of the injuries to Battice and Sullivan would have remained a mystery forever had it not been for a chance conversation with A Company's **John Bellows** sixty years later. He had stepped through the swampy ground and was advancing up the hill towards La Martiniere when he came under machine-gun fire:

I remember stepping on the prong of an S-mine and watching with horror as it launched up in the air... fortunately it didn't go off – which is something I will never forget. However, it did set off a chain reaction of some other mines which wounded some of the other men around me.

Both Bob Battice and Jim Sullivan had been hit by the mines set off by John Bellows – something they reminded him about after the war at reunions. They were both lucky to have survived the mines at Maisy, but they did suffer with their injuries for the rest of their lives.

Jack Burke was down in the swamp looking after them. He continues:

I did what I could by throwing sulphur powder on them from my bag and bandaging them the best I was able. They were lying in the mud and water soaking wet ... it was slushy, ankle deep. We left everything but their rifles. When we got back to the top Lieutenant Parker told me he was going to put me in for the Silver Star ... he never did. We put the wounded onto a 2nd Battalion halftrack as it was positioned just behind the pillbox where we had all the wounded. We had Germans and Rangers there.

As the battle subsided more and more Rangers began tentatively to explore the positions around them. Leaving only sporadic sniping from the edges of the site. Ranger Hurlihy found a German artillery officer's uniform, complete with dagger, and nearby a flag. They later posed for a photograph – no doubt relived that the fighting was over.

Rangers Hurlihy, Rutkoski and Lutick posing on the afternoon of 9 June with souvenirs taken from the Germans at Maisy.

An S-mine, or 'Bouncing Betty', that was dug up in near perfect condition at Les Perruques.

Dr Petrick, accompanying C Company, had pressed a captured German Army doctor into assisting with the treatment of the wounded from the battle. The American troops had found the hospitals and the dispensery during their searching of the batteries and they put the German medical staff to good use. Both the Rangers and Germans were treated equally once the firing stopped and generally the Germans did not wish to cause any problems once captured. There were of course exceptions.

Albert Nyland:

We caught some Germans and took them prisoner, and after the battle we started to take them back to the beach when we came across some US paratroopers who had got lost. I asked them to take eight prisoners back to the beach for us and they agreed ... but they took them into a farmhouse and shot them. The Ranger wounded were also going back to the beach on a horse and cart and one of our medics (Barber) was asked by a Frenchman to look at the dead and dying Germans in his farm. There were a lot of dead pigeons. A lot of the barns would have pigeons in them and when you looked up and heard a rustle of noise you would assume it was a German sniper. We got rid of a lot of pigeons that way!

A Company 5th Battalion veteran Jack Burke standing on the roadway just behind La Martiniere. This is the spot where he put the wounded onto the halftracks to send them back to the beach.

Jim Wilderson:

Whenever we took prisoners we had a central stockade to take them to on the beach ... we would shake them down and take their money. I had a German sergeant and I found out that he was the paymaster for the company. I took this satchel it was full of money and an officer took it away from me. I know he sent it home. I was a corporal and stayed a corporal.

Medical officer Captain Petrick who supervised the treatment of the wounded at La Martiniere.

Jack Burke:

Kalish from A Company took a pile of the Maisy money!

John Raaen:

I didn't send any money home, but my recollection is that if you took the money to any Finance Office it would be converted into dollars. You were then given a money order for the amount and then all you had to do was mail it home. From there we heard that four new millionaires were created through the money orders home!

The Maisy complex had the payroll for the surrounding area as the German payday was 6 June 44. The invasion prevented the money from being disbursed. Sullivan's task force captured the whole payroll. Small amounts were taken by some of the Rangers, more as souvenirs than anything else, thinking that the money was no good. I remember seeing some of it later and pointing out it WAS THE SAME CURRENCY found in our escape and evasion kits. Suddenly it had value. Anybody that had 'liberated' some of the money could go to the local Finance Office and get a money order to send home the money. In the 5th Battalion the holders used it to chase us out of poker games since in real no limit poker the man with the most cash on the table inevitably wins. I had to quit playing poker with those benefitting from the Maisy find.

After capturing the payroll some of it was turned over to the 29th Infantry Division MPs who were following the Rangers to take POWs back to the beaches. However, a strong post-war rumour circulated that a Frenchman from Grandcamp entered the site after the battle and 'liberated' a lot of it for himself before the MPs were involved. Another rumour suggested that Field Marshall Romell had a quantity of gold stored in the Legrande farm buildings in front of Les Perruques, but again this has not been substantiated.

John Raaen:

The money was stacked in 14in square bundles and the Rangers did indeed literally throw it all around. I heard that there 3 or 4 million francs or dollars total value. The story I heard at the time was that it was the payroll for the entire area from the

Vire East to Bayeau. We were told that the Germans paid their troops on the 6th of the month, but the invasion precluded that and the 5th captured the payroll before the Germans had an opportunity to move it. The Germans thought they were mad as the Rangers lit their cigarettes and cigars with the notes.

After resting and reorganising, Major Sullivan's task force proceeded to Osmanville, while John Reville and F Company were sent back to Vierville with the halftracks to help clear the areas around the rear of the beachhead after the battle.

John Raaen:

As an individual I was at the rear of the column and the Germans attacked us with machine guns from a distance. I do remember distinctly passing by one of the Maisy positions and the Rangers were repairing wounds and repairing damaged equipment. Other Rangers had moved out along the Isigny road and were heading towards Osmanville.

Albert Nyland:

That night we bivouacked at Osmanville and we were bombed.

The German command produced a summary of the overall situation of the 352nd Infantry Division at 2200hr on 9 June 1944:

The enemy: we noticed that the enemy troops had gained confidence in themselves, feeling that they were getting the upper hand. This particularly applied to the 29th Infantry Division which had been reinforced by one armoured battalion. True enough a somewhat exaggerated superiority complex could be observed, so as for instance tanks which stubbornly kept rolling forward along main roads without the support of covering parties, and the carefree way in which quarters were taken up once the initial objective had been reached, instead of exploiting successes.

The Germans evaluated the capabilities of the two sides in the Omaha sector on the night of the 9th as follows:

German Side	American Side
Right Sector	
750 infantrymen	2,000 infantrymen
8 piece of heavy artillery	12 pieces of artillery at least
6 pieces of anti-aircraft artillery	
5 tanks	20 tanks
No aeroplanes	12 aeroplanes (almost the whole time)
Central Sector	
800 infantrymen	3,000 infantrymen
6 light pieces of artillery	36 pieces of artillery (at least)
No tanks	An unknown number of tanks
No aeroplanes	12 aeroplanes (almost the whole time)

Left Sector	
700 infantrymen	2,000 infantrymen
No artillery at all	An unknown number of artillery
4 pieces of anti-aircraft artillery	
No tanks	40 tanks
No aeroplanes	12 aeroplanes (almost the whole time)

It was clear that by the evening of the 9th the Germans had lost the area and had virtually nothing left with which to stem the advancing forces. Maisy had literally been the only remaining coastal defence battery to continue firing at the Allies and it too had now been silenced.

German report, 9 June:

The 914 Gren Regt made a report at approximately 0400 hours … enemy tanks had penetrated into Isigny – resistance on a small scale continued at that spot. The commanding officer of the 1st Battalion of the 1352nd Artillery Regiment Major van dem Bergh reported immediately afterwards from the command post of the 914 Gren Regt that when he was about to cross the emergency bridge hard north of Isigny with his battalion – the enemy had already continued his advance with tanks and motor vehicles along the main street of the town in a westerly direction. He had been compelled to abandon his guns and had just arrived at the command post of the 914 Gren Regt with the personnel of his unit (approximately 400 men).

It was therefore clear that on the 9th June the 352 Infantry Division had only fourteen more artillery pieces still available for its approximately 40km wide sector.

The concrete shelters built for the guns at La Martiniere had stood up well to the bombardment. An examination of the casements today reveals virtually no visible damage to their fronts, possibly even indicating that they received no actual direct hits despite all the naval reports to the contrary. However, there is severe cannon and small-arms damage to their rear. As a Ranger said to me, '*We wouldn't be using the back of the bunkers for target practice … they were a threat until we destroyed them – then we stopped firing.*'

John Reville:

Following Maisy we did the mopping up of the beach areas after the battle. I got a jeep and I went back with someone back to where we landed to look for the money to grab some, but it had all gone. Everything had gone.

81st Chemical Weapons' report:

In clearing the enemy from the beachhead, the 81st Chemical Mortar Battalion expended a total of 6,807 rounds of ammunition. Casualties for this period were 11 killed (5 officers and 6 enlisted men), 25 wounded, and 1 captured.

The batteries at Maisy had taken their toll. Major Sullivan and C Company men were wounded by mines and small arms. A Company men were also hit by mines and mortar fire and the following list is taken from John Hodgson's F Company diary, written that evening.

F Company Wounded in Action at Maisy:
Sgt. Antony Muscatello 33251670.
PFC Edward T. Mapes 37467459.
T/5 Nicholas Pasuk 16021197.

Major Sullivan, by now a veteran of three invasion landings, was sent back to the USA with full military honours. However, before this he was awarded the Distinguished Service Cross for 'the fighting at Omaha Beach, the relief of Pointe du Hoc and leading the successful attack on the Maisy Batteries'.

Jim Sullivan and Bob Battice (A Company) lived to a ripe old age, but they did not ever return to their unit and both were severely hampered by the wounds they sustained at Maisy for the remainder of their lives.

Francis Coughlin was wounded on the evening of the 9th. He and some other Rangers had come across four field guns in Osmaville close the the Rangers' rendezvous point. As he attempted to drop a thermite grenade down the barrel of the third of the four guns, it exploded seriously wounding him and killing others. The Germans had placed a live shell halfway up the barrel to boobytrap it and his grenade set it off. He spent six months in hospital and never returned to the Rangers.

Anthony Muscatello recovered from the bullet to his throat after treatment and returned to the Rangers. He was killed in action later that year.

John Hodgson kept the bullet that 'fell into his pocket' and always took it to post-war reunions.

Cecil Gray was given the Purple Heart for his mine injury at Maisy.

Albert Nyland finally had the piece of wood removed from his back in 2007.

Captain John Raaen of HQ Company, 5th Ranger Infantry Battalion on D-Day wrote the following to me in 2008:

I remember writing the After Action Reports for the D-Day operation to show what happened to the 5th Battalion on 9 June 1944. The truth of the matter was that it was the first After Action Report we were asked for and we didn't even know there was to be one. Corps called down and asked for our Action After Report. After Action Report? I didn't understand it and I said, 'What do we put in it?'

I asked Heffelfinger and he said there was an army regulation for it … it may have been a corps reg or a 1st Army reg. I do remember seeing it and being baffled by it. There wasn't enough information in what was required, so it was just an effort to produce the first such After Action Report. There were no examples, no precedents, no coordinates no nothing.

No real instructions, just to describe the actions of the elements of the battalion and include a list of casualties during the day. The whole thing was rather silly because the morning report was more sensible as it had a list of all the people who were wounded and killed ... We just did the best we could with the first one and the company clerk had a typewriter and did the first thing – and we would type it and see how it worked – how it read and then took it up to Heffelfinger and he would comment ... and then he submitted it.

There were so many things we didn't do right, but for our first effort we didn't do too bad.

By the time we reached Brest we were given feedback from above about our first effort.

I would be much more specific about two sites that we were attacking with two companies coming from the north and west with one company coming from the south and I would have identified the companies that participated. Neither Schneider or Heffelfinger were involved in Maisy and neither were interested. They have both been involved in other actions and not Maisy – so their lack of interest would have meant that they were happy with whatever I had written.

Author, in discussion with John Raaen:

Your personal map shows a lack of information and is not detailed.

John Raaen:

The main thing is that at the battalion level – they had the same map as I had with all the enemy fortifications shown on them. They would not be interested in artillery fire and so what we had were S3 maps and they would be different from S2 intelligence officers' maps ... which would show mines, weapons, positions, etc.

Author:

Would you have taken more interest if the fortifcations were marked properly?

John Raaen:

The artillery registration point maps were very useful. They told us where the sites were, but they had no qualitative information about them. If I was a company commander and I received orders to attack target number 5, I would ask the S2 for his information on the site. It would should show mines, wire and extensive information on the area. This info would have been supplied by aerial info and Resistance information.

That is the duty of a company commander to research and get all the information he can on a position he is about to attack. So in theory, Parker, Runge and Wise – they should have been able to have that information. Later on we would identify units down to platoon actions.

When I had the priviledge to meet up with Brigadier General J. Raaen at his home we discussed the evidence now available from my interviews and historical references. I showed him a map and he wrote the following report later and sent it to me. Although not the 'official history of the events of 9 June', it more adequately reflects the actual actions of 9 June 1944, not those recorded as the 'official war department account'.

John Raaen:

Your map is very interesting and useful. Based on it and your text, I have rewritten a part of the story to reflect your findings, since they fit well with my memories and other sources. The way I originally wrote it (the official After Action Report) I had to stretch a few points to make it fit with other sources, but the new version fits much better.

On the morning of D+3, 9 June 1944, A, C and F of the 5th Rangers, still under Major Sullivan, were detached from the 1st Battalion, 116th Infantry. In its advance to the south, the 1st Battalion, 116th Infantry had encountered severe resistance from a German strongpoint at La Martiniere, ¾ mile, SSW of Maisy [52679151], and Les Perruques [53349188], ¾ mile ssw of Maisy. Together, these two connected positions were called the Maisy Battery. The 116th's objective was Isigny not Maisy, so the 1st Battalion, 116th Infantry bypassed the German position. Major Sullivan had three Ranger Companies, two halftracks from the 2nd Ranger Battalion, and Company B, 81st Chemical Weapons Battalion. The latter unit was armed with 4.2in mortars.

During the approach march, I was at the rear end of the column with a small headquarters' element. Crossing through the hedgerows and fields we were taken under long-range machine-gun fire from our right several times. However, we were beyond tracer burn-out and the Germans were never able to reach us. Because of the extensive mine fields protecting the German strongpoint, Major Sullivan decided to attack in a column of companies with A Company in the lead followed by C Company with F Company in reserve. The 58th Armoured Field Artillery Battalion bombarded the Maisy positions in preparation for the 5th Ranger attack.

Support during the attack was provided by the 81st's 4.2in mortars, the two 75mm cannon mounted on the 2nd Rangers' halftracks and the four 81mm mortars. Companies A and F moved down the dirt road just north of gridline 92. This area is quite swampy, and in this swampy area, they came across some dead American paratroopers who had been dropped miles from their intended drop zones. Some had drowned, some had been caught up in trees and gunned down by the German defenders. When opposite (north of) La Martiniere and Les Perruques, the companies wheeled to the left with A Company attacking La Martiniere and F Company, Les Perruques.

Meanwhile, C Company with the cannon platoon from the 2nd Rangers proceeded directly south from Maisy, wheeled right, attacking Les Perruques from the south-east. Major Sullivan controlled the battle from one of the halftracks accompanying C and D Companies. The attack progressed well with some of the German defenders laying down their weapons and surrendering.

However, some German officers, possibly SS, began shouting threats and shooting some of their own men in the back. Despite the mine fields and stubborn resistance, the strongpoint was successfully captured. It contained three 10cm howitzers, large stocks of ammunition and other supplies and about ninety defenders who became POWs. The POWs and the position were turned over to elements of the 29th division.

Ace Parker, the A Company Commander, later told me that, as far as he was concerned, the fight at Maisy was far worse than the Omaha Beach landings of four days before.

After capturing the Maisy Battery, Sullivan's Ranger force marched to a bivouac area west of Osmanville where, at 2000hr, it re-joined the rest of the battalion and turned in for the night in the hedgerows and ditches. The 2nd Ranger Battalion also spent the night in the same area. All was not quiet in Osmanville. Bed Check Charley, a German airplane pilot, paid nightly visits to the battalion area, occasionally dropping bombs.

Several headquarters company men were there.

I hope this helps and that you have no objections to the above rewrite of my story.

It may not be possible 'officially' to amend the original document, but at least now the correct account of what happened on 9 June 1944 is available to historians.

Captain John Raaen – 5th Rangers.

Chapter 11

Challenging a D-Day Myth

Pointe du Hoc did not fire a field gun at anyone on D-Day. So the question then should be, did the Germans leave a huge section of undefended coastline without any static coastal gun battery? The answer is of course they did not. If there were NO field guns at Pointe du Hoc in operation on D-Day, no account can accurately list it as having 6 x 155mm French K418 cannons on 6 June 1944, but all do.

This is simply not correct. It would be like saying that Colonel Rudder's Rangers could have killed Erwin Rommel at Pointe du Hoc on D-Day just because he was once there earlier in 1944. It does not mean he was there on the day, so why do all accounts say that Pointe du Hoc had six guns when on the day there were none at the site. What matters historically is accuracy, not what could have happened, but what did happen.

A US Army intelligence evaluation dated May 1944 reads:

Pointe du Hoc.

586937 – Six 155mm (6.1 inches) French guns, probably type GPF. Range 22,000 yards or more (possibly 25,000 yards). Guns on wheel mountings, the wheels being secured to the central pivot of a concrete emplacement about 40 feet in diameter. Each gun is camouflaged with netting; there is no turret or gun shield. B.O.P. reinforced concrete shelter on headland in front of gun position. Flank OPs – locations unknown; presumably near PTE. Et Raz de la Percée and east of Grandcamp. Shelters and magazines; underground; reinforced concrete, 3 feet, 3 inches to 6 feet, 6 inches thick. Connected with gun emplacement by trenches partly covered over. Huts for off-duty personnel and administrative personnel in rear of gun position. Secondary armament; three (?) 20mm guns in emplacements on roofs of concrete shelters (still under construction). Etc. etc.

This report may seem an accurate appraisal of what was at Pointe du Hoc on D-Day, but, if you read it again you will note it is not right. The position of the six guns will be dealt with shortly, but the most interesting thing is that the intelligence report states that the three shelters (still under construction) have anti-aircraft guns on their roofs.

It is a safe bet to suggest that these were the three 'shelters' indicated overleaf, although we know these are not all shelters – two are casements being constructed for 10.5mm guns. So why does the report suggest they are shelters with AA guns on their roofs? If they had watched them being built they would surely have seen that their construction was interfering with three of the six gun pits already on the site, so why does the report also state that the site still contained six gun pits? Both cannot be true. If the three casements were under construction when the report was written, then the writer must have realised that the casements were being built over and in the way of other pits. This will be explained here in more detail.

The guns of Pointe du Hoc viewed from the air. The observation point is marked in black and above and to its left are anti-aircraft positions circled in white. To the right are the two unfinished casements.

Pointe du Hoc was empty of field guns on D-Day, fact. Casements and pits were camouflaged as a ruse and this ambiguity is often described as the reason that the Rangers had to be sent to attack the site. After all, no one could be sure if they were operational or not. The most common argument heard about Pointe du Hoc is that the Germans moved their guns behind into the fields to protect them a few days before D-Day.

That is nonsense and I feel it is easily disproved. Why would Pointe du Hoc's officers move the guns inland and yet no other battery on the coast do the same? Particularly when the gun batteries were all under attack at some time or other. Nobody else was ordered to move their guns – so why just here? That argument does not make sense.

Perhaps as some suggest, the captain in charge of the unit at Pointe du Hoc decided to move his guns without being ordered, but no order exists in the records of the 352nd Infantry Division to move his guns to the rear. Logically, this is unlikely as well – a professional German officer took orders from his superiors and did not make them up.

Surely the best layout for a static coastal battery to ensure greatest accuracy and indeed its own defence is for it to have its weapons on their own purpose-built concrete pits. Ammunition is protected by the bomb-proof bunkers underground nearby and the gun crews have the most safety. Pointe du Hoc also had its own observation and fire-control position only yards away.

There are no specific reports about Pointe du Hoc firing at D-Day targets in the German 352nd Division reports. Yet reports exist for the batteries at Longues, Crisbecq and Maisy detailing targets, results and problems encountered. If Pointe du Hoc was the 'big coastal battery' in the sector then surely German HQ would be interested in the results of its guns against the huge array of ships within range? Surely there would be radio instructions to the battery to open fire on the enemy. The area commanders would be asking what attempts were being made to destroy the enemy – these radio

A still from the film Rommel made at Pointe du Hoc in early 1944. It clearly shows a 155mm French cannon and no casement being built in front of it.

The same gun position today with the unfinished casement built in front of it. Unfortunately, somebody decided that they would put scaffolding around it to allow visitors to get a better view of the site, thus ensuring that the original character of the building is permanently defaced for future generations.

A close-up of the same gun position taken from the approximate barrel end. It would be impossible to fire directly out to sea from this pit without shooting into the casement. Clearly the pit could not used like this.

This photograph is taken from the US Army official history detailing events at Pointe du Hoc. It shows the six gun pits to be assaulted by the Rangers, the boat numbers and where they land. But it does not indicate that the blockhouses are built over any of these pits. Why not? Possibly because someone has drawn large black circles over them!

reports would exist between Pointe du Hoc and German headquarters, but they do not. However, they exist for Maisy, Crisbecq, Longues-sur-Mer, etc.

To suggest that the Germans did not have radio communication with their forward units in this area is also incorrect. Reports were getting back to HQ about the advance of their counterattacking units at Pointe du Hoc, units that would have liaised with the gunners from behind the Pointe as they passed their positions. No questions came from above to ask why these guns were not operational – why? Is it because HQ was already aware they were not operational and so no demands were made upon them to be firing?

It cannot also be argued logically that the gunners behind Pointe du Hoc were surprised by the landings and simply not ready. German reports, as we have seen, showed the capture of an American Paratrooper lieutenant in the early hours of 6 June. He is said (in German radio reports) to have given the Germans information relating to the invasion on parachute dummies, etc. This information was sent back to HQ by the Germans at Pointe du Hoc – by radio early on – so they would have been under no illusions as to the impending landings.

Another of the casements – you can see the ring of the open gun-pit position in the foreground. The casement has been built over the side of the pit. Internally there are no fittings or mounts in position to allow a gun to be mounted. This casement is not finished. So neither the pit or casement could have been operational on D-Day.

The evidence on the ground is also persuasive. First, the gun pits at Pointe du Hoc need to be examined in detail. In February 1944 Rommel made a famous 'public-relations' film in which he is seen walking around Pointe du Hoc. He is with an army general and a number of K418 French cannons are seen on the concrete pits. Therefore, one has to assume that Pointe du Hoc was fully operational at that time as a 6 x 155mm battery.

On D-Day the guns seen in photographs from Rommel's film are gone. In their place, literally, are large casements under construction. This work had been taking place for some months in 1944, but they were actually unfinished when Pointe du Hoc was assaulted. The Rangers stopped the development at Pointe du Hoc dead, and that is how it remains now. This is helpful from a historical perspective because it allows us to see exactly to what point the construction had progressed by D-Day.

These casements were part of the upgrading work that was being carried out all along the Atlantic Wall and there is nothing usual about that. However, this development is at odds with the present-day perception of Allied reports of what was installed at the Pointe on D-Day. You can clearly see that one of the pits – that was supposed have a gun

Inside one of the unfinished casements. It has no steel fittings to mount a deck gun added yet.

on it two days before D-Day – has a casement built right over where it was. So, one of the six operational pits that the Rangers went to attack, is not capable of even holding a field gun. This leaves five gun pits.

Another, as we have seen, was being built directly in front, leaving four pits. Another pit has the foundations of a casement (which has been started) built on top of the centre of it, so clearly it too did not house a gun on D-Day,

A gun-pit photo clearly showing the round pit being built on by the casement. It was not possible that there was a 155mm gun in the casement or in the pit.

which leaves three operational pits. Another of the pits was destroyed by the RAF on their bombing mission of 22/23 April 1944, which was well documented at the time. Thus two gun pits remain, and could not obviously have housed six guns.

The above-ground, seemingly bomb-proof, naval casements at Pointe du Hoc were being built to house deck-mounted 10.5cm ships guns, as seen below in a similar casement at Jersey. Once finished the casements at Pointe du Hoc would have looked very similar to this.

The two half-finished casements at the Pointe were being built for an identical deck gun, not a gun with wheels and not a gun with two legs 12ft long, which would obviously be too big! The 10.5cm modern German weapon would have sat behind a steel shield. It was similar in fact to those at Longues-sur-Mer, but smaller. This was not a gun that could have been simply wheeled out of a casement and taken away into fields some days before D-Day 'to protect it'.

There are only two operational gun pits for K418 cannons on D-Day and they were both empty when the Rangers got there. So what were the Rangers sent to do and why? Surely Allied intelligence could see that the pits were empty and the casements were not finished from their own reconnaissance? There is more to this than meets the eye, obviously. The main question here is was there something else going on – perhaps politically – which caused Pointe du Hoc to have greater significance on D-Day. In effect, did the assault have a more political or propaganda purpose than simply a military one?

Pointe du Hoc was an obvious promontory in 1944. It is a very clear outline on the landscape and surrounding

A gun position similar to how the Pointe du Hoc guns would have looked when finished.

cliffs and is fairly unmistakable. Erwin Rommel was a highly experienced and clever commander. He is documented as having said that he thought the Allies would land at Vierville, St Laurent and Colleville beaches (collectively now known as Omaha Beach) because they so closely resembled those beaches in Italy that had already been invaded. It is logical to consider that Rommel thought that the Allies would employ similar tactics and equipment developed for the earlier attacks in a similar invasion attempt of Normandy. He also knew that when he allowed himself to be filmed 'showing off' the Atlantic Wall – and in particular Pointe du Hoc, that this activity would not go unnoticed by his opposite number, Supreme Allied Commander Dwight Eisenhower. A film was duly made showing Rommel at Pointe du Hoc and it was released around the world. Today you can see it regularly on the History Channel as part of a larger propaganda film. It shows Erwin Rommel being followed around Pointe du Hoc by a general in a leather coat carrying a clipboard.

By blatantly showing off Pointe du Hoc Rommel was inevitably going to make it a bigger target, and it is reasonable to assume he was fully aware of this. He knew that Maisy was only 2 miles away and covering this section of coast, so logically, why not use Pointe du Hoc as a target to deflect attention from Maisy during its upgrading?

Allied Commander Eisenhower will have seen the film. During a high-level meeting he decided that Pointe du Hoc was 'Target Number 1' – in the whole of the invasion area. That sounds like a logical decision until it is considered alongside other information. The following is a quote from the US Navy Department Library Interrogation after the war of Generalleutnant Dihm concerning Generalfeldmarschall Rommel and the preparation of German defences prior to the Normandy invasion.

My special missions consisted mainly of controlling the work on coastal defences, especially obstacles in the coastal zone and paratroop obstacles. Special assembly areas were set up near the coast for the procurement of the necessary mines, and all usable material, including surplus artillery shells, was brought to the assembly areas.

To thwart bombing attacks, the Generalfeldmarschall ordered the construction along the entire coast of a great number of dummy positions. Dummy installations of widely

One of the Pointe du Hoc gun pits after the battle shows a false wooden gun being viewed by an American serviceman.

different types appeared, varying from heavy batteries to single machine guns. Special orders were given for the realistic and clever construction of these installations and for the improvement of those already existing.

The attempt at deception, which was also intended to simulate the presence of a greater number of units on the coast, was a real success. Thus, numerous attacks by enemy bomber formations were diverted from the actual fortifications.

Erwin Rommel discusses the defences of Pointe du Hoc with his officers. The camera crew captured him walking around the site and it was released to the German public – *Rommel Inspecting the Atlantic Wall.*

The Generalfeldmarschall cherished no illusion that our defensive measures could for long remain unknown to the enemy. The continuous reconnaissance flights of the enemy air force, which could not be prevented, the great number of foreign workers in Organisation Todt and the impossibility of preventing the civilian population from gaining knowledge of the works, all furnished a source of information to the enemy.

As for the batteries near the beaches, the Generalfeldmarschall ordered frequent changes of position, careful camouflage, and the construction of dummy batteries. In the last weeks before the invasion, several of these dummy batteries were bombed heavily, whereas the actual batteries in the vicinity were unharmed.

On the subject of Nazi propaganda, Dihm said the following:

On many of his trips, Rommel was accompanied by reporters and cameramen. He did not intend to put himself in the foreground. He had remained unassuming and modest, but he used his name and his fame as one more weapon. He once said to his chief cameraman, 'You may do with me what you like if it only leads to postponing the invasion for a week.'

Rommel and his generals at Pointe du Hoc.

A staged photo opportunity perhaps?

Rommel inspecting Atlantic Wall defences.

Rommel inspecting camouflaged defences.

Where were these dummy batteries which were 'bombed heavily'? A number of planes exiting over that part of the peninsula dropped their bombs on Pointe du Hoc, so it was bombed on a regular basis for many months before D-Day.

Pointe du Hoc clearly was not operational as a gun battery, but it is often argued that perhaps the Allies did not know and had to make sure. This is understandable to a degree, but when other factors are considered this is not clear cut.

Rommel meets with his Generals.

The following quote is from a letter to Cornelius Ryan by the wartime Resistance chief Jean Marion, mayor of Grandcamp village in 1953. He said, '*The mystery of the Pointe du Hoc guns is this. They had never*

This is a famous photograph clearly showing Pointe du Hoc in flames. The planes are on their way home to England and leaving the French coast.

been mounted. Guns were immobile; had never been installed.' In fact, this is information Marion reported to London by radio on two occasions before D-Day. He wrote to Ryan that from his home in Grandcamp he also '*sent information to London about a battery set to fire on Utah*', which was Maisy – La Martiniere.

The Allies were in full possession of the fact that Pointe du Hoc had not been made operational, not just from their own aerial photographs, but also from the people on the ground. In particular, the people in the Resistance who were making it their business to study everything the Germans were doing.

As soon as Pointe du Hoc became target Number 1 it underwent a series of severe aerial attacks, almost immediately from a number of Allied aircraft and then on a regular basis right up to D-Day. It was allocated ship after ship to fire at it on D-Day and the dedicated force of Rangers were trained and assigned to assault it on D-Day. There was no way Pointe du Hoc was going to remain somewhere that Rommel could show off.

The American After Action Report writes in a rather confused way:

> *Just why the German guns were thus left completely undefended and unused is still a mystery. One theory, based on the fact that some artillerymen were captured that day on the Pointe, was that bombardment caught them in their quarters, and they were unable to get back to their position. All that can be stated with assurance is that the Germans were put off balance and disorganized by the combined effects of bombardment and assault, to such an extent that they never used the most dangerous battery near the assault beaches, but left it in a condition to be destroyed by weak patrols.*

This does not actually make sense as the guns would not, and could not, fit back at the Pointe in the casements being made – so why would the men used to operate the guns be at the Pointe and not within reach of their weapons? It is more likely that these were the gunners who were sent back as defensive infantry to the Pointe during German counterattacks.

Subsequent accounts concerning D-Day include photographs of guns in the field behind Pointe du Hoc and generally state, 'this is one of the missing guns from Pointe du Hoc destroyed by Lomell and Khun'. The most commonly used photograph is the one seen on the right. It is clearly not a gun from behind Pointe du Hoc for a number of reasons. First, the position of the muzzle, approximately 10ft in the air, would have made it very difficult for Ruplinski's patrol to have put a thermite grenade down the barrel, as they say they did. Secondly, if he or Lomell had managed to reach up to do it, they would

This photograph is frequently used to substantiate the suggestion that guns were present in the field behind Pointe du Hoc on D-Day. Gun barrel rased high.

This photograph is often captioned 'Rangers sitting beside one of the 155mm cannons from Pointe du Hoc', which is simply wrong. Again, the breech of this cannon is open, the barrel is in the down position – not up, as described by Lomell, and the hedgerow in the distance is not visible when you are in the position where the guns were located in reality. In addition, the men in the photograph are not Rangers. 'We did not hang around to have our photographs taken', said 2nd Battalion veteran Frank South, and indeed he wondered which Ranger took their camera or dog with them to Pointe du Hoc! These soldiers are not carrying weapons and the gun is not camouflaged in an apple orchard. Need I say more?

have found the grenade rolling out of the bottom of the barrel as the breech block is in open position! The Rangers would have simply shut the breech first and if they had done so it would, by the time of this photograph, have been completely welded up. As you can see in the photograph it is clearly open. Also the trees it is hidden under are not apple trees, but something much larger. Note the lack of camouflage netting.

Jack Burke commented on this photograph in 2010:

Who in the hell would have had a camera at that time. Lomell said they put thermite grenades into the breech of the guns and took off back to the battalion. Someone is using this picture to justify their analysis of a given situation! I'm getting fed up with these so-called 'experts' who have their facts wrong and continue to protect their turf by disregarding what people are telling them, people who were actually involved in fighting.

It is widely acknowledged that Lomell, Kuhn, Ruplinski and his men melted the traversing mechanisms and when possible dropped thermite grenades into the barrels of the guns they found. If that was the case ... and that is what they were trained to do, then why are the breeches of these guns open and why does the elevation of the barrels differ in each photograph? Does that mean that Len Lomell and the other Rangers did not do what they said they did – or are these not the same gun photos? The latter is the most obvious conclusion to me.

The middle image below shows Dwight Eisenhower looking at a gun for a photo opportunity and at a time when he would have been fully aware that the guns had not actually been in the cliff-top position as he thought. The gun has its barrel elevated and its undamaged breech is still open. This is often captioned as 'one of the guns from Pointe du Hoc', but for the reasons stated above it is unlikely, unless the Rangers' story is wrong, and they didn't use thermite grenades.

For the guns to be able to see Utah Beach, as Len Lomell described, then they must have been up on the lane area as seen in the photograph bottom right. It is the only place on the fields to the rear of the Pointe which offers a clear view of Utah Beach as described by Lomell and would match the description of a gun hidden in undergrowth. Beyond this point going forwards there are open fields and behind the lane to the rear is a small apple orchard. For the guns to have been usable they would have had to have been placed along the lane sighted to fire through the hedge towards Utah and not actually in the apple orchard in the field behind. If they were in the field to the rear then there would have been an additional two rows of trees (each side of the lane) to fire through, which would not be sensible.

If you study the route taken by Lomell and Kuhn down the lane and 'straight into the gun position' it is

The same gun – this time from the front. It is clearly not camouflaged in an apple orchard and note that the barrel is now in the down position again.

The same gun taken some time later with its barrel now up.

One of the few places at the field edge where you can clearly see Utah Beach, as described by Len Lomell.

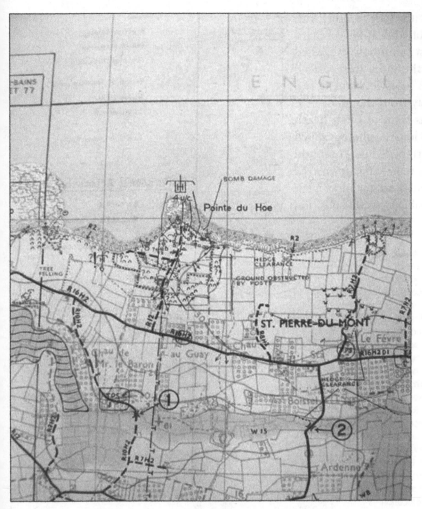

To answer the question, 'Did the Allies know there were troops in this area?', this GSGS map clearly indicates TPS (troop concentration) in this field. The issue is why were the Rangers not told?

most likely that the guns were indeed under cover either in the field edge or on the right-hand side of the lane as they approached, i.e. the field shown overleaf on the map (with white circles). The path taken by Khun and Lomell is indicated by black circles. The reason why the Germans were a distance away from Lomell is explained possibly by their command position being at the bottom of the other apple orchard, down on the lane at the farm. The setting up of any guns along this track would make them accessible and quickly moveable if required, irrespective of what was happening at the Pointe. This position would still offer cover for the guns under the trees while on the lane and under netting in the apple orchard next door. If Ruplinski's patrol was in the other apple orchard to the left on this map, then the guns (had they been set up to fire) would have been firing almost on top of each other to hit Utah Beach, but certainly not aimed at Omaha, as some American After Action Reports state as Omaha Beach cannot be seen from this position. This further fuels the suggestion that they were not set up to fire in this layout, but placed for storage before transportation elsewhere?

The field as it is today (right) with the remains of the apple orchard where it is most commonly suggested that three of the guns were placed (facing south). This location is two hedgerows away from the other field which then has sight of Utah Beach and the previously photographed lane is to the right, while Pointe du Hoc is to the rear. The downward slope of the field does not allow Utah Beach to be visible from this position

All that is left of the Point du Hoc 'Apple orchard', looking towards Utah Beach

The most likely direction taken by Len Lomell from Pointe du Hoc is marked with black circles. Grey circles indicate the best guess as to the position of the two guns Lomell and Kuhn found (if they were) against the hedgerow. Len Lomell told me that he followed a track away from the main road and found the guns in an orchard (not in a hedge). Which would have put them further in the field to the left. Nearer to the other three guns. The track he went down would be the only location which could have had a gate as shown in many post-war photographs and allowed the gun barrel to point towards Utah Beach ... but are the photos with the gun and the gate actually taken at this location – I doubt it. No gate exists along that track today leading into the field. The other three guns would have been in front of Lomell – to the left on this map (in the direction of Utah Beach), under cover in the orchard – just where Lomell described his guns being located. Utah Beach can be seen from this point on the field. These three guns and their ammunition were destroyed by

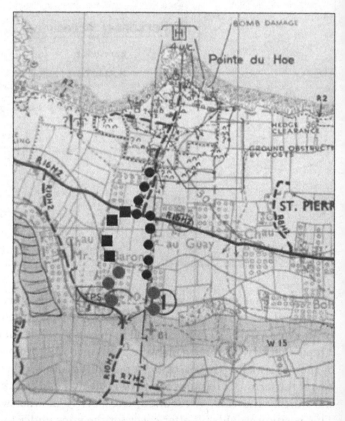

Ruplinski's patrol and it is likely he took the route indicated by the squares to find them – on the other side of the orchard from Lomell.

Therefore an alternative thought is that the guns were not against the gate shown in staged photographs and they were in reality all in the orchard to the left of the track. This is somewhat backed up by the 1944 pre-D-Day GSGS intelligence maps which are clearly marked TPS over the orchard area. TPS on intelligence maps means Troop Concentration – which fits for a group of men and guns hiding in an orchard. This position is only a few hundred yards from their headquarters at the farm.

Obviously the orchard does not have a gate in the middle of it as the apple trees are to the left of the field. So was there actually ever a gate here at this location – as is shown in many photographs. I think it is unlikely.

and yet it is often said that this is where Len Lomell damaged his guns, as they were 'hidden in the apple trees facing Utah Beach'. It is unlikely that the guns were in fact in this field but probably, for the reasons outlined above, they were next to it in the lane and in the field to the right – so more accurately camouflaged 'near the apple trees'.

If you study the same GSGS map carefully upwards to the left side of the Pointe you can see indicated the map symbol for six field howitzers and a question mark. Are these another earlier position of the (now six?) mysterious cannons/howitzers?

Given all the evidence available, it does not seem possible that the guns were set up to fire behind the Pointe. It is more likely, in my opinion, that the guns were hidden in the lane or under trees after being removed from Pointe du Hoc – when the site modifications started to take place. The reason for this is more readily explained when one studies the US post D-Day intelligence report map for the beach area.

The area shown by the words OMAHA in the centre of the map overleaf (at the beachline) indicates that there is no actual German fixed coastal defence battery with an arc of fire covering this stretch of beach. You can see that the three batteries at Maisy 5, 16 and 16A appear to cover to the Vierville exit, and the next battery to the right at Longues-sur-Mer covers only the approach area in front of Omaha Beach simply because its guns could not traverse left any further, because of their directional construction. Until Pointe du Hoc was finished there was actually nothing by way of a fixed coastal artillery unit covering this stretch of beach.

Assuming that the Allies had also figured out this gap existed, this could have been another factor in the Allies selecting this beach for the landings. It was one of the most difficult beaches to have been chosen in terms of the exit terrain and it is well away from the British landings up the coast. In addition, it would make joining up the American and British/Canadian fronts more difficult. It is not unreasonable for intelligence to have surmised that this beach had perhaps been 'missed' out on the German coastal defence plans and that the gap could be exploited. If the Longues-sur-Mer Battery could be neutralised before the landings at Omaha began, then logically the way would be clear for a less-opposed approach and a safer landing on Omaha Beach.

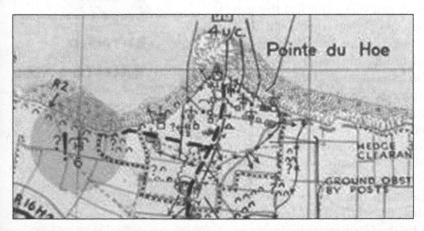

A close-up of the map on p. 284. Note the six field howitzers indicated to the left of the Pointe with a question mark and an exclamation mark next to them.

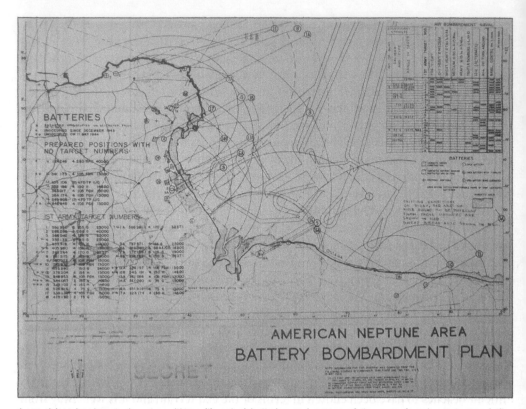

AMERICAN NEPTUNE AREA
BATTERY BOMBARDMENT PLAN

A naval bombardment plan overwritten with actual batteries and ranges of the guns found – not speculation beforehand. This map was produced by naval intelligence in July 1944 after the battle. Maisy's gun ranges are clearly marked with a distance of fire capable of reaching Vierville and covering part of Utah Beach. Pointe du Hoc's guns were shown in red on the original map and do not cover a complete arc – it states alongside that they were not operational or finished. No guns are marked in the fields to the rear of PdH – operational or not. The interlocking fields of fire for the larger batteries covering the US invasion beaches are shown as St Marcouf (Crisbecq), Maisy and Longues sur Mer. Nothing is shown for Pointe du Hoc other than it being under construction. This document remained 'Top Secret' until 2005 – a year after Maisy was 'rediscovered'!

The Germans would, one assumes, have equally been aware that this sector had this gap in beach coverage and perhaps this is why they added another larger 15cm battery at Maisy 16A. The arc of fire for this battery shown on the above map is 'estimated' at 75mm weapons. We now know from evidence dug up at the site of 16A that the guns in this position were more powerful 150mm cannons. Therefore these guns would have covered the 'Omaha gap' and been capable of raining fire directly on the Omaha beachhead, as was witnessed by many.

It is not unreasonable that at a time before the 16A guns were installed, the guns at Maisy could have been seen by the Germans as incapable of

A pair of 150mm German howitzer/cannon wheels dug up at position 16A five years ago.

A German 150mm field cannon.
This example is in Aberdeen Proving
Grounds in the US. Note the wheels.

fulfilling a full beach-defence role along Omaha Beach when turned to point in that direction, then perhaps the five guns sitting behind Pointe du Hoc could have been positioned there to take that area of beach under fire if necessary, just while the Pointe du Hoc Battery was re-developed. However, to do that they would have had to have been moved from where they were on D-Day because they could not see Omaha from the position they were actually found in. Thus further suggesting that the 16A guns fulfilled that purpose.

On two occasions when I spoke to Len Lomell he said the following: '*The guns were big – their muzzles went to hell in the air and their wheels were huge – they were big guns … not the sort of thing you carry around behind a jeep. They were large-calibre howitzers*'.

Although in another interview with me Len said that he didn't know what type of guns the Rangers were looking for in advance. It is also worth noting how high up the

This US Army archive photograph shows an American version of the 155mm cannon, similar to the 'Pointe du Hoc' guns. It is blatantly obvious that this does not have huge wheels or a muzzle, etc.

muzzle is off the ground. He does in the same interview make a few obvious indications as to the type of weapon he found:

1. *He calls it a howitzer, which is a very different type of weapon compared with a cannon – those reported to have been found behind Pointe du Hoc.*

2. *He states that the gun had a muzzle – again not something found on a cannon of this type, but something found on a field howitzer.*

3. *The wheels on a field howitzer are large, whereas the wheels on a cannon, as seen here, are small.*

Obviously these are small discrepancies in the gun types, but possibly significant. The standard German field-howitzer configuration was often four or five horse-drawn or tractored guns – normally placed under camouflage cover in a field position for combat. A position where they could be fired over objects such as trees and down onto a target some miles away, which fits with them being under apple trees. Is it far-fetched to suggest that the guns at Pointe du Hoc had been removed to another coastal location pending the arrival of the new 10.5cm guns – and perhaps that they were placed under apple trees to hide them and/or even that they had already been moved away?

Would it now be far-fetched to suggest that the Germans may have placed a mobile howitzer battery in the trees behind Pointe du Hoc to 'fill the gap' in coverage of the beaches until the Pointe du Hoc Battery was finished? If the guns were placed behind Pointe du Hoc for the purpose of controlling the beaches in that area, then one would have assumed that they would have been some of the first weapons firing on D-Day and that they would at least have been pointing in the right direction. This has long been an issue with historians – why were the guns not firing? I think they were never placed in an operational setting.

Looking for an alternative solution to the events at Pointe du Hoc has resulted in some fascinating incidents that happened close to D-Day coming to light. This is a quote from a discussion with now-retired Brigadier General **John Raaen**, 5th Rangers:

The fields where the guns were found by the Rangers – only a couple of lone apple trees still exist today. Visible in the centre left of the photograph, the treeline to the right of it leads up to the roundabout where the Rangers set up their roadblock.

One other interesting story about the guns in the apple orchard, Lomell's guns. Back in November or December 2001, I was invited to assist the SOCEUR in a tactical walk of the Normandy battle areas. The then assistant manager of the Colleville cemetery also assisted SOCEUR and I got to know him pretty well. He was a history buff and spent much of his spare time digging into the events surrounding PdHoc. He met an old woman who was the daughter (I think that was her relationship) to the owner of the farm in which Lomell found the guns. She was not living at the farm at the time of the invasion, was then very young and evacuated to a safer area by her parents.

The family owned a large house just south of Lomell's field. A group of German officers had commandeered a part of the house for their billets, mess and headquarters. One day, just before the invasion (she was not there), a deranged German soldier burst into the mess and killed and wounded about eight of the officers. My recollection is that it was a grenade explosion. The survivors immediately evacuated the farm.

I often wondered if that headquarters had been the HQ or Fire Control Centre for the PdH Battery and perhaps that their demise might have been the reason the battery was not engaged in firing on D-Day.

Another version of this same story involves a German officer who had gone mad after a heavy bomber attack. He had just found out a few days before that his family had all died in an Allied bombing raid on his home city. He entered the headquarters and detonated a mine in his hands. The subsequent explosion blew out the back wall of the barn creating a large hole. I was told about the hole being 'historic' for those reasons by the elderly lady farm owner in 2005.

Either story – if true, illustrates how a separate incident to the actual invasion could possibly have saved the lives of so many men on the beaches some days later. If the reports of the incident are correct, then perhaps the gunners did not have any officers in position to direct their activities. So they were waiting for targets and instructions.

It was back in Vierville-sur-Mer on the 7th that D Company 81st Chemical Weapons was subjected to one of the heaviest shellings it had ever experienced, as their After Action Report reads:

Several batteries of enemy 150mm artillery, firing from the vicinity of Pointe du Hoc, pounded the centre of town and the road leading to the beach. Heavy casualties were inflicted on the regimental OP group and on a field artillery battalion coming from the beach. An ammunition dump was blown up, scattering small arms ammunition in all directions. This action caused a withdrawal for a time along the highway.

The only artillery batteries capable of firing this size of weapon from this direction on 7 June were the guns at Maisy. From the direction of Maisy to Omaha Beach the shells would have gone past Pointe du Hoc virtually in a straight line into Vierville and in the confusion of battle the 81st men would have assumed the incoming rounds to have come from Pointe du Hoc. They were fully briefed of the dangers presented by that position before landing, yet we know that there were no operational guns at Pointe du Hoc, so they could only have been fired upon by the batteries at Maisy.

Ranger Jack Burke told me sixty years after D-Day that he could '*always tell the direction exactly of an incoming shell by the "spout" it made when it landed. The calibre you could estimate by the noise it made in the air before it hit.*'

A copy of John Raaen's wartime map. He carried this on D-Day and it shows nothing but target numbers 5 and 16 for Maisy. Clearly when he was given the map in England no serious importance was put on this location.

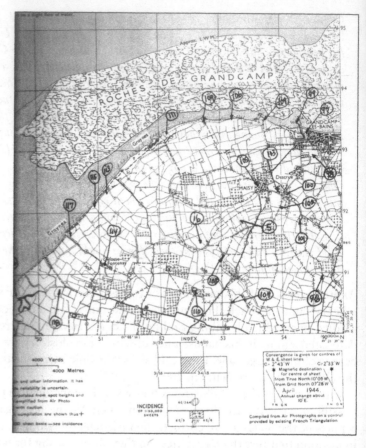

The Pointe du Hoc raid must be examined in detail to ascertain what really happened and why. One hypothesis that has been raised is that possibly Commander Eisenhower sent the Rangers to attack Pointe du Hoc as a propaganda mission, despite being told by intelligence analysts there were no guns there. Did he want to send a clear message to Rommel – 'You build it up and show it off – and we will come and destroy it'? Was it about proving who was the bigger commander? That is possible with hindsight and facts available on the day. This school of thought is aided by the fact that a camera crew was sent with the Rangers to Pointe du Hoc and the local intelligence on the ground was obviously ignored. It is still possible today to see clearly from the air that there were an inadequate number of pits, or casements of the correct size, actually to contain the type of guns the Rangers were sent to destroy. This alone certainly raises more questions than answers.

If the guns destroyed behind Pointe du Hoc had just been removed from the Pointe a few days earlier (as is often suggested), then one would have to question where they had actually come from to the Pointe for this statement to hold water. This is really the specialism of intelligence operatives, so they must have known there was nothing there in advance.

It is quite bizarre that Maisy is marked on GSGS intelligence BIGOT maps well before D-Day and that the site is shown on those maps as twice the size of Pointe du

Hoc, is marked as well armed and well defended. But it was ignored in favour of Pointe du Hoc which was not well armed or by comparison as well defended. Yet Pointe du Hoc was still singled out by Eisenhower for the special attention of the two battalions of Rangers, approximately 1,100 men.

Ranger John Raaen's original ground-troops D-Day map reproduced (p. 290) does not indicate Maisy as being a large site. In fact, it shows only a series of target numbers with no explanation; Maisy being 16, 16A and 5 on his map.

In every interview I have done with Ranger veterans none of them knew anything about Maisy Battery before they were ordered to assault it. To quote Ranger veteran **Frank Kennard** who landed on Omaha Beach with his halftracks:

I have no knowledge of Maisy. In the marshalling area we had the use of a very large three-dimensional map which had every detail of the 2nd Ranger landing area (i.e Vierville exit, Pointe et Raz de la Percée and Pte du Hoc. As far as I can recollect there was no detail of Maisy on it – nor can I recall it ever being named. It wasn't a 2nd Ranger objective and, if all the 2nd & 5th could have come to the Pointe (the initial plan), the Ranger force would have completely 'by-passed' Maisy.

So it was not discussed at all during their detailed and exhaustive briefing sessions and not one of them knew it existed in advance of 9 June, by which time it had been firing for three days.

John Reville:

How could this be a secret for so many years – it didn't make sense that the local people didn't know what was there. Maisy was not any objective of ours.

In a book I read recently the batteries at Maisy were described by the author as 'mundane'. This was an author who did not know the batteries existed before they were 'discovered'. Historians have in some cases just perpetuated the disappearance of the site.

If nothing else, it was a serious failure in Allied intelligence at the time and at worst it is information that was deliberately ignored in favour of the Supreme Allied Commander's wishes that Target No. 1 was Pointe du Hoc. This is backed up by the Allied Intelligence pre-D-Day report NEPTUNE MONOGRAPH CTF122:

*GROUP I: BATTERIES WHICH COVER **BOTH** BEACH AREAS*

Target Number 16 (Les Perruques) 528916 4 x ? 75(mm) Fd (field) Tp (troop) 13,000 (range). Casemates u/c (under construction, facing NNW. Original position at 528915 abandoned: guns moved to temporary position at 531914: late in March 1944 2 casemates were started immediately forward of original emplacements. Range covers only westernmost sector of beach OMAHA and southern half of beach UTAH.

Target Number 5 (La Martiniere) 533918 4 x 155mm H (howitzers) 13,000 (yards range). Open earth revetted pits. Covers only westernmost sector of beach OMAHA and Southern half of beach UTAH.

Target Number 1 (Pointe du Hoc) 586938 6 x 155mm G (cannons). 25,000 (yards range) Open concrete pits, sunken and earth banked. 4 casemates under construction, 2 adjacent to empls (?). 2 & 3 started in April. Range extends beyond limits of both beaches.

This clearly states that targets 16 and 5 could fire at both Omaha and Utah Beaches and well out into the shipping lanes. Target Number 1 has casements 'started in April', two months before D-Day, clearly showing that the intelligence reporters must have realised the Pointe du Hoc guns were not in their original positions from that time.

A number of things are clear now. First, are we to believe that Maisy Battery was ignored by professional photographic observers and decision-makers over many months prior to the invasion taking place? If it was not ignored then by definition it would have to mean that these professionals did their job and their findings were not passed on to D-Day planners. This is an unlikely scenario – they would have passed on all of their information upwards and it was at that stage – a level above, that it would have been used or disregarded for whatever reason.

An alternative view is that the information gathered was not understood to be significant. Perhaps the interpreters did not gauge the size of casements, or they missed that fact that they would not fit anything other than a 10.5cm weapon. Perhaps they missed the fact that the gun pits around them were either built over, in front of, bomb damaged or empty? One has to doubt that was the case in reality. Professionals at all levels will have studied Maisy, which they did as we have seen, so why not attack it as a priority? It was in fact the only battery that engaged both American landing beaches on D-Day and the above report is confirmation that they knew that in advance.

The intelligence members of the French Resistance knew categorically that the PdH site was not operational and their information was ignored. The static flak units surrounding Maisy were attacked and destroyed as we know, so they were well known about and targetted.

It is very difficult to understand that these events happened without someone saying something to someone. After all, to ignore a huge gun battery and to make the decision to go after another one which they were 99 per cent sure was empty not something an intelligence officer would do lightly. They would pass the information upwards and someone then made a decision to ignore Maisy.

Another interesting thing is that in none of the pre-D-Day briefings and post-war papers were the Rangers to look for guns in the fields to the rear of Pointe du Hoc. They were sent to the Pointe itself for the guns, therefore it was a pure accident that they came across guns in fields behind on D-Day.

Dwight D. Eisenhower made the decision to attack Pointe du Hoc as Target Number 1 and therefore the buck stops certainly with him. If Pointe du Hoc was known to be empty prior to 6 June – which by all evidence it was, then he was not attacking an operational target. He could only have been attacking a political target and the very man he personally wanted to beat – Irwin Rommel.

The Rangers' 'second objective' at Pointe du Hoc, the blocking of the Grandcamp–Vierville road is worthy of more detailed examination too. If this was their mission why were they not given large quantities of anti-tank weapons with which to achieve this end? They were not equipped with large numbers of bazookas or large quantities of anti-tank mines, so what purpose was guarding the highway going to achieve? Studying the number of counterattacks launched by the Germans on the Pointe du Hoc position after the Ranger occupation, these attacks were all done on foot by infantry crossing fields and not down the road at all. So what was the purpose of 'guarding the highway'? Also there are no surviving records stating that the Germans had mobile armoured units in the Grandcamp area. Was the 'guard the highway' order just added to pad out the mission?

I looked into a number of other 'pre-H-hour' Normandy assault objectives, for example, Merville Battery, St Marie Eglise town, La Fierre Bridge, Pegasus Bridge – the list goes on. None of these objectives to my knowledge had a film crew sent with them. Is it possible that Eisenhower wanted to record and then show off the sight of Pointe du Hoc being captured for later display?

If it turns out that despite knowing there were no guns at Pointe du Hoc, Eisenhower still sent men to assault it simply as a point-scoring exercise with Rommel, then there would be a lot of explaining to do given the Rangers' casualties at the Pointe. In addition, the hastily ordered unrehearsed assault on the Maisy Battery would need to be justified too.

If Maisy had been deliberately 'wiped off' the historical landscape of the day then someone high up must have been responsible. You cannot just make a large battlefield disappear without someone ordering it to do so. Combat engineers would not bury a large site taking days with bulldozers without being ordered too. They would have had other tasks to carry out in France as the battle advanced and they would simply not have bothered.

But the facts remain, someone ordered the burying of part of the Maisy Battery and that was well before the end of the war and not, before you say it, for the benefit of local farmers. When the local people were given back their land the batteries had simply vanished under tons of soil. When I asked each person or family who had owned a piece of the batteries after the war about its existence, they all said that it was buried before the land was returned to them by the Americans. Everyone who knew about the land locally told me that the land had housed an old anti-aircraft site and was not of any significance. This is simply because the locals did not know what was there.

The crux of the matter is this. Did Supreme Allied Commander Dwight Eisenhower send the Rangers to attack Pointe du Hoc because he was duped by Rommel into thinking that it was a high-priority target? Or did he know it was not the operational position it was made out to be and the attack was a piece of political one-upmanship to be filmed for propaganda purposes? After the battle and after the war why was the battery at Maisy not shown to exist? Why is the battery at Pointe du Hoc always listed in accounts as having six guns when it did not have any on the day?

After the war the Maisy site vanished, buried at Les Perruques and left to the elements above ground at La Martiniere. German prisoners were kept at the site to clear the mines and level the land in conjunction with the US Engineers for some time. Then a good number of the prisoners were sent to camps in Canada.

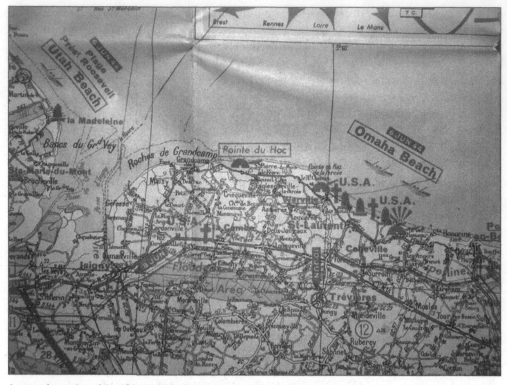

A copy of a portion of the 1946 Michelin Guide to the battlefields. These guides were produced after the war so that families and veterans could return in peacetime to where they fought. This section clearly shows Pointe du Hoc and other gun batteries, but nothing at Maisy, which proves convincingly that by 1946 the site had simply 'disappeared'.

The survey photographs (see p. 298) taken after the war show just how quickly the site vanished.

In 1984 members of the 2nd and 5th Battalions went back to Normandy for the fortieth anniversary of D-Day reunion. At the time of their trip **Lieutenant Jay H. Mehaffey, C Company, 5th Battalion,** was the Battalion Historian. To accompany the trip and by way of a souvenir he wrote up a daily account, which he produced for all the veterans to take home afterwards. The following extract is taken from it:

> *Hotels in France had all been sold out from Cherbourg to Dieppe for two years prior to the 40th anniversary of D-Day. But the Rangers had no problems with accommodation. Len Lomell's great planning had provided rooms in private lodgings for all who did not have hotel space.*
>
> *There isn't space to tell how each Ranger and friend was entertained, wined and dined by our French hosts ... I personally had a five-course sea-food dinner, with wine between each course, and topped off with a snifter of calvados on each of the two nights ... each Ranger can tell a similar story.*
>
> *Tuesday June 5th 1984*

The Rangers and guests assembled at the Deguscuelin Hotel on Tuesday morning for the short bus ride to Pointe to Hoc where a 10.30am rehearsal was scheduled with the White House staff in charge of President Reagan's visit the next day.

There were 62 ex-Rangers on the platform that morning seated in two rows of chairs on each side of the dais from which the president would make his speech. Several dry runs held with the Rangers executing the hand salute and forming up in single file for the walk to the gravel path where the President was scheduled to meet each Ranger on the 6th.

Of course it was impossible for any writing to convey more than a small fraction of the emotions felt by the returning Rangers, particularly for those who were back for the first time in 40 years. For most it was their first visit to the area since D-Day. Dr Tom Petrick the 5th Rangers surgeon recalled his first casualties at the waters edge on Dog White ... Stan Bojara of A Co. recalled the line of trees near Pointe du Hoc where he and part of A Company under Ace Parker wound up on D-Day.

The old LCI-92s rusting hulk is still on dog green where C and D Companies, and part of HQ Company landed ... it was burning and exploding behind us that morning, so it was easy to pin point that location. Herb Epstein of HQ Co. was Col. Schneider's radio man and he recalled General Cota's order to Schneider 'Were counting on the Rangers to lead the way' ... and so was born a legendary slogan.

This was a time for quiet reflection and remembering all the old 5th Battalion returnees. Another highlight of this day was a mass at the Ranger church in Cricqueville behind Pointe du Hoc. The church was filled to capacity with visitors and local people. Albert Nyland another old C Company Ranger pointed out in the church yard 'that's a new steeple' ... the old one was destroyed on D-Day as the Germans used it as an Observation Post.

8pm Grandcamp. The one thing the banquet convinced me of. That after the speeches and the other official back slapping was done by various US officials in attendance, it was the people of Grandcamp and its environs who certainly make me and the other Rangers there feel that any sacrifice they made during the landings was well worth the price.

6th June – the appointment for the Rangers to be at the Pointe was 1.30pm and with the aid of police escorts after we reached the area of Pointe du Hoc in plenty of time. Security was tight and we reached that area of inspection. The President and Mrs Reagan arrived in the landing zone at 2.20pm and were greeted by US Ambassador Galbreath and his wife. They then proceeded to the old German powder magazine where an official of the US battle monuments commission explained the historic nature of the Pointe du Hoc.

The President then examined a gun emplacement before mounting the Rangers' platform where he was greeted by two ex-2nd Rangers who explained the assault to him.

The party then proceeded to the Ranger monument where they were introduced to Mrs Rudder. The 62 Rangers seated on the platform rose and gave the salute as President Reagan walked to the speaker's dais. At 2.30pm June 6th 1984, the President gave his speech – heard around the world.

'We're here to mark that day in history when the Allied peoples joined in battle to reclaim this continent to liberty. For four long years, much of Europe had been

Len Lomell with US President Ronald Reagan.

under a terrible shadow. Free nations had fallen, Jews cried out in the camps – millions cried out for liberation. Europe was enslaved, and the world prayed for its rescue. Here in Normandy the rescue began. Here the Allies stood and fought against tyranny in a giant undertaking unparalleled in human history.

We stand on a lonely, windswept point on the northern shore of France. The air is soft, but forty years ago at this moment, the air was dense with smoke and the cries of men, and the air was filled with the crack of rifle fire and the roar of cannon. At dawn, on the morning of the 6th of June, 1944, 225 Rangers jumped off the British landing craft and ran to the bottom of these cliffs. Their mission was one of the most difficult and daring of the invasion: to climb these sheer and desolate cliffs and take out the enemy guns. The Allies had been told that some of the mightiest of these guns were here, and they would be trained on the beaches to stop the Allied advance.

The Rangers looked up and saw the enemy soldiers – at the edge of the cliffs shooting down at them with machine guns and throwing grenades. And the American Rangers began to climb. They shot rope ladders over the face of these cliffs and began to pull themselves up. When one Ranger fell, another would take his place. When one rope was cut, a Ranger would grab another and begin his climb again. They climbed, shot back, and held their footing. Soon, one by one, the Rangers pulled themselves over the top, and in seizing the firm land at the top of these cliffs, they began to seize back the continent of Europe. Two hundred and twenty-five came here. After two days of fighting, only 90 could still bear arms.

Behind me is a memorial that symbolizes the Ranger daggers that were thrust into the top of these cliffs. And before me are the men who put them there. These are the boys of Pointe de Hoc.

These are the men who took the cliffs. These are the champions who helped free a continent. These are the heroes who helped end a war. Gentlemen, I look at you and I think of the words of Stephen Spender's poem. You are men who in your 'lives fought for life ... and left the vivid air signed with your honor ...'

Forty summers have passed since the battle that you fought here. You were young the day you took these cliffs; some of you were hardly more than boys, with the deepest joys of life before you. Yet you risked everything here. Why? Why did you do it? What impelled you to put aside the instinct for self-preservation and risk your lives to take these cliffs? What inspired all the men of the armies that met here? We look at you, and somehow we know the answer. It was faith, and belief; it was loyalty and love.

The men of Normandy had faith that what they were doing was right, faith that they fought for all humanity, faith that a just God would grant them mercy on this beachhead or on the next. It was the deep knowledge – and pray God we have not lost it – that there is a profound moral difference between the use of force for liberation and the use of force for conquest. You were here to liberate, not to conquer, and so you and those others did not doubt your cause. And you were right not to doubt.

You all knew that some things are worth dying for. One's country is worth dying for, and democracy is worth dying for, because it's the most deeply honorable form of government ever devised by man. All of you loved liberty. All of you were willing to fight tyranny, and you knew the people of your countries were behind you.'

From the cemetery on the 7th of June the 5th Battalion group toured Omaha Beach one more time and placed wreaths at the 5th Battalion Plaque that President Reagan had dedicated the day before. The plaque is on the stone wall that leads out of Vierville exit and toward the Chateau de Vaumical, well remembered by the 5th Battalion and A, B, C companies of the 2nd. The plaque is in a very prominent spot.

For those 5th Rangers who couldn't locate the Maisy Battery East of Grandcamp where C and F companies captured the German payroll and took 200 prisoners let me report: A Richard Brown who lives in Florida and spends his summers in Grandcamp spent his youth playing at the old site. His mother was from Grandcamp and married an American soldier. Mr Brown gave me a personal tour of the old Maisy Battery site and let me say that after a circuitous route to the old bunkers, I doubt that any stranger to the site could ever have found it.

The bunkers are still there and overgrown with weeds. One is filled with garbage, the other two contain farm implements. The Normandy cattle graze all around the area. The trench system that connected the bunkers is gone.

That long approach to the Maisy Battery that was filled with shell craters, barbed wire and mines, is now a grain field, and the road where the halftrack of the 2nd Battalion fired support for the attack is a lone lane path overgrown with foliage.

Jay Mehaffey talks of C and F Companies being at Maisy and yet because of the size of the site, he did not know that A Company were there attacking La Martiniere at the same time. He attacked with the 2nd Battalion halftracks which included HQ men with Sullivan.

A series of photographs taken by a local civil engineer just after the war. He was trying to record what buildings remained at La Martiniere after the German occupation.

Not very clear but this photograph was captioned German graves at Fouchers' Farm.

Debris at the gates to Foucher's Farm.

La Martiniere casements.

A row of more obvious German field graves at Foucher's Farm.

An ammunition tunnel leading up to the casement. It was filled in with the town's rubbish after the war.

A casement and a 622 building start to be enveloped by the surrounding countryside.

Looking into the back of a casement at La Martiniere.

The trenches have long gone behind the casements.

An observation tower for cows!

The front of a La Martiniere casement. Very little damage is evident in the picture.

The rear of a La Martiniere casement showing damage from small-arms fire.

A 622 barely visible in the foreground.

The figure of 200 prisoners is consistent with those figures of men captured at Les Perruques. And this begs the obvious question: why defend a gun position supposedly (according to some historians) that had no guns? Why continue to keep the regional payroll in the centre of an empty site? Why were all the radios still working and the SS defending it if the site had been abandoned? Why were the ammunition bunkers still full of ammunition? The questions go on and on – however, given the number of men and units involved, the battle for the Maisy Battery was one of the most significant battles undertaken in Normandy by the US Rangers. Yet it is not and has never been recognised.

The landowner, Mr Martin, with the same 622 before it vanished.

Coit Coker's account of the evening of 8 June indicates guns still in the vicinity of Foucher's Farm, yet the guns here were supposedly destroyed before the 9th:

> *Enemy artillery shifted onto us again here, one heavy caliber, probably firing from Isigny and the other light caliber, short range probably from vicinity of targets No. 16 (La Martiniere) and No. 108 (Foucher's Farm) about 1500 S and SW of Maisy. Under this artillery fire the battalion dispersed to cover again.*

Brigitte Destores commented, '*I remember the guns still sitting on the gunpits after the battle.*' This again dispels the idea that the site had been vacated of weapons prior to the Rangers' attack.

In 2009, I approached the American Battlefield Monuments Commission to have the men of A and F Companies, 5th Battalion recognised for their heroism at Pointe du Hoc. It is my understanding that this is now being considered four years later and I have put suggestions forward, as have surviving Rangers, to help commemorate the men who took part in the relief of Pointe du Hoc. In 2009 Major General US Army Retired (D-Day Ranger Captain) **John Raaen** wrote to the American Battlefield Monument Commission:

I agree with Gary Sterne that Lieutenant Parker, A Company, 5th Rangers and Lieutenant Reville, F Company, 5th Rangers should be recognised. Parker was the only leader to accomplish the 5th Rangers' mission of reaching Pointe du Hoc on D-Day. His presence there with twenty-two of his men boosted Rudder's force and helped withstand the German counterattacks on the night of D-Day and D+1. Captain Runge and Lieutenant Revelle brought another thirty men or so to the Pointe. Lieutenant Reville ran several patrols for Colonel Rudder including one at about midnight on D+1 which reached the force at St Pierre.

I have pushed and will continue to push the ABMC for a monument to recognise the men of the 5th Battalion for their efforts at Pointe du Hoc.

The situation regarding the 5th Rangers at Pointe du Hoc from 6–8 June can be summed up in this quote from a letter written by **Major Richard Sullivan** to another Ranger veteran:

With the arrival of Ace Parker's platoon and the addition of thirty + men with John Reville's platoon – on D+1, the number of 5th Rangers at the Pointe represented approximately 33 per cent of the force.

While the officers and men of the 2nd Ranger Battalion have so much to be proud of – their fellow Rangers of the 5th Battalion certainly have been equally, if not more honoured for their Combat Service.

In 2006 I was in the company of three of the 5th Battalion A Company men, Daniel Farley, James Gabaree and Jack Burke at Pointe du Hoc. It was a strange feeling to see them quietly walk amidst the hundreds and hundreds of visitors to the site. Such was their modesty, they quietly walked around reading the signs, discussing the battle and their various involvements and they said nothing to the other visitors. I felt for them as they noted that the recognition for the D-Day mission was all directed towards the 2nd Battalion on the signs and there was no mention of their own involvement.

James Gabaree:

Twenty-three rangers fought their way from Bloody Omaha Beach to join the 2nd Rangers at Pointe du Hoc. To our dismay, the dreaded big guns were not in place. I believe the Allied intelligence missed the primary target at Maisy. We were subject to incoming fire from the Maisy fortification until the Rangers captured it on 9 June. After the war, did the Allied intelligence bury their mistake under tons of earth?

Len Lomell:

I never heard of Maisy until sixty years after the war until I visited Grandcamp – somebody mentioned Maisy. I knew nothing about this emplacement in Maisy before or after D-Day. I don't believe any of the Allied intelligence knew anything about it. It didn't figure in our planning or our attack on Pointe du Hoc. It came as a great surprise when I received a letter from the former Mayor of Grandcamp-Maisy and his wife. She translated the article about the discovery of this underground position. They knew nothing about it. I certainly as an American soldier knew nothing about it and I don't think anyone else knew anything about it.

A Company, 5th Battalion veterans at Pointe du Hoc. Daniel Farley, Jack Burke and James Gabaree.

Richard Hathaway:

The thing that surprised me was that the people in Grandcamp didn't know anything about the site.
They knew absolutely nothing. The information was really secret, well hidden from them at the time.

Jack Burke:

I am of the belief that Maisy was a much more important strategic victory than we ever knew.

James Gabaree:

I believe the Allied intelligence designated the wrong primary target in the invasion of Normandy. It should have been the German Maisy Battery rather than Point du Hoc. I do not recall the German Maisy Battery being mentioned in our briefing prior to the invasion.

John Raaen:

We believed that Maisy was a major headquarters as well as an artillery fire base.

Hugo Heffelfinger, Major Infantry, Executive Officer, 5th Ranger Infantry Battalion wrote the following on 9 May 1945:

Statistics for the period of operations on the continent. 6th June 1944 – 9th May 1945.

Prisoners of war during entire period = 4,541
Estimated enemy killed = 1,541
5th Ranger Battle Casualties
Killed in Action = 115　　*Wounded in Action = 552*
Missing in Action = 25　　*Captured in Action = 2*
Total casualties = 694

The battalion started out with approximately 500 men and replacements.

Hopefully this book will enlighten future generations of historians and modern Rangers alike concerning the efforts of both the 2nd and 5th Ranger Battalions in Normandy. I also hope that the ABMC can stand by their commitment to mount a suitable monument that reflects the actions of both Ranger battalions at Pointe du Hoc.

All faults and mistakes within this are purely my own. Trying to cram such a vast subject into one book working to a deadline will inevitably incur mistakes, for this I apologise. One reaches a point when the research has to stop and the writing begin. As time schedules pressed the production of this book, I have been compelled to leave out probably another book's worth of information, which possibly can be published in the future.

If the questions raised here have caused you to think about D-Day history as you know it, then I have done my job. After all, this was the thinking that led to the uncovering of the Maisy Battery in the first place in 2006.

At the time I had a small chuckle to myself. I was in France working on the land when I had a phone call from the then head of the American Cemetery at Colleville. He asked if I had time to show a party of people around Maisy (it was closed off to the public at that time). I of course said yes and we arranged to meet the following day.

The party consisted of two professors from Texas A & M University and a dozen students. I greeted them and then proceeded to give them the 3-hour, gold-plated, top-to-bottom tour of the site and surrounding land. In fairness, at the end of the tour one of the professors, whom I had met some months earlier, said the following: '*First, I have to apologise to you for the way I spoke to you earlier this year – I was a little rude.*' I accepted the apology and said that I didn't remember the incident at all! '*Secondly [and he had a smile on his face], I have to commend you for what you have done … you have single-handedly wrecked seven years of our work on finding the missing guns from Pointe du Hoc – well done!*'

We had a laugh about, it but he was right. Their years of work had never considered that there might be another gun battery in the area and therefore they had fallen into the same trap that everyone else has done – thinking that Pointe du Hoc was the main battery on D-Day, which we now know was not the case.

Perhaps we will never have an exact understanding of the situation on D-Day and as new information arrives all the time I am not arrogant enough to suggest I have got it all right here. The engineers who buried the site are long dead, the people who ordered the site to be levelled are long gone and the reasons why it was allowed to disappear have drifted into obscurity.

One thing is certain, Maisy Battery was there, it did fight, was certainly not 'mundane' and by all reports it gave good account of itself for three days – something that undoubtedly cost a great many Allied lives in both the Utah and Omaha sectors. Rightly or not, this is something for which due respect was well and truly earned the hard way by both the Rangers who assaulted it and the Germans who stood their ground doing their duty.

In fact, if this book has a purpose it is two-fold. First, it is to correct many of the historical works that have presented the battery at Pointe du Hoc as THE defence of the Omaha sector on D-Day, and secondly, to tell the world about the efforts of the sometimes unsung heroes of the entire Omaha landings – the US Army Rangers, for whom I have the greatest respect.

I end the book on a sombre note. If anything is a stark reminder of the ultimate sacrifice many of these brave men went through on our behalf this is it. These following remembrances are from Quentin Aanenson, a 22-year-old P-47 pilot stationed briefly at Englesqueville (between Omaha Beach and Maisy) in the days after D-Day:

During our first two or three weeks after landing in Normandy, a terribly disturbing and distressful situation was taking place below the cliffs of Pointe du Hoc. Bodies of decomposing American soldiers who had been killed during the invasion continued to wash up on shore. We could look down from the bluffs overlooking the English Channel and see them. For the pilots who faced death on every mission, this was particularly upsetting. Some of us had trouble getting this gruesome picture out of our minds, especially when we were lying in our cots at night trying to go to sleep. We could visualise those bodies just a few hundred yards away rolling in the surf.

The graves registration people had moved on by that time – up closer to the front – so there was no one we could call on to retrieve the bodies. One evening our Engineering Officer – a solid, no-nonsense guy – decided something had to be done. He asked several guys to help him, including some of the pilots. We carried 5-gallon jerry cans filled with aviation gasoline -- and several long poles with hooks attached to the ends – down the hill to the beach – then we carried everything to the area where the bodies were piling up. The mood was sombre; there seemed to be a sense of unreality about what we were going to do.

It was a terrible, gruesome ordeal. Most of the bodies were badly decomposed and bloated, but some looked surprisingly normal. We hooked the bodies with the long poles, and pulled them together and piled them up as much as possible. We added as much driftwood to the pile as we could find. In a couple of instances we were able to get their dog tags for identification purposes, but for most of them, there was no way we could make any identification. Then we soaked the whole pile heavily with aviation gasoline.

The engineering officer had us back away, then he paused by the bodies for a minute as if in prayer, finally he ignited the pile. It burned furiously for a short time, then more slowly as the gasoline burned off. The driftwood kept the fire going for some time.

As I watched the fire consume the rotting bodies of these young American boys, I couldn't help but think about their families – and how it would drive them insane if they knew what really had happened to their sons. Better that they should picture their boys being instantly killed by a rifle bullet – and then being given a proper military funeral – with a bugler playing 'Taps' over the grave. But deaths in battle seldom involve dignity. They are horrible, brutal, degrading, and the fact that they died for a good cause cannot sanitise the reality of the circumstances of their deaths.

We slowly drifted away from this horrible scene, but I am sure all of us who were there still carry vivid images of it in our minds.

A few days later I again followed the mine-cleared path to the edge of the bluff and looked down to the water's edge, only to see that our traumatising experience had been for naught. More bodies were rolling in the surf, as the English Channel continued to give up its dead of D-Day.

War is not pretty, it is not glamorous. It is often waged by brave, ordinary men who simply cannot stand by and watch the suffering of others and the failure of either democracy, individuals, countries, or even themselves without trying to help. All the men of the US Army Ranger Infantry Battalions volunteered for their hazardous duties – it was accepted that they were putting themselves slap bang in harm's way. Even now, nearly seventy years later, these men simply see it as them having done their duty.

We owe them a huge debt – and recognising their efforts accurately is only the tip of that iceberg. If this book causes some 'controversy' because people did not know the extent of the Maisy Battery's operations, then it is worth it. I recently received an email from a member of the American military who told he was interested in the Maisy story and that he wanted present-day Rangers to visit the site. He added in his note, 'despite the controversy'. I like to think this book should put paid to the 'controversy' aspect of the Rangers' actions in Normandy.

Now you have all the facts – you can make up your own mind as to the significance of Pointe du Hoc and a little-known place called Maisy in 1944.

Mr Spielberg/Mr Hanks – if you wish to produce a *Saving Private Ryan* Part II then you have it all here. After all, why make up a story when the real thing is much more interesting?

The plaque dedicated to the Rangers at Maisy Battery.

Acknowledgements

Thank you to Brigadier General John C. Raaen for allowing me to spend so much time with him at his home, for his continued support and fine tuning of my work and for his stunning accuracy of memory and clarity of thought. His book *INTACT* (published in 2012) is a valuable resource of first-hand experiences and recollections of this period and should be on your reading list.

I am grateful to Stuart Bryant for his help and discussions about the German dispositions in the sector. His editing, translating and understanding of Fritz Ziegalmann's history of the 352nd Infantry Division proved invaluable as a reference for German thinking at this time.

Special thanks to Kevin McKernon for all his patience and research on my behalf. It is much appreciated – thank you.

Thanks also to Doug McCade at Ohio University who allowed me access to the Cornelius Ryan Papers, an outstanding resource and probably the best collection of first-person combat accounts of D-Day.

A real thank you to all the US Rangers who made me welcome in their homes and spoke to me on the telephone and shared their rembrances. In particular, Francis Coughlin, John Reville, Jack Burke, James Gabaree, Frank Kennard, Frank South, Cecil Gray, James Wilderson, Albert Nyland, Daniel Farley, Lee Brown, Len Lomell, Robert Page Gary, John Hodgson, John Bellows and John Perry.

Thank you to Frank Isidor for his photos and local knowledge of Grandcamp-Maisy, Marc Laurenceau for his boundless support, Monique and Yves Sylvain-Huet for their

A gun pit now restored with a period German howitzer re-fixed in position. You can see the side bunkers for storing ammunition and these were used as troop shelters during the Allied bombardments.

Another gun pit – you can see even without overhead camouflage how the huge howitzer starts to vanish into the landscape.

continual assistance and Jean Marc Lafranc and his wife for their continual work over the years to recognise the Rangers' achievements in 1944.

To Grandcamp mayor Mr Bigot and the villagers of Grandcamp and Maisy for their respect for the Ranger veterans.

Many thanks also to Irene Moore for her help in editing this work. Her friendship with a number of Ranger veterans and her extensive knowledge of the Normandy battlefields have helped ensure that I was on the right track.

Thanks to Tim Roop at www.ww2dday.com for his help with wartime Bigot maps.

There are also many others – too many to mention who have helped along the way – thank you all for your help and support.

Finally, a posthumous thank you to my good friend John Chatel for his friendship and assistance throughout my time in Normandy. Without his help I am sure I would have given up the project many years ago and this book would not have been written. He is greatly missed.

Ranger veterans James Gabaree, Jack Burke and Daniel Farley at the opening ceremony for Maisy Battery.

Index